Ragnar Nurkse (1907–2007)

The Anthem Other Canon Series

The Anthem Other Canon Series is a collaborative series between Anthem Press and The Other Canon Foundation. The Other Canon – also described as 'reality economics' – studies the economy as a real object rather than as the behaviour of a model economy based on core axioms, assumptions and techniques. The series publishes classical and contemporary works in this tradition, spanning evolutionary, institutional, and Post-Keynesian economics, the history of economic thought and economic policy, economic sociology and technology governance, and works on the theory of uneven development and in the tradition of the German historical school.

Other Titles in the Series

Ragnar Nurkse (1907–2007)

Classical Development Economics and its Relevance for Today

Edited by

RAINER KATTEL, JAN A. KREGEL
AND ERIK S. REINERT

ANTHEM PRESS
LONDON · NEW YORK · DELHI

Anthem Press
An imprint of Wimbledon Publishing Company
www.anthempress.com

This edition first published in UK and USA 2011
by ANTHEM PRESS
75-76 Blackfriars Road, London SE1 8HA, UK
or PO Box 9779, London SW19 7ZG, UK
and
244 Madison Ave. #116, New York, NY 10016, USA

British Library Cataloguing in Publication Data
A catalogue record for this book is available from the British Library.

Library of Congress Cataloging-in-Publication Data
Ragnar Nurkse (1907–2007) : classical development economics and its relevance for
today / edited by Rainer Kattel, Jan A. Kregel, and Erik S. Reinert.
p. cm. – (The Anthem Other Canon series)
Based on a conference held in Tallinn, Estonia, on 31 Aug. and 1 Sept. 2007.
Includes bibliographical references.
ISBN 978-0-85728-396-2 (pbk. : alk. paper)
1. Nurkse, Ragnar, 1907–1959–Congresses. 2. Development economics–
Congresses. 3. Economics–Congresses. 4. Economic development–Congresses.
5. Finance–Developing countries–Congresses. I. Kattel, Rainer, 1974-
II. Kregel, J. A. III. Reinert, Erik S., 1949-
HD82.R263 2011
338.9001–dc23
2011020395

ISBN-13: 978 0 85728 396 2 (Pbk)
ISBN-10: 0 85728 396 0 (Pbk)

TABLE OF CONTENTS

PREFACE

This volume is one of two publications that celebrate the centenary of Ragnar Nurkse's birth. The other volume, also published by Anthem and titled *Trade and Development*, reprints the key works of Nurkse.

Ragnar Nurkse was born in Estonia in 1907; he died unexpectedly in Geneva, Switzerland, in 1959. He is one of the early pioneers of development economics, whose works are as relevant today as they were during his lifetime.

This volume is based on a conference that took place in the capital of Estonia, Tallinn (where Nurkse went to school) on 31 August and 1 September 2007.

We would like to thank all the contributors to the volume for the lively discussions during the conference; the Estonian Science Foundation (grant no. 6703), The Other Canon Foundation, Norway and PRAXIS Center for Policy Studies, Estonia, for financial support in organizing the conference; and Ingbert Edenhofer for his editorial help.

The editors.

Ragnar Nurkse (1907–2007)

Chapter One:

THE RELEVANCE OF RAGNAR NURKSE AND CLASSICAL DEVELOPMENT ECONOMICS

Rainer Kattel, Jan A. Kregel and Erik S. Reinert

Every larger undertaking, whenever it unites continuously a certain number of men for a common economic purpose, reveals itself as a moral community.

Gustav von Schmoller, *The Idea of Justice in Political Economy*, 1881.

Introduction

'I do not know', Alexis de Tocqueville says in *Democracy in America*, 'if one can cite a single manufacturing and commercial nation – from the Tyrians to the Florentine and the English, – that has not also been free. Therefore a close tie and a necessary relation exists between those two things: freedom and industry.' Tocqueville expresses what could be called a development truism of half a thousand years from late Renaissance city-states to Marshall Plan and Havana Charter. Indeed, during the Enlightenment, civilization and democracy were understood, through the analysis of people like Montesquieu and Voltaire among many others, as products of a specific type of economic structure. When German economist Johan Jacob Meyenn stated in 1770 that 'it is known that a primitive people does not improve their customs and institutions later to find useful industries, but the other way around', he expressed something which could be considered common sense at the time. We find the same idea – that civilization is created by industrialization or, to put it more specifically, by the presence of increasing returns activities – in the nineteenth century in thinkers across the whole political spectrum from Abraham Lincoln to Karl Marx.

Industrialization 'draws all, even the most barbarian, nations into civilization', as Marx puts it. What might be called the historical development consensus saw, in other words, the aim of development in the creation of middle-income economies – with all the accompanying values and culture that in turn were perceived as highly conducive to further sustained development. However, as Figures 1.1 and 1.2 show, the creation of middle-income economies has become a true rarity in the last three decades.

Apart from East Asia's much-praised experience and the enormous catching up taking place in China and, to a lesser degree in India, the rest of the developing world from Eastern Europe to Latin America and Africa is experiencing strong cognitive dissonance.

While many of these countries have seen significant growth in exports and in foreign capital inflows, their income levels have flatlined since 1980 and in most cases actually dropped in the 1990s. (Figure 1.1)

In fact, compared to highly developed countries, most developing countries were on a steady track towards catching up until the early 1980s; the subsequent decades show continuous and significant catching up – and actual surging ahead in the case of some countries such as Singapore – of East Asian economies. (Figure 1.2; see also Wade 2008) The trends follow rather precisely the changes

Figure 1.1. GDP Per Person Employed, Index (1980 = 100), 1980–2006

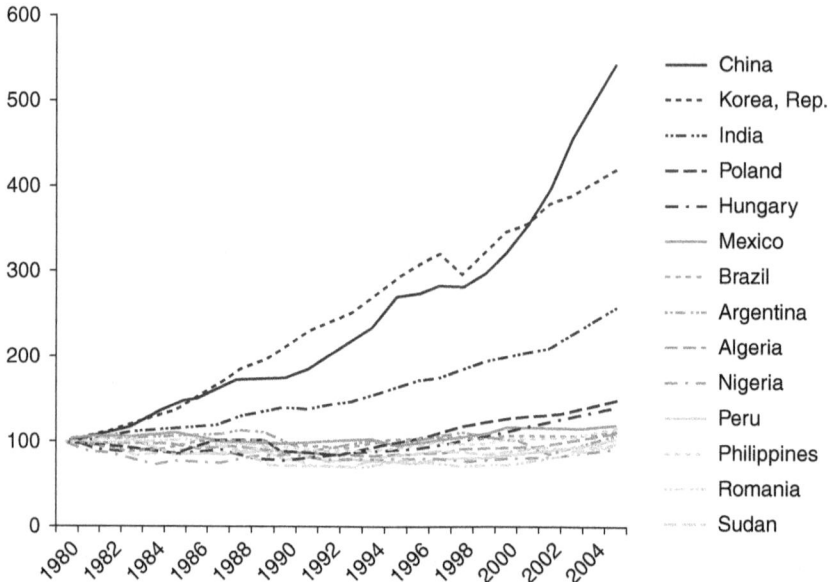

Source: World Bank WDI online database.

Figure 1.2. GDP Per Capita in Selected Developing Countries, 1950–2001 (in 1990 International Geary-Khamis Dollars)

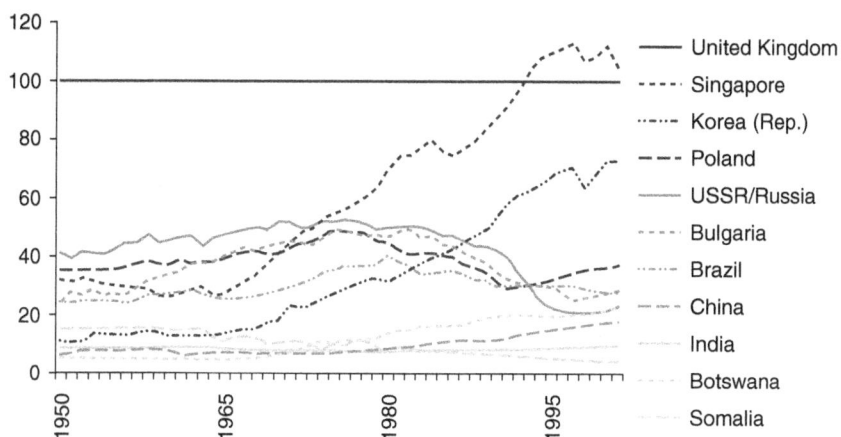

Source: Original data extracted from Maddisson 2003.[1]

in development thinking from classical development economics up to the late 1970s to the Washington Consensus from the 1980s.

Moreover, as Figure 1.3 shows, in recent decades, most developing regions – again with the exception of East Asia – experienced growth rates that go clearly against the more or less positive trend of the last 200 years from a long-term historical perspective. In other words, the world after the industrial revolution has not seen such a dismal development performance. The Washington Consensus in development mainstream seems to be a failure on an unprecedented scale.

Yet, surprisingly, the decades after 1980 have been called the best development decades in a generation (Rodrik 2007, 13–14; Skidelsky 2008).[2] While Amsden (2007, 2) argues, in contrast, that during these same decades, for most developing countries, 'Heaven slowly gave way to Hell', even the most ardent supporters of the Washington Consensus are forced to admit that there is something similar to the 'China price' in the development statistics of the poorer countries from 1980 onward. If one deducts China's and India's growth from the developing countries' data, there is not much as far as growth and development in the rest of the developing world is concerned. And neither China nor India can be counted as showcases of the neoliberal policies propagated by the Washington Consensus. We will return to this later.

As the World Bank itself admits, the rest of the developing countries, notably in Africa, Latin America and some of the former Soviet republics (in Central Asia, Moldova, Ukraine) suffer from heavy doses of a cognitive dissonance between promised growth and the reality of standing still, if

Figure 1.3. Growth Rate of GDP Per Capita of Selected World Regions; Regional Average in Selected Periods Between 1820 and 2001; Annual Average Compound Growth Rate

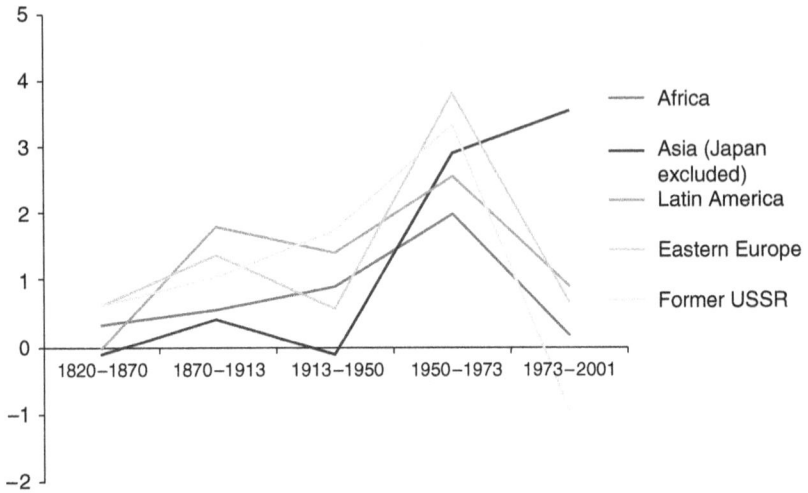

Source: Original data extracted from Maddisson 2003.

they are lucky, or dropping backwards to income levels of earlier decades: 'Whereas Latin America's income per head grew by 10 per cent in the entire 25 years from 1980 to 2005, it grew by 82 per cent in the 20 years from 1960 to 1980' (Amsden 2007, 6; also World Bank 2006; see also Chang 2007).

Latin America diligently followed policy reform suggestions, yet failed to grow, as the World Bank also admits (World Bank 2006, 36–29); Eastern Europe and the former Soviet Union were equally willing to apply the policy reforms, and again, according to the World Bank's calculations, the recession these countries saw in the 1990s and which many are still experiencing, is worse than the Great Depression in the USA and World War II in Western Europe (in both cases, countries affected recovered considerably quicker). In fact, for example, 'even if Ukraine managed to grow steadily at 5 per cent a year, starting in 2002, it would take until 2017 to regain its previous peak – implying a transformational recession of more than a quarter of a century at best.' (World Bank 2006, 33) Indeed, also for most Eastern European countries, the recession was severe and lasted at least 10 years. (Reinert and Kattel 2007, Tiits et al 2008)

Coupled with the change of techno-economic paradigm that completely changed the nature of industrialization (outsourcing) and essentially stripped many maturing and increasingly footloose industrial activities of significant (dynamic) scale economies, Washington Consensus policies emphasising FDI-led growth have created a truly toxic situation for many developing countries where initially the liability destruction was strong and quick but followed by slow asset creation. Thus, 'the failure of the Consensus reform policies lies in the fact that they provided support for the 'destruction' of inefficient domestic industry, but failed to provide support for the 'creative' phase of 'creative destruction' of a real transformation of the productive structure through higher investment and technological innovation' (Kregel 2008). We will return to this topic as well. However, it seems rather obvious that the development community has unlearned how to create middle-income countries.

Yet, there is growing concern and evidence that the current form of globalization not only hurts developing countries that have followed the Washington Consensus policies, but is also harmful to the developed North. The flipside of the unlearning that has taken place in the development community seems to be that we are unlearning how to create middle-class jobs in the developed core countries. For all intents and purposes, nonexisting growth in real wage in USA and Germany over the last decade has given ample reasons to start considering the impact of Washington Consensus trade policies on these countries, the most prominent examples being Samuelson's (2004) and Krugman's (2008) accounts. In 2004, Samuelson argued that continuing globalization and economic integration of world markets in its present form will do permanent harm to high-wage jobs in highly developed countries like the US. In early 2008, Krugman, another celebrity mainstream economist, argued that increased trade between US and developing countries is factually hurting US wages and middle-class jobs and thus increases income inequality. He goes on to prove this not only with US data but also with elaborate modeling.

What Krugman does not realize, or at any rate he does not say it explicitly, is that the problem lies not in the structure or policies of the US economy or even in the growing trade as such, but in the nature of specialization of developing country exports. Specializing in lower-end production or services (also in sectors like ICT) virtually traps developing countries into low-wage jobs and, at the same time, lures the high-wage middle-class jobs away from the developed nations. Thus, while the global production grows, not all countries necessarily benefit from it. And, consequently, 'firms maximize global output but do not necessarily maximize national income' (Palley 2006, 16).

In this introductory chapter, we aim to show, first, how classical development economics, that of Ragnar Nurkse's (1907–1957) generation, epitomized the best development practices of the past 500 years and crafted them into what Krugman (1994) rightly calls high development theory. It is not a coincidence that the post-World War II era, when Nurkse and others ruled the development mainstream, is one of exceptionally good performance for many poor countries. Second, we argue that the alleged death of classical development economics and subsequent rise of the Washington Consensus has to do not so much with increasing modelling in economics, a way of research purposely discarded by many classical development thinkers, as Krugman (1994) claims, but much more with misunderstanding the reasons for East Asia's success and Latin America's demise; we show that the root cause of this misunderstanding – that goes in fact back to 'misreading' key passages in Adam Smith – is the role of technology, or of increasing returns activities, and of finance, in development. Third, we aim to indicate key areas of further research that the current development mainstream should pursue in order to relearn how to create middle-income economies and middle-class jobs.

Classical Development Economics

Pre-Smithian economics saw development as a goal created by increasing returns and innovations in manufacturing and not in agriculture, where stagnant productivity, diminishing returns and monoculture as well as the absence of synergies prevented growth.[3] Furthermore, the targeting, support and protection of manufacturing – that is, of increasing returns activities – were argued in terms of, first, its ability to create wealth; second, its ability to create employment; third, its ability to solve balance of payment problems; and fourth, its ability to increase the velocity of circulation of money. The connection between increasing activities and the creation of more-or-less stable and sustainable states with more-or-less liberal values can be seen as key throughout this entire tradition that reaches until the Marshall plan. Indeed, from as early as Giovanni Botero (1588) and the *Staatsraison* ('reason of state') tradition, there are clear links between economic structure and the viability of states. This tradition was continued by nineteenth-century social scientists and by Friedrich List, directly linking manufacturing and 'civilization'. In fact, already in early German social science, Veit Ludwig von Seckendorff (1626–92) found that Germany did not have the economic basis to create a society like the one observed and so admired in the Dutch Republic. Seckendorff's approach to making the state function better was intimately tied to changing the economic basis of the state itself, its mix of professions and industries and their geographical relocation within the realm. In the tradition started by Seckendorff, the *Fürsten* (Princes) were turned into modernizers by arguing that their *Recht* (right) to govern was accompanied by a *Pflicht* (duty) to modernize and, in effect, in the long term create the conditions where the *Fürsten*, in the end, would be obsolete and the conditions needed for a functioning democracy would have been created. A successful principality carried with it the seeds of its own destruction and the birth of democracy.

The first wealthy states with some kind of republican rule were often islands like Venice and the Dutch Republic. The absence of arable land both led to an absence of a feudal structure and contributed to the creation of a diversified economic structure including activities subject to increasing returns. This makes Florence, with power also by landowners, so interesting. There the *corporazioni* (guilds) and the burghers fought for power among themselves, but very early (twelfth to thirteenth centuries), they had banned the families that owned the surrounding land from participating in politics (these continued to trouble Florence for centuries through alliances with other cities).

There is, then, a long history of trying to move the vested interests of the ruling class from land to manufacturing. The rulers who had a manufacturing strategy also tended to have a policy against the land-owning nobility, starting with Henry VII in England in 1485.

In sum, there are a number of basic principles of development that can be observed in action from fifteenth-century Tudor England to the Marshall Plan. Despite all the theoretical and historical diversity that makes up this tradition of more than 500 years, one very simple formula sums it up rather effectively: a nation is better off with an inefficient industrial (increasing returns) sector than with none at all. Yet, part of this consensus is also the understanding that possessing an industrial sector, however inefficient, should be followed by increased trade in order to create competitive pressure for the industrial sector.

Classical development economics, while in itself a highly diverse group of economic and policy ideas as well as economists, is till today perhaps the best-articulated and theoretically grounded expression of the above-described development consensus. And, as Krugman (1994) argues, the 'irony is that we can now see that high development theory made perfectly good sense after all'.

The group of economists commonly referred to as classical development economists, or pioneers of development or of high development theory, is typically seen to consists of four to six key thinkers: Paul Rosenstein-Rodan, Hans Singer, Arthur Lewis, Albert Hirschman, Gunnar Myrdal and Ragnar Nurkse.[4] While of this group, Nurkse's contribution is the strongest in terms of economic theory, Hirschman's accomplishments are perhaps the most far-reaching in terms of influencing mainstream social science and development. Up to this day, it is relatively typical to find accounts that juxtapose precisely two thinkers as representing almost exactly opposing ideas about development, namely, balanced vs. unbalanced growth. However, as Hirschman later acknowledges, the differences between him and Nurkse were minor at the end of the day, and in large part, they shared a very similar outlook (Hirschman 1984; see also Nurkse 1961, 241ff).

In what follows, we base our brief account mostly on Nurkse's ideas, accompanying them with bits and pieces from the other pioneers, mostly from Rosenstein-Rodan and Hirschman.[5]

The high development theory developed by Nurkse and others rests on two key ideas:

First, financing for development has to come to a large extent from the developing country itself ('Capital is made at home'; Nurkse (1961, 141)).[6]

Second, the key areas to be financed need to exhibit increasing returns in order to trigger dynamics of development or, as Myrdal (1957) argued, virtuous circles of growth.[7]

What makes Nurkse's contribution so important is the fact that he is the only thinker from this group to, first, incorporate both key ideas into a coherent theory of development and, second, to draw clear relationships between these notions.[8] Indeed, this is precisely the reason Nurkse favored the balanced growth approach over the unbalanced one (the difference, simply put, being between whether one industrializes in numerous or just a few key areas): the former was deemed by Nurkse (1961, 241ff) to be financially more stable than the latter.

According to Nurkse, the financing for development has to come mainly from within the country set on development, because financing of growth through either foreign investments or increased trade was largely a historically unique phenomenon confined to the nineteenth century and more specifically to American experience. (See, e.g., Nurkse 1961, 134–136; 282–286). The 'new countries' within and without the British Empire were 'high income countries from the start: effective markets as well as efficient producers' (243). Nurkse thought that it would be nearly impossible for any developing country to repeat such a successful trade- and foreign-financing based growth strategy because America was highly rich in resources, but at the same time populated by a workforce essentially on the same skill level as Britain (143). This unique combination made the American experience non-replicable because in any other circumstance, trade and foreign investment would engender a number of obstacles to development. Namely, first, large parts of such financing would seek to utilize poor countries resources and eventually lock these countries into undiversified economies with a skewed social structure (Nurkse 1961, 100, 137, 144, 248); and second, there is clear danger that significant amounts of foreign financing would end up funding private consumption patterns emulating Western living standards and thus creating balance of payments problems (Nurkse 1953, 66–70).

To sum it up, a growth strategy simply based on trade and foreign financing would leave the poor countries with negative financial flows and undiversified production structure – just like the Washington Consensus, as we will show below – and this amounts to financial fragility or to a Ponzi financing position. The problem with such a strategy is that it relies on foreign financing to balance the current account, and this can take place only under very specific conditions: 'it is only possible to maintain a development strategy based on net imports financed by foreign capital inflows if the interest rates on the foreign borrowing are equal to the rate of increase of foreign borrowing. If interest rates are higher than the rate of increase of inflows … the policy will eventually and automatically become self-reversing as the current account becomes dominated by interest and profit remittances that exceed capital inflows' (Kregel 2004, 11). This, arguably, is what has made various growth efforts in developing countries so difficult to sustain in the last few development decades: many growth strategies are simply based on self-reversing logic, and this is indeed what Nurkse clearly foresaw.

Thus, according to Nurkse, any economic strategy that wants to be sustainable in the long term has to come up with another way of financing the development. What this means, however, is that such a development strategy has to work in a relatively confined environment in terms of capital and skills. Taking into account the financial constraints described above, it is in this context that Nurkse interprets Adam Smith's famous theorem about the size of the market being limited by the division of labor. For Nurkse (1953, 21–25), following Allyn Young's 1928 essay, this theorem indicates that the size of the market is limited by real wages that are, in turn, limited by productivity growth. For Nurkse (Nurkse 1953, 8, 14; Nurkse 1961, 5–9, 27–29, 32), and very clearly for Hirschman and Rosenstein-Rodan (1984), productivity growth is determined by the presence of increasing returns in an economy. Thus, a viable development strategy should aim at establishing a number of increasing returns activities that would become each other's customers and generate the first virtuous circle of growth. The size of the market is limited by the number of increasing returns activities present at the particular market. This dynamics is the essence of Nurkse's balanced growth, but also of Rosenstein-Rodan's big push and, in the end, also of Hirschman's unbalanced growth, expressed in very similar wording.

> The expansion of the market can be realized only through a process of balanced growth, where people in different industries, working with more and better tools, become each other's customers. (Nurkse archives, Box 8; see also Nurkse 1961, 252)
>
> … new producers will be each other's customers, and the complementarity of demand will reduce the risk of not finding a market. Risk reduction is in this sense a special case of external economies. (Rosenstein-Rodan 1984, 213)

Hirschman argues that such an interrelatedness – which he called backward and forward linkages – does not happen simultaneously, but rather in a sequential process of learning and development, and that in this process, the role of public policy or development strategy in setting goals and advancing specific sectors is key.[9] Nurkse's most serious argument against this is that such unbalanced growth will very probably need to rely on foreign financing at some point, as Hirschman (1984, 103) also admits. As we have argued above, due to the specific nature of such foreign financing (extractive in its nature and easily engendering lock-in effects, plus financing the consumption of imported goods), Nurkse (1961, 247–253) was wary that such a strategy would lead to financial fragility. As we have argued above, this proved to be a highly far-sighted concern.

It is important to note that most subsequent accounts of big push and balanced growth theories only emphasize the idea of consorted investments, mostly missing the point that, first, these policy efforts should target increasing returns activities and that, second, the reasoning behind this has to do with financial stability (see, e.g., Easterly 2008).

In order to create increasing returns activities, infant industry protection may be necessary according to Nurkse and others, but it is also more important here to realize that the argument is less about protection but about what is specifically targeted with the protective policies and how: infant creation is more important than infant protection (Nurkse 1961, 247, 257; 1953, 104–105, 109). Indeed, perhaps the key idea behind targeting increasing returns activities is that the resulting virtuous circles of growth (productivity and wage growth) act as barriers of entry for competitors both in terms of private companies but also in terms of regions and countries (See also Reinert 1980, Gomory and Baumol 2004.) The reason is evident in the very logic of balanced growth: virtuous circles of growth relay and create their own demand and financing (Nurkse 1961, 296). Thus, the driving idea behind Nurkse's balanced growth is not simply a set of reasons and/or policies for the creation of diversity in increasing returns activities, but moreover to show that both as a theoretical foundation and as a policy strategy, balanced growth is coherent and sustainable as it shows how long-term growth with financial stability can be achieved and maintained. In sum, Nurkse's balanced growth shows how middle-income nations can be created.

The quest to create middle-income economies as the main goal of development can also be stated differently: how to upgrade developing countries' economic structures *with* raising wages and *without* beggar-thy-neighbor type of policies, for instance, in foreign exchange rates, labor markets, tax rates, and so forth (See also Summers 2008). This, however, is largely the way competitiveness has come to be defined by international organizations like OECD and the European Union. Interestingly, however, this definition of competitiveness comes from a 1985 Reagan administration report *Global Competition: The New Reality* by the President's Commission on Industrial Competitiveness (1985; see Scott and Lodge 1985 as background). Historically, however, this goes back further to the Bretton Woods agreements, in particular the one that established the IMF, where under article I.2, it states the aim of the IMF as follows: 'To facilitate the expansion and balanced growth of international trade, and to contribute thereby to the promotion and maintenance of high levels of employment and real income and to the development of the productive resources of all members as primary objectives of economic policy.' The key background publication for these ideas was the League of Nations publication from 1944 titled *International Currency Experience: Lessons of the Inter-war Period* and mainly written by Nurkse. (See further Urban 2009 in this volume) This does not only show the breadth of Nurkse's influence, but also shows why his and his generation's development ideas are so relevant today: the strategy proposed by classical development economists is, first, based on a historically proven recipe of targeting increasing returns activities and, second, doing so under more or less financially stable conditions. It also shows, however, that following the path of balanced growth makes it clear that there is a need for global balancing rules as well. While the post-WWII era showed that this can indeed be done, the year 2008 has taught that such global financial rules are direly needed again.

Krugman (1994) argues that the decline of high development theory has methodological reasons: 'so why didn't high development theory get expressed in formal models? Almost certainly for one basic reason: high development theory rested critically on the assumption of economies of scale, but nobody knew how to put these scale economies into formal models.' Krugman admits that in particular, Hirschman and Myrdal were consciously against increasing modeling in economics. His own argument that modelling is inevitable in economics is based on two simplifying assumptions: first, science is based on models and second, models need to be mathematical. While both assumptions are, to say the least, debatable (see in particular, Drechsler (2004) for an excellent discussion), putting the blame on the doorstep of high development theory, Krugman along with much of the economics profession completely misses the other side of the story: how model-based economics interpreted post-World War II development stories. As we will argue below, because model-based economics assumed increasing returns and technology from development, it was left with tools Nurkse and others deemed counterproductive when used without targeting precisely the increasing returns activities, trade openness and foreign financing, as the main engines of growth. As the saying goes, if all you have is a hammer, pretty soon all problems look like nails. This is precisely what happened. While high development theory argued for a context-specific approach and tailor-made policies – because economic activities, technology, knowledge and economies of scale change enormously in time and space – the new development consensus on the rise in the 1980s and in full sway to this day argues the opposite: all developed problems are fundamentally alike, and thus, solving them should go by more or less the same policy prescriptions. The success of such an approach lies in the very nature of development: as Hirschman argues, all development presupposes some form of priority setting through policy making (Hirschman 1958). The Washington Consensus did away exactly with this assumption: since all development problems are assumed to be of the same nature, the solutions are bound to be the same as well, and this takes the burden of proof, so to say, away from domestic policymaking.

Washington Follies

It has been more or less thirty years since the alleged death of classical development economics. The 'demise' was precipitated by the onslaught of 'The Age of Milton Friedman,'[10] and by what about fifteen years ago became more widely known as the Washington Consensus.[11] It can be argued that it was truly an intellectual 'counter-revolution', a term used both by the supporters and the critics (see Johnson 1971 and Klein 2007, respectively). The counter-revolution, whatever its ideological core or its public enemies may have originally been (be it development economics proper, Keynesianism or Bastard Keynesianism),[12] was, in its core, aimed at juxtaposing two seemingly different development traditions: East Asia's rise and Latin America's doom in the 1970s and 1980s. However, this was only possible by showing, first, that East Asia's rise was based on using policies based on classical Ricardian comparative advantage thinking and using exports as an 'engine of growth' (see from Balassa 1971 to Rodrik 2006 and World Bank 2008a), and second, that Latin America's problems had its roots in failed or at least mismanaged import substitution industrialization, closely related with the classical development economics (see from Bhagwati 1984 to Rodrik 2007).

In both cases, the counter-revolutionaries or their descendants got it wrong: exports were only a part of the success story in East Asia's rapid rise, and import substitution played only a relatively insignificant part in Latin America's fall.

East Asia's story was told in a way as if feedback linkages and positive externalities emerging in these economies through state-led industrialization played only an exogenous role in development.[13] That is, technology and innovation were simply left out of the story, and a rather simplistic conclusion was drawn: export-led growth is what works in development countries. Latin America's problems, in turn, were seen through a double prism of inflation and rent-seeking, without, however, realizing that increasing foreign private lending in the 1970s also spurred the consumption engine into higher gear, which was bound to lead to the current account problems (through import consumption) and eventually towards long-lasting financial fragility that undermined industrialization efforts, and not the other way around (Kregel 2008). That is, the role of the post-Bretton Woods international financial architecture was ignored and, in fact, together with the newly learned 'lessons' from East Asia about export-led growth, it was precisely the accelerating financial liberalization that was seen as the main source of the much-needed capital for the export-led growth model.[14] Two plus two equals five: development needs foreign investments and exports, and both could be provided by a stable macro-economic environment and liberalized markets. In sum, two misinterpretations ended up providing a new model for development that evolved into the Washington Consensus as a full-fledged ideology and set of policies.

Significantly, both misinterpretations marked a break with a long-standing development tradition reaching back to the Renaissance (see Reinert 2007 in detail) – that was, however, also supported by many if not most neo-classical economists at the time (excellent summary is Evans and Alizadeh 1984) – namely, that infant industry protection is a necessary if not sufficient condition for industrialization and diversification. Also Williamson's (2002) original list of Washington Consensus policies included infant industry protection, and 'a moderate general tariff (in the range of 10 per cent to 20 per cent, with little dispersion) might be accepted as a mechanism to provide a bias toward diversifying the industrial base without threatening serious costs'. Neither made it into the Washington Consensus practices in the 1990s or into its augmented version of the 2000s.[15]

With these misinterpretations, however, not only were real developments misunderstood, equally important is to note that comparing East Asian and Latin American development experiences yields key lessons about the success and failure of development strategies. More precisely, perhaps the key lesson is that protectionism does not equal protectionism. If development history teaches us that infant industry protection is a *conditio sine qua non*, then it is exactly the comparison of two very recent instances of this strategy that can teach us the reasons for success and failure. Indeed, based on these two historical experiences, we can create two 'ideal types' of protectionism. In Table 1.1, we try to distill from vast and diverse historical data and different contexts two such 'ideal types'.

Comparing the two, it is clear that key differences between these 'ideal types' rest precisely in the issues that especially Nurkse, but also other early development economists, thought fundamental to development. First, the idea that development needs specific economic activities that exhibit long-term potential in terms of learning curves, home-market expansion and exports. Such activities provide dynamic increasing returns that in turn create possibilities for continuous upgrading through educational, labor-market and other policies. This is what East Asian countries did; Latin American countries failed to target windows of opportunities in different activities and a need for competitive pressure was underestimated. Second, the failure to create dynamic economies of scale led to financial fragility relatively easily, in particular, when foreign capital inflows and lending became prevalent elements in the development strategy, as happened in Latin America in 1980s.

Table 1.1. **Ideal Types of Protectionism Compared**

East Asian	Latin American
Temporary protection of new industries/products for the world market	Permanent protection of mature industries/products for the home market (often very small)
Very steep learning curves compared to the rest of the world	Learning that lags behind the rest of the world
Based on a dynamic Schumpeterian view of the world – market-driven 'creative destruction'	Based on a more static view of the world-planned economy
Domestic competition maintained	Little domestic competition
Core technology locally controlled	Core technology generally imported from abroad/assembly of imported parts'/ 'superficial' industrialization
Massive investment in education/industrial policy created a huge demand for education. Supply of educated people matched demand from industry.	Less emphasis on education/type of industries created did not lead to huge (East Asian) demand for education. Investment in education therefore tends to feed emigration
Meritocracy-capital, jobs and privileges distributed according to qualifications	*Nepotism* in the distribution of capital, jobs and privileges
Equality of land distribution (Korea)	Mixed record on land distribution
Even income distribution increased home market for advanced industrial goods	Uneven income distribution restricted scale of home market and decreased competitiveness of local industry
Profits created through dynamic 'Schumpeterian' rent-seeking	Profits created through static rent-seeking
Intense cooperation between producers and local suppliers	Confrontation between producers and local suppliers
Regulation of technology transfer oriented towards maximizing knowledge transferred	Regulation of technology transfer oriented towards avoiding 'traps'

These lessons, however, were almost completely missed by the Washington Consensus.[16] Moreover, what is historically significant is the fact that the classical development economists were largely made the culprits of Latin America's problems. It is all the more puzzling when one reads the original works of these authors and looks at the subsequent history; it becomes clear, as we have shown above, that it is their theories that predicted both East Asia's rise (understanding the key role of technology and diversity) and Latin America's doom (understanding financial fragility built into foreign-financing-led growth strategies). Interestingly, Williamson's article on the Washington Consensus ends with doubt and a premonition along similar lines of thought:

A striking fact about the list of policies on which Washington does have a collective view is that they all stem from classical mainstream economic theory, at least if one is allowed to count Keynes as a classic by now. None of the ideas spawned by the development literature – such as the big push, balanced or unbalanced growth, surplus labor, or even the two-gap model – plays any essential role in motivating the Washington consensus ... This raises the question as to whether Washington is correct in its implicit dismissal of the development literature as a diversion from the harsh realities of the dismal science. Or is the Washington consensus, or my interpretation of it, missing something? (2002)

As we have seen in Figures 1.1 to 1.3, Washington Consensus policies not only failed to deliver growth and development to most developing countries, following such policies seems to have been almost a blueprint for falling back rather than catching up. Such an enormous, and as we have shown, historically unprecedented negative impact goes back to two key misunderstandings: first, the role of technology and increasing returns, and second, the role of institutions. However, before we discuss these, it is pivotal to understand that what made the 1990s particularly 'crazy' in terms of development was the coincidence of implementing Washington Consensus policies and the change in techno-economic paradigm. We argue next that this made export-led growth underlying Washington Consensus policies a race to the bottom, or beggar-thy-neighbor environment, because trade and technology were essentially decoupled both in theory and in policies.

Carlota Perez, the inventor of the concept of techno-economic paradigms, has briefly summarized the idea of techno-economic paradigms as follows:

There has been a technological revolution every 40 to 60 years, beginning with the Industrial Revolution in England at the end of the 18th Century; each has generated a great surge of development, diffusing unevenly across the world from an initial core country... . The great wealth creating potential provided by each of them stems from the combination of the new technologies, industries and infrastructures with a set of generic technologies and organisational principles capable of modernising the rest of the economy. The resulting best practice frontier is superior to the previous one and becomes the new common sense for efficiency – a new techno-economic paradigm – that defines the guidelines for innovation and competitiveness. ... The propagation is highly uneven in coverage and timing, by sectors and by regions, in each country and across the world. (Perez 2006; see also Perez 2002)

The paradigms describe how the technological change and innovation of a given period are most likely to take place: organizational forms and finance that are conducive to innovations, what technological capabilities and skills are needed, and so forth. Accordingly, the new ICT-based techno-economic paradigm, coming to full force in 1990s, has engendered key changes in production processes in almost all industries (including many services and agriculture): outsourcing and the resulting geographical dispersion of production functions. These changes have enabled very fast growth in foreign capital inflows into developing countries as well as industrialization (e.g., in terms of growth rates of manufactured and high-tech exports). However, in many cases the outsourcing activities do not exhibit the same dynamics that used to be associated with them in the originating countries – fast and sustained productivity growth, raising real wages, forward and backward linkages – but rather the opposite (For detailed discussion and data, see, e.g., Palma 2005; Cimoli, Ferraz and Primi 2005; Tiits et al 2008). Thus, the key assumption of comparative advantage trade models and theories fell away: even if high technology exports have been growing in developing countries, this does not mean that we deal with similarly dynamic sectors with significant increasing returns (See also Krugman 2008). As a result, increasing global trade easily increases production and investment, but not necessarily global wealth, and, consequently, the allocation of production across the countries may well be globally inefficient (Palley 2006, 10). Due to the changing techno-economic paradigm, integrating developing countries into the world economy has become an increasingly asymmetrical affair in many ways.

Coupled with the change of techno-economic paradigm, Washington Consensus policies emphasising FDI- and export-led growth have created a truly toxic situation for many developing countries, especially in Latin America and Eastern Europe, where liability destruction was strong and quick initially, but was then followed by slow asset creation.

In sum, the Washington Consensus has left many developing countries with an almost completely changed economic and industrial structure that is deeply different from and much less skill- and technology-intensive than the previous structure. This explains the fast growth, but also why they do not catch up with the Asian economies in terms of productivity and income growth witnessed in Figures 1.1 and 1.2.

As we have mentioned, there are two reasons why the Washington Consensus and its descendants run into problems on the level of theory, and in particular, on the level of practical advice, and are constantly criticized by Schumpeterian/ evolutionary/institutional economists:[17] the specific, narrow and eventually misleading understanding of technology and institutions. It is difficult to argue that neither is significant for growth and development, and thus, hardly any economist these days argues against the importance of technology or institutions. Indeed, there is a growing trend to pay rather extensive lip service to both. The latest fashion in development seems to be precisely the mix of 'getting the institutions right' and 'getting the technology right'. Jeffrey Sachs and the World Bank (as proxies for the reigning consensus) advocate that, first, institutional and not simply policy reforms are key to long-term growth, and second, development strategies should be based on technology as one of the key drivers of long-term growth. While both ideas seem very close to what long-term Schumpeterian critics of the Washington Consensus have advocated, in reality there is hardly any change in development advice, and the inclusion of both technology and institutions follows a deeply faulty logic.

While Sachs (2008, 205) argues that 'the very science and technology that underpin prosperity in the rich world are potentially available to the rest of world as well', the World Bank (2008b, 3; see also World Bank 2008a, 18) wonders '[w]hy is it that existing proven technologies are frequently not adopted by people who presumably would benefit most from these technologies'. This is not far from the neo-classical assumption that technology is exogenous to growth since technological development is seen here largely as a linear step-by-step development towards complexity and as essentially open for various competitors to step up and join the ride. This is simply not true. In business terms, this equals arguing that since there is a huge market for computer operating systems, one of the best businesses in town should compete with Microsoft's Windows. That this strategy can be, if at all, taken up perhaps only by Google shows how ridiculous the assumption is that technology is freely available to all.

Seeing technology as yet another neutral ingredient that can be added at will into the development blender gravely misunderstands the process of creative destruction that characterizes capitalist growth. And while the recent publications by the World Bank do actually refer to creative destruction (see, e.g., World Bank 2008a, 26, 44–45), it is usually done in an extremely narrow sense to mean entry of new firms and dissolution of old ones. Technological development is anything but linear and technology is anything but freely available. Path dependencies, linkages, spillovers, externalities, winner-takes-all markets and highly imperfect and dynamic competition make technology an unpredictable, high-risk and possibly high-return endeavour that drives on a tautological logic: technological development feeds on technological development. (See, e.g., Arthur 1994, Perez 2002) Even more importantly, technology is a man-made comparative advantage that creates havoc in the Ricardian comparative advantage model. What technological development shows is that that the key is not trade as such, but what kind of trade and with whom (See Gomory and Baumol 2004, and Palley 2006 for a brilliant discussion). Indeed, trade models without technology and increasing returns advocate a policy environment that is bound to lead to beggar-thy-neighbor policies either through exchange rate depreciations, technological know-how restrictions or the Latin American type of protectionism described above. Palley describes this logic in the following terms:

> First, countries do not benefit from autarky (self-sufficiency) because they lose the benefit of economies of scale. Second, countries still want to retain a more than proportionate share of industry, as this objective restricts global output and drives up prices of goods. Since the countries also export these goods, this objective confers a terms-of-trade benefit that increases income. (Palley 2006, 13)

Models and policies that do not assume increasing returns essentially decouple trade and technology. As we have shown above, successful development from the last 500 years teaches us exactly the opposite: successful trade policy is largely a technology policy.

As far as institutional change is concerned, it has been argued that most developing countries did not reform enough or failed to implement properly Washington ideas: 'meant well, tried little, failed much' (Krueger 2004). The consensus ideas about institutional reform are based on one simple assumption: institutions are 'the rules and norms constraining human behavior' (World Bank 2006, 5). The author most often associated with this line of argument is Douglass North and yet somewhat surprisingly one of the harshest criticisms of the World Bank blend of institutionalism and policy reform comes precisely from him (just substitute, for simplicity's sake, open access societies with developed countries and natural states with poor societies):

> The economists' natural prescription is to suggest that a country 'reform'; that they systematically adopt policies that mimic those in open access order: less regulatory control, absence of monopolies, more secure property rights, improved public goods provision such as education and more markets. Such an approach ignores the fact that natural states adopt limited access policies not just to maximize the incomes of the ruling elite, but because limited access policies address the problem of violence by giving individuals and groups with access to violence an incentive to cooperate. Policies from open access orders – universal, impersonal rights and rule of law – reduce the natural state's ability to control violence. These changes threaten to make people worse off, not better off.... . The transfer of institutions from open access orders to natural states cannot, in and of itself, produce political and economic development. (North, Wallis and Weingast 2008, 15)

North et al. indeed point to a key problem inherent in many of the Washington Consensus ideas about institutions, namely that an institutional setting can be transformed from one society to the next. Such a universal claim makes it possible to reverse the development logic: in any given country, one does not start with problems but rather with solutions. Perhaps the best example is the recent work by the World Bank that advocates openness and context-specific solutions to development problems – but only as long as the diagnosis and solutions are based on the market failure approach (World Bank 2006; World Bank 2008a). This is, of course, a mirror image of the Washington Consensus approach: the latter operates with predefined solutions, the 'new' approach with predefined problems. The Washington Consensus is far from over, it just comes in many new disguises.

Even if it is possible to argue that by now the Washington Consensus has turned into Washington Confusion (Rodrik 2006), there is scant if any evidence that policy advice given to developing countries or analytical work done by the Washington institutions has in substance changed at all (Rodrik also admits this). What is more, there is a growing tendency to deal with symptoms such as mosquito nets, debt relief and the like. It is obviously nonsensical to argue that such activities should not be undertaken. It is, however, equally clear that such palliative pop-star economics, chiefly advocated by Jeffrey Sachs (2004 and 2008) and embodied in UN's Millennium Development Goals, will do almost nothing to put poor countries on a sustainable development track. Quite the opposite, it can also be argued that such treatment of symptoms entraps poor countries into Malthusian boom-bust cycles of population growth and hunger. As Clark (2007, 45) argues, 'the subsistence wage, at which population growth would cease, is many times lower in the modern world than in the preindustrial period... . Given the continued heavy dependence of many sub-Saharan African countries on farming, and a fixed supply of agricultural land, health care improvements are not an unmitigated blessing, but exact a cost in terms of lower material incomes.'

Thus, while the former Washington Consensus writers readily admit to a greater role of technology and institutions in development, their assumptions and conclusions seem to lead right back to the Washington Consensus mode of understanding the development issues. An interesting example is Rodrik's work and, by default it seems, also most recent thinking in the World Bank. Rodrik's suggestions for industrial policies in the twenty-first century are hardly, if at all, compatible with his self-proclaimed neoclassical approach and with his 'growth diagnostics'. While the latter two are obviously based on the concept of market failure (or government failure that causes market failure; the result is the same, namely market failure), most of his policy principles and incentives could have been written by a Schumpeterian economist. Rodrik's (2007, 114–119) policy advice ranges from 'incentives to 'new' activities', through a 'built-in sunset clause' to demanding that 'activities that are subsidized must have the clear potential of providing spillovers and demonstration effects' and to subsidizing R&D and 'general technical training'. Such policies do not necessitate market failure as a concept to understand the need for them; market failure and the neoclassical approach, however, makes the application of these ideas context blind. Clearly, if one assumes a key role for technology in economic growth, one has to give up market failure as a concept, as technologically driven growth is by definition imperfect. Entrepreneurs seek technological innovation in *order* to create market failures. As most economists, Rodrik, too, thinks that the answer lies in better governance to avoid such pitfalls. And, as many before, Rodrik is fundamentally governance blind and does not realize that the same Washington whirlwind of change has swept through policy advice on governance as well (for Rodrik's ideas on governance, see Rodrik 2008).

Indeed, what looked like a set of hardcore economic policies – neutral to politics or morals for that matter, and thus free of rent-seeking, a proper there-is-no-alternative, or TINA (see Hirschman 1984) – was in fact accompanied by a similar sea change in policymaking. Rolling the state back was accompanied by hollowing the state out. This meant that not only did the policy space become strictly defined, but also the way policies were implemented was radically redefined. New public management (NPM) was as fast and furious in its onslaught as the Washington Consensus.

While there is a relatively long tradition of making a caricature out of Weberian or classical bureaucracy that emphasizes rule of law, clear hierarchies, merits and competence (Lynn 2001 for a good overview), what came to be the meeting point for economic policy and governance reforms is the loss of increasing returns or technology from their framework of thinking. While Krugman (1994) and others have documented how mainstream economics lost scale economies due to increasing modelling in the aftermath of WWII, it is interesting that one branch of economics that seemingly retained scale economies, interpreted them in an highly specific way.

From the beginning of their theoretical endeavours, public choice theorists have concentrated upon a specific kind of scale economies, namely, those limited by regulation and/or monopolistic markets. Indeed, one can follow this specific way of understanding increasing returns from Stigler (1951) to Buchanan and Yoon (2008). Public choice theorists go explicitly back to Smith's theorem about the division of labor being limited by the extent of the market and argue that Smith's accomplishment is in the 'replacement of the mercantilist world of monopolies and cartels by competitive markets' (Buchanan and Yoon 2008, 187). It is quite clear that public choice theorists look almost solely at what can be called internal scale economies. In fact, this line of argument (looking only at internal scale economies) can be traced back to Viner's (1937) discussion of trade theory in the 1930s; Viner is similarly worried about the potentially monopolistic impact of internal increasing returns (see also Reinert 1980, 117–121).[18] In this line of argument the increasing returns might engender monopoly rents and stifle competition; consequently, policy focus should not be on creating activities with such returns, or not foremost, but on alleviating the market-limiting impact of such monopoly rents. This, in essence, forms the foundation for the market failure approach discussed above. The entire enormous impact of external and historical increasing returns is left out of the argument, and this has had grave consequences for the way public choice and mainstream economists in general understand the role of the state in economic growth. Since competitive environment is seen as the guarantee for extending market size (and, along the way, lowering prices for consumers) and increasing division of labour, the government's main task is to ensure and maintain such an environment. However, in particular, public choice theory takes it much further than that. Namely, according to this theory, the best way to ensure that government actually looks after the competitive environment is to inject market discipline also into government activities. Thus, the government should outsource and privatize as many activities as possible; there should be markets for public services wherever possible; there should be internal markets within government; public servants should be paid according to their performance, and so forth.

What came to be known in the 1990s as new public management thus has its origins in interpreting increasing returns in a very specific way.[19] The results, however, have been as disastrous for developing as for developed countries. As one commentator puts it, 'as more and more state functions are subcontracted to the private sector, so the state begins to lose competence to do things which once it managed very well... . Government becomes a kind of institutional idiot.' (Crouch 2004, 41) Ironically, the results of NPM reforms are almost the exact opposite of what public-choice theorists intended: instead of lowering socially costly rent-seeking, 'the more that the state withdraws from providing for the lives of ordinary people, making them apathetic about politics, the more easily can corporate interests use it more or less unobserved as their private milch-cow' (Crouch 2004, 19). At the same time, there is strong evidence to suggest that developing countries profit from classical Weberian bureaucratic structures, in particular, in terms of creating long-term administrative capacity, as Weberian administration relies on strict legal principles (government actions are regulated by public law), and there is a strong emphasis on merit, competence and achievement in public service (entrance and promotion based on merit, competences and achievement) and clear hierarchies that enhance accountability.[20] Weberian bureaucracy tends to focus on long-term strategic goals and thus provides, especially, developing countries with direly needed stability in policy planning and design. Indeed, the previous lack of strategic capacities in policymaking is perhaps the strongest reason why many developing countries should be particularly careful in experimenting with most recent administrative reform fashions like 'governing by networks' (see also Schick 1998). However, we see also in developed European countries a growing trend towards what has been termed Neo-Weberian State, where notions of legality and accountability, competence and merit reenter both the academic discourse and actual changes in public sector reforms. (Pollitt and Bouckaert 2004; Drechsler 2005).

It is, however, ironic, but also deeply significant, that in its core, the Washington Consensus and NPM go back to the same misreading of Adam Smith. We use here the term 'misreading' in a rather specific way. This term was coined in the late 1960s by Harold Bloom and denotes a process where authors creatively appropriate phrases, ideas from other authors, in the writing process and mould them into something new, or at any rate something different. Bloom (1997, 5), writing about theory of poetry, writes 'Poetic history ... is ... indistinguishable from poetic influence, since strong poets make that history by misreading one another, so as to clear imaginative space for themselves.' A misreading does not thus connote a negative meaning. Generalizing it into a hermeneutical principle, we can argue that a misreading is the way most theoretical works are read and written. We argue that the history of economic thought has one such key passage, namely Smith's above-mentioned theorem about the size of the market and the division of labour. The importance of the theorem can be easily understood from the famous example Smith himself uses, namely, that of 'the trade of the pin-maker'. According to Smith (1776/1976, 1.1.3), this particular occupation has gone through a transformation from a one-man business into at least 18 distinct operations performed by different individuals, causing productivity per employee to increase from one pin a day to 4,800 pins a day. Such productivity explosions that follow innovations depend, as Smith rightly argued, on extensive trade and, as Smith also admitted, rapid technological development. While most researchers in economics and in related fields agree with the wide-brush description given by Smith, there are strongly varying misreadings about what causes and stimulates such innovations in the private sector. There are essentially two opposing schools of thought: On the one hand, there are scholars in the Schumpeterian/evolutionary/institutionalist tradition who argue that innovations and economic growth in general take place because of knowledge and skill agglomeration and continuous upgrading and technological change that are engendered by highly embedded policymaking of increasing coordination, dialogue and cooperation managed by a highly capable state and administration.[21] On the other hand, there are scholars in neoclassical and public-choice traditions who argue that the main driver behind innovations and growth are trade and competition: the former using the comparative advantage of nations to bring more, better and cheaper goods to consumers (higher efficiency); the latter creating pressures for companies to incessantly innovate and outcompete the competitors, and to push prices downwards in the process (higher efficiency, again).[22] While the differences in details are, of course, greater than described here, it is important to see that both traditions can be traced back to Adam Smith's theorem that the division of labor is limited by the size of the market (1776/1976). The difference is how one understands the theorem: the former school takes it to mean that the division of labour is key (creation of knowledge and technological diversity, and the producer with his capabilities are the main policy goals), the latter school thinks the size of the market is key (the extent of trade and competition, and lower prices for consumers are the main policy goals).

If, instead of accepting Adam Smith as an icon of free trade and laissez-faire under any circumstances, one reads what he says about economic development at an early stage, one will find that he is very much in line with classical development economics, where industrialization is the key recommendation. In his early work, *The Theory of Moral Sentiments*, Adam Smith (1759/1810) argued passionately for 'the great system of government', which is helped by adding new manufactures. Interestingly, Smith argued that new manufactures are to be promoted, neither to help suppliers nor to help consumers, but in order to improve this 'great system of government'.

In fact, it is possible to argue that Adam Smith was also a misunderstood mercantilist, someone who firmly supported the mercantilist policies of the past, but then argued that they were no longer necessary for England. He praises the Navigation Acts protecting English manufacturing and shipping against Holland, arguing 'they are as wise ... as if they had all been dictated by the most deliberate wisdom' and holding them to be 'perhaps the wisest of all the commercial regulations of England' (Smith 1776/1976: I, 486–487). All in all, Smith described a development that had become successfully self-sustained, a kind of snowballing effect, originating in the wise protectionist measures of the past. Only once did Smith (1776/1976, 477) use the term 'invisible hand' in the *Wealth of Nations*: when it sustained the key import substitution goal of mercantilist policies, when the consumer preferred domestic industry to foreign industry. This is when 'the market' had taken over the role previously played by protective measures, and national manufacturing no longer needed such protection. If one cared to look, Adam Smith also argued for tariff protection at an early stage as a mandatory passage point to development as did Friedrich List. Studying economic policy without discussing the context is one of the destructive vices of economic practice.

The key is not which side one chooses, however, but to see that both approaches are not simply complementary to each other, but rather should be seen as following each other in a step-by-step development. This, indeed, is perhaps the greatest legacy of early development economists and Ragnar Nurkse: having synthesized these two broad theoretical schools into a coherent theoretical framework that proved highly successful once applied in real life.

Conclusion: Where Do We Go fom Here?

While the Fall of 2008 marks the end of the neoliberal consensus about globalization and its rules in many ways, it is very much open to debate what direction economic and policy thinking will take from here on. Judging by history, a new development consensus will be in the making for the next decade. Following the classical development economists, what should be the cornerstones of the new consensus?

As a reminder: we have argued that the main development challenge left behind by the Washington Consensus and its affiliates is the difficulty in creating middle-income economies, because of the loss of an activity-specific approach and of increasing returns-based economic policymaking, and loss of how to generate the administrative capacity for development. In addition, the current techno-economic paradigm and financial globalization have enabled the decoupling of knowledge and production, and of production and finance. This has led to an international trade environment where developing countries are in effect engaged in beggar-thy-neighbour types of policies in order to capture increasing returns activities – and in which many of them do not succeed and end up in financially fragile development positions.

The key questions for further research and policy advice can be phrased as follows: how to couple trade, competition and similar policies with targeting increasing returns activities and how to create the financial environment where such activities (and their change) remain in hedged financing positions.

Here we can only demark three key areas where both theoretical and policy advances are necessary to start understanding how to achieve these goals; we argue these are areas where there is relatively little research currently done.

First, the geographical dimension has to be brought back into development economics as well as policy initiatives. While much of the world trade is in fact regional, there are few if any effective regional regulatory and policymaking regimes. Regional policy agenda is pivotal for trade and technology to exchange rate policies (see Wade 2008).

Second, in particular, trade and competition policies (but also other areas, for instance, procurement) should concentrate on targeting increasing-returns activities. There is, however, little research on how this can be done in a development context.

Third, the creation of the administrative capacity to implement policy reforms and in particular, the capacity for targeting activities, should be the focus of context-specific institutional reforms. While there is growing research on how highly developed countries recover from NPM reforms, there is very little research on developing countries.

References[†]

Amsden, Alice. 1989. *Asia's Next Giant: South Korea and Late Industrialization.* Oxford, England: Oxford University Press.

———. 2007. *Escape from Empire: The Developing World's Journey Through Heaven and Hell.* Cambridge, MA/London: The MIT Press.

Arthur, W. Brian. 1994. *Increasing Returns and Path Dependence in the Economy.* Ann Arbor: University of Michigan Press.

Balassa, Bela. 1971. 'Trade Policies in Developing Countries.' *The American Economic Review* 61 (2), Papers and Proceedings of the Eighty-Third Annual Meeting of the American Economic Association. (May, 1971): 178–187.

Bhagwati, Jagdish N. 1984. 'Comment on Raul Prebisch'. In Gerald M. Meier and Dudley Seers, eds., *Pioneers in Development.* Oxford – New York: Oxford University Press, 197–204.

Blecker, Robert A. 2000. 'The Diminishing Returns to Export-led Growth.' Available at http://www.cfr.org/content/publications/attachments/Blecker_Diminish_Paper.pdf

Bloom, Harold. 1997. *The Anxiety of Influence. A Theory of Poetry,* 2nd ed. Oxford and New York: Oxford University Press.

Botero, Giovanni. 1588. *Delle cause della grandezza delle città.* Rome.

Buchanan, James M. and Yong J. Yoon. 2008. 'Public Choice and the Extent of the Market.' *Kyklos* 61 (2): 177–188.

Chang, Ha-Joon. 2007. *Bad Samaritans: Rich Nations, Poor Policies and the Threat to the Developing World.* London: Random House.

Cimoli, M., J. C. Ferraz and A. Primi. 2005. *Science and Technology Policies in Open Economies: The Case of Latin America and the Caribbean.* Santiago: ECLAC.

Cimoli, Mario, Giovanni Dosi, Richard Nelson and Joseph Stiglitz. 2006. 'Institutions and Policies Shaping Industrial Development: An Introductory Note.' LEM Working Paper Series, 2/2006. Available at http://www.lem.sssup.it/WPLem/files/2006-02.pdf

Clark, Gregory. 2007. *A Farewell to Alms: A Brief Economic History of the World.* Princeton: The Princeton University Press.

Crouch, Colin. 2004. *Post-Democracy.* Cambridge: Polity.

Drechsler, Wolfgang. 2004. 'Natural vs. Social Sciences: On Understanding in Economics'. In Erik S. Reinert, ed., *Globalization, Economic Development and Inequality: An Alternative Perspective.* Cheltenham/Northampton, MA: Edward Elgar, 71–87.

———. 2005. 'The Rise and Demise of the New Public Management.' *post-autistic economics review* 33. Available at http://www.paecon.net/PAEReview/issue33/ Drechsler33.htm

---

[†] All websites accessed last in January 2009.

Easterly, William. 2008. 'Can the West Save Africa?' NBER Working Paper Series, No 14363. Available at http://www.nber.org/papers/w14363.pdf

Evans, David and Parvin Alizadeh. 1984. 'Trade, industrialisation, and the visible hand.' *Journal of Development Studies* 21 (1): 22–46.

Evans, Peter B. and James E. Rauch. 1999. 'Bureaucracy and Growth: A Cross-National Analysis of the Effects of 'Weberian' State Structures on Economic Growth.' *American Sociological Review* 64 (5): 748–765.

Galbraith, James K. 2008. 'The Collapse of Monetarism and the Irrelevance of the New Monetary Consensus.' The Levy Institute of Bard College, Policy Note 1/2008. Available at http://www.levy.org/pubs/pn_08_1.pdf

Gomory, Ralph E. and William J. Baumol. 2004. 'Globalization: Prospects, Promise and Problems.' *Journal of Policy Modeling,* 26 (4): 425–438.

Hirschmann, Albert O. 1958. *The Strategy of Economic Development.* New Haven: Yale University Press.

———. 1984. 'A Dissenter's Confession: 'The Strategy of Economic Development' Revisited.' In Gerald M. Meier and Dudley Seers, eds., *Pioneers in Development.* Oxford/New York: Oxford University Press, 87–111.

Huang, Yasheng. 2008. *Capitalism with Chinese Characteristics: Entrepreneurship and the State.* Cambridge: Cambridge University Press.

Johnson, Harry G. 1971. 'The Keynesian Revolution and the Monetarist Counter-Revolution.' *The American Economic Review* 61: (2), Papers and Proceedings of the Eighty-Third Annual Meeting of the American Economic Association (May, 1971): 1–14.

Klein, Naomi. 2007. *The Shock Doctrine: The Rise of Disaster Capitalism.* New York: Metropolitan Books.

Kregel, Jan A. 2004. 'External Financing for Development and International Financial Instability.' G–24 Discussion Paper Series, United Nations. Available at http://www.unctad.org/en/docs/gdsmdpbg2420048_en.pdf

———. 2008. 'The Discrete Charm of the Washington Consensus'. The Levy Economics Institute of Bard College Working Paper No 533. Available at http://www.levy.org/pubs/wp_533.pdf

Krueger, Anne O. 2004. 'Meant Well, Tried Little, Failed Much: Policy Reforms in Emerging Market Economies.' Available at http://www.imf.org/external/np/ speeches/2004/032304a.htm

Krugman, Paul. 1994. 'The Fall and Rise of Development Economics.' Available at http://web.mit.edu/krugman/www/dishpan.html

———. 2008. 'Trade and Wages, Reconsidered.' Available at http://www.princeton.edu/~pkrugman/pk-bpea-draft.pdf

League of Nations. 1944. *International Currency Experience: Lessons of the Inter-War Period.* League of Nations.

Lynn Jr., Laurence E. 2001. 'The Myth of the Bureaucratic Paradigm: What Traditional Public Administration Really Stood For.' *Public Administration Review* 61 (2): 144–160.

Madisson, Angus. 2003. *The World Economy. Historical Statistics.* Paris: OECD.

Nurkse, Ragnar. 1953. *Problems of Capital Formation in Underdeveloped Countries.* Oxford: Oxford University Press.

———. 1961. *Equilibrium and Growth in the World Economy.* Gottfried Haberler and Robert M. Stern, eds. Harvard Economic Studies CXVIII. Cambridge, MA: Harvard University Press.

North, Douglass, John Wallis and Barry Weingast. 2008. 'Violence and Social Orders: A Conceptual Framework for Interpreting Recorded Human History.' In *Governance,*

Growth, and Development Decision-Making. Washington; World Bank. Available at http://siteresources.worldbank.org/EXTPUBLICSECTORANDGOVERNANCE/Resources/governanceandgrowth.pdf

Myrdal, Gunnar. 1957. *Economic Theory and Underdeveloped Regions.* London: Duckworth.

Palley, Thomas. 2006. *Rethinking Trade and Trade Policy: Gomory, Baumol, and Samuelson on Comparative Advantage.* The Levy Economics Institute of Bard College, No 86.

Palma, Gabriel. 2005. 'The Seven Main 'Stylized Facts' of the Mexican Economy Since Trade Liberalization and NAFTA.' *Industrial and Corporate Change* 14 (6): 941–991.

Perez, Carlota. 2002. *Technological Revolutions and Financial Capital: The Dynamics of Bubbles and Golden Ages.* Cheltenham: Elgar.

———. 2006. 'Respecialisation and the Deployment of the ICT Paradigm: An Essay on the Present Challenges of Globalization'. In R. Compañó, C. Pascu, A. Bianchi, J.-C. Burgelman, S. Barrios, M. Ulbrich, I. Maghiros (eds.), *The Future of the Information Society in Europe: Contributions to the Debate.* Seville, Spain: European Commission, Directorate General Joint Research Centre.

Pollitt, Christopher and Geert Bouckaert. 2004. *Public Management Reform. A Comparative Analysis.* 2nd ed. Oxford: Oxford University Press.

President's Commission on Industrial Competitiveness. 1985. *Global Competition. The New Reality.* The Report of the President's Commission on Industrial Competitiveness, volume1.

Rauch, James E. and Peter B. Evans. 2000. 'Bureaucratic structure and bureaucratic performance in less developed countries.' *Journal of Public Economics* 75: 49–71.

Reinert, Erik S. 1980. *International Trade and the Economic Mechanisms of Underdevelopment.* Cornell University, University Microfilms.

———. 2007. *How Rich Countries Got Rich … and Why Poor Countries Stay Poor.* London: Constable.

Reinert, Erik S. and Rainer Kattel. 2007. 'European Eastern enlargement as Europe's attempted economic suicide?' The Other Canon and Tallinn University of Technology Working Papers in Technology Governance and Economic Dynamics, no. 14. Available at http://tg.deca.ee/files/main//2007070309122525.pdf

Rodrik, Dani. 2006. 'Goodbye Washington Consensus, Hello Washington Confusion? A Review of the World Bank's Economic Growth in the 1990s: Learning from a Decade of Reform.' *Journal of Economic Literature* XLIV: 973–987.

———. 2007. *One Economics, Many Recipes. Globalization, Institutions, and Economic Growth.* Princeton/Oxford: Princeton University Press.

———. 2008. 'Thinking about governance.' In *Governance, Growth, and Development Decision-Making.* Washington; World Bank. Available at http://siteresources.worldbank.org/EXTPUBLICSECTORANDGOVERNANCE/Resources/governanceand growth.pdf

Rosentsein-Rodan, Paul N. 1984. 'Natura Facit Saltum: Analysis of the Disequilibrium Growth Process.' In Gerald M. Meier and Dudley Seers, eds., *Pioneers in Development.* Oxford/New York: Oxford University Press, 207–221.

Sachs, Jeffrey. 2004. *The End of Poverty. How Can We Make It Happen In Our Lifetime.* New York: The Penguin Press.

———. 2008. *Common Wealth: Economics for a Crowded Planet.* New York: The Penguin Press.

Samuelson, Paul. 2004. 'Where Ricardo and Mill Rebut and Confirm Arguments of Mainstream Economists Supporting Globalization.' *Journal of Economic Perspectives* 18 (3): 135–146.

Schick, Allen. 1998. 'Why Most Developing Countries Should Not Try New Zealand's Reforms.' *World Bank Research Observer* 13: 123–131.

Shleifer, Andrei. 2008. 'The Age of Milton Friedman.' Available at http://www.economics.harvard.edu/faculty/shleifer/files/friedman3.3.pdf

Schmoller, Gustav von. [1881] 1893–4. *The Idea of Justice in Political Economy*. Annals of the American Academy of Political and Social Science 4: 697–737.

Scott, Bruce and George C. Lodge, eds. 1985. *US Competitiveness in the World Economy*. Boston, MA: Harvard Business School Press.

Skidelsky, Robert. 2008. 'Gloomy about Globalization'. *New York Review of Books* 55 (6) April 17. Available at http://www.nybooks.com/articles/21259

Smith, Adam. [1776] 1976. *An Inquiry into the Nature and Causes of the Wealth of Nations*. London: Methuen and Co. Available at http://www.econlib.org/LIBRARY/ Smith/smWN.html

———. [1759] 1810. *The Theory of Moral Sentiments*. London: A. Millar.

Sombart, Werner. 1949. 'Sociology: What It Is and What It Ought to be an. Outline for a Noo-Sociology'. *The American Journal of Sociology* 55 (2): 178–193.

Stigler, George J. 1951. 'The Division of Labor is Limited by the Extent of the Market.' *Journal of Political Economy* 59: 185–193.

Summers, Lawrence. 2008. 'A strategy to promote healthy globalisation'. *Financial Times* May 4. Available at http://www.ft.com/cms/s/0/999160e6-1a03-11dd-ba02-0000779fd2ac. html?nclick_check=1

Tocqueville, Alexis de. 1876. *Democracy in America*. 2 vols. 6th ed. Boston: John Allyn.

Toye, John. 1987. *Dilemmas of Development. Reflections on the Counter-Revolution in Development Theory and Policy*. Oxford: Blackwell.

Tiits, Marek, Rainer Kattel, Tarmo Kalvet and Dorel Tamm. 2008. 'Catching up, pressing forward or falling behind? Central and Eastern European development in 1990–2005.' *The European Journal of Social Science Research* 21 (1) March: 65–85.

Urban, Scott. 2009. '*International Currency Experience* and the Bretton Woods System: Ragnar Nurkse as Architect.' In this volume.

Viner, Jacob. 1937. *Studies in the Theory of International Trade*. Clifton, NJ: Kelly.

Wade, Robert. 2004. *Governing the Market: Economic Theory and the Role of Government in East Asian Industrialization*. 2nd ed. Princeton: Princeton University Press.

———. 2008. 'Financial Regime Change?' *New Left Review* 53 (September–October). Available at http://www.newleftreview.org/?issue=287

Williamson, John. 2002. 'What Washington Means by Policy Reform.' Available at http://www.iie.com/publications/papers/paper.cfm?ResearchID = 486 (Updated version of his 1990 article.)

———. 2008. 'Williamson versus the Washington Consensus?' Available at http://www.growthcommissionblog.org/content/williamson-versus-the-washington-consensus

World Bank. 2006. *Economic Growth in the 1990s: Learning from a Decade of Reform*. Available at http://www1.worldbank.org/prem/lessons1990s/

———. 2008a. *The Growth Report: Strategies for Sustained Growth and Inclusive Development*. Available at http://www.growthcommission.org/index.php?option = com_content &task = view&id = 96&Itemid = 169

———. 2008b. *Science, Technology, and Innovation. Capacity Building for Sustainable Growth and Poverty Reduction*. Available at http://go.worldbank.org/GEYA2NRGW0

Young, Allyn. 1928. 'Increasing Returns and Economic Progress.' *The Economic Journal* 38: 527–542.

Chapter Two:

LIFE AND TIME OF RAGNAR NURKSE

Kalev Kukk and Kalle Kukk

To introduce this article on Ragnar Nurkse, here are selected entries about him from four different national encyclopedias:

NURKSE (Ragnar), économiste américain (1907–1959). Il a particulièrement étudié la croissance dans les pays sous-développés et les problèmes monétaires internationaux. Il prône la diversification dans certaines branches de production comme stratégie de développement. On lui doit, notamment, *Problems of Capital Formation in Underdeveloped Countries* (1953). (*Grand Dictionnaire Encyclopédique Larousse*. 1984. Vol. 17, 7494; France)

    NURKSE, RAGNAR, 1907–59, estnisk nationalekonom, verksam vid Nationeras Förbund 1934–45, därefter professor vid Columbia University, New York. N:s forskning rörde internationell ekonomi och utvecklingsekonomi. I sitt mest kända verk, *Problems of Capital Formation in Underdeveloped Countries* (1953), driver N. tesen att u-länderna bör eftersträva en balanserad tillväxt. (*Nationalencyklopedin*. 1994. Vol. 14, 309; Sweden)

    NURKSE RAGNAR (1907–59), ekonomista amer., pochodzenia est.; 1934–45 pracowal w Lidze Narodów; 1945–54 prof. Columbia University w Nowym Jorku; zajmowal się problemami pieniądza (*International Currency Experience: Lessons of the Inter-War Period* 1944), handlu, 'zaklętogo kręgu ubóstwa', zrównowazonego wzrdstu; *Problems of Capital Formation in Underdeveloped Countries* (1953). (*Nowa encyklopedia powszecka PWN*. 1997. Vol. 4, 554–555; Poland)

    NURKSE, RAGNAR, amer. economist estonskoga podrijetla (Virn, Estonija, 5. X. 1907 – Le Mont-Pèlerin, Švicarska, 6. V. 1959). Prof. na Sveucilištima Columbia i Princeton. Bavio se monetarnom ekonomikom te ekon. Rastom zemalja u razvoju. Značajnija djela: *Uvjeti medunarodne monetarne ravnotež e* (*Conditions of International Monetary Equilibrium*, 1945), *Tijek I kontrola inflacije* (*The Course and*

Control of Inflation, 1946), *Problemi formiranja kapitala u nedovoljno razvijenim zemljama* (*Problems of Capital Formation in Underdeveloped Countries*, 1953), *Ravnoteža I rast u svjetskoj privredi (Equilibrium and Growth in the World Economy*, 1961). (*Hrvatska Enciklopedija*. 2005. Vol. 7, 796; Croatia)

Ragnar Nurkse's early years

Ragnar Nurkse is the most famous economist of Estonian origin. According to the local parish church register, he was born on 5 October 1907 (or 22 September in the old calendar) in the small village of Käru (in Rapla, respelled Raplamaa, county nowadays) about 100 km south of the Estonian capital Tallinn. In some documents, his birthplace has been recorded as another village of the same name, Käru in Viru (respelled Virumaa) county, but the parish register is clear that he was born in Raplamaa county.

His father, Wilhelm Nurkse (born 1883 in Vatku, Viru county, died 1933 in Edmonton, Canada), was at the time of Ragnar's birth the forester of Käru estate, and later the overseer of the same estate. Ragnar's mother, Victoria Clanman-Nurkse (born 1882, died 1964 in New York), descended from Estonian Swedes (*estlandssvenskarna*) who lived mainly on the West coast of Estonia and on different islands until the end of World War II. She came from a very intellectual family – her father Johann Klanmann (Klanman, Clanman) was at the time of Victoria's birth a teacher in a small school in Võnnu about 10 km from Haapsalu and later (1888–1910), the teacher on the small island of Naissaar (Nargö) populated by Swedes (Aman 1992, 83–84). Victoria Nurkse had a gymnasium education and later studied voice at La Scala in Milan.

In 1917 Ragnar Nurkse left Käru for Tallinn to continue his education there. In 1918 he began studies in the Tallinn Cathedral School (*Domschule zu Reval*). This was the time of the Estonian Freedom War against Bolshevik Russia and the buildup of the young country and post-war stabilization of Estonian economy (See, e.g., Valge 2006). The *Domschule* was a highly accepted school at that time. He graduated in 1926 with best honors and could, according to the Secondary School Act, enter the university without entrance exams. According to the school diploma, he had already begun to study economics at the *Domschule*. He also studied music at Tallinn Conservatoire of Music and graduated from the conservatoire as a student of Professor Peeter Ramul (piano) in 1927 with best honors.

In autumn 1926 Nurkse entered the University of Tartu, Faculty of Law, which included economics. He took only one exam there – in general law with highly renowned Professor Jüri Uluots (the last Prime Minister of Estonia before Soviet occupation in 1939–1940), getting *maxime sufficit* (excellent) grades. On 11 September 1928 he tried to pass the exam in political economy with Professor

Mikhail Kurtshinsky, but according to the minutes, unsuccessfully (*Estonian Historical Archives: Collection 2100, Inventory 10, Unit 160*). This was the first paradox in his life as a famous economist. At the same time, he was looking for an opportunity to study further in the United Kingdom and asked for support from the Ambassador of the Republic of Estonia in London, Dr. Oskar Kallas (who was a well-known folklorist). In a letter dated 1 October 1927, Dr. Kallas confirmed that he would get Nurkse a position as a trainee with the Honorary Consul of Estonia in Leith, Scotland, Adolph Ellingsen, and recommended for Nurkse 'to take an Estonian cargo vessel, which is cheaper', to Scotland (according to the family remembrances he indeed worked his way to the United Kingdom on a cargo ship from Estonia). In 1928 Nurkse worked as a secretary for Ellingsen (*Eesti välisteenistus* 2006, 182). During this period, his parents emigrated from Estonia to Canada in 1928, seeking better opportunities.

On 12 May 1929 he sent a letter from Edinburgh to the Dean of the Faculty of Law of University of Tartu and asked to postpone exams until autumn: 'Unfortunately I could not come to Tartu to take exams at the end of spring term as I am engaged here, and my duties do not allow my departure; besides, I am taking a course at the University of Edinburgh, and it would be difficult to interrupt it' (*Estonian Historical Archives: Collection 2100, Inventory 10, Unit 160*).

Ragnar Nurkse did not return to the University of Tartu, where he was formally a student, until 1 November 1929. In 1929 Nurkse started to study economics at the University of Edinburgh, which has always been a prestigious centre for economic studies. He graduated from Edinburgh in 1932 with a first-class degree, again with excellent honors. Nurkse considered himself a student of the late Professor and Director-General of the BBC, Sir Frederick Wolff Ogilvie (Nurkse 1935, VI). Professor Ogilvie himself regarded Nurkse as his most outstanding student (Hemming 1959). In Edinburgh, Nurkse continued his musical studies with Professor Sir Donald Francis Tovey and appeared regularly as a very fine performer on harpsichord and pianoforte in public concerts in Edinburgh and Glasgow, including radio broadcasts on the BBC.

In 1932–1934 Nurkse continued his studies in Vienna. He was awarded a Carnegie Fellowship to study at the University of Vienna where he visited the lectures. According to his *Meldungsbuch* (student register book) he studied with Professor Ludwig von Mises (theory of money), Dr. Gottfried von Haberler and Oskar Morgenstern (main problems of economics). This was the peak time of the second wave of Austrian School of economics. He was a participant in Mises's renowned *Privatseminar* (Haberler 1961, 20). Many of his fellows later became eminent professors of renowned universities in United Kingdom and in United States: e.g., Friedrich August von Hayek (London School of Economics and Chicago University), Gottfried von Haberler (Harvard University), Fritz Machlup (John Hopkins University and Princeton

University), Oskar Morgenstern (Princeton University) and Paul Narcyz Rosenstein-Rodan (Massachusetts Institute of Technology).

In Vienna, he published his first article *Ursachen und Wirkungen der Kapitalbewegungen* [*Causes and Effects of Capital Movements*] (Nurkse 1934) and first monograph on the same subject *Internationale Kapitalbewegungen* [International Capital Movements] (Nurkse 1935) published by *Österreichisches Institut für Konjunkturforschung*, which was founded by Mises and Hayek. In 1938 this book was translated into Japanese. According to Ragnar Nurkse (1935, V) himself, this piece of research was an attempt to handle international capital flows in the context of general economic theory in a comprehensive and systematic way. This research was strongly influenced by Bertil Ohlin and 'Austrians', particularly by Haberler and Machlup. Later, Haberler has classified these publications as pre-Keynesian (Haberler and Stern 1961, X).[1] In Vienna, Nurkse's close friendship with Haberler started and continued until Nurkse's death. This friendship was not affected by different views on exchange rate regimes (See, e.g., James and Bordo 2001).

League of Nations

In Vienna, on his own initiative and with the support of references from the Universities of Edinburgh and Vienna, Nurkse successfully applied for a job in the Secretariat of the League of Nations in Geneva. On 24 January 1934 the Secretary-General of the League of Nations, Joseph Avenol, sent Nurkse a letter informing him of a one-year service contract: 'I am glad to be able to offer you an appointment as a temporary official on the Secretariat of the League of Nations, in the capacity of Member of Section. The appointment will date from the 1st May, 1934, and is made for one year. You will be on probation during the first six months of your service. Your salary will be at the rate of 11,400 Swiss francs per annum' (*Estonian State Archives: Collection 957, Inventory 8, Unit 1321*). After the completion of the probation period, Nurkse was offered a long-term service contract for seven years. Secretary-General Joseph Avenol informed August Schmidt (later Torma), the Permanent Delegate of Estonia to the League of Nations of the decision in a letter dated 1 March 1935. He remarked highly on the work accomplished by Ragnar Nurkse and asked for understanding and support with an unexpected problem. As an Estonian citizen, Nurkse had to complete mandatory military service. But a prerequisite of the new service contract was that he should not interrupt his service in the League of Nations because of military service. The Chief Commander of the Estonian Army, Lieutenant General Johan Laidoner, gave his decision in a statement dated 23 July 1935: 'If Nurkse will not show up to the service he will be considered a defector and will be taken to court' (*Estonian State Archives: Collection 957, Inventory 8, Unit 1321*).

This dispute between the Ministry of Defence and Ministry of Foreign Affairs, where the biggest advocate for Nurkse was the Minister of Foreign Affairs, Julius Seljamaa, resulted in a very positive evaluation of Ragnar Nurkse. Alexander Loveday, the head of the Financial Section and Economic Intelligence Service of the League of Nations, presented in a letter dated 22 June 1935 to August Schmidt an outstanding characterization of the 27-year-old Nurkse:

> Nurkse is, in my opinion, a real discovery and likely to prove of very real value to the League, once we are placed in a position to be able to give him a contract. He has what is, in fact, unexpectedly rare, exactly the quality of mind that is suited to our Intelligence work here, as well as an exceptional knowledge of languages and a first-class education. He has proved himself quite unusually useful to me as, on account of his ability and training and also his quickness, I can turn him from one subject to another as pressure of work demands in a manner for which nobody else working in the Section is really fully adapted. (*Estonian State Archives: Collection 957, Inventory 8, Unit 1321*)

Nurkse continued his service as Member of Section (a position providing diplomatic immunity in Switzerland) under Loveday. The Financial Section and Economic Intelligence Service of the League of Nations was the first major international research institution in the social sciences. He contributed regularly to publications of the League like *Monetary Review*, *The Review of World Trade* and *World Economic Survey*. Unfortunately, it is not possible to identify his writings in those publications – these were written anonymously. Throughout the years, Loveday's remarkable team included several laureates of the Nobel Prize in Economics: Jan Tinbergen, James E. Meade and Tjalling C. Koopmans. John Bell Condliffe, Marcus Fleming, Folke Hilgert, Jacques Polak and Louis Rasminsky, for example, were also part of the team (James and Bordo 2001, 7).

From 21 to 24 August 1937, when Joseph Avenol visited Estonia, Nurkse was a member of the accompanying delegation. In Tartu the daily *Postimees* interviewed him and introduced Ragnar Nurkse to the readers, noticing that Nurkse was 'one of these few Estonians who have an excellent foreign education' (*Rahvasteliidu peasekretär Tartus* [Secretary-General of League of Nations in Tartu] 1937).

From 17 July to 2 August 1939 Nurkse visited Estonia for the last time on vacation. World War II started one month later, and on 17 June 1940 the Soviet Union occupied Estonia. Nurkse lost his homeland forever and Estonia its greatest scientist of the 20th century for more than 50 years.

Loveday's Economic and Financial Department was transferred to Princeton following the joint invitation of Princeton University, The Rockefeller Foundation and the Institute for Advanced Study. Nurkse landed in the United States on 13 September 1940. In a letter to Dr Mary Rankin (University of Edinburgh) dated 30 March 1941, Nurkse wrote that they 'are also expected to give some thought to problems of postwar reconstruction.' His own 'official work is still mainly on questions on currency, banking and finance'. In the same letter he described his academic dreams:

> It seems almost ridiculous in present circumstances to bring up the question of my dissertation. But I do not want to give up the idea of a PhD. The upsetting events of last year prevented me from doing much work on it. But some work I have done, nevertheless. To complete the dissertation this year is out of the question; I need one more year for it. But I am sending the matriculation fee to Edinburgh for 1940/41, so that there will be, I hope, no interruption in my status as a PhD student. (See also Bass, Chapter 9 in this volume)

Nurkse had been a PhD student at the University of Edinburgh since 1938.

International Currency Experience

The results of Nurkse's research in Princeton were published under the auspices of the League of Nations as *International Currency Experience: Lessons of the Inter-War Period*, which became his first 'classic' (Nurkse 1944). Chapter VI, *Exchange stabilization funds* (143–161), was written by Professor William Adams Brown, Jr., but the rest of the book is credited to Ragnar Nurkse. This work is an analysis of the development of monetary systems between the two World Wars as a valuable lesson. In his preface to the book Loveday wrote:

> The purpose of this volume is to consider the lessons that may be learnt from the story of international monetary relations during the inter-war period. No other period of equal duration affords so great of variety of experience; in no other period were so many experiments deliberately or fortuitously undertaken; in no other period was the influence of extraneous events on monetary relations or of monetary policy on economic conditions greater. ... The story is related in bold outline and the evidence is collated and analyzed in such a manner as to throw the major facts and sequences of events into perspective and with the object of deriving from those facts and sequences the conclusions that would appear to be of major importance for the formulation of policy in the future. (Ibid., 4)

Loveday was right. *International Currency Experience: Lessons of the Inter-War Period* played a very important role in building up the postwar international monetary arrangement, the Bretton Woods system. This book was distributed and 'was circulating in roneographed form to the delegations arriving in the summer of 1944 for the preliminary meeting at Atlantic City that prepared the agenda for the United Nations Monetary Conference at Bretton Woods' (James and Bordo 2001, 7).

Nurkse also took part in the Bretton Woods conference. He was the alternate to Alexander Loveday, the Head of delegation of the Economic, Financial and Transit Department of the League of Nations. Their colleague, Rasminsky, belonged to the Canadian delegation.

For many economists (e.g., Anthony M. Endres, Grant A. Fleming, Harold James, Michael D. Bordo, Sergei Moiseyev), Nurkse has been one of the leading architects or influential supporters of the Bretton Woods system (beside John Maynard Keynes and Harry Dexter White). Anthony M. Endres (University of Auckland) has written:

> When Ragnar Nurkse's study for the League of Nations entitled *International Currency Experience* (1944) was distributed to delegates at the United Nations Monetary and Financial Conference at Bretton Woods in July 1944, his conclusions would have been scarcely surprising and indeed widely accepted. As the last major economic research contribution of the League, Nurkse's study contained all the fundamental tenets of the Bretton Woods agreement. ... The formal Bretton Woods Agreement follows all the elements of Nurkse's study of *International Currency Experience*. (Endres 2005, 14, 19)

The chapter *International Finance and Exchange Rate Policy* in his and Grant A. Fleming's (Australian National University) book *International Organizations and the Analysis of Economic Policy, 1919–1950* is a pure and detailed approach of Nurkse's *International Currency Experience* and *The Course and Control of Inflation: A Review of Monetary Experience in Europe after World War I* (1946; Endres and Fleming 2002, 169–197).

Professors James and Bordo (2001, 7) share the same opinion. Moiseyev (2007, 182–184) from Moscow University underlines, first of all, Nurkse's huge influence on the project of the Bretton Woods system: 'This man was Ragnar Nurkse.' In her obituary of Nurkse, Margaret Hemming (1959) wrote: 'It [*International Currency Experience*] provided a valuable background to the discussions proceeding at that time for postwar international economic reconstruction' (1959). Professor Erik Lundberg from Stockholm University has said *International Currency Experience* as a report is 'the best available one we have of the lessons of international monetary relations during the inter-war period' (Nurkse 1959, 7). The same was also underlined by Endres more than 40 years later: 'Nurkse [*International Currency Experience*] represents the best example of a thorough historical study of the international financial system in the interwar years. Nurkse brought to the fore the benefits of studying international financial "experience" as opposed to idealistic plans for reforming international financial agreements' (Endres 2005, 217 For James (Princeton University), Nurkse's *International Currency Experience* is 'the most influential academic statement' on this field (James 1996, 38). According to Professors Hans-Joachim Jarchow and Peter Rühmann (University of Göttingen), Nurkse's critique on floating exchange rates in this book was the initial point for everlasting discussion on topic 'floating *versus* fixed exchange rates' (Jarchow and Rühmann 1993, 198).

From the Princeton period also came *Conditions of International Monetary Equilibrium* (Nurkse 1945), the last of four well-known essays published by the Finance Section of Princeton University in 1943–1945. This paper has been reprinted many times, including in the memorial volume *The International Monetary System: Highlights from Fifty Years of Princeton's Essays in International Finance* (Kenen 1993, 1–24).

In 1946 Nurkse's second 'classic', *The Course and Control of Inflation: A Review of Monetary Experience in Europe after World War I*, was issued. Actually, Nurkse wrote Part I, *Analysis of Inflation Problems and Policies* (1–84); the author of Part II, *Survey of European Currency Stabilizations* (85–132), was A. Rosenborg, Head of the League of Nations Mission in the United States. In this book Nurkse proved that inflation is a monetary phenomenon: 'a country's money supply must always be under the control of the State. Private demands for fresh money can always be rejected; not so the demands of the State itself … government deficits were the primary cause of inflation, any appraisal of policies for combating inflation must center around the possible methods of reducing such deficits' (*The Course and Control of Inflation* 1946, 9, 68). This statement is essentially 'equal' to the famous quote of Milton Friedman, 'Inflation is always and everywhere a monetary phenomenon.' At the same time, he was pointing to the danger of expected inflation: 'When a price rise goes on for some time, however, it tends to create expectations of a further rise' (ibid., 7).

The League of Nations era was over. Discussions were held in London in 1945 on how to transfer Nurkse's department to the new organization (United Nations). In his letter to Rankin on 20 August 1945 Nurkse wrote:

Whatever the outcome of these discussions, I do not intend to seek employment in the new organization; and I intend to leave the service of the old League as soon as the inflation memorandum is completed. I have twice tried to resign from the League during the war (once in 1940 and the other time in 1943) and was each time prevailed upon to stay on. Now that war is over, I am free to resign. This makes it possible for me to take up my work on the PhD thesis at the point where I left it in 1940 or 1941. (I have of course done some work on the subject of my thesis since then, but no really continuous work.)

He was hoping 'that I may be allowed to resume my work for the PhD with two more years' time to complete it. ... In any case I shall have ample time, facilities and resources [in Princeton at the Institute for Advanced Study] to complete my study for the Edinburgh PhD.'

In 1946 Ragnar Nurkse married Miss Harriet Berger (1916–1978) of Englewood, New Jersey, whom he met on the ship from Lisbon to New York in 1940.

Columbia University

In 1945 Ragnar Nurkse was appointed visiting lecturer in Economics at Columbia University. It was a part-time appointment, running from the end of September 1945 to the end of May 1946. This appointment involved an advanced course on monetary economics. In the aforementioned letter (1945) to Rankin, Nurkse wrote: 'I am glad to have this appointment, as the subject is interesting, and it will give me some teaching experience. I am curious to find out whether I am any good at teaching, and whether I shall like it! At the moment, I rather look forward to it.'

At the same time he also wrote to Rankin: 'I may even to be able to visit you in Edinburgh next summer. I feel, however, that I had better not leave this country (except for short trips) until I have obtained US citizenship, which will be in about 2 years. Otherwise I should be a stateless or 'displaced' person abroad.' Nurkse was still a citizen of Estonia, which was incorporated violently into USSR. The validity of his Estonian foreign passport was extended for the last time by the Estonian Consulate General in New York on 22 April 1946.

However Nurkse finally decided to turn to an academic career. From 1946 to 1948 he was a Member of the Institute for Advanced Study in Princeton. Although Nurkse was offered a high position in the International Monetary Fund where his former colleagues Polak and Marcus Fleming already worked, he accepted a professorship at Columbia University. In 1947 Nurkse was appointed an Associate Professor of International Economics, and moved from Princeton to New York. In 1949 he was promoted to full Professor at Columbia University. However, Nurkse never did receive the doctoral degree.

His publications and experiences were for Columbia University more valuable than a formal PhD degree. The lack of a PhD degree for such a famous Professor was quite exceptional. This could be taken as the second paradox in his academic life.

In the beginning of his new academic career he continued to research the problems of international economics. As Member of the Institute for Advanced Study, Nurkse (1947) wrote his remarkable paper *Domestic and International Equilibrium*. This paper was published for the first time in the memorial volume of John Maynard Keynes edited by Seymour E. Harris (Harris 1947) and was, according to Haberler (Haberler and Stern 1961, X), his most Keynesian essay. It makes sense to agree with Haberler, although it is possible to follow a very clear influence of the Austrian School in this article as well. Interestingly, *Domestic and International Equilibrium* is the only paper written by Nurkse that has been translated into Estonian.

Gradually Nurkse turned to the area of development economics and was a key person in this field as well. According to Professor Irma Adelman (1999, 4), University of California at Berkeley, 'the classical development theorists' were Arthur Lewis, Paul Rosenstein-Rodan, Ragnar Nurkse, Raul Prebish, Albert Hirschman and Harvey Leibenstein. For George Pagoulatos (2003, 14) 'from the late 1940s and through the 1950s and 1960s the pioneers of the developmentalist school' were first and foremost Ragnar Nurkse, Paul Rosenstein-Rodan, Arthur Lewis, Walt Whitman Rostow and Albert Hirschman.

Nurkse has been one of the main authors of the doctrine of balanced growth, and according to Stanford University Professor Tibor Scitovsky (1987, 178), 'the foremost and most influential advocate of balanced growth'. He did not favour the idea of central planning and never minimized the role of international trade; e.g., 'There is no need to sacrifice the benefits of international trade for the sake of maintaining a stable satisfactory level of domestic activity. ... It is utterly senseless to create employment by reducing the level of economic efficiency.' (Nurkse 1947, 53–54) Domestic growth and international trade 'are really friends, not enemies' (Nurkse 1957, 257).

His third 'classic' *Capital Formation in Underdeveloped Countries*, which was published in 1953 grew out from his lectures held in Rio de Janeiro (1951) and Cairo (1952). This work was linked first and foremost to Latin America and translated into Spanish (many editions) and Portuguese soon afterwards: Spanish in 1955 (*Problemas de formación de capital en los países insuficientemente desarrollados*, Mexico) and Portuguese in 1957 (*Problemas de Formação de Capital em Países Subdesenvolvidos*, Rio de Janeiro). *Capital Formation in Underdeveloped Countries* was translated later into Polish (*Problemy tworzenia kapitału w krajach gospodarczo słabo rozwiniętych*, 1962, Warszawa), Indonesian (*Masalah Pembentukan Modal di Negara-negara yang Sedang Membangun*, 1964, Jakarta), Italian (*La formazione del capitale nei paesi sottosviluppati*, 1965, Torino), French (*Les problèmes de la formation du capital dans les pays sous développés*, 1968, Paris) and Japanese. The Czech translation *Problematika tvorby kapitálu v hospodársky málo vyvinutých zemích* exists as teaching material at the University of Economics in Prague (1965). In these years, Nurkse was, in Latin America, a 'hot name', like Jeffrey Sachs in the 1990s.

Obviously, Nurkse has played a very important role in creating close relations between Columbia University and Latin America. In fact, the well-known 'Chicago boys', Ministers of Finance of Chile Jorge Cauas (1975–77) and Hernán Büchi (1985–89) were actually nurslings of Columbia University. Professor Kaushik Basu (1987, 687), Cornell University, has written in *The New Palgrave. A Dictionary of Economics*: 'Nurkse's other important (and, in my opinion, more important [than *International Currency Experience*]) book was *Problems of Capital Formation in Underdeveloped Countries*.' It was the same book (4) that turned Nurkse's expression, 'A country is poor because it is poor', into a brand. A year earlier he had started the article *Some International Aspects of the Problem of Economic Development* with the same sentence (Nurkse 1952, 571).

In 1954–55 Nurkse spent a sabbatical year in Europe, at Nuffield College, Oxford. In 1958 he was elected Fellow of the American Academy of Arts & Sciences. The following year he was offered a Professorship of Economics and the position of Director of the International Finance Section at Princeton University. He wrote to formally accept the position at Princeton only a week before his death.

In 1958–59 Nurkse was awarded a Ford Foundation Research Scholarship. He spent that year mostly working at the United Nations library in Geneva, but also gave lectures in Paris and Rome. In April 1959 he was invited to Stockholm to deliver the *Wicksell Memorial Lectures* on the topic of international trade. According to Haberler (1960, 97; see Nurkse's writings in Appendix), these lectures were 'a most important contribution … to the two fields of economics, international trade and economic development, which he so much enriched in several books and a long series of articles …. They are a gem of the *genre* of economic literature, "the combination of history and theory", in which he was a master.' These lectures (Nurkse 1959) were published posthumously.

After returning to Geneva from Stockholm Nurkse took a walk on the slopes of Mont Pèlerin above Lake Geneva on 6 May 1959. There he suddenly collapsed and died of a heart attack. Ragnar Nurkse is buried in Vevey in St. Martin cemetery.

His most well known students are Robert M. Stern, Professor Emeritus at the University of Michigan (PhD in 1958; see his memories in the box) and the late Frank Isaiah, Professor in the School of Advanced International Studies at John Hopkins University (1960).

Robert M. Stern, Professor Emeritus of Economics and Public Policy, University of Michigan:

I had the privilege of studying under Professor Nurkse in the PhD program in economics at Columbia University. I took his course on International Economics as well as his course on International Capital Movements in 1955–56. It was on the basis of these two courses that I decided to specialize in international economics. It is no exaggeration to say that Nurkse was a marvelous teacher. His lectures were models of clarity and rigor, and he was always open to questions both in class and during his office hours.

After completing my PhD oral exams in 1956, I was faced with the need to choose a dissertation topic. At the time, I was interested in international commodity problems and sought Nurkse's assistance in developing a dissertation proposal. I remember vividly how we discussed different topics and his suggestion that I might write on issues of US agricultural surplus disposal and trade policies. He guided me along in our periodic meetings, and he was of great help in reading and commenting on my research. It is to his credit that I was able subsequently to publish five papers based on my dissertation.

I continued to work on international commodity problems after completing my PhD, focusing especially on measuring the price responsiveness of primary commodity producers in a variety of settings, including rice and jute in India, Egyptian cotton, West African cocoa, and Malayan natural rubber. Thereafter, I concentrated on empirical research in international trade, beginning with a study of the Ricardian model of comparative advantage, using American and British data on trade and wages and productivity that built upon material covered in Nurkse's course. My research interests over the past decades have spanned both international trade and international finance, which is something that I can attribute to Nurkse's influence since his own research and publications similarly spanned both aspects of international economics.

On a more personal note, I had occasion in late 1958 to assist Nurkse in Geneva in compiling historical data on international capital flows in connection with the preparation of his *Wicksell Lectures* that he delivered in Stockholm in April 1959, shortly before his untimely death. At the time, I was a Fulbright scholar studying econometrics in Rotterdam with Henri Theil. When Nurkse asked if I could come to Geneva for a couple of weeks to work with him, I welcomed the opportunity. During my stay in Geneva, we met each day to discuss my data collection and how it would fit into the preparation of his lectures. I look back on this experience with nostalgia and warmth as one of the high points of my academic career.

After Nurkse died, Professor James Tobin of Yale University, who was on leave in Geneva and was a close friend of Nurkse, called me in Rotterdam and asked if I would be able to come to Geneva to help Mrs Nurkse organize his papers. This was a sad occasion, needless to say, and I was glad to be of assistance to Mrs Nurkse in a time of need. It turned out later that I was able to work with Gottfried Haberler of Harvard University and a close friend and associate of Nurkse going back to his time in Vienna and in the League of Nations Secretariat, in assembling Nurkse's collected papers and publishing them in 1961 as a Harvard Economic Study entitled *Equilibrium and Growth in the World Economy: Economic Essays by Ragnar Nurkse.*

24 December 2007

The untimely death of Ragnar Nurkse was a shock for everyone, a sudden end to his short but very successful scholarly career. Obituaries were published in the *New York Times* (7 May), *The Times* (13 May), *Vaba Eesti Sõna/Free Estonian Word* (New York, 28 May) and other papers and journals.

In 'Prof. Ragnar Nurkse. An Able Economist', Margaret Hemming (1959) wrote:

Nurkse was unusually gifted, no less as a musician than as an economist. In his early years he studied music at the Conservatoire of Music at Tallinn and later in Edinburgh under Professor Donald Tovey: he was himself a very fine pianist. An unusually modest and retiring man on public occasions, he had, nevertheless, an extraordinary gift for making and retaining friends. Through the unusual chance of birth and the vicissitudes of postwar history, Ragnar Nurkse lived and felt at home in very many countries and languages. He could speak at ease in Estonian, Russian, Swedish, English, German, and French. He was a true citizen of the world.

'Prof. Dr. Ragnar Nurkse. In memoriam' (*Vaba Eesti Sõna/Free Estonian Word* 1959):

Professor Nurkse was not just highly rated by his students but also an economist of outstanding international renown. It is evident that there has to be an underlying reason for such domestic and international fame – a reason sweeping along crowds of students, a reason differentiating one researcher from another. In brief, we can say that the reasons include in-depth knowledge of international economic theory and practice, original ideas, clear and authentic vision of problems, bold and constructive prognosis, logical presentation skills, and last but not least – his attractive personality.

His senior colleague at Columbia University, Professor James W. Angell (1960), said in his memorial minute at the meeting of the Faculty of Political Sciences, May 1960, the following words: 'Few academic men of his age [Ragnar Nurkse died at the age of 51] were as widely and favourably known. But it was Nurkse's personal qualities that particularly endeared him to his hosts of friends in all parts of the world, and for which he will be especially remembered. He was lucid, patient and encouraging to his students; generously helpful with his colleagues; modest and almost apologetic about his own achievements and honors.'

In 1965 the Ragnar Nurkse Chair in Economics was established at Columbia University. Charles P. Issawi (1965–77) and Ronald E. Findlay (1977 to the present) have both held this chair.

In 1961 Nurkse's long-time close friend Professor Gottfried Haberler and distinguished student Robert M. Stern (Haberler and Stern 1961) compiled a memorial collection of his economic essays *Equilibrium and Growth in the World Economy* that includes a selection of Nurkse's articles. In 1964 this book was translated into Spanish (*Equilibrio y crecimiento en la economía mundial*, Madrid). Many of Nurkse's books and articles have been translated into other languages or reprinted later (see his writings in the Appendix); the last edition of the Spanish translation of *Capital Formation in Underdeveloped Countries* was issued, for example, in 1985. One can find his personal article in the remarkable *The New Palgrave* (Basu 1987, 687–88; and later editions) and in Mark Blaug's (1999, 842–43; and earlier and later editions) *Who's Who in Economics*; also in Michel Beaud`s and Gilles Dostaler´s (1993) *La pensée économique depuid Keynes: Historique et dictionnaire des principaux auteurs*. Nurkse's works have continued to be discussed in the literature up to the present (e.g., Endres and Fleming 1998; James and Bordo 2001; Bass 2007).

It is proper to summarize the work of Ragnar Nurkse as an eminent economist and scholar with words of Professor Jacob Viner from Princeton University: 'Everything Nurkse wrote had distinction. He has contributed to the international economics field special qualities of novel insights, enlightening balancing of speculative reasoning with empirical evidence, original applications of the standard analytical tools. His ideas have had marked influence on other workers in the international aspects of the economic development field, and have been made the center of discussion for much of the recent literature.' (Haberler and Stern 1961, cover)

On 5 October 2007, the centenary of his birth, a memorial sponsored by the Bank of Estonia was dedicated to Ragnar Nurkse in his place of birth in Käru. On the same day, the Estonian Post released a stamp and First Day Cover in his memory.

Acknowledgement

We would like to thank the sons of Professor Ragnar Nurkse, Peter and Dennis Nurkse, for valuable materials from their family archive, used in writing this article.

References

Adelman, Irma. 1999. *Fallacies in Development Theory and Their Implications for Policy.* Department of Agricultural and Resource Economics and Policy. Division of Agricultural and Natural Resources. University of California at Berkeley. Working Paper No. 887.

Aman, Viktor. 1992. *En bok om Estlands svenskar. 4. Kulturhistorisk översikt.* Stockholm: Kulturföreningen svenska odlingens vänner.

Angell, James W. 1960. Memorial Minute, read at a meeting of Faculty of Political Science, Columbia University (unpublished).

Bass, Hans A. 2007. 'Ragnar Nurkse (1907–1959): Balanced Growth und die Rolle der Kapitalbildung im Entwicklungsprozess.' *Entwicklungspolitik: Information Nord-Süd* 11 (2–3), 58–60.

Basu, Kaushik. 1987. 'Nurkse, Ragnar.' In John Eatwell, Murray Milgate and Peter Newman (eds). *The New Palgrave. A Dictionary of Economics.* Vol. 3. London, New York and Tokyo: Macmillan Press, Stockton Press and Maruzen Company, 687–688.

Beaud, Michel and Gilles Dostaler. 1993. *La pensée économique depuid Keynes: Historique et dictionnaire des principaux auteurs.* Paris: Seuil. English edition: Michel Beaud and Gilles Dostaler. 1997. *Economic Thought Since Keynes: A History and Dictionary of Major Economists.* London and New York: Routledge, 366–367.

Blaug, Mark (ed.). 1999. *Who's Who in Economics: A Biographical Dictionary of Major Economists.* 3rd edition. Cheltenham, UK and Northampton, MA: Edward Elgar Publishing, 842–843.

The Course and Control of Inflation: A Review of Monetary Experience in Europe after World War I. 1946. Princeton: League of Nations. Economic, Financial and Transit Department.

Eesti välisteenistus. Biograafiline leksikon 1918–1991. 2006. Tallinn: Välisministeerium.

Endres, Anthony M. 2005. *Great Architects of International Finance: The Bretton Woods Era.* London, New York: Routledge.

Endres, Anthony M. and Grant A. Fleming. 2002. *International Organizations and the Analysis of Economic Policy, 1919–1950.* Cambridge: Cambridge University Press.

————. 1998. *Ragnar Nurkse's Rule-Based Approach to International Monetary Relations: Complementarities with Chicago.* The University of Auckland, Department of Economics. Working Paper Series, No. 183.

Estonian Historical Archives: Collection 2100, Inventory 10, Unit 160. Tartu.

Estonian State Archives: Collection 957, Inventory 8, Unit 1321. Tallinn.

Haberler, Gottfried. 1961. 'Mises's Private Seminar.' *The Mont Pelerin Quarterly* 3, 20–21.

————. 1960. 'Nurkse on Patterns of Trade and Development.' *The Review of Economics and Statistics* 42 (1), 97–99.

Haberler, Gottfried and Robert M. Stern (eds). 1961. *Equilibrium and Growth in the World Economy: Economic Essays by Ragnar Nurkse.* Cambridge, Massachusetts: Harvard University Press.

Harris, Seymour E. (ed.). 1947. *The New Economics: Keynes' Influence on Theory and Public Policy.* New York: Alfred A. Knopf.

Hemming, Margaret. 1959. 'Prof. Ragnar Nurkse. An Able Economist.' *The Times* 13 May.

James, Harold. 1996. *International Monetary Cooperation Since Bretton Woods.* Washington DC, Oxford, New York: International Monetary Fund, Oxford University Press.

James, Harold and Michael D. Bordo. 2001. *Haberler versus Nurkse: The Case for Floating Exchange Rates as an Alternative to Bretton Woods.* University of St. Gallen, Department of Economics. Discussion paper no. 2001–08.

Jarchow, Hans-Joachim and Peter Rühmann. 1993. *Monetäre Außenwirtschaft. II. Internationale Währungspolitik.* 3rd edition. Göttingen: Vandenhoeck & Ruprecht.

Kenen, Peter B. (contributor). 1993. *The International Monetary System: Highlights from Fifty Years of Princeton's Essays in International Finance.* Boulder: Westview Press.

Moiseyev, Sergei R. 2007. *Mezhdunarodnye valytno-kreditnye otnoshenya.* 2nd edition. Moscow: Delo i Servis.

Nurkse, Ragnar. 1959. *Patterns of Trade and Development.* Wicksell Lectures 1959. Stockholm: Almquist & Wicksell.

———. 1957. 'Balanced and Unbalanced Growth.' Reprinted in Haberler and Stern 1961, 241–278.

———. 1953. *Problems of Capital Formation in Underdeveloped Countries.* Oxford: Basil Blackwell.

———. 1952. 'Some International Aspects of the Problem of Economic Development.' *The American Economic Review* 42 (2), Papers and Proceeding of the Sixty-fourth Annual Meeting of the American Economic Association, 571–583.

———. 1947. 'Domestic and International Equilibrium.' Reprinted in Haberler and Stern 1961, 41–71. Estonian translation: Ragnar Nurkse. 2004. 'Sise-ja rahvusvaheline tasakaal.' *Akadeemia* 5, 976–1007.

———. 1945. *Conditions of International Monetary Equilibrium.* Essays in International Finance, No. 4. Princeton, N. J.: Princeton University.

———.1944. *International Currency Experience: Lessons of the Inter-War Period.* League of Nations. Economic, Financial and Transit Department. Princeton, NY: Princeton University Press.

———. 1935. *Internationale Kapitalbewegungen.* Wien: Julius Springer.

———. 1934. 'Ursachen und Wirkungen der Kapitalbewegungen.' *Zeitschrift für Nationalökonomie* 5 (1), 78–96.

Pagoulatos, George. 2003. *Greece's New Political Economy: State, Finance, and Growth from Postwar to EMU.* Basingstoke, U. K.: Palgrave, Macmillan.

'Prof. Dr. Ragnar Nurkse. In memoriam.' 1959. *Vaba Eesti Sõna/Free Estonian Word* (New York) 28 May.

Rahwasteliidu peasekretär Tartus. 1937. *Postimees* 23 August.

Scitovsky, Tibor. 1987. 'Balanced Growth.' In John Eatwell, Murray Milgate and Peter Newman (eds). *The New Palgrave. A Dictionary of Economics.* Vol. 3. London, New York and Tokyo: Macmillan Press, Stockton Press and Maruzen Company, 177–179.

Valge, Jaak. 2006. *Breaking Away from Russia: Economic Stabilization in Estonia 1918–1924.* Acta Universitatis Stockholmiensis. Studia Baltica Stockholmiensia 26. Stockholm: Almquist & Wiksell International.

Appendix

The Writings of Ragnar Nurkse[2]

Books and Pamphlets

Internationale Kapitalbewegungen. 1935. Wien: Verlag von Julius Springer.
Japanese translation: 1938.

International Currency Experience: Lessons of the Inter-War Period. 1944. Princeton, N. Y.:
Princeton University Press. [Except Chapter VI *Exchange stabilization funds* (143–161),
which is written by Professor William Adams Brown, Jr.]
Reprinted 1947 by United Nations.
French edition: *L'expérience monétaire internationale: Enseignements de la période d'entre les deux
guerres*. 1944. Genève: Société des Nations.
Spanish edition: *Experienca monetaria internacional: lecciones del período de entreguerras*. 1945.
Geneva: Sociedad de las Naciones.
Japanese translation: 1953.
Chapter II, 'The Gold Exchange Standard,' is reprinted in Barry Eichengreen (ed.).
1985. *The Gold Standard in Theory and History*. New York: Methuen; Barry Eichengreen
and Marc Flandreau (eds). 1997. *The Gold Standard in Theory and History*. 2nd edition.
London, New York: Routledge, 262–288.

Conditions of International Monetary Equilibrium. 1945. Essays in International Finance, No. 4.
Princeton, N. J.: Princeton University Press.
Reprinted in: *Readings in the Theory of International Trade*. 1949. Philadelphia: Blakiston
Company, 3–34; William R. Allen and Clark Lee Allen (eds). 1959. *Foreign Trade and
Finance: Essays in International Economic Equilibrium and Adjustment*. New York: Macmillan,
296–312 (partial); Peter B. Kenen (contributor). 1993. *The International Monetary System:
Highlights from Fifty Years of Princeton's Essays in International Finance*. Boulder: Westview
Press, 1–24; Robert Z. Aliber (ed.). 2001. *International Finance*. Vol. II. Cheltenham:
Edward Elgar Publishing.

The Course and Control of Inflation: A Review of Monetary Experience in Europe after World War I.
1946. Princeton, N. Y.: Princeton University Press. [Part I, *Analysis of Inflation Problems
and Policies* (1–84), is written by Ragnar Nurkse.]

Some Aspects of Capital Accumulation in Underdeveloped Countries. 1952. *National Bank of Egypt,
Fiftieth Anniversary Commemoration Lectures*. Cairo, 66. Incorporated in *Problems of Capital
Formation in Underdeveloped Countries*. 1953. Oxford: Basil Blackwell.

Problems of Capital Formation in Underdeveloped Countries. 1953. Oxford: Basil Blackwell.
Reprinted in: *Problems of Capital Formation in Underdeveloped Countries, and Patterns of Trade
and Development*. 1967. New York: Oxford University Press.
Chapter I ('The size of the market and the inducement to invest') is reprinted in:
Development and Society. 1964. New York: St. Martin's Press, 91–96; Shanti S. Tangri and
Peter H. Gray (eds). 1967. *Capital Accumulation and Economic Development*. Boston: D. C.
Heath & Co., 62–68.
Chapters I and II ('The size of the market and the inducement to invest' and
'Population and capital supply') are reprinted in Amitava Krishna Dudd (ed.). 2002.
The Political Economy of Development. Vol. I. Cheltenham: Edward Elgar Publishing.
Spanish translation: *Problemas de formación de capital en los países insuficientemente desarrollados*.
1955. Mexico: Fondo de Cultura Económica.
Portuguese translation: *Problemas de Formação de Capital em Países Subdesenvolvidos*. 1957.
Rio de Janeiro: Editôra Civilização Brasileira.

Polish translation: *Problemy tworzenia kapitalu w krajach gospodarczo słabo rozwiniętych.* 1962. Warszawa: Państwowe wydawnictwo Naukowe.

Indonesian translation: *Masalah Pembentukan Modal di Negara-negara yang Sedang Membangun.* 1964. Jakarta: Bhratara.

Italian translation: *La formazione del capitale nei paesi sottosviluppati.* 1965. Torino: Einaudi.

Czech translation: *Problematika tvorby kapitálu v hospodářsky málo vyvinutých zemích.* 1965. Vysoká škola ekonomická v Praze. (Mimeographed teaching material.)

French translation: *Les problèmes de la formation du capital dans les pays sous développés.* 1968. Paris: Cujas.

Japanese translation: n.d.

Patterns of Trade and Development. 1959. Wicksell Lectures 1959. Stockholm: Almquist & Wicksell.

Reprinted by Oxford: Basil Blackwell (1961); reprinted in Gottfried Haberler and Robert M. Stern (eds). 1961. *Equilibrium and Growth in the World Economy: Economic Essays by Ragnar Nurkse.* Cambridge, Massachusetts: Harvard University Press, 282–336; *Problems of Capital Formation in Underdeveloped Countries, and Patterns of Trade and Development.* 1967. New York: Oxford University Press.

The first lecture 'Contrasting Trends in the 19th and 20th Century World Trade' is reprinted in: James D. Theberge (ed.). 1968. *Economics of Trade and Development.* New York: John Wiley & Sons, 85–102 (partially) Richard S. Weckstein (ed.). 1968. *Expansion of World Trade and the Growth of National Economies.* New York: Evantson and London: Harper & Row, 21–44.

Polish translation: *'Dynamika handlu a kierunki rozwoju.'* In Ragnar Nurkse. 1963. *Wpływ Obrotów Międzynarodowych na Rozwój Gospodarczy.* Warszawa: Państwowe wydawnictwo Economiczne, 98–162.

Spanish translation: 'Patrones de comercio y de desarrollo.' 1964. In Ragnar Nurkse. 1964. *Equilibrio y crecimiento en la economía mundial.* Madrid: Rialp, 320–380; 'Modelos de comercio y desarrollo.' 1971. James D. Theberge (ed.). 1971. *Economía del comercio y desarrollo.* Buenos Aires: Amorrortu, 113–132. (The first lecture 'Contrasting Trends in the 19th and 20th Century World Trade.')

Haberler, Gottfried and Robert M. Stern (eds). 1961. *Equilibrium and Growth in the World Economy: Economic Essays by Ragnar Nurkse.* Cambridge, Massachusetts: Harvard University Press.

Spanish translation: Ragnar Nurkse. 1964. *Equilibrio y crecimiento en la economía mundial.* 1964. Madrid: Rialp.

Wpływ Obrotów Międzynarodowych na Rozwój Gospodarczy. Wybór pism. 1963. Warszawa: Państwowe wydawnictwo Economiczne.

Papers

'Ursachen und Wirkungen der Kapitalbewegungen.' 1934. *Zeitschrift für Nationalökonomie* 5 (1), 78–96.

English translation: 'Causes and Effects of Capital Movements.' In Gottfried Haberler and Robert M. Stern (eds). 1961. *Equilibrium and Growth in the World Economy: Economic Essays by Ragnar Nurkse.* Cambridge, Massachusetts: Harvard University Press, 1–21. Reprinted in John H. Dunning (ed.). 1972. *International Investment. Selected Readings.* Harmondsworth: Penguin Books, 97–116.

Spanish translation: 'Causas y efectos de los movimientos de capital.' In Ragnar Nurkse. 1964. *Equilibrio y crecimiento en la economía mundial.* Madrid: Rialp, 17–38.

'The Schematic Representation of the Structure of Production.' 1935. *The Review of Economic Studies* 2 (3), 232–244.

Reprinted in Gottfried Haberler and Robert M. Stern (eds). 1961. *Equilibrium and Growth in the World Economy: Economic Essays by Ragnar Nurkse*. Cambridge, Massachusetts: Harvard University Press, 22–40.

Spanish translation: 'La representación esquemática de la estructura de producción.' In Ragnar Nurkse. 1964. *Equilibrio y crecimiento en la economía mundial*. Madrid: Rialp, 39–58.

'The Future International Bank Position of the United States, as Affected by the Fund and Bank.' 1945. By Walter Gardner, Discussion by Ragnar Nurkse. *The American Economic Review* 35, 291–294.

'Domestic and International Equilibrium.' 1947. In Seymour E. Harris (ed.). *The New Economics: Keynes' Influence on Theory and Public Policy*. New York: Alfred A. Knopf, 264–292.

Reprinted in: William R. Allen and Clark Lee Allen (eds). 1959. *Foreign Trade and Finance: Essays in International Economic Equilibrium and Adjustment*. New York: Macmillan, 239–255 (partially); Gottfried Haberler and Robert M. Stern (eds). 1961. *Equilibrium and Growth in the World Economy: Economic Essays by Ragnar Nurkse*. Cambridge, Massachusetts: Harvard University Press, 41–71.

Spanish translation: 'Equilibrio nacional e internacional.' In Ragnar Nurkse. 1964. *Equilibrio y crecimiento en la economía mundial*. Madrid: Rialp, 59–91.

Estonian translation: 'Sise- ja rahvusvaheline tasakaal.' 2004. *Akadeemia* 5, 976–1007.

'International Monetary Policy and the Search for Economic Stability.' 1947. *The American Economic Review* 37 (2), Papers and Proceedings of the Fifty-ninth Annual Meeting of the American Economic Association, 569–580.

Reprinted in: Gottfried Haberler and Robert M. Stern (eds). 1961. *Equilibrium and Growth in the World Economy: Economic Essays by Ragnar Nurkse*. Cambridge, Massachusetts: Harvard University Press, 72–86.

Japanese translation: 1953.

Spanish translation: 'La política monetaria internacional y el objetivo de la estabilidad económica.' In Ragnar Nurkse. 1964. *Equilibrio y crecimiento en la economía mundial*. Madrid: Rialp, 92–107.

'The Domestic Economy of Western Europe: Resources and Needs.' 1950. In Howard S. Ellis. *The Economics of Freedom*. New York: Council for Foreign Relations, 17–41.

'Western Europe and Shortage of Dollars.' 1950. In Howard S. Ellis. *The Economics of Freedom*. New York: Council for Foreign Relations, 61–62.

'Problemas de formação de capitais em países subdesenvolvidos.' 1951. *Revista Brasileira de Economia* 5 (4), 1–190. (Portuguese translation by João B. Pinheiro of six lectures delivered in English; short French and English summaries follow Portuguese text.) Incorporated in *Problems of Capital Formation in Underdeveloped Countries*. 1953. Oxford: Basil Blackwell.

'Some International Aspects of the Problem of Economic Development.' 1952. *The American Economic Review* 42 (2), Papers and Proceeding of the Sixty-fourth Annual Meeting of the American Economic Association, 571–583. Incorporated in *Problems of Capital Formation in Underdeveloped Countries*. 1953. Oxford: Basil Blackwell.

Reprinted in: A. N. Agarwala and S. P. Singh (eds). 1958. *The Economics of Underdevelopment*. Bombay, London: Oxford University Press, 265–271.

Polish translation: 'Niektóre międzynarodowe dnia dzisiejszego rozwoju gospodarczego.' In Ragnar Nurkse. 1963. *Wpływ Obrotów Międzynarodowych na Rozwój Gospodarczy*. Warszawa: Państwowe wydawnictwo Economiczne, 13–30.

German translation: 'Einige internationale Gesichtspunkte des Problems der wirtschaftlichen Entwicklung.' In Erich Streissler and Monica Streissler (eds). 1966. *Konsum und Nachfrage*. Köln, Berlin: Kiepenheuer & Witsch, 302–308 (partially).

Portuguese translation: 'Alguns aspectos internacionais do desenvolvimento econômico.' In A. N. Agarwala and S. P. Singh (eds). 1969. *A economia do subdesenvolvimento*. Rio de Janeiro: Forense, 263–277.

'The Cyclical Pattern of Inventory Investment.' 1952. *The Quarterly Journal of Economics* 66 (3), 385–408. Review article of Moses Abramovitz. 1950. 'Inventories and Business Cycles, with special reference to Manufacturers' Inventories.' New York: National Bureau of Economic Research.

'Notas sobre o Trabalho do Sr. Furtado Relativoa a 'Formação de Capitais e Desenvolvimento Econômico.'' 1953. *Revista Brasileira de Economia* 7 (1), 67–78. [English summaries, 78–87]

Spanish translation: 'Formación de Capital y Desarrollo Económico: notas sobre el estudio de Furtado.' 1953. *El Trimestre Económico* 20 (Abril–Junio), 292–305.

'The Problem of Currency Convertibility Today.' 1953. *International Economic Outlook* 25 (3), 61–78.

'A New Look at the Dollar Problem and the U. S. Balance of Payments.' 1954. *Economia Internazionale* 7 (1), 46–60. (With Italian, French, German and Spain summaries, 60–64). Reprinted in Gottfried Haberler and Robert M. Stern (eds). 1961. *Equilibrium and Growth in the World Economy: Economic Essays by Ragnar Nurkse*. Cambridge, Massachusetts: Harvard University Press, 87–103.

Spanish translation: 'La política monetaria internacional y el objetivo de la estabilidad económica.' In Ragnar Nurkse. 1964. *Equilibrio y crecimiento en la economía mundial*. Madrid: Rialp, 92–107.

'Period Analysis and Inventory Cycles.' 1954. *Oxford Economic Papers* (N. S.) 6 (3), 203–225. Reprinted in Gottfried Haberler and Robert M. Stern (eds). 1961. *Equilibrium and Growth in the World Economy: Economic Essays by Ragnar Nurkse*. Cambridge, Massachusetts: Harvard University Press, 104–133.

Spanish translation: 'Análisis secuencial y cyclos de inventarios.' In Ragnar Nurkse. 1964. *Equilibrio y crecimiento en la economía mundial*. Madrid: Rialp, 126–158.

'International Investment To-Day in the Light of Nineteenth Century Experience.' 1954. *The Economic Journal* 64 (256), 744–758.

Reprinted in William R. Allen and Clark Lee Allen (eds). 1959. *Foreign Trade and Finance: Essays in International Economic Equilibrium and Adjustment*. New York: Macmillan, 472–487; Gottfried Haberler and Robert M. Stern (eds). 1961. *Equilibrium and Growth in the World Economy: Economic Essays by Ragnar Nurkse*. Cambridge, Massachusetts: Harvard University Press, 134–150; Amar Narain Agarwala and Sampat Pal Singh (eds). 1969. *Accelerating Investment in Developing Economies*. Oxford University Press, 492–507; Mira Wilkins (ed.). 1977. *Issues and Insights on International Investment*. New York: Arno Press, 745–758.

Polish translation: 'Investycje międzynarodowe dnia dzisiejszego w świetle doświadczeń XIX wieku.' In Ragnar Nurkse. 1963. *Wpływ Obrotów Międzynarodowych na Rozwój Gospodarczy*. Warszawa: Państwowe wydawnictwo Economiczne, 31–50.

Spanish translation: 'La inversión internacional en la actualidad a la luz de la experiencia del siglo XIX.' 1954. *Revista de Economia Politica*. May 1953–December 1954, 155–173; and in Ragnar Nurkse. 1964. *Equilibrio y crecimiento en la economía mundial*. Madrid: Rialp, 159–176.

'The Relation between Home Investment and External Balance in the Light of British Experience, 1945–1955.' 1956. *The Review of Economics and Statistics* 38 (2), 121–154.

Reprinted ('Balance-of-Payments Policy at Full Employment') in William R. Allen and Clark Lee Allen (eds). 1959. *Foreign Trade and Finance: Essays in International Economic Equilibrium and Adjustment.* New York: Macmillan, 363–371 (partially); Gottfried Haberler and Robert M. Stern (eds). 1961. *Equilibrium and Growth in the World Economy: Economic Essays by Ragnar Nurkse.* Cambridge, Massachusetts: Harvard University Press, 151–220. Spanish translation: 'La relación entre inversión interna y equilibrio externo a la luz de la experiencia británica, 1945–1955.' In Ragnar Nurkse. 1964. *Equilibrio y crecimiento en la economía mundial.* Madrid: Rialp, 177–252.

'Internal Growth and External Solvency.' 1955. *Bulletin of the Oxford University. Institute of Statistics* 17 (1), 38–50.

'Balanced Growth on Statistic Assumptions.' 1956. *The Economic Journal* 66 (262), 365–367. Reply to Marcus Fleming's review of *Problems of Capital Formation* in *The Economic Journal* 65, 1955.

'Foreign Aid and the Theory of Economic Development, American Aid: A Reappraisal.' 1956. *Proceedings of the Annual Fall Sessions of the National Academy of Economics and Political Science.* Special Publications Series No. 12 (16–17 October), 5–9.

'Fluctuations in Exports of Primary Products.' 1957. In *Contribuçoes a Analise do Desenvolvimento Economico*, written in honor of Eugenio Gudin. Rio de Janeiro: Agir, 251–265.

'Productive Investment and the Balance of Payments: The British Case.' 1957. *The Review of Economics and Statistics* 39 (1), Note by Thomas Balogh, 84–88, Replay by Ragnar Nurkse, 88–90.

'Reflections in India's Development Plan.' 1957. *The Quarterly Journal of Economics* 71, 188–204.
   Reprinted in Gottfried Haberler and Robert M. Stern (eds). 1961. *Equilibrium and Growth in the World Economy: Economic Essays by Ragnar Nurkse.* Cambridge, Massachusetts: Harvard University Press, 221–240.
   Spanish translation: 'Reflesiones sobre el Plan de Desarrollo en la India.' In Ragnar Nurkse. 1964. *Equilibrio y crecimiento en la economía mundial.* Madrid: Rialp, 253–274.

'Excess Population and External Prospects.' 1957. *The Scientific Monthly* 85 (2), 81–85.

'Excess Population and Capital Construction.' 1957. *The Malayan Economic Review* 2, (2) 1–11.

'Excess Population and Capital Construction.' 1958. *The Malayan Economic Review* 3 (April), 58–59. Comments by Sir Sidney Caine, Replay by Ragnar Nurkse.

'The Conflict between 'Balanced Growth' and International Specialization' and 'Some Reflections on the International Financing of Public Overhead Investments.' 1957. Lectures on Economic Development. Istanbul University, Faculty of Economics and Ankara University, Faculty of Political Sciences.
   Reprinted ('Balanced and Unbalanced Growth') in Gottfried Haberler and Robert M. Stern (eds). 1961. *Equilibrium and Growth in the World Economy: Economic Essays by Ragnar Nurkse.* Cambridge, Massachusetts: Harvard University Press, 241–278.
   Spanish translation: 'Crecimiento equilibrado y desequilibrado.' In Ragnar Nurkse. 1964. *Equilibrio y crecimiento en la economía mundial.* Madrid: Rialp, 275–316.
   Polish translation: 'Wzrost zrównoważony I wzrost nieżrównoważony.' In Ragnar Nurkse. 1963. *Wpływ Obrotów Międzynarodowych na Rozwój Gospodarczy.* Warszawa: Państwowe wydawnictwo Economiczne, 51–97.

'Trade Fluctuations and Buffer Policies of Low-Income Countries' and 'Epilogue.' 1958. *Kyklos* 9 (2), 141–154, 244–265.
   Reprinted in Carl K. Eicher and Lawrence Witt. (eds). 1964. *Agriculture in Economic Development.* New York, Toronto, San Francisco and London: McGraw-Hill, 311–322.

'Trends in World Trade.' 1959. *Kyklos* 12 (1), 1–26. (Review of *Trends in International Trade*, A Report by a Panel of Experts, GATT. 1958. Geneva.)

Reprinted ('The Export Lag of Primary Producing Countries') in Walter Krause and F. John Mathis (eds). 1968. *International Economics and Business: Selected Readings*. Boston: Houghton Mifflin, 92–98 (partially).

'Notes on 'Unbalanced Growth.'' 1959. *The Oxford Economic Papers* (N. S.) 11 (3), 295–297. (With notes signed by J. R. Hicks.)

Reprinted in Gottfried Haberler and Robert M. Stern (eds). 1961. *Equilibrium and Growth in the World Economy: Economic Essays by Ragnar Nurkse*. Cambridge, Massachusetts: Harvard University Press, 278–281.

Spanish translation: 'Notas sobre el 'crecimiento desequilibrado''. 1964. In Ragnar Nurkse. 1964. *Equilibrio y crecimiento en la economía mundial*. Madrid: Rialp, 316–319.

'Le Commerce des Pays Sous-Développés et les Conditions Internationales de Croissance.' 1959. *Convertibilité, multilatéralisme et politiques de stabilisation*. Cashiers de l'Institut de Science Économique Appliquée. Paris: ISEA, 19–45. [French translation of 'The Trade of the Poor Countries and the International Economics of Growth.' Lecture given at the ISEA in December 1958.]

'Comments on Professor Jacob Viner's paper 'Stability and Progress: The Poorer Countries' Problem.'' 1958. In Douglas Hague (ed.). *Stability and Progress in the World Economy*. First Congress of the International Economic Association, held in Rome in 1956. London: Macmillan, 69–77.

'La Teoría del comercio internacional y la política de desarrollo.' 1960. In Howard S. Ellis and Henry C. Wallich (eds). *El Desarrollo Económico y América Latina*, trabajos y comentarios presentados en la Conferencia de la Asociación Económica Internacional celebrada en Rio de Janeiro en agosto de 1957. Mexico and Buenos Aires: Fondo de Cultura Económica, 278–312.

English edition: 'International Trade Theory and Development Policy.' 1961. In Howard S. Ellis and Henry C. Wallich (eds). *Economic Development for Latin America: Proceeding of a Conference Held by the International Economic Association*. London: Macmillan, 234–263.

Reprinted ('The Theory of Development and the Idea of Balanced Growth') in Alan B. Mountjoy (ed.). 1971. *Developing the Underdeveloped Countries*. London: Macmillan, 115–128.

'Further comments on Professor Rosenstein-Rodan's paper 'Notes on the Theory of the ?Big Push'.' 1961. In Howard S. Ellis and Henry C. Wallich (eds). *Economic Development for Latin America: Proceeding of a Conference Held by the International Economic Association*. London: Macmillan, 74–78.

Spain edition: In Howard S. Ellis and Henry C. Wallich (eds). 1960. *El Desarrollo Económico y América Latina*, trabajos y comentarios presentados en la Conferencia de la Asociación Económica Internacional celebrada en Rio de Janeiro en agosto de 1957. Mexico and Buenos Aires: Fondo de Cultura Económica.

Book Reviews

Cassel, Gustav. 1933. *Spara eller icke spara*. Stockholm: Kooperativa förbundets bokförlag; Myrdal, Gunnar. 1933. *Konjunktur och offentlig hushallning*. Stockholm: Kooperativa förbundets bokförlag. In *Zeitschrift für Nationalökonomie* 5 (3). 1934, 393–95.

Papi, Giusepe Ugo. 1933. *Escape from Stagnation*. London: P.S. King & Son. In *Zeitschrift für Nationalökonomie* 5 (3). 1934, 396–97.

Heilperin, Michel A. 1932. *Monnaie, Crédit et Transfert*. Paris: Recueil Sirey. In *Zeitschrift für Nationalökonomie* 6 (1). 1935, 120–21.

Arnold, Arthur Z. 1937. *Banks, Credit and Money in Soviet Russia*. New York: Columbia University Press. In *The Economic Journal* 48 (189). 1938, 81–83.

> Reprinted in Gottfried Haberler and Robert M. Stern (eds). 1961. *Equilibrium and Growth in the World Economy: Economic Essays by Ragnar Nurkse*. Cambridge, Massachusetts: Harvard University Press, 339–341.

> Spanish translation: In Ragnar Nurkse. 1964. *Equilibrio y crecimiento en la economía mundial*. Madrid: Rialp, 381–383.

Buchanan, Norman, S. 1945. *International Investment and Domestic Welfare: Some Aspects of International Borrowing in the Post-War Period*. New York: Henry Holt and Company. In *Political Science Quarterly* 61 (2). 1946, 254–256.

> Reprinted in Gottfried Haberler and Robert M. Stern (eds). 1961. *Equilibrium and Growth in the World Economy: Economic Essays by Ragnar Nurkse*. Cambridge, Massachusetts: Harvard University Press, 342–345.

> Spanish translation: In Ragnar Nurkse. 1964. *Equilibrio y crecimiento en la economía mundial*. Madrid: Rialp, 384–388.

Halm, George N. 1945. *International Monetary Cooperation*. Chapel Hill: University of North Carolina Press. In *The Journal of Political Economy* 54 (2). 1946, 179–180.

> Reprinted in Gottfried Haberler and Robert M. Stern (eds). 1961. *Equilibrium and Growth in the World Economy: Economic Essays by Ragnar Nurkse*. Cambridge, Massachusetts: Harvard University Press, 346–347.

> Spanish translation: In Ragnar Nurkse. 1964. *Equilibrio y crecimiento en la economía mundial*. Madrid: Rialp, 388–390.

Schwenter, Jürg J. 1945. *Kapitalexport und zwischenstaatliche Warenbewegungen, eine theoretische Betrachtung*. Bern: Rösch, Vogt & Co. In *The Journal of Political Economy* 55 (5). 1947, 479.

Dehem, Roger. 1946. 'Emploi et revenus en économie ouverte. Théorie et application à l'évolution belge et britannique de 1919 à 1939.' In *The Journal of Political Economy* 55 (6). 1947, 616–618.

Mikesell, Raymond F. and Hollis B. Chenery. 1949. *Arabian Oil: America's Stake in the Middle East*. Chapel Hill: University of North Carolina Press. In *The Journal of Political Economy* 58 (4). 1950, 265–266.

Wilcox, Clair. 1949. *A Charter for World Trade*. New York: The Macmillan Company. In *Political Science Quarterly* 64 (4). 1949, 616–618.

> Reprinted in Gottfried Haberler and Robert M. Stern (eds). 1961. *Equilibrium and Growth in the World Economy: Economic Essays by Ragnar Nurkse*. Cambridge, Massachusetts: Harvard University Press, 348–351.

> Spanish translation: In Ragnar Nurkse. 1964. *Equilibrio y crecimiento en la economía mundial*. Madrid: Rialp, 390–394.

Hawtrey, Ralph G. 1950. *The Balance of Payments and the Standard of Living*. London and New York: Royal Institute of International Affairs. In *The American Economic Review* 41 (3). 1951, 483–484.

Meade, J. E. 1951. *The Theory of International Economic Policy. Vol. I: The Balance of Payments*. London, New York and Toronto: Oxford University Press; and *The Balance of Payments: Mathematical Supplement*. 1951. London, New York and Toronto: Oxford University Press. In *Political Science Quarterly* 67 (4). 1952, 604–608.

Reprinted in Gottfried Haberler and Robert M. Stern (eds). 1961. *Equilibrium and Growth in the World Economy: Economic Essays by Ragnar Nurkse*. Cambridge, Massachusetts: Harvard University Press, 352–356.

Spanish translation: In Ragnar Nurkse. 1964. *Equilibrio y cr ecimiento en la economía mundial*. Madrid: Rialp, 394–399.

Viner, Jacob. 1951. *International Economics*. Glencoe: The Free Press. In *The American Economic Review* 68 (1). 1952, 978–979.

Reprinted in Gottfried Haberler and Robert M. Stern (eds). 1961. *Equilibrium and Growth in the World Economy: Economic Essays by Ragnar Nurkse*. Cambridge, Massachusetts: Harvard University Press, 360–362.

Spanish translation: In Ragnar Nurkse. 1964. *Equilibrio y crecimiento en la economía mundial*. Madrid: Rialp, 403–406.

Chang, Tse Chun. 1951. *Cyclical Movements in the Balance of Payments*. New York, London: Cambridge University Press. In *Political Science Quarterly* 68 (1). 1953, 141–142.

Robbins, Lionel. 1954. *The Economist in the Twentieth Century and Other Lectures in Political Economy*. London and New York: Macmillan. In *The American Economic Review* 45 (3). 1955, 437–438.

Humprey, Don D. 1955. *American Imports*. New York: The Twentieth Century Fund. In *Political Science Quarterly* 71 (1). 1956, 138–139.

Meade, J. E. 1955. *The Theory of International Economic Policy. Vol. II: Trade and Welfare*. London, New York and Toronto: Oxford University Press; and *Trade and Welfare: Mathematical Supplement*. 1955. London, New York and Toronto: Oxford University Press. In *Political Science Quarterly* 71 (3). 1956, 459–462.

Reprinted in Gottfried Haberler and Robert M. Stern (eds). 1961. *Equilibrium and Growth in the World Economy: Economic Essays by Ragnar Nurkse*. Cambridge, Massachusetts: Harvard University Press, 357–359.

Spanish translation: In Ragnar Nurkse. 1964. *Equilibrio y crecimiento en la economía mundial*. Madrid: Rialp, 399–403.

Chapter Three:

NURKSE AND THE ROLE OF FINANCE IN DEVELOPMENT ECONOMICS

Jan A. Kregel

Nurkse, Early Development Theory and Modern Monoeconomics

Ragnar Nurkse was part of a group of early theorists of economic development who questioned orthodox Ricardian trade theory as the basis for development policies: 'In many of the less developed countries today the dominant practical question is whether the available investment funds ... should be used to provide activities specialized along lines of comparative advantage internationally or diversified so as to provide markets for each other locally.' He noted that this 'clash of prescriptions on the policy plane reflects ... a gap between the neoclassical allocation economics and ... growth economics' (Nurkse 1961b, 235–6). The emphasis on growth economics engendered a debate over whether 'balanced' or 'unbalanced' growth was the best strategy for developing countries to support growth through industrialization. In difference from modern discussions of development, there was a general agreement amongst economists that industrialization was the most efficient means of supporting economic development.[1]

Ragnar Nurkse, along with Paul Rosenstein-Rodan, was the most important and influential advocate of 'balanced' growth as a means to support the industrialization of 'undeveloped' (to use Oscar Lange's terminology; Lange 1946) economies.[2] It was taken as given that a developed economy was an industrial economy. Nurkse and Rosenstein-Rodan supported balanced growth with what might be called 'classical' arguments concerning long-run determinants of the interaction between demand and supply, in particular those advanced by Allyn Young and Josef Schumpeter in the 1920s, joined to an historical analysis of the changing structure of international trade and payments in the twentieth century.

While borrowing from the then novel Keynesian ideas, they were considered to apply primarily to the short-run problems facing industrialized developed economies, and thus, although correct, not directly relevant to the problems under consideration. They also considered reference to the development experiences of Latin America in the nineteenth century to be inappropriate in the changed international economic conditions that emerged after 1920. These early debates were in marked difference from current development discourse dominated by what Albert Hirschman has called 'monoeconomics',[3] the belief that there is a single correct economic analysis that can be applied to all economic problems – to developed and developing economies alike. The fact that it has become the basis of the so-called Washington Consensus, amplified in the 'structural adjustment policies' that place conditionality on the loans of the multilateral financial institutions, suggests that Nurkse's challenge to orthodoxy was lost and that the orthodox strategy based on optimal allocation through international market-driven comparative advantage in free and open trade and financial markets is generally accepted.

The Consensus gained support from the performance of the newly industrializing Asian economies in the 1980s (compared to the failure of the hyperinflating Latin American economies) and by the improved performance in the early 1990s of countries (such as Mexico, Brazil and Argentina) that embraced the approach. However, the outbreak of financial crisis in Mexico in 1994, then in Asia in 1997, followed by Brazil in 1999 and Argentina in 2001 raised doubts about its theoretical underpinning. This has been reinforced by the decline in growth rate trends and sluggish employment creation that has accompanied the policy. In particular, the idea that countries could develop on the basis of eliminating barriers to trade and liberalizing financial markets was based on a theoretical contradiction. As Nurkse (1961b) pointed out in the earlier debates, in classical Ricardian trade theory the benefits from comparative advantage specialization that result from the static comparison of a country moving from autarchy to free trade presumes the full utilization of immobile productive factors such as capital and labour. It is not evident that it applies to trade in both goods and financial assets in a dynamic context. Additional theoretical justification is required to join the free flow of capital with the benefits of free trade in goods.

The theoretical justification for the free international flow of productive capital is also based on the static analysis of the benefits obtained from an improved allocation of capital to its most productive uses across countries. However, it rests on the assumption that the market mechanism can identify and respond to differential rates of return created by international differences in factor intensities. In the context of developing countries, this requires not only that factor intensity can be calculated and compared across countries, but that intensity is higher in developed than in developing countries and that the return to capital is inversely related to capital intensity. After the capital theory debates of the 1960s, it is clear that none of these conditions are theoretically robust.

Further, the stylized facts of most developed countries show substantial and persistent unemployed resources and throughout the postwar period, capital flows have, in general, been from developing to developed countries rather than the opposite. This suggests that a review of Nurkse's theory might be beneficial in discovering the lacuna in the current monoeconomics of development. In particular, Nurkse's theory may help in assessing the benefits of a policy of directed industrialization that were taken as given in the earlier debates. It is interesting to note the current ignorance of these early debates, and in Nurkse's work in particular, exhibited by proponents of the modern monoeconomics. This is especially visible in criticisms of a recent book by Erik Reinert (2007) advocating an approach to development via industrialization similar to that advanced by Nurkse and other early development economists. They suggest that his approach should be criticized as nineteenth-century economics (although Nurkse rejected this approach) or as inapplicable because it advocates protectionism (also rejected by Nurkse) or the failure of a particular form of industrialization through import substitution applied in Latin America (considered by Nurkse no longer feasible).[4]

Given this tendency to argue about slogans rather than theory, in revisiting Nurkse's position on the question of finance for development, I am going to suggest that a better way to understand the point that was under discussion would be to abandon the slogans of protection versus markets and instead, draw a distinction between those such as Nurkse, who believed that development was basically demand constrained, against his (and Reinert's) critics who believe development to be supply constrained.[5]

Learning from History and Geopolitical Conditions

In contrast to the current monoeconomical view of trade and capital flows in the development process, Nurkse placed emphasis on the fact that both theory and policy were historically conditioned. An important example may be found in his recognition of different historical patterns of development. Nurkse refers to the unique nature of the nineteenth century experience of foreign investment. It was associated with the migration of people from Europe to the great 'empty' plains in other temperate regions. Both capital and labour migrated in a complementary search for higher earnings in the new settlement, rich in natural resources. As others working in the area, he used Folke Hilgerdt's terminology – 'regions of recent settlement', noting that they were favoured by a rapidly expanding demand for their primary products.

This tended to raise real incomes directly by improving their barter terms of trade, which, in a time of reduced transport costs, was not incompatible with improving commodity terms of trade for the industrial centres as well. This gave comparatively advantageous employment to any increases in the domestic labour force or capital stock. It also tended to mobilize dormant resources and draw them into economic activity for export production. It also helped by attracting to those areas a part of the increase in capital and labour that was taking place in the dominant centres of growth. Rapidly increasing external demand encouraged the application of capital and improved techniques to primary production for export, often including the creation of domestic infrastructure that was of benefit to the development of other sectors of the economy. This constituted what Nurkse, echoing Dennis Robertson's enunciation of *trade as the engine of growth*, identified as the nineteenth century pattern of development called *growth through trade*, a pattern that appears to lie behind the Washington Consensus.

Development Theory and Development Reality: Cognitive Dissonance?

Nurkse notes ironically that in this period when there were important flows of both capital and labour from Europe to other continents, Ricardo's static classical theory of comparative advantage, based on the immobility of productive factors, dominated academic discourse. While Nurkse admits that this cumulative, dynamic process by which growth in the centre was transmitted to the periphery may have improved the international allocation of resources, it was the dynamic impact on growth that was dominant. By the end of the 1920s, this dynamic engine had started to stall and the industrial centre was no longer transmitting its growth to the developing countries through an increase in the demand for their primary exports. Again, with irony, Nurkse (1953, 121) notes that in the 1930s as the 'classical assumption of international immobility of productive factors had become almost perfectly valid in fact', Bertil Ohlin was proposing the incorporation of international factor mobility into his theory of international trade. Nurkse (1953, 120) concluded that 'economic theory tends inevitably to lag behind the actual course of events'. It was for these reasons that he stressed the inapplicability of the static approach of classical trade theory, instead favouring a dynamic approach of cumulative causation based on the analysis of the evolution of international demand relative to the expanding resources of developing countries. He thus placed major emphasis on the continual increase in the productive or potentially productive resources in underdeveloped countries, believing that no useful purpose was served by continuing to discuss matters of trade and development on the classical assumption of a constant stock of productive factors. Development cannot be a question of the optimal distribution of scarce resources when developing countries are experiencing a continual expansion of their productive resources.

Although Nurkse believed that this nineteenth century process, in which demand from the centre supported exports of the periphery, would always play a role in the development process, he was convinced that the industrial countries' demand for a wide range of primary commodities could not be maintained at a rate sufficient to absorb the expansion of labour and capital in developing countries. He thus believed that the major problem facing developing countries experiencing rapid growth in their labour force and capital stock would be the failure of external demand from the industrialized countries for primary exports to keep pace with the expansion of resources in developing countries. His particular concern was that international conditions had changed in the twentieth century in ways that would prevent the continuation of this cumulative process as developed country's demand for primary exports slowed.

Similar to Hans Singer, Raul Prebisch and Gunnar Myrdal, he reached the conclusion that in such conditions it would be useless to commit additional resources to increase production in the traditional export sectors given the inelastic demand that traditional exports were likely to meet. It was thus the changed international conditions of the postwar economy that made it imperative for developing countries to find an alternative strategy to exports of primary commodities determined by comparative advantage and financed by capital inflows from the industrialized countries.

Nurkse (1954, 746) also notes that the success of the nineteenth century pattern of development was based on the fact that roughly two-thirds of global capital flows went to the 'regions of recent settlement' and that they were drawn by the movement to these regions of largely European emigrants with a 'capital-minded milieu, ... culturally prepared for the use of western equipment, methods, and technique'. He also notes that very high proportion of the foreign investments – 'no less than three-quarters of the total was in public or public-utility investments' (1954, 747), concentrated in 'a process of capital widening' (Nurkse 1953, 748). However, in the twentieth century, when the United States took over as the source of international capital flows, it was largely to substitute for the movement of labour, not to complement it, and to be dominated by private flows concentrated in mineral extraction and other areas that responded to the demand of the capital exporting countries. This was basically because of the lack of profitability of investing in the domestic market due to its small size and development. He thus concludes that 'it seems unlikely that direct investment alone can become anything

like an adequate source of international finance for economic development'
(1953, 754).

In addition, he noted that the implementation of Keynesian policies in the
twentieth century had by and large eliminated the need for developed countries
to use foreign lending as a means of supporting domestic demand. This meant
that there was no longer any economic reason for capital to move from
developed countries to provide finance for developing countries. Developing
countries would thus face the problem of finding alternative sources of finance
for the mobilization of their underemployed domestic resources. This raised the
possibility that developing countries might best concentrate on policies that
produced domestic demand creation without relying on external resources.

New Conditions Require a New Development Theory

Despite the success of the nineteenth century pattern of development, Nurkse
took it as given that primary production for export could no longer provide
support for development in the twentieth century and that international capital
flows could no longer play the supporting role that they had in the nineteenth
century. Given this breakdown in the pattern of development that had prevailed
in the nineteenth century, the question facing developing countries was how to
mobilize their ever-growing labour force and capital resources.

Nurkse noted that one market-driven solution would be for factors of
production to migrate from the less-developed countries to the centres of growth
in the industrial economies where they would earn higher returns. While it seems
quite clear that capital has in fact taken this path in many countries, after the
1930s this became increasingly difficult (if not impossible) for labour,[6] and thus,
simply aggravated the mismatch between the growth of their primary exports
and the growth of population.

The Obvious Answer: Internal Growth through Domestic Industrialization

Instead, he proposed what he considered a more realistic alternative. If demand
conditions for a wide range of primary products were not conducive to growth
and if external capital could not provide support for development, then, in
addition to their primary exports, which (as already noted) he believed would
always be part of a successful development strategy, developing countries should
embark on a path of internally led growth through domestic industrialization.
He notes the existence of an influential school of thought in support of
industrialization, today much expanded by the historical research of Erik
Reinert, that suggests that this position has been dominant among successful
industrializers since the 1600s, if not earlier.[7]

While this argument for industrialization is similar to that put forward by Prebisch and Singer, it is important to note that Nurkse places greater emphasis on the long-term shifts in international demand than on any trend decline in the terms of trade for developing countries. Indeed, he suggests that in the long run, 'a change in the terms of trade tends to induce shifts in production and in the distribution of resources, which will tend to reverse or counteract the changes in the terms of trade', such that the 'long-term trends in international demand need not be reflected fully, if at all, in changes in the terms of trade' (Nurkse 1961, 243–4).

Facing a lack of sufficient demand for primary commodities and no necessary financial flows from developed countries, developing countries faced the problem of how they could achieve industrialization. For Nurkse, this could be reduced to the question of achieving a sufficient rate of capital accumulation. This leads to the basic question behind any strategy of industrialization – how to finance the required capital formation to support industrialization in the absence of sufficient external capital inflows. Nurkse notes that policies to support domestic industrialization depend on whether the domestic economy was similar to the former 'regions of recent settlement' with low domestic population growth, or whether it more resembled the former colonies with excess labour and rapid population growth. He concentrates on the latter, representing the majority of developing countries in Africa and Asia.

Capital Supply for Industrialization – Disguised Unemployment

In his simple and direct method of approach, Nurkse puts this question as follows: Where is the food to come from to feed the workers who will be employed to build the capital goods to create an industrial sector? While there is always some (and often much more than generally recognized) voluntary saving among the rich urban commercial and landowning classes of poor countries, this is unlikely to be sufficient to support industrialization.[8] These savings could be supplemented by measures to reduce the 'conspicuous consumption' of these higher-income classes through formal restrictions or fiscal policy measures, but these are likely to be difficult to enforce. Thus, given the shortfall of voluntary saving out of existing incomes, poor developing countries will be doomed to a vicious cycle of poverty unless they can find alternative sources. This has been the traditional approach to development that considers developing countries as supply constrained, and the way to lift this constraint has been to look for ways to attract an inflow of capital from abroad.

But Nurkse differs from the traditional approach, noting that external finance will not only be uncertain (for reasons already discussed above), it is likely to be inadequate to needs, especially given the experience of the poorest of developing countries in attracting foreign investment. Further, he notes that it may be unnecessary since there is a third potential source of resources to feed the workers on the new investment projects. Among a country's available domestic resources, Nurkse notes that the widespread existence of 'disguised unemployment' also represents 'disguised saving' potential.[9]

While disguised unemployment was introduced in the economic literature by Joan Robinson in a discussion of the definition of unemployment in developed countries,[10] Nurkse adapts the concept in providing the answer to the supposed supply constraint on the ability of developing countries to finance capital formation in support of industrialization.

Constraints on Supply for Industrialization

In an analysis that follows the lead of Rosenstein-Rodan (and foreshadows the subsequent approach of 'unlimited supplies of labour' proposed by Sir Arthur Lewis), but is closer to what became the Cambridge approach to growth and distribution, Nurkse explains the idea again in simple physical terms. If existing 'unproductive' surplus labourers in the countryside are being supported by the 'productive' labourers who produce more than they consume, then this difference only represents 'virtual' saving from the point of view of the economy as a whole because it is fully consumed by the 'unproductive' workers. If the 'unproductive' workers (who contribute nothing to total output) could be employed to produce new capital goods, then the 'virtual' savings could be transformed into effective saving, and capital could be created without requiring any decrease in the overall level of consumption of any individual in the economy. The supply of 'finance' for the accumulation of capital could then be provided internally simply by mobilizing the disguised unemployed into productive employment. No formal creation of finance or provision of ex ante savings is required other than the reallocation of underemployed labour to capital construction projects. The only condition is that there is disguised unemployed labour that can be employed in the production of capital goods without a fall in total agricultural output.

Nurkse highlights the difference between this proposition and traditional Keynesian theory, suggesting that it represents an intermediate position between the classical and the Keynesian analysis of the relation between saving and investment. Rather than an increase in the rate of capital formation requiring a reduction in consumption (as in the classical analysis that presumes full employment of resources) or an increase in investment expenditure producing an accompanying increase in saving via the multiplier to match it, the employment of disguised unemployed labour to increase capital formation creates capital without a reduction in consumption or an increase in saving via the multiplier.

The difference from Keynesian theory is important and often misunderstood. In difference from the multiplier analysis that is dynamic, Nurkse's argument concerning the increased supply of saving is purely static. The higher level of saving is the result of the higher level of income that results from the increased output per head of the disguised workers when in productive employment, since both productive and unproductive workers consume as much as before; the average propensity to consume for all workers remains equal to unity,[11] but the propensity for personal consumption by productive workers is below unity. The point of the argument is not to explain the relation between investment and saving, but simply to highlight an unexploited source of resources that can be costlessly made available for capital formation through a rearrangement of employment. Here Nurkse (1953, 49) follows classical economists such as Hume (and Keynes as well) when he notes that, in his view, 'labor is the real source of wealth, and the supply of capital, we now see, can be increased by making use of unemployed labor. It can be increased, not only for extensive, but also for intensive investment for economic development.'

Nurkse also highlights the difference between his approach and traditional discussions of excess population and high population growth creating an increased need for capital. In this approach, a calculation is made of the amount of capital 'required' for the productive employment of both the annual increase in the labour force and the existing surplus labour. The extremely large figures that result from such calculations lead to what appears to be the obvious conclusion that domestic saving capacity will be insufficient to needs and, thus, external savings will be required. Consequently, this approach reaches the diametrically opposed conclusion to Nurkse – that developing counties will have almost exclusive reliance on external resources rather than focusing on the saving potential that is concealed in the existence of disguised unemployment.

But this discussion refers only to the supply side and supports the idea that the constraints on development are not to be found on the supply side. However, in order to make supply effective requires policy on the demand side or a discussion of the incentives to invest that will be capable of putting the disguised unemployed to work to produce capital goods. In his analysis of the demand side of the problem, Nurkse introduces the idea of balanced expansion.

Demand Constraints on Capital Supply for Industrialization

Those economists who argued in favour of industrialization through balanced growth based their discussion of the inducement to invest on Allyn Young's

1928 extension of Adam Smith's dictum that the division of labour depends on the extent of the market.[12] This position incorporates both demand and technical progress since Young points out that the 'the principal economies which manifest themselves in increasing returns are the economies of capitalistic' production and the economies of more capital-intensive methods of production, 'even more than the other forms of the division of labor, depend upon the extent of the market – and that, of course, is why we discuss them under the heading of increasing returns' (Young 1928, 531). He then notes that 'under conditions of increasing returns and when the demand for each commodity is elastic, in the special sense that a small increase in its supply will be attended by an increase in the amount of other commodities which can be had in exchange for it, an increase in the supply of one commodity *is* an increase in the demand for other commodities, and it must be supposed that every increase in demand will evoke an increase in supply,' thus ensuring a high level of demand across a range of industries will provide an increasing surplus due to increasing returns that will be available for capital accumulation. The problem is how to generate this generalized process of expansion.

Following an argument used by Rosenstein-Rodan, Nurkse notes that this cannot be done by an individual entrepreneur. With an argument that parallels that used by Keynes in establishing the possibility of underemployment equilibrium, it notes that if disguised unemployed workers are given employment producing shoes, but do not spend all their wages on shoes, then the shoe factory cannot recover its costs and will make losses; the higher level of employment will not be maintained. But, if 'unemployed workers are taken from the land are put not into one industry, but into a whole series of industries which produce the bulk of the goods on which the workers spend their wages, what is not true in the case of one shoe factory would become true in the case of a whole system of industries: it would create its own additional market, thus realizing expansion of the world output with the minimum of disturbance of the world markets' (Rosenstein-Rodan 1943, 205–6).

This is the genesis of the idea of 'balanced' expansion; investment in a range of activities will produce incentives in terms of sales and profits that would not be present if only a single entrepreneur were to start production.[13] In addition, initiating a range of activities produces scale economies that increase the surplus available for investment that would not be reaped if only a single entrepreneur was active.[14]

Although Nurkse adopts a similar argument to explain the need for balanced expansion, he does not support Rosenstein-Rodan's extension of the idea to a 'big push' (see Nurkse 1961c), instead he refers to developing countries with disguised unemployment as exhibiting 'underdevelopment equilibrium', a condition he considers analogous to the Keynesian 'underemployment equilibrium'. Just as in Keynes's theory, the problem is not on the supply side, nor is it a question of deficient savings; the problem is to create the inducements to mobilize the potential savings for capital accumulation locked in disguised unemployment. He considers the basic problem facing developing economies in generating balanced expansion to be the small size of the market due to the low level of income.

This creates problems for any individual entrepreneur seeking to employ disguised unemployed labour to produce capital goods since there will be no demand for them. However, following Young and Rosenstein-Rodan, Nurkse notes that this conundrum can be resolved if there is a more or less general application of capital to a range of different industries. This would result in an overall enlargement of the market, as people working with more and better tools in a number of complementary projects become each other's customers.

This shifts the problem to the means by which an economy can achieve balanced expansion. Here Nurkse refers to Schumpeter's (1961) *Theory of Economic Development* as the template for the general theory of economic expansion. In Schumpeter's theory, it is the individual entrepreneur that is at the centre of the inducement to invest, but Nurkse notes that the success of new innovations depends on their propagation through the entire economy in a wave of new applications in sectors that are not directly connected with the initial innovation. The problem is that developing economies generally lack the entrepreneurial talent or the technical expertise to induce this type of Schumpeterian expansion.[15] Thus, while any substantial application of capital by an individual entrepreneur in any particular industry may be blocked or discouraged by the limitations of the preexisting markets, this problem can be overcome if there is a wave of capital investments in a number of different industries. In this way, the market difficulty (and the drag that it imposes on individual incentives to invest) is removed or, at any rate, alleviated by means of the dynamic expansion of the market through investment carried out in a number of different industries. Such balanced growth thus creates externalities, not only in terms of generating demand, but also in the form of Youngian technical progress that increases the productivity of capital.

While Nurkse grants that expansion in one area will have positive income and expenditure effects through the multiplier and induce expansion in other industries, if other producers are not also expanding autonomously this will slow down the expansion of the industry that took the initial act of expansion. Thus, it would be more expedient if every sector were expanding spontaneously without waiting for the demand signal to arrive from the rest of the system. Nurkse's principle of balanced expansion is then simply a means of accelerating the overall rate of output growth. He also notes that this simply amounts to promoting increases in output that are diversified in accordance with domestic income elasticities so as to provide markets internally for each sector of production, in contrast to output expansion for export, which is determined by international comparative advantage.

Here, Nurkse can be understood as setting out the requirements for a 'virtuous circle' of development, in contrast to his description of the 'vicious circle of poverty' that Myrdal was to develop into a 'cumulative theory of economic development.'[16]

Although he tends to favour analysis in real terms when discussing the supply side, when he deals with demand, Nurkse always argues in terms of value productivity, not physical productivity. He notes that an investment that is undertaken by a single entrepreneur may have a very low or even negative marginal value productivity, while the same investment undertaken in conditions of balanced growth may have a much higher positive marginal value productivity. Again, it is important to note the emphasis on the impact of the level of aggregate demand on productivity, but also that the process is not the same as would be found under the multiplier.

Finally, following the Keynesian lead, he believed that there was no independent market force that would bring about this result, making the State the obvious choice to promote balance expansion. Yet Nurkse had no inherent belief in any inherent superiority of the State in economic affairs. Indeed, in his writings he repeatedly stressed that he was indifferent to the way in which balanced growth was achieved, simply noting that it was required if the capital accumulation potential of disguised unemployment was to be achieved.

> How is this to be achieved? Autonomous advance involving capital investment in different branches simultaneously may come about though the infectious influence of business psychology, through the multiplier effects of investment anywhere which can create increased money demand elsewhere or through deliberate control and planning by public authorities. The widely held view that balanced growth necessarily calls for programming strikes me as dubious. Indeed, as a means of creating inducements to invest, balanced growth can be said to be relevant primarily to a private enterprise system. (Nurkse 1961b, 247)

He also noted that 'the balance-growth principle can be and has been interpreted too literally. Producing a little of everything is not the key to progress' (Nurkse 1961, 249). This position was reinforced in posthumously published notes commenting on an article proposing 'unbalanced' growth:

> I am now inclined to think that it might be well to distinguish between balanced growth as a method and balanced growth as an outcome or

objective. Even zigzag growth must have balance as its ultimate aim, in the sense of output expansion in accordance with national income elasticities of demand. I am inclined to be 'liberal', accepting as alternative possibilities: central planning; generally optimistic expectations, leading to spontaneous advance on a wide front; or the 'disequilibrium' method of zigzag growth in successive industries or sections, each tugging the other along by signals given by the price mechanism. (Nurkse 1959, 296)

Finally, it is important to note that Nurkse made a sharp distinction between the balanced expansion support for the accumulation of productive capital and the investment in infrastructure. Nurkse notes that:

The case for diversified investment [in balanced expansion] ... stands in sharp contrast, first of all, to the great concentrations of capital needed for public overhead facilities such as transport and electric power. The notion of balanced growth ...is a limited one, confined to the horizontal pattern of supply and demand for consumables. It is not applicable in any simple way to the relationship between the overhead facilities sector and the consumer goods sector, which is essentially a vertical relationship, since the basic services like transport and power are significant chiefly as producers' services.[17]

Alternative Paths of Domestic Industrialization

Thus, given the potential for capital accumulation inherent in the high level of disguised unemployment and the possibility of mobilizing it through balanced expansion, Nurkse notes there are at least two possible ways in which the capital may be employed in industrialization: to produce manufactures for export to the industrial countries or to produce manufactures mainly for domestic markets. With premonition of the debates that would come to surround import substitution, he noted that neither strategy implied elimination or reduction of exports of the primary commodities that countries naturally produce.

Industrialization for Export

Nurkse points out that industrialization to produce manufactures for export to developed, industrialized countries is to be recommended over production for domestic consumption because it relies on foreign demand and, thus, does not require the extensive improvements in productivity and incomes in domestic agriculture to support domestic demand. Further, it does not necessarily depend on expansion of total demand abroad for the type of goods to be exported because developing countries can initiate a Schumpeterian-type process in which they will be the low-cost producers that displace high-cost suppliers in the industrial countries, allowing them to move into more productive activities such as skilled services, engineering and chemistry. However, he does note that this approach does have some serious drawbacks.

Even if there is substantial disguised labour, technical qualifications and work experience may not be appropriate to the creation of an industrial sector. There may be a wide gap, or discontinuity, between the traditional primary products and the new manufactured goods for export. Perhaps more serious is the necessity of the older industrial countries adopting commercial policies that support, or at least do not discriminate against, developing country exports of manufactures. But, Nurkse notes, such support cannot be relied upon with certainty. The difficulties encountered in providing such policies through the International Trade Organization, and more recent experience in the WTO, suggests that this position was prescient.

As a result, developing countries seeking to build a base of manufacturing exports would be driven to concentrate on simple manufacturers, such as textiles, where resistance to new suppliers might be less robust. However, while this may solve one problem, it creates another; in industrialized economies these sectors are usually experiencing declining demand so that existing producers in the advanced economies must of necessity be injured and displaced if such exports are to be increased. That export markets are found through displacement of existing high-cost suppliers in the industrialized countries also acts against introduction of supportive commercial policies in developed countries.

Industrialization for Domestic Consumption

The possible resistance from developed countries to opening their markets suggests the alternative strategy – production of industrial output for domestic consumption. However, Nurkse notes that this approach may face even greater difficulty, since demand for the manufactured goods output of the new industrial sector will have to be generated internally, in particular from the agricultural sector, through increased productivity to improve purchasing power. Since in most underdeveloped countries agriculture is not an open, innovative sector, this transformation cannot be relied upon to happen in response to market incentives alone. He notes that the necessary improvement in agricultural organization, including land ownership policies, may require a revolution in the countryside, affecting the lives of the great mass of the people.

Domestic industrialization also requires an expansion of the concept of balanced expansion. The symbiosis between agricultural and manufacturing necessary to support domestic industrialization fits naturally with the concept of balanced growth. Nurkse first notes that the development of the manufacturing sector may be stymied by the failure of the agricultural sector to produce a marketable surplus. In just the same way as a single entrepreneur in manufacturing may fail because of an absence of the necessary inputs and purchasers of other entrepreneurs in other sectors, the same occurs if agricultural workers are too poor to buy the output of manufactures.

Is this Import Substitution Industrialization?

Nurkse recognizes that promoting the industrial production of manufactures for home consumption in underdeveloped countries will always be considered by critics as import substitution. However, he takes pains to counter this characterization by pointing out that domestic output expansion can occur in the sectors producing domestic goods that do not normally enter into foreign trade, as well as in those areas that compete with imports from abroad. More importantly, he suggests that domestic industrialization can mean the substitution of capital goods imports for consumption goods imports. A country can still increase its imports of capital equipment by cutting down its imports of consumer goods without directly substituting them with domestic production.

Industrialization with Limited Supplies of Labour

Nurkse's analysis is built around the concept of 'disguised' unemployment in agriculture in countries with high rates of population growth. However, for completeness, he notes that not all poor developing countries face such conditions. For countries without a potential surplus to exploit, a different approach will be required. Of particular importance will be the ability of the agricultural sector to produce a surplus to provide demand for the industrial sector. If this cannot be achieved through the movement of labour between sectors, it will have to occur through technical progress in the agricultural sector. In the tradition of Singer, Prebisch and Myrdal, he notes that it is not the case that there is no technical advance in agriculture. He refers to the impact of changes in crops and the introduction of crop rotation in England in its period of early industrialization – 'The Turnip Effect'. However, he limits his recommendations to policies to improve agricultural productivity and does not follow the above-mentioned economists in suggesting policies to adjust the terms of trade facing primary commodity exporters.

Demand Constraints – The Demonstration Effect and the External Finance Constraint

In the traditional view, the existence of an external constraint on a country's development is evidence of a scarcity of resources, a supply constraint. Nurkse takes a rather different view, emphasizing the impact of unequal wealth and income distribution between developed and developing countries on demand and the operation of the international adjustment mechanism. Even if a country succeeds in mobilizing its domestic resources in support of capital accumulation for industrialization, the gap in income levels may create an autonomous increase in the domestic propensity to consume that diverts resources from capital accumulation. In an extension of Dusenberry's demonstration effect, Nurkse notes that developing countries will tend to have higher levels of consumption for equivalent levels of GDP than the already advanced economies experienced during similar stages in their development process. He argues that international income disparities will continually cause gaps in the balance of payments of developing countries that will tend to be financed by international income transfers rather than by measures to reduce imports of luxury consumption goods – this to the detriment of the ability of balanced expansion to support capital accumulation.

Further, he argues that since there is no automatic economic mechanism to ensure these compensating transfers, in the absence of governmental direction, there is no reason for private capital movements to meet a country's external financing needs. Indeed, chronic or recurrent balance of payments difficulties are likely to act as a deterrent to private inflows and may even cause movements that increase the financing gap. Nurkse notes that the gold standard was, in theory, supposed to produce an automatic adjustment mechanism for external imbalances, but it was employed mainly by the advanced industrial countries and thus did not provide a solution for developing countries. Since most developing countries were too poor to hold reserves balances sufficient to allow them to smooth cyclical, short-term fluctuations in payments balances, they found it difficult to apply the rules of the game of the gold standard system. Given the low priority developing countries place on holding sufficient international reserves, Nurkse identifies a natural tendency towards disequilibrium in the balance of payments between rich and poor countries that is not caused by differences in productivity, but by the difference between the poor countries' propensity to spend and their capacity to produce. He notes that in these circumstances, applying the classical gold standard prescription for balance of payments adjustment –reducing demand to stop inflation accompanied by devaluation of the exchange rate – may not work because it has no impact on these structural factors. This creates a constraint on the ability of balanced expansion to support domestic resource mobilization, because even if capital transfers automatically cover the external financing requirement, there is no guarantee that they will be used to support capital formation.

Supplementing Domestic Resources with External Capital

Despite his skepticism on the size and ability of external finance to supplement domestic resources, it would be a mistake to believe that Nurkse completely rejected that external investment could play a role in the development process. He considered that external investments could contribute, but only after the process of domestic mobilization of disguised unemployment resources had been initiated through balanced growth. It is thus instructive that he gave little importance to Hans Singer's argument that foreign investment was really an extension of the lender's economy and had little impact on the development of the recipient country, by pointing out that private investment was the minor part of international investment, the majority being in government fixed-income lending to finance infrastructure.[18]

In support of his 'academic' argument that it might be more efficient for underemployed resources in developing countries to move to developed countries, he notes that the rate of return on a single investment in isolation would be much lower than if it took place in conditions of balanced growth. Thus, returns on investment in an economy before the balanced growth process gets underway would be insufficient, except for monopoly rights for mineral extraction and the exploitation of primary products. However, once balanced expansion has been initiated, the expected marginal value product of investment projects will increase above those available in developed countries and provide attractive possibilities for foreign investors. He thus concludes that foreign investment can play little role in the process of mobilizing disguised unemployment into capital accumulation, but once this process takes place, foreign capital can make a contribution to the further development of the domestic manufacturing sector.

Nonetheless, Nurkse remained skeptical about the potential size of such flows. As noted above, although Keynesian analysis had shown the favourable income and employment effects of foreign investment upon the developed economy lender, it also showed how domestic borrowing could maintain a steady level of employment in any advanced industrial country without the need of foreign investment. Thus, industrialized countries no longer needed to transfer their surplus output to the world's poorer regions to achieve their domestic policy goals. He also notes that even if such transfers did occur, they would be determined by the domestic requirements of the lender, not by the needs of the recipient country, and might have a perverse impact on the less-developed country recipients.

Nurkse thus argues that the economic case for the international transfer of resources through direct investment could not depend on its role in countercyclical policy, but should be made to stand on its contribution to development. He felt that the emphasis that was placed on functional finance in postwar Keynesian policies had cleared the way for the analysis of the developmental aspects of the international movement of capital.

A Developmental Approach to International Capital Movements

Nurkse starts by noting that the development dimension of capital movements should focus on capital as a factor of production. The geographical redistribution of capital determined by the principle of real income maximization should thus cover both net investment and the redistribution of the existing capital stock. The analysis of mobility of capital as a factor production would then be based on recognition of the differences in capital-labour-land ratios in different countries, the technical forms that capital should assume in response to different relative factor endowments, the relations between capital movements, and population growth and migration.

Nurkse points out that while external investment may support the level of activity in the short run, in the long term the return flow of income and amortization may cause difficulty. He refers to Domar's (1950) theoretical analysis of the problem that suggests that under certain conditions these difficulties may not exceed the benefits. However, he notes that Domar's analysis deals with debt service rather than distinguishing the different impact of interest payments and amortization of capital on the development process.

As far as the capital account is concerned, Nurkse joins those who argue that from a development perspective, net repayment of capital should not be necessary, nor should it be expected before the creditor and debtor countries have changed their place and their relative scale of economic development.[19] While individual loans will be repaid, if the economy is experiencing balanced expansion, an increasing amount of new loans will be granted so there will be a net increase in lending, not net repayment. Repayment of foreign loans would not take place until and unless the fundamental conditions of the two economies reversed themselves so that in the creditor economy the propensity to save falls short of domestic investment needs and the opposite occurs in the debtor economy.

After noting the reciprocal nature of the conditions facing the developed creditor and undeveloped debtor country, Nurkse follows the earlier discussion of the transfer problem, dividing the payment of interest by the debtor country into a budgetary or collection problem and a transfer problem. The budget problem requires a positive return in domestic currency of the country in which the investment has been made. This will depend directly or indirectly on the productivity of the investment and thus, on whether balanced expansion is taking place.

Two conditions must be met to resolve the transfer problem: The first is that the foreign loans finance productive investment that increases real national income and provides a return in domestic currency that covers interest. The second (and, in Nurkse's opinion, separate) condition is an export surplus to produce the foreign exchange necessary to service the loan. Nurkse points out that theoretically, it is not necessary that the foreign investment lead directly to an increase in exports, or provide direct substitutes for import, in an amount equal to the interest charges. He argues that the foreign investment projects should be determined by their marginal productivity so that the as external capital becomes available, it should be invested to yield the highest possible return, taking into account any external economies created by the project, as well as the direct commercial yield. The particular goods that are exported to create the external surplus to allow the payment of interest should be determined by comparative advantage. No particular relation is required between the marginal productivity of the capital schedule and the comparative costs schedule. On the presumption that there is no diversion of resources into additional consumption, there should be no difficulty in the servicing the lending.

> The people who buy the new product in the home market, as long as they buy out of their income and not from inflationary sources, must necessarily divert their expenditure from other goods, including imported goods. Therefore, even if the industry does not produce anything that replaces goods previously imported, but produces a net addition of new goods for sale in the domestic market, there is no inherent reason for the balance of payments difficulties to arise, always provided that the sale of the extra goods is not financed by means of inflation. There is no reason why foreign investment should be deliberately kept away from industries producing additional goods for the domestic market. (Nurske 1953, 137–38)

However, this solution also requires the cooperation of the creditor country that must be willing to adopt a liberal commercial policy that allows the debtor access to its markets. Nurkse also notes that a country that becomes dependent on external capital runs a risk of a change in sentiment or expectations leading to a financial crisis. Since a capital-exporting country has no legal obligation to renew old loans or grant new loans, a simple decline in lending, combined with the legal amortization requirements on existing loans, may lead to a capital reversal that may be unrelated to any change in the real returns earned on the investments. The case is more risky in the case of short-term credits that can be withdrawn on demand or on short notice.

Foreign Aid as Supplement to Domestic Resources?

Unilateral aid provides an alternative external source of resources. Nurkse confronts the problem of unilateral transfers from two points of view: resolving the problems associated with private investment flows, and assuring that aid is used to support additional capital formation. He notes that in many cases, private flows have become international unilateral transfers because of subsequent default. However, he also notes that this is not a very efficient solution, since default interferes with the continuity of the flow of capital and that their occurrence is not linked to development needs. Better to use unilateral grants-in-aid. However, he notes that intergovernmental grants are inevitably instruments of foreign policy and such transfers as may occur will be based on political expediency, expressing doubt that intergovernmental capital transfers are inherently more stable and reliable than the private capital movements.

In a reflection that foreshadows modern concerns for global governance, Nurkse points out that

> If we lived under a world government, automatic transfers from the richer to the poorer parts of the globe would occur as a matter of course through the fiscal mechanism. We have no world government. On the other hand, if we depart from the automatic market mechanism of private capital movements, or if this mechanism fails to function, there are no objective, nonpolitical criteria for guiding the flow of funds. The problem of devising a system of international grants is a political problem and, in the nature of the case, political considerations cannot be kept out of it. A system of international grants-in-aid does not stem from the economic mechanism of the market; nor does the principle of progressive taxation. Both are based, of necessity, on political value judgments. (Nurkse 1953, 80)

Nurkse notes that the pattern for such judgments could be based on a mechanism that tends to automatically produce transfers of resources from the richer to the poorer regions within a given country. This fiscal mechanism represents a way in which economic development may be financed in the poorer regions of a given country. It depends on progressive taxation resulting in interregional income transfers that are accepted by taxpayers in the rich and the poorer regions.

They are acknowledged as a natural consequence of the principle of ability to pay and as part of the fiscal system in which this principle is embodied. Nurkse views unilateral income transfers as an imperfect approximation to redistribution that occurs within a country automatically and would take place across countries at different levels of development if they were under a world government.

Quite apart, however, from the inconvenient but inevitable political aspects of international gifts and grants, Nurkse questions whether such transfers provide a solution to the problem of capital accumulation in underdeveloped countries. Even if they fill the gaps in the balances of payments of low-income countries, do they offset the handicap that the demonstration effect imposes on the domestic saving capacity of these countries? Such transfers may be desirable on general grounds. They spring, in part, from the tensions produced by the disparities in living levels, and serve to mitigate these disparities. The question is whether they meet the needs of capital development.

In this respect, Nurkse stresses that a country's capacity to absorb foreign aid for investment may be much more limited than its unlimited ability to increase current consumption. The limits are due to a country's backwardness, from a lack of various overhead facilities in the early stages of development and the fact that capital development schemes usually require large movements of people, as well as of material goods. In underdeveloped countries, mobility is impeded by lack of transport, housing and public facilities of all kinds – without deliberate efforts to extend the local bottlenecks, any added provision of external resources, even if directed into the investment sector in the first instance, will directly spill over into consumption. The earmarking of foreign loans or grants to specific investment projects may do something to ensure the productive use of funds, but is not by any means a sure remedy. Only where there is no domestic saving at all to start with will such earmarking be fully effective. It is not otherwise an infallible method of increasing the rate of investment, for it cannot prevent a substitution of external for domestic sources of finance.

Nurkse and Modern Development Alternatives

Nurkse provides a fresh alternative view to current monoeconomics that says that all that is required is getting the supply side right and the market will produce economic development. By placing the emphasis on the demand constraints to development, Nurkse provides an alternative perspective to elucidate many of the vexing problems of development. In some quarters, this approach is getting a second hearing. For example, his concern with mobilizing underutilized domestic labour resources is now reflected in official documents, such as the 2005 Global Summit Declaration. As economists come to recognize the failure of the market to transfer resources from developed to developing countries, well before real growth theory, Nurkse explained the reasons for low productivity and low returns in investments that would lead to a market tendency to negative net transfers of resources. His skepticism concerning a possible return to the kind of capital flows that are largely directed by governments and focused on infrastructure, leads to the natural conclusion that the only road to development is through domestic industrialization based on mobilization of disguised labour resources. But this is not antitrade or antimarket: 'The traditional pattern of development through production for expanding export markets is not to be despised and not to be discouraged. ...all opportunities in this direction are [to be] fully exploited, [but] conditions for this type of growth do not ... appear to be as promising as they were a hundred years ago' (Nurkse 1961b, 239).

Nurkse always allows for the forces of the market and international trade to play a role, but he also recognizes that international goods markets are not freely competitive and the market may not always work to the benefit of developing countries. In the tradition of Myrdal (and subsequently, Kaldor), he notes the importance of cumulative causation in the development process and the necessity for government to set that cumulative process in motion to create a virtuous circle of development. He further notes the paradox of the domestic transfer of resources from rich to poor and the necessity of some form of global governance to ensure this transfer on a global basis. In the absence of such a global mechanism, governmental aid must take its place. But, he notes, even if it were to occur, weak domestic demand conditions make it difficult for aid to be other than palliative in the vicious circle of poverty.

There are alternative voices in the development debate that echo these themes. The Other Canon,[20] through the work of Erik Reinert, has stressed the importance of the rite of passage for developing countries of domestic industrialization. Nurkse enriches that discussion by reminding economists of an alternative source of increasing productivity that relies on externalities of market size that exist independently of those due to the exploitation of technical economies that are achieved at large scale. It is important to note that Nurkse took this as the obvious conclusion of his reading of the changed economic conditions after 1920 – a position echoed in the work of Raul Prebisch.

Nurkse also followed Prebisch in drawing another conclusion from the change in geopolitical and historical conditions – the impact of the demonstration effect leading to excessively high consumption aspirations in the developing countries' elites, reducing the incentive for increasing investment. For both, this was a structural problem that was difficult, if necessary, to resolve. Nurkse emphasizes the importance of directing disguised unemployment to the formation of capital goods, yet remains uncommitted regarding the institutional mechanism that should bring it about. It is clear that he recognized that market forces could not be relied upon to reach this goal. One possible mechanism has been proposed, by The Center for Full Employment and Price Stability,[21] through a statutory programme of guaranteed government employment to ensure that the resources represented by the unemployed are mobilized for the good of the community. The benefits from these programmes would result independently of the kind of socially useful activities they promote. They can be directed towards public infrastructure with high employment content, as in proposals made by the ILO, or towards rural development, as in the recent Indian government legislation to provide guaranteed minimum employment for workers in the rural sector. They can also be used to promote other goals, such as increasing the skill level of the labour force or promoting gender equality. In this broad sense of providing social and economic capital, the programme would be precisely what Nurkse recommends to provide the basis for the use of disguised unemployment to support the capital accumulation required for domestic development.

Nurkse does not provide much technical discussion of the provision of finance for the implementation of the schemes to employ disguised unemployment. His discussions of the balance of payments adjustment mechanism do suggest that he is not in favour of fixed exchange rate policies for poor developing countries. His skepticism concerning the need for foreign savings, and likely size and ability of foreign aid or direct investment, suggests that he believes financing can be provided by internal means. In this respect, his approach may be considered to be close to the German Chartalist school of Knapp (recently amplified by Mosler (1995) and Wray (1998)) that suggests that an economy that employs flexible exchange rates and eschews external borrowing may achieve a degree of monetary sovereignty that eliminates an external constraint on domestic demand. This frees the way for both a policy of balanced expansion and the guaranteed employment of disguised labour.

Finally, it is important to note Nurkse's preference for his strategy of industrialization for export, a policy that has been followed by most successful Asian developing countries. However, he also notes that after this strategy has been employed, it may be necessary to shift to a strategy more dependent on domestic market growth. This is precisely the problem that has plagued Asian countries, starting with Japan – how to shift from external demand-driven growth to domestic demand-driven growth, when high capital accumulation and savings are no longer necessary and Keynesian domestic demand policy becomes relevant.

References

Alter, Gerald M. 1961. 'The Servicing of Foreign Capital Inflows by Underdeveloped Countries.' In Ellis 1961, 139–167.

Amsden, Alice. 1989. *Asia's Next Giant: South Korea and Late Industrialization*. New York: Oxford University Press.

Avramovic, Dragoslav (assisted by Ravi Gulhati). 1958. *Debt Servicing Capacity and Postwar Growth in International Indebtedness*. Baltimore: Johns Hopkins University Press.

Cherney, Hollis. 1955. 'The Role of Industrialisation in Development Programs.' *American Economic Review* 45 (May), 40.

Domar, Evsey. 1950. 'The Effect of Foreign Investments on the Balance of Payments.' *American Economic Review* 40 (December), 805–26.

Ellis, Howard S. (assisted by Henry C. Wallich) (ed.). 1961. *Economic Development for Latin America*: Proceedings of a Conference held by the International Economic Association. London: Macmillan.

Griffin, Keith. 1969. *Underdevelopment in Spanish America*. Cambridge, MA: MIT Press.

Haberler, Gottfried and Robert M. Stern. 1962. *Equilibrium and Growth in the World Economy*. Cambridge, MA: Harvard University Press.

Hirschman, Albert O. 1981. *Essays in Trespassing*. Cambridge: Cambridge University Press.

_____. 1958. *The Strategy of Economic Development*. New Haven: Yale University Press.

Keynes, John M. 1946. 'The Balance of Payments of the United States.' *The Economic Journal* 56 (222), 184.

Lange, Oscar. 1946. 'Economic Progress and Full Employment.' *Annals of the American Academy of Political and Social Science* 246 (July), 92.

Lewis, Sir Arthur. 1964. 'Development Economics in the 1950s.' In Gerald M. Meier and Dudley Seers (eds). *Pioneers in Development*. New York: Oxford University Press for the World Bank, 121–147.

Mosler, Warren. 1995. 'Soft Currency Economics.' *Journal of Post Keynesian Economics* 20 (2), 167–82.

Myrdal, Gunnar. 1956. *Development and Underdevelopment: A Note on the Mechanism of National and International Economic Inequality*. Cairo: National Bank of Egypt, Fiftieth Anniversary Commemoration Lectures.

Nurkse, Ragnar. 1961a. *Patterns of Trade and Development*. The Wicksell Lectures for 1959. New York: Oxford University Press.

_____. 1961b. 'International Trade Theory and Development Policy.' In Ellis 1961, 234–274.

_____. 1961c. 'Further Comments on Professor Rosenstein-Rodan's Paper.' In Ellis 1961, 74–78.

_____. 1959. 'Notes on 'Unbalanced Growth'.' *Oxford Economic Papers* 11 (3), 295–97.

_____. 1957. 'Reflections on India's Development Plan.' *The Quarterly Journal of Economics* 71 (2), 190.

_____. 1954. 'International Investment Today in the Light of Nineteenth-Century Experience.' *The Economic Journal* 64 (December), 746.

_____. 1953. *Problems of Capital Formation in Underdeveloped Countries*. New York: Oxford University Press.

Reinert, Erik. 2007. *How Rich Countries Got Rich … and Why Poor Countries Stay Poor*. London: Constable & Robinson.

Robinson, Joan. 1936. 'Disguised Unemployment.' *The Economic Journal* 46 (June), 226.

Rosenstein-Rodan, Paul. 1943. 'Problems of Industrialisation of Eastern and South-Eastern Europe.' *The Economic Journal* 53 (June–September), 202.

Schumpeter, Joseph A. 1961. *The Theory of Economic Development*. Oxford: Oxford University Press.

Singer, Hans. 1960. 'Balanced Growth in Economic Development: Theory and Practice.' Reprinted in *International Development: Growth and Change*. New York: McGraw Hill, 1964, 39–54.

Streeten, Paul. 1959. 'Unbalanced Growth.' *Oxford Economic Papers* 11 (June), 167–190.

Wray, L. Randall. 1998. *Understanding Modern Money: The Key to Full Employment and Price Stability*. Cheltenham, UK and Northampton, MA: Edward Elgar Publishing.

Young, Allyn. 1928. 'Increasing Returns and Economic Progress.' *The Economic Journal* 38 (December), 527–542.

Chapter Four:

EARLY DEVELOPMENT THEORY FROM SUN YAT-SEN TO RAGNAR NURKSE

Maiju Johanna Perälä

Introduction

Though Rosenstein-Rodan's (1943) 'Problems of Industrialisation of Eastern and South-Eastern Europe' is often attributed as being the work that initiated the birth of development economics as a field, as argued by Chakravarty (1983), a broader reading of the relevant literature shows that the theoretical formation of development economics and the discussion on the pertinent ideas began much earlier as a thorough theoretical and history of thought analysis of Allyn Young's classical endogenous growth vision shows (see Perälä 2002, 2006). Interestingly, there are other earlier contributions in the field of economic development consistent with the classical endogenous growth process, most notably a number of contributions by Sun Yat-sen: *San Min Chu I: The Three Principles of the People* (1953a), *The International Development of China* (1922), and *Fundamentals of National Reconstruction* (1953b),[1] some written over four decades and published nearly two decades before the heralded work by Rosenstein-Rodan, to which a mere mention or limited recognition exists in the contemporary economics literature.[2] Given the breadth of his development analysis and writings, Sun Yat-sen, though largely neglected by the profession, can be considered to be one of the earliest pioneers of economic development.

Given that Sun Yat-sen was much more of a development practitioner than an academic economist, interesting aspects in his development perspective are apparent. Most notably, his analysis is not limited by the theoretical body of thought or motivated by the shortfalls of the neoclassical economics analysis that was gaining prominence within the academic economic circles at the time and has become dominant especially during the latter half of the twentieth century.

The ultimate focus of his writings and work was to uplift China from the state of underdevelopment to equal status among other world nations, to achieve a sustained improvement in the standards of living of the Chinese nation. Because of this, his vision of development is comprehensive and balanced and he was able to anticipate many central issues of the postwar development economics. Sun Yat-sen's framework of analysis of the development problems and challenges is consistent with the classical endogenous growth process, a vision that theoretically culminated in the analysis of the relevance of increasing returns on economic growth by Allyn Young (1928).[3] Though the early development theorists Paul Rosenstein-Rodan and Ragnar Nurkse sought to analyze economic conditions that clearly violate the basic neoclassical assumptions (equilibrium adjustment, market clearing and perfect competition) in the context of developing economies and hence, could not be explained by the neoclassical model, given that their analysis was motivated by the criticisms and the shortfalls of the neoclassical economics, they had a more narrow standpoint in explaining the relevant economic phenomenon, despite the fact that they also were highly influenced by classical economics and approach.

The differences in perspective and motivations have led to important distinctions in the underlying theoretical views, as Sun Yat-sen (1922) more openly recognizes the role of demand in enhancing the process of development, while the later development pioneers Rosenstein-Rodan and Nurkse, though recognize the demand side as a part of the development and growth process in general and in terms of specifically affecting the dynamics of capital formation, their policy prescriptions are supply-side oriented, in line with the 'capital fundamentalist' view predominant at the time, which probably is a reflection of the influence of neoclassical economic analysis that has solely resorted to analyzing the process of economic development and growth from the supply-side perspective.

Young's views are similar to the latter two pioneers of development, as his primary focus is on the role of capital accumulation in generating externalities that promote endogenous growth; these externalities operate on both supply and demand sides, though he leaves the relevant policy aspects entirely without a discussion. His other contributions indicate that his vision for growth- and development-promoting policies to sustain and promote endogenous growth would potentially entail a broader range of measures than mere supply-side investment promotion policies, as he argued in reference to business enterprises that growth is like an evolution of a living organism, which cannot by itself, if left to the competitive forces alone, assure that balance is achieved on the market (Young 1999, 416). Policies needed to achieving the market balance that is necessary for classical endogenous growth are not limited to supply-side policies.

Of the recognized development and growth pioneers, Allyn Young (1928) focuses on describing the endogenous growth process in a vibrant industrial economy, neglecting the underdevelopment viewpoint, while Ragnar Nurkse's (1953) theory is based on a more comprehensive view of the economic development process affecting the developing countries, recognizing both the demand and supply sides in the capital accumulation process. Though recognizing the potential for a virtuous circle of growth, Nurkse focuses on the case of persistent underdevelopment, since he is preoccupied with explaining the dynamics perpetuating economic stagnation. Perälä (2002, 2006) has argued and shown that the case analyzed by Nurkse is 'the other side of the coin' of the classical endogenous growth process as envisioned by Young (1928), who retained the most balanced view in describing an active endogenous process, though given that it was mostly a theoretical description of the growth process itself, it is unclear about the relative balance and the role of economic policy measures needed. In essence, it leaves the policy discussion open and the appropriate development policy can be anything that best enables the classical, market-driven endogenous growth process. Sun Yat-sen's vision, given the absence of theoretical limitations, is more broad-based in that, though focusing on the underdevelopment experience of China and how to promote the development of an economy from subsistence level to a higher income level, he is able to relate his analysis to the development process and experience of more advanced economies, to the cases of success, while at the same time, adopting the needed policies to the conditions of the low-income, subsistence economy. Sun Yat-sen's vision entails an in-depth understanding of the development and growth process consistent with the classical endogenous growth process, with focused context-specific development policy recommendations geared towards the welfare maximization of the Chinese population.

In discussing the development pinoeers vision on economic development and growth, the chapter proceeds in chronological order discussing Sun Yat-sen, after which Allyn Young's endogenous growth vision is presented. While beginning with a brief reference to Paul Rosenstein-Rodan's theory of the big push, next the paper focuses its discussion on Ragnar Nurkse's theory of vicious circle and balanced growth,[4] after which the differences in the development and growth visions are discussed and the concluding remarks are provided in the last section.

Sun Yat-sen's View on Development and Growth

Though much more appreciated by the political scientists and historians than economists during the postwar era, Sun Yat-sen, based on the breadth of development analysis and original contributions as evidenced by his writings, can be considered to be one of the earliest pinoeers of the twentieth century modern development economics. Given his writing style and the timing of his writings, not much can be said about what economic works or perspectives influenced Sun Yat-sen's development view, apart from those perspectives and influences that are apparent from his economic development analysis.[5] Despite this, the Western influence on his thought through his education and life experience is clear. Sun Yat-sen was born in 1866 in Southern China, in a village close to Macao and Hong Kong, which exposed him to Western influences from the Portuguese and British colonies nearby, especially through trade and economic relations. At an early age, he moved to Hawaii to receive an education that was conducted in English and his further schooling in Hong Kong by the missionaries was Western influenced. During his medical school years at Canton Hospital Medical College (1886–1887) and then the College of Medicine for Chinese in Hong Kong (1887–1892), Sun Yat-sen held revolutionary thoughts from early on and aspired to bring modernization to China in the form of political and economic development, an inspiration that grew in him over time and was enriched by his foreign travel (or the period of exile) in the Western European countries and the United States.

Sun Yat-sen was deeply motivated by the aspiration to further the economic development of China via a broad-based development programme and plan, as evidenced by his work, most notably by his book, *The International Development of China*, published in 1922, which outlines and discusses concrete plans and policies to promote China's economic development and growth. His vision of economic development and growth, especially its necessity for China and the needed policies to promote it, is elaborated at a more general political, economic and philosophical level in the *San Min* lectures that were given in 1924 at the National Senior Normal College in Gwangdung and first published in English in 1927. The lectures are an elaboration on Sun Yat-sen's development principles and doctrines as well as an assessment of the present development situation of China that he already began forming during his exile in Europe in 1897 and their core ideas were published as the 'Kuomintang Declaration' in 1923 (Dr. Sun Yat-sen Memorial Hall).

Sun Yat-sen's development thought entailed in the above-mentioned works emerged over time through his work in political and economic policymaking and organizational involvement as well as through his lifelong reading and research from foreign to ancient Chinese texts in economics, politics, history, philosophy and religion. Though up until this contribution he has not been recognized as a development pioneer,[6] his economic development insights are thoughtful and ahead of his time, as he anticipated many of the core notions and discussions that were to follow in modern development economics, especially during the second half of the twentieth century.

The *San Min* lectures focused on discussing the political and economic development needs of China and are based on three principles (or concepts): nationalism, democracy and livelihood (the standard of living). While his lectures on nationalism and democracy are more political in nature, after discussing the political aspects, Sun Yat-sen closely connects the economic development process and prospects on the relevant aspects of economic nationalism that enable the society to gain cohesion as well as confidence in their path towards self-sustained development and growth. The last aspect, livelihood or national welfare, focuses on analyzing the needed improvements to achieve a meaningful standard of living or to acquire sustained gains in development. This last part of *San Min* principles consists of four lectures on national welfare and people's livelihood, landownership and 'regulation of capital', the food problem and other basic necessities, such as clothing. It is clear that in terms of his economic analysis, Sun Yat-sen focuses on initiating development in a subsistence economy via promoting agricultural productivity increase through capital and infrastructure investments as well as land reform, while also addressing the provision of basic needs related to food, shelter and clothing. The relevant context of his economic analysis is clear and, as a consequence, so are his policy prescriptions and vision, all of which conform to the classical endogenous growth vision, seeking to expand the market and promote self-sustained economic development and growth of agricultural and manufacturing sectors alike for the purpose of reducing poverty.

Furthermore, in *The International Development of China*, Sun Yat-sen argues for the significance of public works, as a concrete way to enhance the economic development of the country, geared towards enhancing the agricultural sector development as well as the industrial one. He holds a relatively balanced view between the importance of both sectors, though his policies promoting agricultural productivity increase are especially important given that at the time, the majority of the Chinese population was living in rural areas relying on subsistence agriculture. His account of China's early development is interesting, as from his study it is evident that the development achieved historically is not directed by or solely an outcome of politics. Rather, it is a response to the economic development needs combined with a specific geography and its advantages, such as the extensive waterways that enabled cheap and fast transport between the different regions of a diverse and natural resource-rich economy. The role of the development of waterways through extensive river networks was already brought forward as one important factor promoting China's development (Smith 1776). Consistent with Smith's perspective, Sun Yat-sen provides an extensive discussion on the further development of the waterways to meet the modern needs to promote agricultural and industrial development (Yat-sen 1922, 58). He promotes the development of waterways for transport, flood control and irrigation to ensure an increase in agricultural productivity and to enhance intracountry trade between different regions within China as well as international trade. When discussing the international linkages that promote development, Sun Yat-sen highlights the need for international loans as a means to finance canal development and other infrastructure building, given their central role in development and the shortage of domestic funds.

Despite the fact that he held revolutionary views during his early years, Sun Yat-sen's (1922, 79) development view is not based on socialist economic organization and he does not advocate socialist policies. He recognizes the importance of competition and rural development as opposed to monopoly and rural underdevelopment, discussing them through developed country examples. Sun Yat-sen argues for the public ownership of natural monopolies in the provision of utilities. Furthermore, having his development context of a subsistence, agriculture-reliant economy in mind, Sun Yat-sen did not overemphasize industrial development as the only way to proceed, as many development pioneers did, or what has also been the emphasis of Soviet development programmes, which lead to the immiseration of the agricultural sector, especially in the developing world, as a consequence of the development policy failures or the outright neglect of the agricultural sector's needs with urban sector dominating the policy makers perspectives. Clearly influenced by the country experience and conditions, based on which he formed his view on development, the relative importance of rural development becomes evident for the sake of expanding the market and promoting endogenous growth process. Furthermore, in discussing the investment in developing the waterways, he does point out their role in increasing agricultural productivity through flood control as well as improved irrigation and hence, the focus on agricultural development promotion also remains in this aspect of the transport infrastructure investment.

As mentioned, China, at the time, was at a very initial stage of development in terms of its structural transformation as the agricultural sector dominated the economy, a condition explicitly emphasized by Sun Yat-sen. Therefore, though Sun Yat-sen seeks to promote industrial development via various policies, such as infant-industry protection, capital investment and technological development, providing incentives for modernization, he refrains from neglecting the necessity of improving the productivity and output of the agricultural sector that he views as a complement for industrial sector development. In this respect, he is distinct from other early development pioneers who emphasized industrial sector development strategies, often at the cost of agricultural sector development or while neglecting the role of agricultural sector in the process of economic development. In promoting industrial and trade policies and infant-industry protection, Sun Yat-sen anticipates the theoretical arguments that were to follow in modern development economics and development planning from the times of the early development theory to its contemporary contributions, and avoids the shortcomings of these early contributions in promoting balanced development of a subsistence economy without the neglect of the agricultural sector.

The theoretical economic discussion on development needs by Sun Yat-sen bears similarity to the theoretical notions discussed by the early development theorists Rosenstein-Rodan and Nurkse, yet entails significant departures as well as original thought. Sun Yat-sen describes a phenomenon that can be called a 'dynamic mirror effect' of Say's law, operating and initiating from the demand side.[7] Sun Yat-sen (1922, 29) argues that 'needs create new needs', a mere demand-side perspective apparent from his subsistence-economy development vision, a distinct departure from Rosenstein-Rodan's and Nurkse's emphasis that 'supply creates its own demand' following the law by Jean-Baptiste Say (1803). The economic phenomenon theorized by Sun Yat-sen initiates from the demand side, entailing a behavioural externality,[8] in that expanded needs constitute an enlargement of demand that in the end are satisfied and fulfilled by supply. According to Perälä (2007a), the recognition of the consumer-side behavioural changes reveals that Say's law operates differently at different income levels. It has less strength or is likely to be inoperative at low-income levels,[9] while it may be observed at higher income levels, where endogenous growth in present production is combined with production and marketing strategies based on expected markets and demand, rather than actual demand, as is the case at low income levels.

In formulating his development views, Sun Yat-sen was not limited by the neoclassical method of analysis nor the classical economic perspective, as he did not adhere to Say's law as other development pioneers did. Rosenstein-Rodan and Nurkse, though reacting against and being critical of the neoclassical methods, were much more orthodox, classical in terms of their analysis and possibly limited by their theoretical training or to an extent had internalized the neoclassical way of analysis, despite the fact that they were able to provide a critical view and were capable of recognizing the limitations of the approach in analyzing the development experience of low-income economies.

The growth signal initiates on the demand side and its strength on the demand side is stronger and more in line with the economic incentives that predominate within market economies. This perspective, consistent with Sun Yat-sen's view, has been lost in much of early development theory as well as mainstream postwar economic development and growth analysis. It is important to note that despite holding some revolutionary views, Sun Yat-sen's view on the economy confirms with capitalism, though with some socialist influence on the policy side, similarly to the Nordic development perspective, as his development promotion policies are based on more egalitarian economic and social opportunity,[10] with a relatively balanced vision between the importance of agricultural and industrial development via government policy that leads to a balanced broad-based market expansion that promotes endogenous development and growth within the economy.

Allyn Young's Endogenous Growth Vision

Towards the end of the 1920s, right before the Great Depression, Allyn Young (1928) formalized his vision of growth based on increasing returns, a complex, dynamic process generated endogenously, within the economic system. Though arguing that he merely extends Smith's dictum 'the division of labour is limited by the extent of the market', Young modernizes and extends the notion to a comprehensive description of growth dynamics in a modern developed economy or rapidly developing capitalist economy. Young's motivation for writing the 1928 article has widely been considered to have been a critique of general equilibrium methods.[11] Perälä (2002, 2006) has challenged this view by arguing that it is rather to present his dynamic vision of growth, incorporating the role of the market size and increasing returns fuelled by external economies – growth dynamics not captured by the theoretical methods used by his contemporaries.

Following Marshall, Young (1928, 527) defines internal economies as those captured generally when a market expansion allows a firm to broaden its production scale, while external economies can be visualized through changes in industrial organization at the macroeconomic level. Though using the classical method of analysis by providing examples of a micro-level phenomenon in order to associate to and explain a macroeconomic phenomenon, Young conscientiously abstracts away from a firm-level technical viewpoint to a macroeconomic perspective in order to analyze long-run economic growth. He argues for the importance of this in terms of analyzing increasing returns and dynamic external economies that generate and promote economic growth at the aggregate level, as he believes that 'these economies lie under our eyes, but we may miss them … if we try to make of *large-scale* production … any more than an incident in the general process by which increasing returns are secured and if accordingly we look too much at the individual firm or even, … at the individual industry' (Young 1928, 531; italics in the original).

Young's perception of the division of labour is a broader phenomenon than that of Smith and entails a complex, dynamic growth mechanism. While understanding the broad dimension of the labour division process, Young chooses to focus his discussion on following aspects: the incorporation of indirect (roundabout) production methods, the incorporation of capital in the production process, and the industrial division of labour, the industry, sectoral and macroeconomic level changes in industrial organization. His discussion on the former concept is a detailed account of the phenomenon generating external economies, productivity increase and growth at the firm and sectoral level, while the latter views the phenomenon from an aggregate, macroeconomic perspective where his main emphasis remains, given his focus on long-run development and growth effects of increasing returns and externalities. In Young's view, much of modern economic history, more specifically the economic development of advanced, industrialized economies, can be attributed to the process of securing these returns at the aggregate level.[12]

At the firm level, Young points out that complex production processes are simplified, and incorporation of capital (or machinery) to implement the simplified production phases is facilitated. That is, it is easier to introduce machinery to execute simple repetitive, routine-like tasks, than it is for complex ones. The essence of Young's first 'variation on the theme' can then be summarized as the most important consequence of the division of labour. While simplifying the production processes, the division of labour fuelled by an expansion of the market enables capital to be incorporated into the production process, increasing output and productivity, which in turn extends the market,[13] and hence, leads to a further division of labour reinforcing this circular phenomenon and stimulating economic progress.

Furthermore, Young (1928, 531) adds that these economies, 'even more than the economies of other forms of the division of labour, depend upon the extent of the market.' The most important economies that beget increasing returns are generated through the application of capitalistic production methods and are external in nature.[14] Given that they exhibit higher implementation costs, they more strongly depend on the market size to render them more feasible than any other types of economies derived from the division of labour. Young's growth process entailing primary and secondary economies describes an industrial diversification process at the firm and industrial levels from consumption to capital goods production, fuelled by external economies that are driven by the expansion of the market and incorporation of capital into the production process that increases productivity. His view entails market-based interdependencies (or dynamic pecuniary external economies) between firms and industries, as any new development in an industry or an increase in the market for goods in one industry has the potential to spill over to other industries and to initiate similar mechanisms, which in turn provoke the phenomenon further.[15] The mechanism is promoted through competition, an inherent part of the classical view on the economy, that promotes market expansion via purchasing power increase due to competitive price-setting as well as diffusion of pecuniary and technological (nonpecuniary) externalities leading to generalized increasing returns while, at the same time, limiting internal returns at firm level.

Young (1928, 533) is explicit in his definition of the market, which he considers to be determined by purchasing power rather than area or population.

He further elaborates that recognizing this leads to the observation that 'capacity to buy depends upon capacity to produce. In an inclusive view, considering the market not as an outlet for the products of a particular industry and therefore external to that industry, but as the outlet for goods in general, the size of the market is determined and defined by the volume of production.' Though his wording emphasizes the demand, the market side, it touches on Say's Law without adhering to it – in Young's words, the production volume determines and defines the size of the market. The volume of production, in turn, is influenced by the scope of the division of labour and hence by the market size.

In essence, the process is cumulative and generates endogenous growth. This circularity of disequilibrating forces within the economic system gives occasion for economic growth and progress in Young's vision. An extension of market initiates the mechanism by deepening the division of labour and facilitating the application of capital, which further extends the market through an increase in output. Hence, there is clearly feedback or direct interrelation between supply and demand.

Though he views the process as uneven, disequilibrating, Young's vision encompasses continuity and progress, in that he does not highlight the aspects that might lead to a general failure of the type experienced during the Great Depression.[16] He does, however, make explicit that defining the market in this way as '– an aggregate of productive activities, tied together by trade – carries with it the notion that there must be some sort of *balance*, that different productive activities must be proportioned one to another' (Young 1928, 533; emphasis added). Hence, in this way he does recognize the necessity of balance and, implicitly, when this condition is not fulfilled, the possibility of maladjustments within the market, though a case of market failure is not analyzed by him.[17] His view is a complement to Ragnar Nurkse's vision of development and growth; Nurkse focussed on analyzing the same economic dynamics, though from the perspective of an underdeveloped economy.

Young recognizes the relatively strict conditions underlying his endogenous growth process, indicating that they are not necessarily met in reality:

> Moving away from … abstract considerations, so as to get closer to the complications of the real situation, account has to be taken … of various … obstacles. The demand for some products is inelastic, or with an increasing supply, soon becomes so … Then there are natural scarcities, limitations or inelasticities of supply … [in addition to which] progress is not and cannot be continuous. The next important step forward is often initially costly, and cannot be taken until a certain quantum of prospective advantages has accumulated. (Young 1928, 535)

Hence, Young does recognize that there can be significant impediments to the growth mechanism, such as fixed costs and inelasticities of supplies and demands, and that the role of stage of development is important.

Young considers growth process to be of a disequilibrium nature. It does not proceed at an even rate, rather, it varies across industries and depends on factors such as industrial organization and its capacity to adjust, as well as pure luck as various forces coincide, since the process is influenced by 'trial and error'. Further hindrances to the process are created by the inflexible nature of human capital and the time needed to accumulate capital. These impediments, however, are merely mentioned by Young and he does not explicitly consider them leading to a market failure, a case that preoccupied early development theorists such as Paul Rosenstein-Rodan and Ragnar Nurkse.

Young argues that 'certain quantum of prospective advantages' is often required before the growth process may be able to continue, which can be interpreted that a certain stage of development (or a level of institutional development) for a country is needed for his market-based growth mechanism to function smoothly. He points out factors, such as the discovery of natural resources and their new uses and the growth of knowledge, that reinforce the presence of increasing returns and hence, resorts to a more 'macro' level perspective in his discussion that supports such an interpretation. Nevertheless, it is clear that Young's growth vision assumes a certain level of institutional development in a country in order for the market-driven growth mechanism to operate efficiently. Interestingly, Sun Yat-sen, Rosenstein-Rodan and Nurkse relaxed this stage of development assumption and focused their attention on economies in which this endogenous growth-generating mechanism was not observed (or was not functioning in a balanced fashion). In doing so, the latter two coincidentally highlighted in their theories what Young viewed as the obstacles for the process of growth – inelasticities in supplies and demands and presence of indivisibilities (and fixed costs) – as the conditions preventing these economies from experiencing self-sustaining growth. The emphasis on scarcity of supply and demand and the insufficiency of market and imbalances were the focus of Sun Yat-sen, who analyzed the growth process within a unified framework in which the stage of development recognition is inherent.

Later, it will be shown that it is precisely the failures of these conditions in less-developed economies on which the early development theorists such as Rosenstein-Rodan and Nurkse focused as they sought to explain the absence of economic growth in the developing world. Hence, it is argued that Young and these development pioneers in essence describe different aspects of the same growth model.

Ragnar Nurkse's Vicious and Virtuous Circles of Development

The contribution that is generally attributed to have ignited postwar development economics literature, Rosenstein-Rodan (1943), is a policy-oriented discussion focusing on jump-starting the process of development of an underdeveloped economy. The theoretical notions introduced, especially the theory of the big push that the contribution begins formulating, were much in their infancy at the time and were clarified by his later contributions, Rosenstein-Rodan (1961) and (1984), though as a whole they still consist of a rather fragmented body of development literature when not read and understood in the proper development and economic theory context. According to Rosenstein-Rodan, a large coordinated development effort is made necessary by the inherent presence of complementarities and externalities between industries that are more prevalent in the developing than developed market economies. The presence of indivisibilities and inelasticities in supplies and demands, created by pecuniary and technological externalities,[18] created obstacles for the process of development and to overcome them, a sufficient expansion of the market via development policy is needed. Rosenstein-Rodan applied the classical endogenous economic growth analysis as represented by the work of Young to the case of underdevelopment, a case unanalyzed by the latter author, and this focus of analysis was soon followed by other modern development economics pioneers, such as Ragnar Nurkse, who formulated his theory of the vicious circle and virtuous circle of development; the latter has also been known as the balanced growth doctrine, which in essence captures the classical endogenous growth process previously discussed. Ragnar Nurkse (1953), following Rosenstein-Rodan's focus with a more theoretically oriented and comprehensive discussion on the central economic dynamics involved in persistent underdevelopment, provides a much clearer vision of economic stagnation and potential for cumulative growth, and hence it is taken as the point of reference to compare and contrast to the theoretical notions set forth in classical endogenous growth theory à la Young as well as Sun Yat-sen's development vision for a large, low-income, subsistence economy.

Following the core notion of economic development and growth analysis since the time of the Industrial Revolution, that industrialization is associated with economic development, with sustained improvements in the standards of living, Ragnar Nurkse (1953, 10) emphasizes the problems of achieving growth through capital accumulation, which he considers neither automatic nor spontaneous. With this in mind, he first sets the scene for what can be called a theory of stagnation, or a vicious circle of poverty, after which he proceeds to discuss his theory of growth, or virtuous circle of development. According to

Nurkse (1953, 4), a vicious circle of poverty, 'a circular constellation of forces tending to act and react upon one another in such a way as to keep a poor country in a state of poverty', is a possible, even likely dynamic in a capital-poor country, resulting in the persistence of underdevelopment. The concept clearly describes the presence of economic forces that can keep a country stagnated at a low-income equilibrium, a state in which the cumulative growth process, taken as given in Young's classical endogenous growth vision, is no longer automatic and natural outcome of economic interactions. At low income levels, potentially growth-promoting incentives are distorted in a fashion that they create forces that perpetuate the status quo and prevent the cumulative growth process from igniting, leading to a vicious circle of poverty and underdevelopment. According to Nurkse, it is most detrimental to development when the process of capital accumulation is affected by such distorted economic dynamics, given its central role in promoting economic development and growth, leading to sustained increases in standards of living through the advancement of economies from early stages of development with predominantly agricultural production orientation to more advanced stages of development via industrialization.

Nurkse (1953) formalizes the possibility for a low investment level and capital accumulation spiral through supply- and demand-side dynamics, directly affecting the investment and accumulation process in low-income economies. [19] The supply-side argument for a low level of investment in an economy stems from a country's small amount of savings, caused by its low income level combined with the inability to save and make available funds for investment. The low income level is, in turn, a result of low productivity, which is a direct consequence of small amounts of capital used in the production process due to low past capital investment, again a consequence of the low domestic savings that has been available in the economy for financing the needed capital investment.

The demand-side argument for stalled capital formation manifests itself through a process similar to that discussed by Young and Rosenstein-Rodan. Namely, low inducement to invest is caused by the small size of the market, which leads to the market's low capacity to absorb goods and hence, to a low expected market for manufacturing goods depressing investment incentives, a direct consequence of low income level in the economy due to its low productivity. Like in the supply-side argument, low productivity is a direct indication of low levels of capital used in the production process, attributable to the weak investment stimulus prevailing in the economy, again due to small market size and low expected market for goods.

Common to both demand and supply sides is the low income level of the country, caused by the low level of productivity determined by the lack of capital used in the production process due to low past investment and accumulation. Though he discusses both sides of the capital accumulation spiral, Nurkse notes that the supply side is generally more emphasized than the demand side without explaining the justification for this and rather just adopts this perspective in his analysis. His position is in accordance with the 'capital fundamentalist' thinking that dominated early development economics contributions as well as the postwar economic growth contributions. As a matter of fact, his analysis accentuates the importance of the supply side up to a point that prevents him from considering a generalized market expansion as a stimulus to growth, central to classical endogenous growth process, according Young's theory as well as inherent in Sun Yat-sen's development vision.

The lack of incentive to invest due to the small size of the market, the small expected market for goods, is at the heart of the demand-side explanation (Nurkse 1953, 6). Nurkse follows Young and Rosenstein-Rodan in assuming that the size of the market influences the incentive for a private individual or a firm to invest, in approximating the expected market and sales for their goods, making direct reference to Young (1928). Though he does not make reference to the role of labour division in the understanding of the accumulation process, the mechanism through which the constraint on economic growth takes place is similar to Young's view of the cumulative, endogenous process of growth generated in the presence of positive externalities in an economy. Perälä (2002, 2006) argues that Nurkse, in his theory, describes the 'other side of the coin' by explaining how this cumulative, endogenous growth process can fail, as a consequence of the vicious circle of poverty, leaving a country stagnated at a low income level. In essence, Perälä (ibid.) makes explicit recognition that the classical endogenous growth theory and the early development theory as represented by the works of Rosenstein-Rodan and Nurkse are analyzing the same development and growth process from different perspectives, advanced and underdeveloped economies, respectively, a fact that has not been commonly recognized within the literature up until now. The recognition of this literature improves our contemporary understanding of the originality of early development theory contributions like Ragnar Nurkse's theories, as well as helps us understand the relevant economic insights of development and underdevelopment that persistently affect and challenge the endogenous growth process that leads to a development path with sustained increases in the standards of living, sustained development gains.

A market expansion in Young's view via the deepening of labour division, within Nurkse's framework can be considered, via an increase in expected market for goods, to increase the inducement to invest leading to the increased use of capital in the production process that directly increases output productivity, resulting in a higher income level and further increases in the market, and so on. Where Young does not make a stern division between supply and demand sides, a characteristic of classical economic analysis, and hence refrains from limiting himself to a one-sided perspective in his analysis, early development theorists are more 'neoclassical' in their approach,[20] in that though acknowledging the relevance of both sides and making extensive reference to the market-side, explicitly as well as via the recognition of pecuniary externalities, they retain their policy prescriptions limited to a supply-side solution that is an indirect method of expanding the size of the market rather than the direct demand-side policies that would lead immediately to actual and expected market enlargement.

Nurkse argues that two major factors contribute to the formation of vicious circle dynamics within an economy. First, he discusses how capital investment is necessarily 'lumpy', characteristic of relatively large units that are indivisible. In the context of a relatively small market, the mere fact that the application of capital is in relatively large units entailing large fixed costs and requiring relatively large investment, increases the risk to invest and thus reduces the incentive to do so, especially at low income levels. Given that this fixed investment component leads to increasing returns at the firm level, as firms are able to capture internal economies with increases in output, as well as at the industrial and macroeconomic level, through positive pecuniary and technological (nonpecuniary) external economies from across-the-board capital investment, output and productivity increases and ongoing production condition changes operating through market mechanism and/or directly affecting the firms. Second, at early stages of development, this phenomenon is coupled with inelasticities of demands, inherently more prevalent on smaller markets, and hence, the risk of capital investment is augmented as the firms' markets, as well as expected markets, are more unstable, inherent of greater contractionary possibilities and with less expansionary potential through positive pecuniary externalities, as this inelasticity leads to smaller quantity-demanded increases to be induced by any given price reduction, and, as a consequence, the market incentive to invest in capital equipment is further reduced.

After explaining his theory of stagnation, Nurkse proceeds to explain his solution for the vicious circle dilemma and turns to his theory of economic growth, also known as the 'doctrine of balanced growth'. Nurkse is explicit in that the circular forces have a potential in generating self-sustaining growth like in Young's vision of classical endogenous growth. The doctrine of balanced growth entails a method of expanding the size of the market and, in this way, reinvigorating investment incentives that were previously suffocated, thus enabling the economy to embark on the path to development and growth. The notion of balance is essential, as the demands faced by industries are interdependent due to the 'diversity of human wants'. Hence, given that a supply-side policy is advocated by Nurkse, he argues for a broad-based investment in the manufacturing sector that through the productivity increases and employment generated would lead to a demand-side expansion of the market and hence the essence of Say's law would hold, a broad-based expansion of the market would be achieved indirectly by stimulating the supply.

Though neglecting the direct role of market expansion in initiating self-sustained growth, explicit focus and central driving mechanism of growth, according to Young in his theory, much of Nurkse's vision of stagnation and growth is nevertheless similar to the process of growth envisioned in classical endogenous growth theory. First, the notion of industry interdependence and the necessity for balance is present in both visions, given that they assume the aggregate notion of Say's law, which, in the presence of the diversity of human wants, can only hold when a certain level of economic activity (or level of development) is assumed and has been achieved. '[An] aggregate of productive activities, tied together by trade – carries with it the notion that there must be some sort of balance, that different productive activities must be proportioned to one another' (Young 1928, 533). Though like Rosenstein-Rodan, Nurkse adopts a supply-side bias when considering the potential for a sustained market expansion via policy, as mentioned, seeking to achieve it indirectly rather than using a direct demand-side measure. The notion of balance is also inherent in the development vision of Sun Yat-sen, though he advocates both supply- and demand-side policy measures to promote economic development in a subsistence low-income economy with equal emphasis on agricultural and industrial development. Given the focus on capital accumulation and industrialization, this latter aspect, the sectoral balance in development, was not the focus of analysis of Young or Rosenstein-Rodan; Nurkse hence, to an extent, contributed to the neglect of the agricultural sector, though the classical endogenous growth theory and economic development process can be considered at a level of generality that does not prevent its application to agricultural sector development via capital accumulation and investment into agricultural production and productivity increase, and as such, is consistent with Sun Yat-sen's development perspective. Similar to the industrial investment, capital investment in agriculture leads to a productivity increase and an expansion of the market, either via agricultural wage increase or the generalized purchasing power, market increase, due to a decline in agricultural output prices, most importantly that of food that at low-income levels are the greatest part of consumption expenditure from the wages, hence expanding the market for industrial products.

The similarity between the theoretical contributions of Young, Nurkse and Rosenstein-Rodan, is that they all entail a possible presence of generalized increasing returns. Similarly to Young, Nurkse considers external economies generated by generalized market expansion perhaps the most important factor leading to increasing returns. 'It may be that the most important external economies leading to the phenomenon of increasing returns in the course of economic progress are those that take the form of increases in the size of the market' (Nurkse 1953, 14). These externalities can be both types, pecuniary and technological (nonpecuniary). Hence, both envision the possibility for cumulative, self-sustaining growth, though given the differing research foci of Young and Nurkse, the former author's focus is on describing how this growth is endogenous, generated within the system, in an economy in which the market mechanism entails the required dynamism and conditions for progress at higher income levels, while the latter's focus is on describing the difficulty of initiating the before-mentioned process in an economy in which the growth-generating mechanism has failed at a low income level. The process of development is not viewed in this theoretical form in Sun Yat-sen's work and hence, increasing returns are not directly addressed though the development vision is in line with the achievement and initiation of sustained endogenous growth similar to the before-mentioned authors.

Nurkse argues that the supply side of the capital accumulation spiral is a more important obstacle to the process of growth and development than the demand side. When discussing the supply side, though occasionally referring to the smallness of domestic market causing depressed investment incentives in reference to its relevance to the infant industry argument and how it influences the nature of foreign direct investment flows, Nurkse refrains from considering that a general expansion of consumption is beneficial to growth, a counterintuitive argument from the perspective of classical endogenous growth. His emphasis on the supply side focuses his attention on the problem of accumulating investment funds, and any such funds that are directed to consumption instead of saving, slows the process of capital accumulation and hence economic growth, a clear departure from Young's vision. He argues that 'the general economic problem … is to direct as much as possible of the increment in real income into saving and to allow as little as possible of it to go into an immediate increase in consumption' (Nurkse 1953, 146–7). Clearly, the continuous interaction between supply and demand, their endogeneity, that promotes dynamic growth in Young's theory is missing in Nurkse's analysis, which leads him to make his argument that a sustained market expansion can only be achieved indirectly via a supply-side measure through an increase in productivity resulting from an increased usage of capital in the production process.

A critical difference in these two views is the degree of efficiency assigned to the market in producing long-run growth and improvement in standard of living. Young assumes that any market expansion, whether propagated from the demand or supply side, generates a deepening of labour division, which induces investment in capital and hence, results in a higher level of it to be used in the production process increasing productivity and so on.

The endogenous growth mechanism in Young's view is initiated via an impulse generated in the market and hence, driven by the incentives prevailing on it. These incentives are assumed to be compatible with the long-run growth of the economy. Nurkse (and Rosenstein-Rodan) begins with a premise that the prevailing market incentives are such that they do not generate endogenous growth. They then seek to alter the state in such situations and argue that capital accumulation is required in order to generate a productivity increase and hence, an increase in the income level and an expansion of the market is expected to follow. Though this latter perspective is not technically incorrect, from the dynamic perspective, the sequence of phenomena, the relevant economic processes and their relations, lack realism, especially at low income levels. Say's law is assumed to hold, which is unplausible at low income levels and rather, a direct market expansion that allows the 'dynamic mirror effect' of the law to promote production incentives via market mechanism and hence leads to increases in production (supply) and further expansion of the market is consistent with classical endogenous growth process that captures the process of development and growth more realistically.

Therefore, despite the differing emphasis in the process of growth and development and the ensuing supply-side policy bias that dominated Nurkse's work (as well as Rosenstein-Rodan's), the theoretical thought of Nurkse can be considered to bear a mechanism similar to Young, though describing the exact opposite. Bringing the obstacles to this cumulative growth process as described by Young (inelasticities of demands and supplies and indivisibilities) to the forefront of the capital accumulation spiral enables Nurkse to relax the stage of development assumption and in this way allows, for an occasion to broaden this theory of cumulative growth to account for the development or, rather, the underdevelopment experience of the developing world, a case that was not considered by Young.

Another significant difference in the emphasis between these two authors or, perhaps more accurately, between Young and much of early development economics literature, is in their views of whether or not long-run growth can be generated via policy. Young explicitly refutes the capability of 'an industrial dictator' in generating a transformation of a country into an industrialized one in a matter of years and hence, he might be viewed as expressing his 'scepticism' for the role of industrial policy in generating growth.[21] However, in commenting on the growth of economic system with reference to cities, Young highlights the evolutionary nature of the economic system and points to its inability to guide itself indeterminately.

American cities have only recently come to realize, what most European cities learned a long time ago, that a city's growth must be planned, that it must not be left to the haphazard forces of shopkeepers' competition and real estate speculation. A city is like a living organism, but unlike a healthy unitary organism, it does not have within itself those magical properties which preserve a due balance of the parts and organs and which prevent the development of abnormalities and excrescences. (Young 1999, 416)

Therefore, perhaps a more appropriate interpretation of Young's views with respect to the role of policy in facilitating the long-run growth of economic systems, is that he wishes to emphasize the significance of the time required and the challenges for policy in generating an industrial transformation in an economy via the growth mechanism that he describes. Early development theorists, in turn, uniformly express a firm belief in development planning, in a form of a coordinated investment across sectors, to embark an economy on a self-sustaining growth path. One possible explanation for the differences in emphasis in views between these authors, as conveyed by these particular contributions, with respect to the role of policy or its capacity to generate growth might be explained by the fact that Young's contribution was written before the Great Depression, a generalized market failure without a parallel in modern economic history that highlighted the role of macroeconomic policy in revitalizing economic growth and ignited the Keynesian revolution within economics, while the early development theory contributions were written after it. Though this might be one of the factors that contributes to the latter's solid belief in 'the power of policy', it must be recognized that this timing, in turn, puts the early development theory contributions in a notably less flattering position when considering the shift in emphasis to the supply side as was adopted by them. Writing practically at the height of the Keynesian revolution in economics, early development theory downplayed, if not outright neglected, the demand side's importance in generating growth. Though, when considering the fact that much of modern growth theory adopts a similar 'bias', the emphasis chosen by them can much more easily be understood as a reflection of the dominant perspective in the economic analysis of our time, an influence of neoclassical economic analysis as applied to economic development and growth.

The Evolution of Development Thought from Sun Yat-sen to Ragnar Nurkse

Sun Yat-sen's development thought anticipated development economics theories on many fronts. His development writings addressed issues such as infant-industry protection and industrialization and the theories of dependence in the international trade and finance aspects, arguments that were to arise to dominate the development discourse of the South from the early postwar era until mid-1980s. Sun Yat-sen's work contains clear influences of and is consistent with classical economic analysis of development and hence, in its approach is also related to the early development theory as represented by the works of Rosenstein-Rodan and Ragnar Nurkse. Given that he wrote a decade before Allyn Young and over two decades before the field of development economics was initiated, Sun Yat-sen can be considered to be one of the first pioneers of modern development economics, though he is hardly known to the profession of Western academic economists and has not been recognized as a development economics pioneer. His approach to development is broader than that of the pioneers that followed him, given that he was limited by his training. Though classical in his approach, his understanding of development was not through particular economic laws and concepts, classical or neoclassical, and motivated by their criticisms and shortfalls. Rather, he sought to communicate and explain the development state and needs through the classical economic laws and processes whenever they corresponded to the realistic state of China's development, whether in history or in the present. Sun Yat-sen's perspective is characteristic of a perspective consistent with a continuum of development and growth from prehistoric times to the contemporary period and future, based on a thorough understanding of the historical socioeconomic development of China to the present period and the needed improvements for the future.

Young's perspective, though long-run in nature, hence related to Sun Yat-sen's very long-run development perspective, is more focused on describing the central dynamics promoting endogenous growth in an advanced market economy. Young points out the necessary conditions upon which the rate of growth hinges – sufficiently elastic demand and supply for each commodity and the absence of major indivisibilities – and implicitly assumes that a certain level of development underlies the market-driven growth process to generate endogenous growth. Despite recognizing the necessary conditions for growth and the fact that in some cases the growth mechanism does not operate smoothly, Young fails to analyze the case of an underdeveloped economy, a focus that was adopted by the early development theory during the post war era, in a sense a focus regained in economic analysis of the twentieth century when considering the work of Sun Yat-sen.[22]

Comparing the works of Sun Yat-sen to the Western development pioneers, that two perspectives emerged separate from each other is interesting, as not much direct communication between them existed, given the stage of development of research facilities at the time as well as the difference in the time periods between writing and publishing these works. While Sun Yat-sen, through education, written work and travel experiences, was influenced by the Western economists from Smith up until his contemporaries, as well as the contemporary state of economies and events, the growth and development pioneers have neglected his work and writings as has much of the modern economics research profession.[23]

Sun Yat-sen's development view can be considered to be a fusion of a world view based on Confucian philosophy as well as that of the Western thinking. He combines the oriental mentality with that of the Western, and hence, provides a more broad-based vision on development than Rosenstein-Rodan, who had difficulties in clearly articulating and formulating his theory of the big push; and Ragnar Nurkse was focused on the dynamics of the capital accumulation process. In comparison to the development and growth view of Allyn Young, highly related to the early development theory as it represents its classical counterpart, Sun Yat-sen discusses his development view in relating and formulating his policies for a developing economy, China, based on the development experience of the Western industrialized economies, while also fitting his analysis to the economic and political development history and context of China. Hence, the recognition of the stage of development is inherent in his analysis, while it remains a major distinction between Young's and Rosenstein-Rodan's and Nurkse's focus of analysis.

Sun Yat-sen's work can be considered to be ahead of his time in terms of the context sensitivity of his economic development analysis, as only recently some gains towards this direction have been achieved in the development paradigm that has emerged towards the end of the 1990s. Based on this study as well as the recent research on Sun Yat-sen, it may be argued that this context sensitivity or specificity got lost in the economic analysis of the postwar era with the emergence of the dominant schools of thought, with contending and competing perspectives, that have dominated, especially, the theoretical developments in economic analysis at the cost of dynamic contextual understanding and sensitivity to country-specific economic development and growth needs.[24] Evidence of this can be considered to be the postwar development experience of the developing countries that varies from one country to another influenced by historical development and institutions, more often than not defying the standard theoretical economic insights and policy recommendations; yet the theoretical policy prescriptions to address the development challenges and recommendations up until recently have been rather standard, one-size-fits-all approach reaching its height during the mid-1980s when the Washington Consensus emerged to combat developing country economic instabilities and imbalances.

Concluding Remarks

This chapter has extended the history of thought narrative on the origins of development theory by investigating the development and growth vision that the early development pioneers had from Sun Yat-sen to Ragnar Nurkse. The relationship between classical growth theory and the early development theory as represented by the works of Paul Rosenstein-Rodan and Ragnar Nurkse has recently been analyzed and discussed by Perälä (2002, 2006). This paper extends the before-mentioned work by revealing the related broad-based development insights brought forward in Sun Yat-sen (1922) and compares them to the development visions of the more known development and growth economics pioneers, Allyn Young and Ragnar Nurkse. Young's cumulative growth process influenced the thinking of the most noted early development theory pioneers, Rosenstein-Rodan and Nurkse, who theorized on the problem of underdevelopment and the challenge of achieving balanced growth, while Sun Yat-sen's impact on the development theory that arose to dominate the economic development thinking in underdeveloped countries has previously been underinvestigated.

Interestingly, this so-far-unrecognized development pioneer anticipated much of the topics and issues central to the postwar development experience and hence, has relation to various topics and theories of economic development. Thus, his writings remain relevant even within contemporary development economics discourse and bear especially relevant insights in terms of the ability to adopt and apply relevant economic insights to development problems and challenges of a specific country. While less theoretically oriented in his discussion, especially relative to Ragnar Nurkse, Sun Yat-sen bridges his ideas closely to the actual development experience and the policies needed to uplift a country from a subsistence level to a higher income level to be able to catch up with the industrialized economies. The two recognized development economics pioneers, Rosenstein-Rodan and Nurkse, as well as Young, sought to build their views at a more theoretical level with reference to real-life development and growth experience and economic dynamics, though focusing on different stages of development along the continuum of growth consistent with classical endogenous theory and perspective of growth. In his approach to development analysis, Sun Yat-sen adopts a perspective consistent with classical economics approach, that is, he focuses on the microeconomic phenomenon or on a particular topic and tries to bridge to the macroeconomic level or to provide a comprehensive vision of development for a low-income economy. Furthermore, his analysis is of a very long-run nature, grounded in Chinese economic and political history and hence, provides an analysis consistent with the continuum on the economic development of China from ancient times to his contemporary period as well as projecting to contemporary and future needs to achieve an advanced economy status. While the two development and growth pioneers retain their level of analysis more at the macroeconomic level, focusing on the initiation and dynamics of endogenous economic growth via capital accumulation, though making different stage of development assumptions. Of these two contributions, while vibrant endogenous growth process is Young's emphasis, Nurkse provides the most comprehensive theoretical analysis, given that he recognizes both possible types of dynamics, vicious and virtuous circles of development, inherent in the classical endogenous growth process.

References

Chakravarty, Sukhamoy. 1983. 'Paul Rosenstein-Rodan: An Appreciation.' *World Development* 11 (1), 73–75.

Dr. Sun Yat-sen Memorial Hall. *Chronology of Dr. Sun Yat-sen.* Taipei: Dr. Sun Yat-sen Memorial Hall.

Ellis, Howard S. (ed.). 1961. *Economic Development for Latin America: Proceedings of a Conference Held by the International Economic Association.* London: Macmillan.

Gregor, James and Maria Hsia Chang. 1982. 'Marxism, Sun Yat-sen, and the Concept of 'Imperialism.'' *Pacific Affairs* 55 (1), 54–79.

Lai, Cheng-chung and Paul B. Trescott. 2005. 'Liang Qichao, Sun Yat-sen, and the 1905–1907 Debate on Socialism.' *International Journal of Social Economics* 32 (12), 1051–1062.

Lewis, Arthur. 1988. 'The Roots of Development Theory.' In Hollis Chenery and T. N. Srinivasan (eds). *Handbook of Development Economics*, Vol. I. Amsterdam: North Holland, 28–37.

Lin, Sein. 1974. 'Sun Yat-sen and Henry George: The Essential Role of Land Policy in Their Doctrines.' *American Journal of Economics and Sociology* 33 (2), 201–220.

Marshall, Alfred. 1920 [1890]. *Principles of Economics.* London: Macmillan.

Nurkse, Ragnar. 1961. 'Further Comments on Professor Rosenstein-Rodan's Paper.' In Ellis 1961, 74–78.

———. 1953. *Problems of Capital Formation in Underdeveloped Countries.* Oxford: Basil Blackwell.

Perälä, Maiju Johanna. 2007b. 'On Classical Method of Economic Analysis and the Contemporary Relevance of Classical Economics.' Working paper.

———. 2007a. *A Development Pioneer Unappreciated: Sun Yat-sen's Thought on Economic Development.* Unprocessed manuscript.

———. 2006. 'Looking at the Other Side of the Coin: Allyn Young and the Early Development Theory.' *Journal of the History of Economic Thought* 28 (4), 461–488.

———. 2002. *Essays on Economic Development and Growth.* University of Notre Dame dissertation.

Rosenstein-Rodan, Paul N. 1984. 'Natura Facit Saltum: Analysis of the Disequilibrium Growth Process.' In Gerald M. Meier and Dudley Seers (eds). *Pioneers in Economic Development.* New York: Oxford University Press, 207–21.

———. 1961. 'Notes on the Theory of the 'Big Push.'' In Ellis 1961, 57–78.

————. 1943. 'Problems of Industrialisation of Eastern and South-Eastern Europe.' *Economic Journal* 53 (210/211), 202–211.

Say, Jean-Baptiste. 1803. *Traité d'économie politique, ou, Simple exposition de la maniére don't se forment, se distribuent et se consomment les richesses.* Paris: Chez Antoine-Augustin Renouard.

Schiffrin, Harold. 1957. 'Sun Yat-sen's Early Land Policy: The Origin and Meaning of 'Equalization of Land Rights.'' *Journal of Asian Studies* 16 (4), 549–561.

Smith, Adam. 1992 [1776]. *An Inquiry into the Nature and Causes of the Wealth of Nations.* Chicago: Encyclopaedia Britannica, Inc.

Weaver, William. 1939. 'The Social, Economic, and Political Philosophy of Dr. Sun Yat-sen.' *Historian* 1 (2), 132–141.

Yat-sen, Sun. 1953a. *San Min Chu I: The Three Principles of the People.* Taipei: China Cultural Service.

————. 1953b. *Fundamentals of National Reconstruction.* Taipei: Sino-American Publishing Co. Ltd.

————. 1922 [1929]. *The International Development of China.* New York and London: G. P. Putnam's Sons.

Young, Allyn A. 1999. 'Big Business: How Economic System Grows and Evolves Like a Living Organism.' In Perry G. Mehrling and Roger J. Sandilands (eds). *Money and Growth: Selected Papers of Allyn Abbott Young.* London and New York: Routledge, 411–420.

————. 1928. 'Increasing Returns and Economic Progress.' *Economic Journal* 38 (152), 527–542.

Chapter Five:

THE ROOTS OF UNEQUAL EXCHANGE: MIHAIL MANOILESCU AND THE DEBATE OF THE 1930s

Joseph L. Love

The concept of Unequal Exchange played a large role in the debates on economic development in the quarter century after 1950, and it surfaced in three traditions – Latin American structuralism (Raul Prebisch, Hans W. Singer), Marxism (Arghiri Emmanuel) and Dependency (Andre Gunder Frank, Samir Amin).[1] Yet Unequal Exchange made its first formal appearance in the work of Mihail Manoilescu, the Romanian trade theorist who challenged neoclassical trade theory between the two world wars. His place in the trade debate is often ignored in the postwar discussions of Unequal Exchange.[2]

A man of many parts, Mihail Manoilescu had an international reputation as a theorist of corporatism as well as an economist. Yet it also seems that he wanted to succeed at politics more than at anything else – he was ''furiously ambitious', in the words of the British Ambassador to Romania in 1940,[3] and Manoilescu was a stereotypical Balkan politician in his opportunism. Born in 1891, Manoilescu came from a modest background. His parents were secondary school teachers at Iasi, the capital of Moldavia. Manoilescu studied engineering at the School of Bridge and Highway Construction at Bucharest and led his class every year.[4] There he also became a friend of the future King Carol II. Manoilescu received his engineering degree in 1915, and during the First World War worked in the National Munitions Office. His energy, cleverness and ability to form useful connections allowed him to become Director-General of Industry in 1920 and to organize the first industrial exhibition of Greater Romania in 1921 (Manoliu 1936, 10). This was the beginning of his campaign to stimulate Romanian industrial development.

A rising star in the government of General Alexandru Averescu from 1927, Manoilescu gained a reputation for both efficiency and articulateness, virtually running the country's ministry of finance as undersecretary. Having ingratiated himself with the new king, Carol II, Manoilescu was named Minister of Public Works, then Minister of Industry and Commerce, and in May 1931 was appointed Governor of the National Bank. Yet in July 1931 his meteoric rise in politics came to an abrupt halt when he refused to authorize National Bank credits for a major commercial bank belonging to one of the king's cronies and the bank failed.[5] Manoilescu's services in high government circles were not sought again until the crisis of 1940, when Germany followed the USSR in seeking to shrink the Greater Romania that had emerged in 1919.

Mihail Manoilescu was also prominent in a number of private organizations and served, at various times, as president of the national civil servants' society, president of the national engineers' association, president of the congress of the national industrialists' association (UGIR) and president of the Romanian Chamber of Commerce. Under Romania's quasi-corporatist constitution of 1923, he represented the Chamber of Commerce in the Romanian senate. He also participated in various meetings of the International Chamber of Commerce, as well as attending other pan-European conferences, lecturing in different parts of Europe, and in 1930 representing Romania at the League of Nations in Geneva. As a politician, he founded a corporatist party in 1933. The Romanian theorist was proud of his acquaintance with Mussolini. Manoilescu was also on good terms with some of the intellectual and pseudointellectual figures in Nazi Germany – notably Werner Sombart and Alfred Rosenberg. His work as political theorist also impressed Antonio Salazar, the dictator of Portugal, and the Portuguese law professor Marcelo Caetano, Salazar's future successor, during the Romanian's visit to Lisbon in 1936.[6]

As a personality, Manoilescu had certain gifts: He was deemed handsome and personally charming, so much so that one unsympathetic commentator gibed that had Manoilescu chosen to become a screen actor, cinema would have profited, and politics would have lost nothing. (Diamandi [1936?], 266, 271) The same writer accused Manoilescu of political corruption, and foreign observers agreed.[7] If true, however, this trait would hardly have distinguished him in the Romania of the 1930s, in which milieu *smecherie* (imaginative peculation or embezzlement) was widely admired.

Manoilescu's opportunism in politics is well documented, and he changed political orientations and parties several times. In 1937 he won a seat in the Romanian Senate on the ticket of the Iron Guard, then called 'All for the Country'. Yet his backing for the only local fascist party to achieve power by its own action, outside Germany and Italy, was probably based on opportunism rather than conviction, as was his timely antisemitism.[8] In 1940, following the fall of France and the Soviet seizure of Bessarabia in June, King Carol II again called on Manoilescu, this time to direct Romania's foreign affairs. But in August, under heavy Nazi pressure, he acquiesced in a new national disaster as the Romanian signatory to the 'Vienna Diktat', whereby Hungary obtained half of Transylvania. Within a week of the Diktat, his political career had ended in disgrace, and King Carol had lost his throne.

Despite this debacle, Manoilescu remained loyal to the Axis cause, and his politics affected his economic views in the late thirties and early forties. He turned away from his long and passionate defence of allegedly scientific protectionism in favour of Nazi policy, which emphasized Romania's agricultural complementarity with Germany. Romania was to be part of the agricultural hinterland of the 'Grossraumwirtschaft' (Greater German Economic Space). The Manoilescu of the War years argued that within the German system Romania would receive higher prices for her exports than she would on the international market (e.g., Manoilescu 1942a, 50). He offered no evidence for this contention and in fact, Germany exploited the resources of Romania ruthlessly.[9]

Bucharest was liberated in August 1944; Romania immediately joined the Allies; and Manoilescu was jailed in October. He remained in prison until December 1945, awaiting trial for his role in the loss of Transylvania. The ex-Foreign Minister was cleared of charges five months later, partly, perhaps, because Romania had regained its pre-1940 frontiers with Hungary. Manoilescu then proceeded to write his memoirs. But in December 1948 he was again incarcerated by the newly consolidated Communist regime. The politician-theorist died two years later as a result of prison-induced ailments and was condemned posthumously for pro-Axis press articles written during the war. Because of his Axis sympathies, Manoilescu's works were banned by the postwar regime; but a generation later, his economic works, which anticipated many Third World claims, aspirations and indictments, were mentioned in official publications as an important Romanian contribution to the analysis of underdevelopment.

Manoilescu's treatises in economics and political theory have a didactic tone, sometimes featuring whole paragraphs in italics. In economics, Manoilescu was self-taught, having an engineering background. He became interested in economic theory as a result of his work in the secretariat of finance, reorganizing the Romanian tariff structure in 1927 to favour industrial protection (Manoilescu, 'Memorii,' 55).

Manoilescu's *Theory of Protectionism and International Exchange* (1929), translated from French into five other languages, including Spanish and Portuguese, already had repercussions in his own day in Brazil and in other countries where Iberian languages were spoken, and he was proud of his reputation as an economic theorist in South America. His *Century of Corporatism* (1934) was equally well known there.

Manoilescu's ideas appeared in a period of much greater receptivity to heterodoxy than in the prewar era. The concept of economic planning, which was widely discussed in East Central Europe in the interwar years, had grown less out of the Russian Revolution than the 'Kriegswirtschaft' of Germany and the other belligerent powers in the latter years of the First World War (Neumark 1936, 51). A growing penchant for planning meshed with a rising tide of economic nationalism in the region, focusing on industrialization and exacerbated by capital flight, as foreign investors disinvested in the 1930s (See Kofman 1990, especially 207). Furthermore, in the twenties and thirties, corporatist industrialists shared an 'ideology of productivity'. In Italy, for instance, 'Technocratic accents ... became the rhetoric of the industrial leadership as it pushed for lower labor costs [i.e., lower wages] in the name of productivity and rationalization' (Maier 1975, 567).

Yet, a rising rate of monopolistic combination did not necessarily halt the spread of industrialization beyond Western Europe and the United States – on the contrary. Manoilescu was not unique in his day in perceiving that the Depression, by inducing protectionist reactions among the Great Powers, was stimulating the diffusion of manufacturing beyond the highly industrialized states.[10] But industrialization was a long-run proposition, and in the shorter run, Romania, along with other agricultural-exporting countries, had already begun to experience the 'price-scissors' problem – a widening gap between industrial and agricultural prices – in the latter 1920s. The scissors opened farther and cut deeper in the 1930s.

The decline of prices for agricultural commodities relative to those for manufactured goods had two principal medium-term causes, both growing out of the War: One was the effort by the major industrial countries of continental Europe to achieve self-sufficiency in wheat production in the twenties, hedging against another international conflict; the other was technological advance, notably the diffusion of the tractor, in high-productivity, agricultural-exporting nations, a process stimulated by the vital need for grain during the Great War.

The issue remained, however, why industrial prices did not fall as well, given the greatly expanded manufacturing potential of the belligerent powers and the tendency for industrialization to spread to new countries. During the Great Depression, many economists noticed that industrial prices tended to be downwardly rigid, and the causes of the latter phenomenon were identified as early as 1927 by the Swedish economist Gustav Cassel in a report for the League of Nations. Cassel pointed to monopolistic tendencies in the labour and manufactures markets of the industrial West.[11] 'From 1913, a very serious dislocation of relative prices has taken place in the exchange of goods between

Europe and the colonial world …' owing to these monopolies, he wrote in 1927.[12] These causes were reiterated in an Economic Committee report of the League in 1935 (League of Nations 1935, 9). The latter document further pointed out that agricultural producers could not control supply as readily as their industrial counterparts, and individual farmers sometimes increased quantities of goods offered for sale to make up for falling unit prices – thereby exacerbating the problem. Thus, individual interest conflicted with group interest.[13]

Manoilescu recognized, as Gustav Cassel had before him and Raul Prebisch would later, that in times of depression, industrial prices were 'sticky' because of the power of organized labour, compared to its unorganized counterpart in farming in the agricultural-exporting countries. Nevertheless, the 'imperative of the [world] crisis', he proclaimed, was for the industrial countries, whose terms of trade had improved dramatically since 1913, to adjust their export prices downward relative to those of their agricultural trading partners by lowering wages and profits; meanwhile, manufacturing in agricultural countries should be protected by 'exaggerated' tariffs – presumably as a reprisal (Manoilescu 1933b, 6–8, 15).

As economist – as opposed to politician – Manoilescu's chief concern was with the relationship between the purchasing power of a unit of labour expended in producing a good traded on the world market in terms of the labour of other workers abroad – a concept later developed as the 'double factorial terms of trade'. Manoilescu held that labour productivity in industry (manufacturing and mining) was superior to that in agriculture, by a ratio of four or more to one, in empirical studies.[14] This superiority owed to 'specific capital', i.e., the capital per worker, which was much higher in industry than that in agriculture. Specific capital also indicated the 'degree of mechanization' in a given industry (or economic activity).[15]

Using data for 1937 in the final edition of his treatise on production and trade (published in Romanian), Manoilescu calculated that average industrial wages in Romania were 4.6 times greater in industry than those in agriculture; capital per worker ('specific capital') was 4.1 times greater; and labour productivity was 4.6 times greater. Yet the average rate of profit was only 1.8 per cent greater in industry than in agriculture.[16] Employing data from the Ministry of National Economy to measure productivity and profitability for specific industries, Manoilescu found that there was no correlation between general profitability and productivity; rather, capital per worker 'determined' (i.e., was highly correlated with) productivity. For Manoilescu, these findings and the small spread between profit rates in industry and agriculture noted earlier showed that the individual interest in profit could and did in fact diverge from the 'national' interest in productivity (Manoilescu 1986, 127). Manoilescu apparently did not know the work of A. C. Pigou, who had demonstrated in *Wealth and Welfare* (1912) and *The Economics of Welfare* (1920) that differences owing to indivisibilities in capital-intensive forms of production could arise in social and private marginal net product (Robinson 1987, 876–79). Later, Paul Rosenstein-Rodan would use such indivisibilities and the external economies to which they give rise, to argue for a state-led 'big push' to overcome structural deficiences in the economies of underdeveloped countries.[17]

Manoilescu, like Marx, Ricardo and other classical economists, accepted the labour theory of value, although the Romanian thought there were 'qualitative' differences between labour inputs that were explained by the amount of capital per worker, and that these differences were stable over time. They could therefore be used to establish a hierarchy of economic activities (i.e., branches of production) (Manoilescu 1986, 13–37). Manoilescu further developed a 'coefficient of quality', showing which industries could produce a given value of output with minimum inputs of labour and capital. Such a coefficient could be used by state planners to rank industries, and the concept could be modified to measure agricultural productivities as well.[18]

Since labour productivity was manifestly so much greater in industry than in agriculture, '... the passing of backward agricultural states from agricultural occupations to those of industry offers a greater advantage [to them] than to industrial countries.'[19] As labour moved from agriculture to industry, in the longer run, however, Manoilescu believed a tendency toward the convergence of agricultural and industrial productivities would occur, and those of the United States already revealed this tendency.[20]

Until such convergence occurred, low-productivity labour in agriculture should be moved to high-productivity manufacturing; or, in its precise formulation, stated in neoclassical terms: When the marginal productivity of labour in agriculture approaches zero, surplus labour should be moved to manufacturing or other higher-productivity activities. The Romanian theorist was remembered in postwar development theory primarily for this, the 'Manoilescu argument', which remained a hotly debated subject. Viewed from the perspective of costs of production, the argument could be put differently: The large gap between (traditional) agricultural and industrial wages, reflecting a large productivity differential, was an impediment to industrialization that could be offset by a compensatory tariff on, or subsidies for, industrial goods. This argument was later developed by Kurt Mandelbaum, Raul Prebisch and the Nobel Laureate, W. Arthur Lewis.[21]

Manoilescu adapted his formulae to measure productivity of land as a factor of production, and therefore yield per hectare,[22] but he made no effort to measure the productivity of services; thus, he could only measure the value of physical product. He apparently believed that commerce (the major component of services) did not produce wealth, but only redistributed it, although he allowed that commerce produced 'relative utility' as opposed to the 'absolute utility' of production.[23]

In the matter of international trade, the issue for Manoilescu was not comparative advantage, as for Ricardo, since this theory 'prescribed' a division of world labour into industrial and agricultural specialists; rather, the issue was whether a given economic endeavour within a country had a labour productivity higher than the national average. If it did, its development should be encouraged (Manoilescu 1986, 279; 1929, 183). Specialization in traditional agricultural pursuits required four to ten hours of Romanian labour to purchase the product of a single hour of English labour. Thus, international trade was a swindle. Protection for industry was justifiable, not just in terms of Friedrich List's 'infant industry' argument, by which an enterprise would take advantage of economies of scale and external economies over the intermediate run to bring costs down to internationally competitive levels; rather, protection was justified because a sheltered industry that had a labour productivity higher than the national average of economic activities was a boon from its first day of operation.[24] Further, for Manoilescu protection was a valid policy for the longer as well as the short term, if differentials in productivities across different economic activities persisted.[25] The more the productivity of a given good exceeded the average national productivity, the more the domestic price of that good could justifiably exceed the foreign price (Manoilescu 1929, 161).

To engage in agricultural exports, Manoilescu argued, a country's comparative advantage in domestic agriculture over its foreign counterpart must be greater than the 'intrinsic superiority' in labour productivity of industry over agriculture within the country (Manoilescu 1986, 234). Such cases were rare, Manoilescu thought, since agriculture in Romania and other underdeveloped countries with dense populations was primitive in technique and was consequently labour intensive. If the comparative advantage in domestic agriculture over that of a foreign country (or 'all other countries') was zero, and if labour productivity in domestic industry was four times greater than that in agriculture, then the inferiority of domestic labour productivity over its foreign counterpart could be 75 per cent 'without the solution of industrial production ceasing to be advantageous' (Manoilescu 1986, 262). Further, if the price of a good produced in an agricultural country were three times that of its foreign counterpart, and its labour productivity were greater than the highest labour productivity of any other national product, then a tariff of 200 per cent (to bring the foreign and national goods to the same price level in the local market) 'would be justified in practice and in theory': This, because of the growth in national income that the production of the new good would effect (Manoilescu 1986, 288).

In the long run, the productivity gains for agricultural countries, whose incomes would rise, would benefit the industrial countries, with which the former would now trade more extensively (Manoilescu 1986, 351). Thus, the industrialization of backward countries 'has nothing in common with autarky',[26] although it was at odds with the 'free trade' doctrines of the League of Nations (Manoilescu 1986, 362).

As noted above, Manoilescu distinguished between profitability and productivity: The former criterion guides the actions of individual entrepreneurs, while the latter should be the cynosure of nations, as directed by the state. In (high productivity) industry, workers receive high incomes, creditors to industrial enterprises receive high rates of interest, the state receives large tax revenues and entrepreneurs obtain high profits. In (low productivity) agriculture, even when the product can compete at the world price and the capitalist farmer receives a large income, 'the benefit to the nation (that is, the sum of individual benefits to workers, creditors, the state and entrepreneurs) is small in comparison with the national benefit obtained in industry' (Manoilescu 1986, 89). The assumption of the 'liberal school' that there was a coincidence between profitability and productivity was false (Manoilescu 1941, 2).

In a variety of forums Manoilescu emphasized the exploitation inherent in international trade. In a brash moment he wrote, 'It is scientifically absurd to speak of growing rich by one's own work only. [It is] only by organizing and exploiting others' labour that anybody can become rich.' The same fact held true for nations as well as for individuals, he inferred (Manoilescu 1931, 2). Because the exchange of industrial goods for agricultural products and raw materials on the world market was a cheat – *un marché de dupes*, he called it (Manoilescu 1940b, 331) – Manoilescu demanded the replacement of an allegedly outmoded 'socialism of classes' by a 'socialism of nations', the Romanian's way of expressing the notion that the modern world was divided into 'proletarian' and 'plutocratic' nations.[27] He thus anticipated demands by Third World governments in the 1970s for a New International Economic Order, and the Romanian's path toward the new order was basically the same as theirs: If the First World did not agree to a major shift in the international relative prices of industrial and agricultural goods, the backward agrarian countries should industrialize through protectionist policies.[28]

Manoilescu's economic programme today would be described as state-directed import-substitution industrialization. Presumably, if the agrarian country succeeded in transforming itself into an industrial nation, it could – and would be advised to – follow the practice of presently industrialized countries, and ultimately export manufactures. But Manoilescu does not seem to have made such a strategy explicit;[29] he preferred to emphasize the long-run gains from expanded trade to be reaped by the currently industrialized countries,[30] and did not consider the implications for those countries even further behind in the race toward high productivities than the ones that would adopt his policies. If he had, this fact might have strengthened the political appeal of his argument, since the later a country jumped on the bandwagon, the fewer the countries that would remain to exploit through unequal exchange.

Although Manoilescu's *Theory of Protectionism* was published in six languages by the latter 1930s and was well received in a few journals,[31] as a whole, the economics profession in the 1930s greeted Manoilescu's theses with hostility.[32] Bertil Ohlin (1931, 34–35), perhaps the leading neoclassical trade theorist of the 1930s,[33] criticized Manoilescu's assumptions: Why should the average productivity of all national industries be considered representative of that of the export industries? What justified the assumption that the price level of factors is everywhere equal, when it was known that money wages in the United States were more than ten times higher than in Romania? Why did Manoilescu only consider labour productivity in his calculations and ignore capital and land? (Manoilescu did consider these two factors, in theory, and gave formulae for their measurement, but only attempted to obtain cross-country empirical data for labour productivity.) As for Manoilescu's definition of productivity, 'It goes without saying,' Ohlin remarked, 'that the output per worker does not provide any test as to productivity, as the quantity of other productive factors used per worker is widely different in different industries.' Wages, Ohlin (1931, 35) argued, were a better measure of labour productivity across industries. In addition, Ohlin observed, Manoilescu's assumption of constant costs and fixed prices on the world market, in the face of changing trade relations, led to the absurd conclusion that 'it would pay to produce only manufactured goods and import agricultural products' in his 'agricultural country' (36). Ohlin's 'fundamental criticism', however, was that, as Manoilescu assumed that factors of production can move from activities with low productivities to those with high productivities, the benefits from protection arise from the allegation that protection causes the transfer. But why, Ohlin asked, did this transfer not occur *without* protection, since price signals should favour the industries with higher productivities?[34]

Jacob Viner, the leading trade theorist in the United States in the 1930s, agreed with Ohlin's critique, but thought he had conceded 'too much'[!] to Manoilescu. If domestic prices or wages were higher in one economic activity than in another, one had to consider the *reason* for it, which might well be artificial wage rates through trade union monopoly. Viner agreed that protection of manufactures could raise the real income of a country if it had a comparative labour advantage in manufacturing, and if trade union monopoly kept wages so high in industry that imports could underprice domestic manufactures. But he pointed out that free trade could achieve the same end, by forcing a reduction in industrial wages and revealing true comparative advantages in market prices. Viner dismissed Manoilescu's book with the judgment, 'The task of finding an intellectually satisfactory economic defense of protection still awaits achievement and has not been carried forward by this attempt.'[35]

In 1937, five years after writing his review of *The Theory of Protectionism*, Viner published a major theoretical volume, defending and extending the neoclassical theory of international trade. Among his contributions was the 'liberation' of the doctrine of comparative costs from the labour theory of value, accepted by Ricardo and some non-Marxist economists into the 1930s, including, of course, Manoilescu (See Baumol and Viner Seiler 1979, 784–85). In his *Studies in the Theory of International Trade*, Viner argued that 'the association of the comparative cost doctrine with the labor cost theory of value' was a 'historical accident'. Most classical economists other than Ricardo expressed real costs as ultimately subjective phenomena – what were later called 'disutilities' (e.g., the postponement of consumption or the irksomeness of labour) – though '… they generally assumed that disutilities were proportional to quantities of the services of the factors [of production] …' Yet, a later writer, Nicholas Georgescu-Roegen, was skeptical that Viner had had the last word.[36]

Not only was Manoilescu attacked in Western Europe and the United States, in Romanian academic circles Manoilescu's theses were probably contested more than they were accepted in the 1930s. A sharp critic of both *Theory of Protectionism* and *Century of Corporatism* was Gheorghe Tasca, Rector of the Academy of Commercial and Industrial Studies in Bucharest and a former Minister of Commerce and Industry.[37] Tasca, a liberal anti-fascist with doctorates in both law and economics from the Sorbonne, reiterated several of Ohlin's arguments. A striking point of his own, aimed more at Manoilescu's nationalist credentials than his economic analysis, began with the concession that his opponent might be right that a Romanian peasant gave ten days' labour for one day's labour embodied in a manufactured product purchased abroad. However, since Manoilescu allowed that national manufacturing industry was only one-fourth as productive as foreign competing industries, the same Romanian peasant, under a closed economy, would have to exchange forty days' labour instead of ten, to acquire the same industrial product![38]

A critical but more favourable review of the expanded German edition of Manoilescu's *Theory of Protectionism*, published in 1937, was that of Michal Kalecki. The Polish economist, then working in England, was regarded in the postwar period as one of the leading macroeconomists of his generation and an authority on economic development. While noting with interest Manoilescu's assertion that capital per worker rather than the quantity of labour expended determines prices, as per Ricardo, Kalecki criticized Manoilescu for not using neoclassical criteria for economic optima, based on the marginal productivity of labour and capital. He further noted that if Manoilescu's 'specific capital' was the key to high levels of productivity, new capital investments had to be obtained at the expense of some other economic activity, and asked if capital-starved agriculture would provide it. Nonetheless, Kalecki agreed with Manoilescu's policy prescription of protection for new industries as a means of engendering capital formation and employment in underdeveloped countries (Kalecki 1938).

Nor did Manoilescu find wide acceptance of his theses in Hitler's Germany, whose economists, as well as political leaders, he was courting, beginning with Werner Sombart.[39] Carl Brinkmann, reviewing the German edition of Manoilescu's treatise on trade in 1938, criticized the Romanian's approach to trade theory as outdated and static, based as it was on the classicals' treatment of comparative costs, the labour theory of value, and average costs, whereas modern theory was based on comparative prices, modern (neoclassical) value theory, and marginal costs.[40] Otto Frölich gave Manoilescu's theses equally bad marks in the same journal, *Weltwirtschaftsliches Archiv* (Fröhlich 1938, 288–308).

Other strictures could be made about Manoilescu's supply-side economics. As services at the end of the twentieth century loomed ever larger both in national product and international trade, the Romanian economist's omission of the tertiary sector appeared as an increasingly serious weakness in his theory.[41] Another problem is inconsistency in his voluminous writings, and it is sometimes difficult to separate Manoilescu's economic policy flipflops (e.g., for or against commodity price agreements in international trade as the prime objective; for or against autarky) from sudden turns in his theoretical analysis, since the latter type of volta-face sometimes appeared in academic journals as well as in the shriller polemics of his corporatist review, *Lumea Noua*. Asserting that the advantage of industrial countries in international trade falls secularly and 'continuously', Manoilescu (1986, 347) took no note of the fact that the sharp and sustained depression of agricultural prices from 1925 to 1935 had not been 'predicted' by his theory. Further, the allegation that international trade was the *basis* for the wealth of Western countries (Manoilescu 1929, 103) implicitly conflicted with his observation that rich countries trade less with poor countries than with each other (Manoilescu 1986, 350). In the latter case, who was exploiting whom?

Manoilescu nonetheless had an important insight about the development process that was expanded and rigorously formulated by the American economist Everett Hagen in 1958. After considering longitudinal and cross-country data showing that wages (a measure of productivity) were consistently higher in manufacturing than in agriculture, Hagen demonstrated theoretically that '... protectionism raises real income, relative to free trade, if the increase under protection in the aggregate cost of the industrial product to its buyers is less than the increase in income to the factors which shift from agriculture to industry.' At the empirical level, citing the cases of the United States, Japan, the Soviet Union and – perhaps less convincingly – Brazil, Colombia and Mexico, Hagen wrote, 'The broad historical record suggest that protectionism may have accelerated economic development.'[42] Hagen traces the origins of his thesis to insights by Gottfried Haberler and Jacob Viner, but not to Manoilescu, whom he also mentions (Hagen 1958, 496–97).

On the matter of the evolution of the world economy, it is clear that the Romanian trade theorist – or as Ronald Findlay prefers to call him, the Romanian 'writer' (Findlay 1980, 70) – failed to take into account the dynamism of modern industrial capitalism. Manoilescu's assumption of static costs and prices implied a static technology, and had he lived into the 1960s he would have seen that developed countries' control of technological innovation made irrelevant much of the diffusion of industrial production to the Third World. Productivities in the dynamic sectors of manufacturing were still *relatively* low in Third World countries, and the income gap between developed and underdeveloped countries was not obviously closing.

Beyond his shortcomings as a theorist, Manoilescu's political activity and inconsistency in his advocacy of economic policies probably diminished the currency of his writings as an economist after World War II. It seems probable that, given his reception in parts of both agrarian Europe (including Iberia) and Latin America, Manoilescu would have attracted more attention as a precursor of development economics had it not been for his politics. In 1937 he was elected on the Iron Guard ticket to the Senate, and in 1938 he saw political opportunity in an association with Nazi Germany. Up to that time, as a professor of economics at the Polytechnic in Bucharest and in many venues abroad, mostly of an academic nature, Manoilescu defended the thesis of the closed economy. He now began to support Hitler's 'Grossraumwirtschaft', and though he was subsequently anything but consistent, Manoilescu renounced his thesis on international trade see numerous examples in Love 1996, 258, note 54).

Finally, to understand Manoilescu's influence, we must give some attention to the economic aspects of his political thought. In his own day, Manoilescu was as well known for his theory of corporatism as for his economic theses, although – and perhaps significantly – after the defeat of fascism, he judged *The Theory of Protectionism* to have been his most important work (Manoilescu. 'Memorii,' 601). For his contemporaries, *The Century of Corporatism* was equally influential, if one may judge by its reception in Iberia and Latin America (See sources in Love 1986). Our interest concerns the relation between his political and economic views and the ways in which his political propositions contributed to the diffusion of his economic theses. There was such a relation, as is implicit in the judgment of the Brazilian demographer Josue de Castro that Manoilescu was a 'Neo-St.-Simonian', emphasizing the pro-planning, pro-industrialization, elitist and organicist elements in St.-Simon's thought (Castro 1968, 79).

Indeed, had the Romanian's political associations in the late thirties and the War years been less closely associated with Romanian fascism and the aspirations of the Third Reich, his focus on the double factorial terms of trade, the 'Manoilescu argument' that disguised unemployment in agriculture should be remedied by moving idle labour to industrial activities, and his model of internal colonialism[43] – all might have been more influential in Third World nations in the postwar era. In any event, his writings may have helped create a favourable reception for the theories and programmes of Raul Prebisch and the UN Economic Commission for Latin America in the 1950s.

Manoilescu's contention that the value of agricultural and industrial labour would tend to converge in the long run (contrary to Prebisch) conflicted with his assumption of constant prices and constant costs for his 'agricultural countries' in international trade. If, as Roxana Bobulescu has recently pointed out, the Romanian had instead assumed falling costs and increasing returns to scale for protected industries, his argument would have approximated that of Frank Graham, who defended sustained protection for industries with increasing returns (Graham 1923; Bobulescu 2003, 119).

This shift would also have brought Manoilescu closer to recent developments in growth theory. Before 1990, the standard explanation of economic growth was that of Robert Solow (1956, 65–94), whose independent variables included only labour and capital. Yet, in empirical regressions, the two together 'explained' less than half of measured growth, leaving technology in a black box (the 'residual'). In recent years, however, the theoretical problem appears to have been solved, chiefly through the work of Paul Romer. His model of economic growth, published in 1990, incorporated technology (and therefore new knowledge), rather than seeing it as exogenous.[44] Romer showed how bringing in technology could explain the widely observed, but hitherto unprovable phenomenon of increasing returns to scale, contrary to the standard assumption of constant returns, used by Solow. This was the case because technology raises total output through positive externalities without any obvious limits. Romer, like Murphy, Shleifer and Vishny, stresses the importance of Total Factor Productivity (largely based on knowledge and technology) rather than labour and capital. Romer further showed that private-firm technological innovation had important spillovers, lowering the costs of future innovation for competitors (Helpman 2004, 44). Romer's work thus potentially 'legitimates' the position of Graham and, by extension, that of Manoilescu, adding the assumption of diminishing costs.

References

Baumol, William J. and Ellen Viner Seiler. 1979. 'Jacob Viner.' *International Encyclopedia of the Social Sciences*. Vol. 18. New York: Macmillan, 784–785.

Bobulescu, Roxana. 2003. 'Protectionism in Retrospect: Mihail Manoilescu (1891–1950?).' *Brazilian Journal of Political Economy* 23 (4), 114–123.

Brinkmann, Carl. 1938. 'Mihail Manoilesco [sic] und die klassische Außenhandelstheorie.' *Weltwirtschaftliches Archiv* 48 (part 2), 273–287.

Cassel, Gustav. 1927. *Recent Monopolistic Tendencies in Industry and Trade: Being an Analysis of the Nature and Causes of the Poverty of Nations*. Geneva: League of Nations.

Castro, Josue de. 1968 [1960]. *O livro negro da fome*. 3rd edn. Sao Paulo: Brasiliense.

Condliffe, J. B. 1933. 'Die Industrialisierung des wirtschaftlich rückständigen Länder.' *Weltwirtschaftliches Archiv* 37, 335–359.

Corradini, Enrico. 1973 [Ital. orig. 1910]. 'Principles of Nationalism.' In Adrian Lyttelton (ed.). *Italian Fascisms from Pareto to Gentile*. London: Cape, 146–147.

Diamandi, Sterie. [1936?] *Galeria oamenilor politici*. Bucharest: Cugetaria.

Eatwell, John et al. (eds). 1987. *The New Palgrave. A Dictionary of Economics*. Vol. 3. London: Macmillan.

Findlay, Ronald. 1980. 'On W. Arthur Lewis' Contributions to Economics.' *Scandinavian Journal of Economics* 82, 62–79.

Fröhlich, Otto. 1938. 'Wirtschaftliche Rechtfertigung des Zollschutzes?' *Weltwirtschaftliches Archiv* 48 (part 2), 288–308.

Georgescu-Roegen, Nicholas. 1987. 'Manoilescu, Mihail.' In Eatwell et al. 1987, 299–300.

Graham, Frank. 1923. 'Some Aspects of Protection Further Considered.' *Quarterly Journal of Economics* 37 (February), 199–227.

Hagen, Everett E. 1958. 'An Economic Justification of Protectionism.' *Quarterly Journal of Economics* 72 (4), 496–514.

Helpman, Elhanan. 2004. *The Mystery of Economic Growth*. Cambridge, MA: Harvard Belknap.

Kalecki, Michal. 1938. Review of M. Manoilescu. *Die nationalen Produktivkräfte*. *Economic Journal* 48, 708–711.

Kofman, Jan. 1990. 'Economic Nationalism in East Central Europe in the Interwar Period.' In Henryk Szlajfer (ed.). *Economic Nationalism in East-Central Europe and South America: 1918–1939*. Geneva: Droz, 191–249.

Lampe, John, and Marvin Jackson. 1982. *Balkan Economic History, 1550–1950: From Imperial Borderlands to Developing Nations*. Bloomington, IN: Indiana University Press.

League of Nations [Société des Nations]: Comité Economique. 1935. *Considérations relatives à l'évolution actuelle du protectionnisme agricole: 20 mai 1935*. Geneva: League of Nations.

Lewis, W. Arthur. 1954. 'Economic Development with Unlimited Supplies of Labour.' *The Manchester School of Economic and Social Studies* 22 (2), 139–191.

Love, Joseph L. 1996. *Crafting the Third World: Theorizing Underdevelopment in Rumania and Brazil*. Stanford, CA: Stanford U. Press.

———. 1986. 'Manoilescu, Prebisch, and Unequal Exchange.' *Rumanian Studies* 5, 125–133.

Maier, Charles. 1975. *Recasting Bourgeois Europe: Stabilization in France, Germany, and Italy in the Decade after World War I*. Princeton, NJ: Princeton U. Press.

Manoilescu, Mihail. 'Memorii.' 1991, 1993. MS. (1946–48); 'Urmare la 'memoriile mele.'' MS. (1947). Later published as *Dictatul de la Viena: Memorii. Iulie–August 1940*; *Memorii*, 2 Vols. [Ed. by Valeriu Dinu.] Bucharest: Enciclopedica.

————. 1986. *Fortele nationale productive si comertul exterior: Teoria protectionismului si a schimbului international.* Bucharest: Stiintifica. [Romanian edn of Manoilescu. *Théorie du protectionnisme*, 1929, revised in 1940].

————. 1942a. 'Economia Romaniei in Europa unita.' *Lumea Noua* 11, (1–6), 47–54.

————. 1942b. *Rostul si destinul burgheziei romanesti.* Bucharest: Cugetarea.

————. 1941. 'Productivitatea si rentabilitatea in economia romaneasca.' *Buletinul Institutului Economic Romanesc* 20, (1–6), 1–31.

————. 1940a. 'Le triangle économique et social des pays agricoles: La ville, le village, l'étranger.' *Internationale Agrarrundschau* (6), 16–26.

————. 1940b [1933]. 'Curs de economie politica.' Scoala Politehnica. Revised and expanded version, mimeo.

————. 1937. 'Doctrinele si teoriile noastre in lumina criticei.' *Analele Economice si Statistice* 20, (3–5), 26–92.

————. 1934a. *Le siècle du corporatisme: Doctrine du corporatisme intégral et pur.* Paris: Alcan.

————. 1934b. 'Autarhia economica.' *Analele Economice si Statistice* 17 (7–9), 11–26.

————. 1933a. 'Criza agricola in cadrul international.' *Viata Agricola* 24 (3), 113–127.

————. 1933b. *L'impératif de la crise.* Bucharest: Chambre de Commerce Internationale.

————. 1931. 'European Economic Equilibrium.' In *Royaume de Roumanie: Ministère de l'Industrie et du Commerce; Correspondance Economique Roumaine* 13 (2), 1–15.

————. 1929. *Théorie du protectionnisme et de l'échange international.* Paris: Alcan.

Manoliu, Florin E. 1936. *Bibliographie des travaux du Professeur Mihail Manoilesco* [sic] *précédée d'une biographie et suivie de la nomenclature des études critiques suscitées par ces travaux.* Bucharest: Luceafarul.

Meisner, Maurice. 1967. *Li Ta-chao and the Origins of Chinese Marxism.* Cambridge, MA: Harvard U. Press.

Morgenstern, Oskar. 1937. *The Limits of Economics.* London: W. Hodge.

Murphy, Kevin M., Andrei Shleifer and Robert Vishny. 1989. 'Industrialization and the Big Push.' *Journal of Political Economy* 97 (5), 1003–1026.

Neumark, Fritz. 1936. *Neue Ideologien der Wirtschaftspolitik.* Vienna: Deuticke.

Ocampo, Jose Antonio and Maria Angela Parra. 2003. 'Returning to an Eternal Debate: The Terms of Trade for Commodities in the Twentieth Century.' *CEPAL* (series *Informes y estudios especiales*) (5). At http://www.eclac.cl/publicaciones/Secretaria Ejecutiva/3/LCL1813PI/lcl1813i.pdf (Accessed 19 August 2007).

Ohlin, Bertil. 1931. 'Protectionism and Non-Competing Groups.' *Weltwirtschaftliches Archiv* 33, (part 1), 30–45.

Paiusan, Robert and Daniela Busa. 1990. 'Manoilescu et Tasca. Leur Polémique.' *Revue Roumaine d'Histoire* 29, (3–4), 291–320.

Popisteanu, Cristian, Dumitru Preda and Mihai Retegan. 1982. '22 octombie 1931: O joie neagra.' *Magazin Istoric* 16 (1), 38–44.

Robinson, Austin. 1987. 'Pigou, Arthur Cecil.' In Eatwell et al. 1987, 876–879.

Romer, Paul M. 1990. 'Endogenous Technological Change.' *Journal of Political Economy* 98 (5, part 2), 71–102.

Rosenstein-Rodan, Paul. 1984. 'Natura Facit Saltum: Analysis of the Disequilibrium Growth Process.' In Gerald M. Meier and Dudley Seers (eds.). *Pioneers in Development.* New York: Oxford, 207–221.

Solow, Robert M. 1956. 'A Contribution to the Theory of Economic Growth.' *Quarterly Journal of Economics* 70 (1), 65–94.

Tasca, Gheorghe. 1937. 'Liberalism si corporatism.' *Analele Economice si Statistice* 20 (1–2), 1–69.

'Unequal Exchange.' At http://en.wikipedia.org/wiki/Unequal_exchange (Accessed 16 August 2007).

Vasile, R. 1979. 'Economia Romaniei in timpul celui de-al doilea razboi mondial.' In Nicolae Marcu (ed.). *Istorie economica*. Bucharest: Didactica, 368–391.

Viner, Jacob. 1937. *Studies in the Theory of International Trade*. New York: Harper.

———. 1932. Review of Mihail Manoilesco [sic]. 'The Theory of Protection and International Trade.' *Journal of Political Economy* 40, (1), 121–25.

Warsh, David. 2006. Knowledge and the Wealth of Nations: A Story of Economic Discovery. New York: Norton.

Chapter Six:

NURKSE AND THE EARLY LATIN AMERICAN STRUCTURALISTS: A REFLECTION ON DEVELOPMENT THEORY, INDUSTRIALIZATION AND THEIR RELEVANCE TODAY

*Annalisa Primi**

Introduction

The open economies context implies increasing globalization and interdependence between countries and a reconfiguration of industrial powers and, hence, of prevailing international equilibria. The rise of China and India are only two examples of this tendency.[1] At the same time, we are facing the emergence and the consolidation of new technological paradigms, mainly information technology, biotechnology and nanotechnology, which are engendering a radically different meaning and scope of what has been traditionally called 'industrialization'. The borderline between science and business is continuously redefined, and it is increasingly less sharp.[2] Intangibles and knowledge are more and more relevant, and the reshaping of intellectual property regimes at a global scale amplifies this tendency.[3]

This set of broad reconfigurations of dominant actors, prevailing technological paradigms and new international trade and production rules redefines the opportunities and the constraints for development, which, unfortunately is still a goal to be reached in many regions of the world. Reports on the state of the world

* The author is grateful to Mario Cimoli and Wilson Peres for their comments to a previous version of this paper and for the numerous and interesting discussions on the Latin American structuralisms and development. The usual disclaimer applies.

abound with figures showing the persistency of poverty, the marginal participation of developing countries to global trade and the poor quality and articulation of production structures in developing economies.

Classical development economists shared the perception that developing economies differ in major structural ways from developed economies, mainly, in their dependence on exporting primary products, and in their technological backwardness (Prebisch 1950, Hirschman 1958, Myrdal 1956, Nurske 1953a, Lewis 1954, among others). They recognized that the specificities of the socioeconomic structures of developing economies would have affected their patterns of integration to world trade. Export-led growth would have not, per se, led to development. These authors, even though their views differ in various aspects, identified development with diversification of production structures, involving a shift of labour from low-productivity agricultural activities to more productive industrial sectors, and as a deep transformation of leading socio-institutional structures.

Development, in this view, meant the creation of sectoral backward and forward linkages, based on cumulative processes and incentives generated by recurrent imbalances between sectors (Hirschman 1958). Nowadays, their diagnosis of the principal problems of developing countries is, unfortunately, broadly still alive, as it is their main message (i.e., the imperative of industrialization). There is a need to analyse contemporary problems and to propose solutions that go beyond the mere replication of past, and yet obsolete, policies, but that must also go beyond the 'palliative' economics and the prevailing 'access to assets' discourse (Reinert 2007). Development theory should nowadays, as in the fifties, link production structure transformation, productivity growth and employment generation. In this context, the reflection on classical development ideas responds to the urgency of finding appropriate questions, and hence, solutions for development.[4]

Regrettably, contemporary development challenges are not so dissimilar, in general terms, to the problems faced by developing economies in the early fifties. At the aggregate level, backward production structures oriented to natural resources extraction and primary commodity exports, low skilled labour, poor local value added and scarce technological content of domestic production, weak local institutions and fragile states still characterize production processes and socioeconomic structures in developing economies, or in marginal areas of emerging economies (CEPAL 2007; UNCTAD 2006, 2007).

Even after decades of international cooperation for development and thousands of reports on development, the risk is, as Reinert rightly warned in his recent book, to experience a collective backslash in memory on how to create a rich nation (Reinert 2007). There are common threads linking the pre-Smithian economic literature, classical development theory and the experience of various countries at different points in time. A common trait was the shared view that industry was the main locus for learning and technological accumulation and diffusion. Hence, building a rich nation would have meant producing and exporting mainly manufacturing goods.

This paper is far from calling to a sterile replication and transplantation of economic models from one context or country to another. It tackles the importance of recognizing common traits in development trajectories, as well as the existence of specific and unique circumstances (what in modern language have been called windows of opportunity[5]) in development. In particular, amongst the various contributions of the pioneers of development theory, this article focuses on Nurkse and the Latin American structuralists. In 2007 we celebrated 100 years since Ragnar Nurkse's birth. In 2008 we are celebrating the 60 years of the foundation of the United Nations Economic Commission for Latin America and the Caribbean, which has been the cradle of Latin American structuralism. In economics, as in lives, anniversaries are not fundamental, but they help to reflect on advancements, obstacles and goals still to pursue. This paper, far from being an exhaustive survey, is rather a reflection on some classical development ideas and on their relevance for today.

Both Nurkse and the Latin American structuralists developed their theories starting from the identification of the patterns of trade and growth in the world economy; patterns that, according to them, would not have, per se, favoured capital accumulation in backward areas. From those observations derived the balanced growth theory (Nurkse 1957) and the structuralist approach to development (Prebisch 1950). However, the interest in development theory gradually faded in the subsequent decades; the financial and debt crisis of the eighties, which diverted the attention from development to 'macroeconomic stability', the coming into power of conservative administrations in many advanced economies, and the rise of the market-friendly policies approach and the Washington Consensus contributed to delegitimize development policies,[6] as they had been implemented in the previous decades. The role of the State, 'State interference', started to be the object of serious critiques.[7] 'Policy' (industrial, technological, etc.) became a sort of 'bad word', not to be pronounced in decent political discourses.

After the decade of the nineties, when the best development policy was not to have a development policy, there has been a growing consensus on the (easy) issue of adopting different solutions for different problems. Much of the discussion in the post-Washington Consensus focused on banning the revival of 'old' policies that were considered 'inefficient'. New challenges and reshaped contexts require new institutional designs and policy instruments. No men of good sense would apply the same solution to different problems. However, this obvious statement presents the risk of being converted into a naïve attitude that disregards historical evidence and experience. No one, nowadays, would subscribe the one-size-fits-all strategy in any development field (industrial, technology, trade, intellectual property policies). However, it is much more difficult to propose specific solutions in each of those domains.

For example, with the emergence of new technological paradigms countries are facing the challenge of choosing where and how to participate in those new paradigms; and a look at the history might help in shaping current policy options.[8] Nowadays, unfortunately, many economists and policymakers have lost the capacity of looking at development through a 'vision' that should still have production, employment and productivity at its heart. At present, we are facing an interesting political scenario, with progressive forces gaining grounds in emerging and developing economies, while they are losing weight in more advanced economies. There has also been a (slow) return of policies for development and an upsurge in their political and social acceptance.[9] However, the contemporary debate on development still suffers from what Nurkse (1957) recognized in the 50s: 'The clash of prescriptions on the policy plane reflects what looks like a deadlock on the theoretical level also.'

Prebisch (1950, 1) affirmed that 'in economics, ideologies usually tend either to lag behind events or to outlive them.' However, early development thinkers tried to reduce the gap between the theoretical discussion, real dynamics and political tendencies. We should do the same. Development has never been a deferrable dream. But new technological paradigms and current political leaderships require concrete and nondeferrable choices. And a reflection on Nurkse and the structuralists views might help to bring the development of production capacities back onto the agenda, to increase the legitimacy of policies and to support policy targeting.

The first section briefly introduces the Latin American structuralism. The second section, which constitutes the main body of the article, analyses, Nurkse and the structuralists' views on development focusing on three main issues: (1) the expression of the discontent with the 'monoeconomic' approach, (2) their views on patterns of industrialization, trade and growth and (3) the role of the state. The third section concludes, emphasizing the relevance of some early development economics contributions to the contemporary debate.

The Latin American Structuralism: A Brief Overview

A complete analysis of the body of literature commonly known as the Latin American structuralism goes beyond the scope of this paper. What suffices here is to highlight the essence of the Latin American development synthesis, with a special emphasis on the seminal works of the two main early structuralists, Raul Prebisch and Celso Furtado.

Much of the Latin American development economics is linked to what is commonly known as the '*pensamiento cepalino*', an expression used to identify the body of theory and evidence elaborated in the newly born UN Economic Commission for Latin America, founded in 1948 in Santiago de Chile.[10] To understand the origins of the Latin American structuralism and its contribution to development economics, it is important to have in mind the context in which those analyses had originated.

After the Second World War, the world (i.e., the developed world) was experiencing a process of reconstruction, which induced rapid expansion and reindustrialization; traditional exports, where thought to regain their dynamism, and the Ricardian standard trade theory of specialization based on static comparative advantages was the main theoretical reference. Until that time, there had been no 'development theory', simply because development was not an issue. Since then, a continuously expanding frontier allowed countries to trust in the prevailing 'international bonanza' for their growth and development. The two World Wars and the dramatic crisis of 1929 reshaped international equilibria and posed new challenges for development. With the 'central' countries mostly focused on their industrial and political reconstruction, the Latin American countries found themselves with the need to create incentives for industrialization responding to the 'real needs' of their economies.

However, as Bielschowsky (1998) states, those who were interested in industrializing the countries of the (peripheral) region faced a 'theoretical vacuum'. Standard trade theory was not suitable; it left no room for the industrialization of Latin America. Those countries, abundantly endowed with natural resources and cheap labour, should have followed the (invisible hand of the) market, pursuing specialization in activities intensive in the use of their relative abundant factors. The body of evidence elaborated by the early structuralists, such as Prebisch and Furtado, represented the theoretical framework for justifying the industrialization effort embraced by the governments of the countries of the region. The structuralism represented the 'peripheral' contribution to development theory.[11]

According to Hirschman, the seminal work of Prebisch on the 'Economic development of Latin America and its principal problems' published in 1950 appears as the '*manifiesto*' of the Latin American development tradition. This seminal work paves the way for the generation of a specific development programme for the countries of Latin America in clear contraposition with the principal body of literature prevailing in the 'centre'. That work laid the basis for the introduction of some of the key (and still relevant) concepts in the south-led structuralist development debate: (1) dynamic and increasing returns form industrialization versus specialization in primary products and the structural heterogeneity of peripheral countries (2) the trade multiplier and the role of technical change; (3) demand and supply constraints to capital accumulation; (4) the role of the state and (5) the relationship between production structure specialization, social configuration and income distribution.

In the structuralist view, development is a long-term process that is not subject to automatic adjustments. The structuralists analysed the modus operandi of the relationship between income distribution, production structure and consumption patterns, underlining the relevance of the demand constraint in capital accumulation, in opposition with the prevailing 'monoeonomic' approach that focused only on the supply constraint.[12]

The structuralist methodological framework implied an analysis of stylized facts. The periphery was identified as vulnerable since it was primarily specialized in exports of natural resource based products and services that were facing a scarcely dynamic external demand, and specialized in imports of dynamic goods and services. The peripheral status also implied a peculiar characteristic of the domestic social structures that showed consumption patterns and technological demands that regularly exceeded the domestic capacity of rent generation, thus engendering a tendency towards structural external disequilibrium.

An appropriate interpretation of the Latin American structuralism sees it as a unique body of literature emerged in a specific context with the objective of dealing with specific 'real' problems. The ECLAC thinking was oriented to elaborate a framework to propose solutions for the puzzling issue of how to develop a nation (a region) in a context characterized by huge asymmetries and disparities between the region and the rest of the world. Development, in that 'real' connotation, was conceived as something more that sustained output growth; the development *problematique* was characterized as a multifaceted issue concerning output growth, employment generation and income distribution. Development was identified, in a Schumpeterian way, with the transformation of socioeconomic systems continuously creating and disrupting alliances deriving from the characteristic of the production and consumption functions. The structuralist approach framed the need for public policies in support of industrialization, also considering the positive effect of industrialization on income distribution.

The whole theoretical apparatus was elaborated starting from the recognition of the asymmetry between Latin America and 'the rest of the world.' Through the lenses of the 'centre-periphery' relationship, the structuralists analysed development with an historical structuralist approach (Bielschowsky 1998). They recognized the relevance of history and path dependency, analyzing the mechanisms through which the conditions in the centre feedback on the development path in the periphery.[13] Technical change is seen as one of the major determinants of the development trajectory in the long run. The centre is considered to be in a position that allows it to capture the benefits of technical progress through two main channels. On the one hand, the countries of the 'centre' are able to appropriate the rents of the technical progress that takes place in their economies, thanks to knowledge and productivity spillovers derived from their endogenous technological capabilities. On the other hand, those countries capture the benefits of the technical change that takes place in the economies of the periphery, which, given their production structure specialization, is translated into lower prices for their export commodities. Given the 'structural features' of the countries of the region, and considering their prevalent pattern of integration with the more advanced economies, industrialization (and the generation of endogenous technological capabilities) appeared as the principal means to develop the countries of the region. The import substitution industrialization strategy responded to the need of reorienting the specialization pattern of the region towards the generation of endogenous technological and production capacities.

During the 50s the newly born commission focused on the analysis of international trade patterns, highlighting the vulnerability of the regional position. The analysis focused on the structural domestic conditions and the determinants of growth and development, technical change, employment generation and income distribution; the recognition of the secular tendency towards a reduction in the terms of trade and the evidence of structural imbalances in the trade balance, led to prioritize on the analytical side, the study of the perverse effects of the prevailing specialization patterns, which were seen as the causes of the trade deficits and as the determinants of the prevailing structural heterogeneity. On the policy prescription side, the discourse focused on the import substitution policies. One of the main structuralist messages is the need to distort market prices in order to allow development to take place given the structural characteristics of the periphery with respect to the centre.

In this respect, it is useful to make a clarification. Contrary to a common and simplistic approach, the ECLAC ideas where far from promoting autarky. The advocacy for infant industry protection and for the state governance of the industrialization process was conceived as a mean to overcome the structural barriers to development deriving from the peripheral status. The early structuralists theories were dynamic in nature, and conceived development as a process of accumulation, not only of capital but of capabilities, that was influenced and conditioned by external constraints and opportunities; i.e., the 'pensamiento cepalino' started from the recognition of integrated economies, and hence elaborated a theoretical framework to overcome the problems of development given the asymmetrical characteristics of the global economic system in which the economies of Latin America were integrated (Prebisch 1950, 1964; Furtado 1952).

Developing a Nation: Principal Problems and Hints for Solutions

In the polarized discussion on how to develop a nation, Nurkse and the Latin American structuralists are usually pulled together due to their common Keynesian matrix and for their heterodox approach towards economic development. However, beyond some similarities, there are also divergences between these two stances. In this respect, it is interesting to recall the debate between Celso Furtado and Ragnar Nurkse at the beginning of the decade of the 50s, which has been published at that time by the Revista Brasileira de Economia (RBE) of the Getulio Vargas Foundation, and that has been recently entirely republished by the Celso Furtado International Center for Development Policies (Centro Internacional Celso Furtado 2007).

In 1951 the Estonian economist gave a cycle of six lectures in Rio de Janeiro on the problems of capital formation in developing countries. The Brazilian Economic Review published the articles, originating an extensive debate between the Nurkse and the team of economists working under the leadership of Prebisch in the newly born Economic Commission for Latin America. Celso Furtado was in charge of elaborating the answer to the Nurkse conferences, and he did so in quite a critical way, dismissing many passages of Nurkse's ideas. Nurkse, on his turn, answered back, thus amplifying the *querelle*. The main divergences rooted in the different weight given to the demand as a structural constraint for capital accumulation, the diverse assumptions regarding the role of technical change and knowledge and the structuralists concern with the 'practical and managerial aspects' of 'how to do things', which was clearly beyond Nurkse's concerns. On the contrary, the economists working at ECLAC were critically interested in 'what' to do and 'how' to do it, in terms of institutional arrangements and policies.

The cycle of conferences created the occasion for confronting alternative voices in development economics. The first conference focused on market size and investment incentives as determinants of capital accumulation. Nurkse mentioned the relevance of demand constraints in the process capital accumulation in developing economies. According to him, in developing economies, there is a vicious cycle that links low productivity with reduced real wages and adoption of capital-intensive production processes. The way to interrupt this vicious cycle is the process of 'balanced growth', i.e., the simultaneous expansion of different lines of production (industries), so that each industry would represent a market for the other, solving the problem of limited market size.[14] In this view, underdevelopment is identified with the scarcity of capital with respect to population and natural resources.

Nurkse starts clarifying that his interest is related to the international aspects of development, since those issues are relevant to the US. Hence, he will not address the question of technological capabilities in capital formation; he will focus only on physical capital formation. Technical change is seen as a mere mechanical aspect of increments in the stock of capital (Centro Internacional Celso Furtado 2007, 21). The starting hypothesis of Nurkse is the fact that in the world there is a great deal of technical knowledge that might be profitably applied in production processes in developing economies, if there was enough available capital in order to support capital demand (Centro Internacional Celso Furtado 2007, 21). What he proposes to discuss is 'the incentive to invest as it presents itself to the entrepreneur, i.e. the conditions that determine the demand for capital goods' (Centro Internacional Celso Furtado 2007, 41).

According to Nurkse, in early development stages, limited market size constraints entrepreneurial demand for capital. Hence, the structural barrier to capital accumulation is the scarcity of real purchasing power in the domestic market. The argument goes this way: most of goods can be sold in developing economies at such reduced scale that there is no incentive for the entrepreneur to produce them (actually most of the necessary installed capacity would be subutilized). Nurkse's argument is different form the small economies one. He makes the relevant point that market size is not determined by the physical size of the country. The main determinant of market size is productivity. And productivity directly derives from the amount of capital used in production. All flows in a circular connection. The identification of this vicious cycle, leads him to affirm that the theory of stagnation must be replaced by a theory of development. Nations must not accept the 'underdevelopment' state as a sort of divine mandate, and secondly, historical experiences show that development actually occurred in given nations at given points in time, hence there must have been something that had inverted the tendency of the vicious circle, he says. Nurkse makes explicit reference to the theory of economic development of Schumpeter, flagging the fact that in the Schumpeterian interpretation, innovations, even though generated in a specific sector of the economy might induce spillover effects in a high number of entrepreneurial activities, increasing investment incentives (Schumpeter 1934).[15]

In the Schumpeterian theory the key agent is the entrepreneur. Nurkse recognizes that that theory was elaborated to explain development in occidental capitalistic societies. In other societies, there might be other agents that should promote the creative destruction process. In this respect, he cites the example of Japan, where the state has been the primary force in prompting national industrial development.[16]

However, Nurkse, is not interested in the 'methodological issue' of whether it should be the state or the private sector as the major player in organizing the production processes to spur development (this is a major difference with the structuralist who were directly involved in policy planning and who were primarily concerned with how to promote industrialization in developing economies). Nurkse is interested in the economic nature of the solution of the problem of capital formation, not in its administrative solution.

Contrary to classical theory, which predicts that the marginal productivity of capital should be higher in countries where capital is scarce relative to other factor endowments (like population and land), Nurkse considers that those economies, given their 'underdeveloped' status might precisely lack or face a reduced demand for capital. However, even though he stresses the existence of demand and supply constraints in capital accumulation in developing economies, he explicitly says that the constraints on the demand side are less severe and more easily remediable than the barriers arising from the scarcity of capital supply (Centro Internacional Celso Furtado 2007, 40).

The second conference addressed the topic of income inequality and saving capacity. Nurkse presented an analysis of the effect of the US consumption pattern on the consumption patterns of developing economies, identifying in the Duesenberry demonstration effect, one of the elements that contributed to depress capital formation in developing countries. Nurkse framed the tendency of individuals (and countries) to live constantly beyond their means, in the new theory of consumption stressing the interdependency between individual consumption preferences. At the same time, he also explicitly quotes Prebisch and his analyses of the vicious cycle that undermines productivity and growth dynamisms in Latin America. Both Prebisch and Nurkse highlight the effect of consumption patterns in more advanced economies on consumption patterns in developing countries. According to Nurkse, international capital flows can not be considered, per se, a solution for the problem of capital accumulation; there is a need for coordination measures in order to ensure that those capital flows will be used productively and not used for financing luxury and emulative consumption.

The third lecture pointed to analyzing the internal sources of capital formation, flagging the role of the available mass of 'sub- or underemployed' that could be seen as a potential reserve of resources to be employed in production activities to boost economic development.[17] The fourth seminar tackled the issue of foreign direct investment and its relation to capital formation. Direct business investment might represent an important external source of capital formation; however, this effect can be jeopardized first, by the fact that most foreign investment is directed to export activities and not to production for domestic markets, due to limited domestic market size. Second,

Nurkse recognizes that direct business investment flows would likely have to be inferior to the investment patterns of the previous decades. In their turn, international loans and grants are seen as relevant external sources of capital formation, once the economy disposes of mechanisms guaranteeing that they are going to be directed to the financing of production of 'social overhead capital' and not spent on consumption.

The fifth conference tagged the controversial issue of trade policy as a tool for boosting capital formation. Nurkse questions the capacity of import substitution measures to act as incentives for investments in production activities. Also, he tries to analyse under which conditions the restriction of consumption of imported goods leads to capital formation. Nurkse states that considering the structural features of developing countries, the creation of industrial capabilities is more important than the protection of infant industries. According to him, disposing of measures to protect infant industries will not, per se, stimulate investment in the generation of those industries. In addition, he notes that tariff protection would only help already strong actors, not weak ones, thus inducing an adverse selection effect. In terms of solutions, Nurkse considers that imposing restrictions to imports of luxury goods for arresting the demonstration effect in domestic consumption patterns is less effective than the introduction of mechanisms to induce compulsory savings though tailored public finance management.

Making a strong and quite critical point, Nurkse criticizes the use of trade policy as a leeway for prompting savings for capital accumulation, making explicit the fact that is much more consensual to introduce direct subsides or manage tariffs than to manage fiscal policies and impose taxes on rents to finance capital accumulation. According to him, the use of tariffs for capital accumulation treats the symptoms instead of the causes of the underdevelopment of production capabilities. In the last talk, professor Nurkse concentrates on the analysis of the problems related to international financial movements.

Furtado responds to the publication of the six lectures of Nurkse with an article entitled 'Capital formation and economic development' (Furtado 1952). Furtado, whose article also expresses the ECLAC perspective, focuses on three main issues: the issue of market size, the demand constraints and the role of the state. He starts by recognizing that Nurkse's contribution represents one of the most serious efforts from the economists of the developed world to try to understand and analyse the problems of development in underdeveloped economies.

Even though both authors express the need for a development theory, they differ in the interpretation of the Schumpeterian theory. Actually, Furtado criticizes Nurkse's personal vision of the Schumpeterian theory. He also disagrees with Nurkse in the definition of market size. According to Furtado, if we consider the possibility of exporting to foreign markets, the demand constraints emerging by market size as described in Nurkse disappear. Market size can be increased, not only by increasing real purchasing power in the domestic economy, but through external market expansion, Furtado affirms.

This point is particularly interesting since it flags a common misperception regarding the early structuralist theory. ECLAC has been strongly criticized for the supposed 'inward looking industrialization strategy'; however, as Furtado states, external markets were seen as necessary and useful ingredients for capital accumulation in developing economies. Yet, since no automatic adjustment was considered to take place, there was a need to manage the timing and the form of external trade in order to orient it in support of domestic industrialization. Furtado clearly states that the problem of market size as the main constraint for growth and development fades when considering the potentiality of the external market. It is interesting to note that in this discussion, it is Furtado who calls for trade as an engine for growth and industrialization. Nurkse, in his response, ironically says that he would be the last to deny the importance of foreign trade for developing economies. However, he affirms that it cannot be said that countries are not developing due to lack of incentives deriving from foreign trade, since at that time, international trade was expanding (Nurkse 1953b). Again on this point, Furtado asserts that market is 'small' in relation to 'something specific', which in this case is the kind of capital used in production. Hence, there is no need for introducing the most modern capital in the production process; the simple mechanization of production would bring about a huge change in the process of production. Actually, he ironically says that the simple introduction of the 'wheel' would make production more productive in Brazil! At the same time, the Brazilian economist also recognized that technical change is costly, saying that, usually, capital modernization would imply increasing costs in the short term and not reduced costs of production in the short term.

Regarding the theory of balanced growth, Furtado interprets Nurkse's points in a narrow way. Furtado criticizes Nurkse for assuming that the process of development would be naturally induced in developing economies by the initiatives of Schumpeterian entrepreneurs, who would have been prone to invest in production, thanks to the mutual incentives arising from simultaneous investments in different production lines. Sarcastically, Furtado says that it is difficult to imagine, as Nurkse seems to suggest, that developing economies might 'levantarse pelos próprios cabelos'. Furtado stresses the fact that the socioeconomic traits of developing economies might hamper not only the initial availabilities of resources for production investments, but also the willingness to invest, and the very existence of the entrepreneurial class.

Furtado is concerned with the creation of production capabilities. And he emphasizes the constraint exercised on that process by the existing dualism between developed and developing economies. Furtado states that in developed economies, growth derives from accumulation of scientific knowledge and from increased capabilities in applying new knowledge to production, i.e., technical progress; while in developing economies, the principal engine of growth would be the assimilation of prevailing production techniques. However, while this point is quite close to Nurkse's starting assumption that there is much technical knowledge available for developing countries' technological upgrading, Furtado's and the structuralist's subsequent analyses deepened the study of the barriers to the absorption of exogenously generated knowledge and sustained the need to create endogenous technological capabilities.

In the analysis of consumption patterns, Furtado and Nurkse have similar visions, and the former recognizes Nurkse's contribution in including the consumption demonstration effects and the interdependency of individual consumption preferences into the new theory of consumption. In reviewing the analysis of investments and the balance of payments, Furtado highlights the importance of Nurkse's contribution in stressing the relevance of the social marginal productivity of investment and not only of the private marginal productivity. Furtado also acknowledges the importance of considering fiscal policy as a strong tool for inducing savings in developing economies, a point that even though it was present, was not so explicit or highlighted in the seminal works of the structuralists.

Nurkse replies to Furtado's comments with his article, 'Notes on the work of Celso Furtado on capital formation and economic development' (Nurkse 1953b). Nurkse clearly sates that even though he recognizes that capital formation is constrained both on the demand and the supply side in developing economies, he considers the constraints arising from the lack of supply more relevant than those deriving from the absence of the demand. Nurske stresses that his thesis regarding market size as a determinant of lack of demand for capital in developing economies rests on the consideration that consumption is inelastic given prevailing low level of incomes in developing countries in addition to the problems of technical discontinuities and indivisibilities in more capital investment production processes. In response to Furtado's critique regarding the utility of the Schumpeterian theory for explaining development in contemporary developing economies, Nurkse clarifies the misinterpretation and makes it explicit that both authors agree that given the prevalent structural conditions of developing economies in their times, no private and spontaneous entrepreneurial effort would support capital accumulation. Actually, Nurkse openly recognizes that given the structural characteristic, there is a room for state intervention in order to organize production and coordinate entrepreneurial efforts.

The cycle of the Brazilian conferences and the subsequent debate in the *Brazilian Economic Review*, represent the most direct and open confrontation between the Estonian development economist and the structuralists. However, beyond the direct *querelle* between them, it is interesting to explicitly confront their stances on three main topics that are of extreme relevance for contemporary development theory: the discontent with the 'monoeconomic' approach; industrialization, trade and growth patterns; and the role of the state.

The Discontent With the 'Monoeconomic' Approach

Nurkse and the Latin American structuralists express a clear discontent with the prevailing 'monoeconomic' approach. In their framework, different 'contexts' or 'structures' require different approaches.[18] According to them, orthodox trade theory lacks the capacity to capture the dynamics of capitalistic development in developing economies. Most of the assumptions of standard theory fail to capture the adjustment mechanisms that actually take place in the economy, hence jeopardizing its predictive capacity. Both Nurkse and the Latin American structuralist analyses were meant to be 'reality-based', in the sense that the theory was seen as a necessary framework to understand and analyse reality, and to offer normative solutions for its principal problems, i.e., they both followed an inductive approach (Nurkse 1953a, 1956, 1959a; Prebisch 1950, 1981; Furtado 1956a, 1956b, 1961).

Nurkse and the structuralists put the events, the 'stylized facts' (*hechos estilizados*), as founding premises for the theory. So theories should be, according to them, not in contrast with a common sense view of the reality, echoing the Shumpeterian exhortation of 'looking around your self' for building theoretical frameworks able to reflect real dynamics (Prebisch 1950; Furtado 1956a). In line with this, Nurkse, in his 1935 article on 'The schematic representation of the structure of production', criticized the linear representation of the production process as in the Hayekain view, stressing the fact that this vision is not able to grasp the essential element of the differences in the 'techniques' of production. The main objective of Nurkse is to 'examine the adequacy of that picture [the standard representation of the production function] as a representation of reality, and to contrast it with a different view of the productive process that, although it might claim to be commonsense view, has perhaps been unduly neglected' (Nurske 1935, 22).

They also recognized the relevance of historical experience anticipating the concepts of path-dependency and windows of opportunity.[19] Actually, Nurkse, in 'Balanced and unbalanced growth', invites the reader to take a look at the past experience and 'see how economic growth in certain areas was induced through international trade' (Nurkse 1957). At the same time, Nurkse and the strucuralists denied the existence of automatic adjustments in socioeconomic structures, criticizing the equilibrium mirage (Nurkse 1935; Furtado 1956a; Prebisch 1950, 1981).

'Economists have paid too little attention in the past to the relation of economic progress to the business cycle. The general body of economic doctrine has centred on the analysis of economic equilibrium, and industrial fluctuations have come to be treated simply as oscillations about a basic stationary equilibrium position. A contraction of demand may tend to perpetuate and reinforce itself thorough the circular paths of the productive system. The monetary processes are always conditioned by the technological characteristics of the structure of production' (Nurkse 1935). 'Prices, especially of finished consumer goods, do tend to be sticky. Sooner or later of course they respond to any substantial and lasting change in market conditions. But in the short run is not perfectly fluid…. Uncertainty and imperfect foresight will be readily accepted' (Nurkse 1954, 117).

In the same way, Prebisch states that 'In Latin America reality is undermining the out-dated schema of the international division of labour, which achieved great importance in the nineteenth century and, as a theoretical concept, continued to exert influence until very recently. Under that schema, the specific task that fell to Latin America, as part of the periphery of the world economic system, was that of producing food ad raw materials for the great industrial centers. There was no place within it for the industrialization of the new countries' (Prebisch 1950, 1).

Prebisch recognized the soundness of the theoretical reasoning of the standard international trade theory; however, he says that 'it is usually forgotten that it is based upon an assumption that has been conclusively proved false by facts' (Prebisch 1950, 1). The fallacy of the classical assumption of the distribution of technical progress benefits to the whole community derives, according to Prebisch, from the generalization of the concept of 'community'. It is conceivable to assume that the benefits of technical progress in the long run will tend to reduce disparities within the industrializing centres. However, it is not so realistic to assume that the benefits of increased international trade will be evenly distributed in the long run among all social groups and classes in the 'periphery'.

The structuralist discontent with the standard economic theory derived from the role that that theory assigned to the countries of Latin America: they should specialize in natural resources and labour-intensive activities according to their comparative advantages, disregarding income elasticities of imports and exports, domestic consumption patterns and endogenous accumulation of technological capabilities. 'The case of the Latin American countries must therefore be presented clearly, so that their interests, aspirations and opportunities, bearing in mind, of course, their individual differences and characteristics, may be adequately integrated within the general framework of international economic cooperation' (Prebisch 1950, 2). In line with it, Nurkse (1957) affirmed that 'Much of the conventional theory of trade seems to me to be based on a very understandable, yet analytically illegitimate generalization of the 19th century experience, an experience which in some ways was unique. The theory of international specialization as such is a static analysis.' There was a need to frame development from a different perspective.

Patterns of Industrialization, Trade and Growth

In opposition to the prevailing approach, both Nurkse and the Latin American structuralists developed a vision of their own to analyse the relationship between industrialization, trade and growth. Actually, 'The dominant practical question in some of less developed countries is whether the available means, limited as they are, should be used to promote activities (a) specialized along lines of comparative advantage internationally or (b) diversified as to provide markets for each other locally. Some less-developed countries think that they cannot rely on an external demand for their primary products, a demand which is usually inelastic with respect to price. The clash of prescriptions on the policy plane reflects what looks like a deadlock on the theoretical level also' (Nurkse 1957).

The option of specializing according to comparative advantages was not suitable. The call for industrialization derived from the exhaustion of the previous growth model based on sustained foreign demand for national production from the centre. At the same time, there was a clear recognition of the qualitative differences in the organization of production and in the redistribution of income generated by industry and by primary production. In the Latin American *Manifiesto*, Prebisch (1950) explains the mechanisms through which the 'centre', specialized in technology-intensive production, is in a position to capture the benefits of technical progress due to the advances in productivity of its domestic production. The centre also appropriates the benefits of technical progress in the periphery, since in primary activities, technical progress takes the form of reduced prices for export products.

Industrialization would have allowed developing economies to capture the benefits of increasing international trade. 'Industrialization is not an end in itself, but the principal mean at the disposal of those countries of obtaining a share of the benefits of technical progress and of progressively raising the standard of living of the masses' (Prebisch 1950, 2).

In addition, building industrial capabilities and deepening primary exports were not seen as alternative solutions. The 'industrialization of Latin America is not incompatible with the efficient development of primary production' (Prebisch 1950, 2). 'The more active Latin America's foreign trade, the greater the possibility of increasing productivity by means of intensive capital formation. The solutions does not lie in growth at the expense of foreign trade, but in knowing how to extract, from continually growing foreign trade, the elements that will promote economic development' (Prebisch 1950, 2). Actually, '... the Keynesian approach demonstrates that any single country can and should do something to realize these conditions (optimal division of labour and full employment) within its borders without hurting its neighbours and without throwing away the gains form international trade' (Nurkse 1947).[20]

Foreign direct investments were identified as important sources of capital supply, at least in early stages. Even though there is no guarantee that FDI would automatically translate into production investments engendering linkages with domestic production, regulations and controls are needed, because market incentives, contrary to mainstream view, would not lead FDI to act as sources of capital accumulation in developing economies (Prebisch 1950; Nurkse 1956). However, capital accumulation was constrained also by demand. Export-led growth would not automatically reduce income disparities between the centre and the periphery.

'The social aim of industrialization might well be jeopardized if too large a part of the increase were to be devoted to increasing consumption or to a premature slackening of productive effort' (Prebisch 1950, 44). Moreover, 'capital formation has to overcome a strong tendency towards certain type of consumption that are often incompatible with intensive capitalization' (Prebisch 1950, 4). Both Nurkse and the structuralists recognized the conflict between the need for capital accumulation and the desire to assimilate patterns of consumption and ways of life of more advanced economies, which in contrast, had achieved them gradually as long as they developed their industrial capabilities. Actually, in Latin America 'the characteristic lack of savings is the result, not only of this narrow margin, but in many cases of its improper use' (Prebisch 1950, 37). Savings in Latin America did not grow as expected according to increases in income, given the Duesenberry demonstration effect.

At the same time, income inequality turned out to be a structural barrier for development, constraining domestic demand. Stagnant real salaries triggered down consumption growth, reducing the capacity to generate a local market in the periphery. The structure of domestic demand constrains the expansion of dynamic industries, jeopardizing development. Moreover, it puts pressure on the trade balance, increasing the propensity to import goods that are not available in the domestic market (Nurkse 1953a, 1957; Furtado 1952, 1956a; Prebisch 1950). However, the demand constraint is considered less relevant and less difficult to solve with respect to the supply constraint in the analysis of Nurkse, as we already pointed out in the previous section.

Both Nurkse and the structuralists considered that 'In general, economic growth through trade can hardly be expected to narrow the gap in income levels between the center and the periphery. Nevertheless, unbalanced and unsteady growth through foreign trade is surely much better than no growth at all.' But since 'it is no longer so certain that less developed countries can rely on economic growth being induced from the outside through an expansion of world demand for their exports of primary commodities. It is not surprising that countries should be looking for other solutions' (Nurkse 1957). However, while the structuralists called for industrialization through import substitution, for Nurkse (1957), 'the solution seems a balanced pattern of investment in a number of different industries, so that people working more productively, with more capital and improved techniques, become each other's costumers. A pattern of mutually supporting investments in different lines of production can enlarge the size of the market and help to fill the vacuum in the domestic economy of low income areas. This is in brief the notion of balanced growth.'

The Role of the State

As it is manifest from the evidence presented so far, there is more room for state intervention in the structuralist approach than in Nurkse. Indeed, Nurkse was not interested in the 'practical' question of how to industrialize a nation. His attention was focused on which mechanisms would have better induced capital accumulation and productive investments in backward economies. On the contrary, the structuralists were critically interested in proposing policies for creating those incentives. However, as has been already stated, Nurkse openly recognizes that given the structural characteristic of backward economies, there might be a room for state intervention in order to organize production and coordinate domestic entrepreneurial efforts (Nurkse 1953b). His pragmatism also led Nurkse (1947, 52) to affirm that 'from the point of view of a national economy creating employment through an export surplus is just like digging holes at home. It is possible to adopt import restrictions not to reduce them but to prevent them from growing. People often tend to regard a policy measure as either good or bad in all circumstances. In reality, it all depends.'

Actually, it is fair to say that both in the frame of Nurkse and that of the structuralists, given the specific circumstances of developing economies, *the state has a role to play*. Even though, for the structuralists, state intervention roots on different assumptions ,the state should correct excessive asymmetry in income distribution; it might absorb labour, it finances production and in some cases it is also a direct producer in key technological and production areas (Prebisch 1950; Furtado 1956a).

On his turn, Nurkse (1947) leaves much less room for state intervention. He clarifies that even though 'according to some writers the balanced growth argument implies that the market mechanism is eliminated and that investment must be effected according to a coordinated plan. This opinion seems to me dubious. Governments will end by creating white elephants and intolerable disproportions in the structure of production. It is private investment that is attracted by markets and that needs the inducement of growing markets. In my presentation balanced growth is an exercise in economic development with unlimited supply of capital, as in Lewis's model with unlimited supply of labor.'

In Nurkse, the role of the state is basically confined to what in current languages would be named the 'market failure' approach.[21] In fact, he was sceptical about import substitution policies. He stressed the fact that infant creation was far more important that infant protection. However, the disagreement on the issue of 'creating' versus 'protecting' industries appears to be more a 'terminological' divergence than a substantial one. In the structuralist approach, the import substitution strategy, at least in its original conception, was indeed conceived to create the conditions for the generation of technological and production capacities, and not to 'protect' already established rents and positions.

Nurkse nuances his position on the role of the state when it comes to public utility works, or what he calls social overhead capital. Public utility projects involve high sunk costs that have to be sustained before the economy might make full use of those installations. 'They [public utility works] are built ahead of demand partly for this reason, that is, because of technical necessity due to indivisibilities but possibly also as a result of a deliberate policy of public authorities or of the speculative exuberance of private promoters' (Nurkse 1956, 1957). Recognizing the gap between the time of construction and the time of profitable operation, Nurske (1956) opens up a space for direct state intervention in the provision of 'services, transport, power, water supply, which are basic for any productive activity, [and] cannot be imported from abroad and require large and costly installations ... It is conceivable that some of these public works would turn out to be white elephants. But the risk has to be taken. Any form of capital investment is in the last analysis an act of faith.'

The overview presented so far frames two development theories that, beyond some divergences, are indeed similar in their main message: lack of industrial capabilities hampers output and productivity growth, and adversely affects income distribution; hence, developing countries should embrace an industrialization strategy. In terms of development strategies, Nurkse and the early structuralists focus on different topics, but they agree on one key issue: there are structural constraints to development that are proper to backward economies and that should, in one way or another, be tackled in order to create the conditions for development. Underdevelopment is not a 'natural' stage of the development process; it is a specific feature, with peculiar traits, that is proper to given areas at given times. Hence, as Nurkse noted in the first Brazilian conference, there is a need to substitute the prevailing 'stagnation theory' with a 'theory of development' that should identify the forces that in the past pushed the economies out of their supposed steady state, braking the vicious cycle. Table 6.1 presents a taxonomy of the theory of economic development of Nurkse and the structuralist, flagging the main similarities and differences analysed so far.

Concluding Remarks

In the last decades, the discipline of development economics evolved unfortunately more than its object of study.[22] The concept of economic development itself changed. Nowadays it includes, explicitly, additional dimensions to output growth (living conditions, well-being and even democratic level of institutions are often included in international rankings on the state of development in the world). However, underdevelopment is still a reality in much of the economies, and in many areas of emerging or developing economies. Still, low productivity, informality, low quality of domestically produced goods and services, low salaries and low-skilled labour force characterize all developing countries' socioeconomic structures.

After a period (the nineties) in which industrialization for developing countries was a taboo, nowadays it is again politically correct to call for industrialization as a way out of poverty for developing countries. Expenditures for the generation of scientific, technological and production capabilities are seen as investments for the countries' development, at least in governments' declarations and plans. However, much has to be done in this sense. The new technological paradigms, such as information technology, biotechnology and nanotechnology, entail radically new forms of doing business, of creating and adding value to production and of exchanging the newly generated intangible value. These paradigms open opportunities for development, in creating new sectors and new production activities. But, at the same time, they present a big challenge to developing economies. The risk of being marginalized and locked out is high, since these paradigms are increasingly intensive in accumulated specific technical knowledge and capabilities.

Developing countries should invest *now* in generating the capacities to cope, understand and operate with these new paradigms, even though the generation of these capacities is a long term process. Furthermore, in addition to the classical development theory idea that progress derived from increased use of capital in production, which in turn was determined by domestic market size and real purchasing power of domestic market, the structuralist and the more recent evolutionary contributions point to the fact that domestic technological capabilities are determinant not only because they create the conditions for the demand for capital in domestic markets, but because they also represent the necessary absorption capacity that the system requires in order to profit from exogenous technological opportunities.[23]

Development is undoubtedly related to the accumulation of knowledge and technological capabilities, and it is much more so in the new technological paradigms. However, nowadays, as in the fifties, 'here, as in many other cases, our knowledge of the economic structure of the Latin American countries, their cyclical form of growth and their possibilities is limited. If a scientifically impartial investigation of such questions could be carried out and the training encouraged of economists capable of grasping new economic phenomena, foreseeing the problems involved and cooperating in the search for solutions, a service of incalculable value would be rendered to the economic development of Latin America' (Prebisch1950, 59). Actually, how does learning take place in developing economies, how do firms generate, appropriate and trade knowledge, under which conditions public-private partnerships (so much advocated nowadays) do work or fail, these and many more questions need to be explored within the lenses of development theory in order to go beyond rhetoric in the contemporary development discourse.

The debate between static comparative advantages and dynamic ones is far from ended. In this sense, the message of classical development theory is more than alive today. 'Frequently the objection is made: but why use machinery? Why adopt capital-using methods in areas where labor is cheap and plentiful? Why not accordingly employ techniques that are labor intensive instead of capital intensive? The answer is obvious. As an adaptation to existing circumstances including the existing factor proportions, the pursuit of labor-intensive methods with a view to economizing capital may be perfectly correct, but the study of economic development must concern itself with changing these circumstances, not accepting them as they are. What is wanted is progress, not simply adaptation to present conditions' (Nurkse 1956).

A look back at the pioneers' works in development economics might help us to try to avoid being captured in sterile debates, as has happened and still happens many times, on the fact that new problems needs new solutions. This is quite obvious and clear. A look at the history of development economics shows us that it has always been obvious that solutions must be tailored to specific cases and contexts. However, what was also clear, and what tends to be collectively forgotten, is that there are some recurrences in economic

Table 6.1. **Nurkse and the Latin American Structuralists: A Taxonomy of Early Development Theories**

	Nurkse	Early Structuralists (Prebisch and Furtado)
Definition of development	Industrialization (capital accumulation) Sustained output growth.	Sustained output growth + increasing income equality Socio-economic transformation of production and political structures.
Methodological approach	Discontent with the 'monoeconomics' approach and with the assumption of standard international trade theory. Historical-structuralist and inductive approach.	
Demand-side constraints for capital accumulation	Low income small market, small incentive to invest, limited used of capital goods, low productivity, low income. Demonstration effect. Interdependency of individual consumption preferences and adverse effect of domestic consumption patterns on capital accumulation in developing economies. Demand constraint is less relevant than the supply constraint.	Demand constraint might be extremely relevant in explaining investment and savings decisions of peripheral countries.
Supply-side constraints for capital accumulation	Low income, small savings, lack of capital goods, low productivity, low income. Foreign aid, grants and loans might be useful but there is a need for policy coordination in order to ensure the investment in production activities. Foreign direct investment as source of capital supply: (1) might not be available in the required amount; (2) is primarily directed to export activities and not to the domestic market.	Foreign direct investment as source of capital supply usually presents few linkages with the domestic economy, does not increase automatically endogenous technological capabilities.
Trade multiplier and growth	Developing economies cannot uniquely rely on trade for fostering capital accumulation and growth, especially considering current trends in world trade.	Explicit reference to qualitative differences of production activities. Income elasticity of peripheral imports, deriving from asymmetry in specialization patterns, hampers the positive effects of exports growth on output growth.

	Balanced Growth.	Import Substitution Industrialization.
Industrialization		
Technical progress	Exogenous. There is sufficient amount of knowledge to be applied to domestic production; lack of demand and supply of capital constraint the incorporation of available technologies/capital in domestic production.	Technical progress originates increasing returns and allows increasing productivity and output growth. There is a need to create endogenous technological capabilities to create the conditions for appropriating innovation rents (support to domestic capital goods production).
Role of the State	The focus is on the economic nature of the solution of the problem of capital formation, not in its administrative solution. However, developing economies might require state intervention to coordinate production investment decisions, given the limited size of domestic market.	The State has a primary role. It corrects excessive asymmetry in income distribution, it might absorb labour, it directly finances production and technological development, it is a direct producer in key technological and production areas.
Social overhead capital	Need for public provision and/or financing.	
Trade Policy	A tailored fiscal policy is preferable to tariff management. The use of tariffs treats the symptoms but not the cause of lack of incentives for capital formation.	Import Substitution Strategy to generate incentives for the creation of domestic production and technological capabilities.

Source: Author's elaboration.

trends, that there are trajectories of capabilities' development that might be of help in elaborating contemporary development strategies (Cimoli, Dosi, Nelson and Stiglitz 2006; Reinert 2007). History should not be seen as a source of guidelines to apply, but as a precious source of information on the evolution of socioeconomic systems.

Beyond the importance of adopting an historical-structuralist approach, beyond the attention paid to the capacity of a theory to explain real dynamics, beyond the incipient recognition of the relevance of technical change and of the demand side in capital accumulation, the main legacy of Nurkse and the structuralists is the identification of development with a 'change' of current status quo, a change induced by industrialization, i.e., by the introduction of new products and methods of production.

Development was not seen as a deepening of given features, or as a 'maximizing' effort with respect to given conditions. Development was identified as a process of transformation of socioeconomic structures. And it should be even more so nowadays, when the new technological paradigms are increasing the rate at which the transformation of socioeconomic systems occurs. Restoring the view of development as 'change' of current circumstances, and treating explicitly the role of uncertainty and indivisibilities in structural and technical change, would help to free the debate from naïve discussions on 'efficiency', on the need to avoid 'duplicity of efforts' and on 'maximizing advantages'. It would also, hopefully, contribute to shifting the attention to 'effectiveness' of policies, to selective targeting, to the creation of basic and frontier capabilities, just to mention some issues. Matching insights from classical development theory with the advances in the literature on how knowledge is accumulated and transferred within and between systems could also contribute to create a coherent theoretical framework for development in which, for example, investments in the creation of scientific and technological capabilities in information technology, biotechnology and nanotechnology would appear not only *justifiable*, but *necessary*, for developing economies, as for frontier countries.

References

Adelman, I. 1999. *Fallacies in Development Theory and their Implications for Policies*, Working Paper, no. 887, Department of Agricultural and Resource Economics and Policy Division of Agricultural and Natural Resources University of California at Berkeley.

Arthur, W. B. 1989. 'Competing Technologies, Increasing Returns and Lock-in by Historical Events,' *Economic Journal* 99 (1), 116–131.

Atkinson, A. B. and J. E. Stiglitz. 1969. 'A New View of Technological Change.' *The Economic Journal* 79 (315), 573–57.

Bell, M. and K. Pavitt. 1993. 'Technological Accumulation and Industrial Growth Contrasts between Developed and Developing Countries.' *Industrial and Corporate Change* 2, 157–210.

Bhagwati, J. 1988. *Protectionism*. Cambridge, MA: MIT University Press.

Bielschowsky, R. 2006. 'Celso Furtado's Contribution to Structuralism and their Relevance today.' *ECLAC Review* 88, 7–15.

––––––. 1998. 'Cincuenta años del pensamiento de la CEPAL: una reseña.' In CEPAL 1998.

CEPAL. 2007. *Progreso técnico y cambio estructural en América Latina*. Santiago, Chile: CEPAL/IDRC.

––––––. *Cincuenta años de pensamiento en la CEPAL*. Santiago, Chile: CEPAL, Naciones Unidas-Fondo de Cultura Económica.

Chang, Ha-Joon. 1994. *The Political Economy of Industrial Policy*. London: Macmillan Press.

Centro Internacional Celso Furtado de Políticas para o Desenvolvimento, 2007. *Memórias do desenvolvimento*, Rio de Janeiro, ano 1, n. 1, June, 2007.

Cimoli, M. and G. Dosi. 1995. 'Technological Paradigms, Patterns of Learning and Development: An Introductory Roadmap.' *Journal of Evolutionary Economics* 5, 243–268.

Cimoli, M. and A. Primi. 2008. *Technology and Intellectual Property: A Taxonomy of Contemporary Markets for Knowledge and their Implications for Development*. LEM Working Paper Series, 2008/6.

Cimoli, M., G. Dosi, R. Nelson and J. Stiglitz. 2006. *Institutions and Policies Shaping Industrial Development: An Introductory Note*. LEM Working Paper Series, 2006/2.

Cohen, W. and D. Levinthal. 1990. 'Absorptive Capacity: A New Perspective on Learning and Innovation.' *Administrative Science Quarterly* 35, 128–152.

Dahlman, C. 2007. *Development Strategies of China and India: Lessons for Brazil*. Santiago, Chile: ECLAC, United Nations.

David, P. 1985. 'Clio and the economics of QWERTY.' *American Economic Review* 75 (2), 332–37.

Dosi, G. 1988. 'Sources, Procedures and Microeconomic Effects of Innovation.' *Journal of Economic Literature* 26, 1120–1171.

Fajnzylber, F. 1983. 'La industrialización trunca de América Latina', Mexico, DF, Editorial Nueva Imagen.

Furtado, C. 1985. 'A Fantasia organizada' Rio de Janeiro: Paz e Terra.

––––––. 1961. *Desenvolvimento e subdesenvolvimento*. Rio de Janeiro: Editora Fundo de Cultura. Reprinted in CEPAL 1998, 229–271.

––––––. 1956a. 'El análisis marginal y la teoría del subdesarrollo.' *El Trimestre Económico* 23 (4), 438–447.

––––––. 1956b. 'Ensayo de interpretación histórico-analítica del desarrollo económico.' *El Trimestre Económico* 23 (2), 151–176.

––––––. 1952. 'Formação de capital e desenvolvimento ecônomico.' *Revista Brasilera de Economia* 6 (3), 7–45. Republished in Centro Internacional Celso Furtado 2007.

Haberler, G. and R. M. Stern (eds). 1961. *Equilibrium and Growth in the World Economy. Economic Essays by Ragnar Nurkse*. Cambridge, MA: Harvard University Press, 1961.

Hirschman, A. O. 1981. *Essays in Trespassing*. Cambridge, MA: Cambridge University Press.

––––––. 1958. *The Strategy of Economic Development*. New Haven: Yale University Press.

Krueger, A. 1990. 'Government Failure in Development.' *Journal of Economic Perspectives* 4 (3), 9–23

Lewis, W. A. 1954. 'Economic Development with Unlimited Supplies of Labor.' *Manchester School of Economic and Social Studies* 22, (2), 139–191.

Marshall, A. 1890. *Principles of Economics*. London: Macmillan.

Myrdal, G. 1956. *The Political Element in the Development of Economic Theory*. Cambridge, MA: Harvard University Press.

Nelson, R. 1959. The simple economics of basic scientific research, The Journal of Political Economy, 67 (3), 297–306

Nurkse, R. 1959b. 'Notes on 'Unbalanced Growth'.' Oxford Economic Papers 11 (3), 295–97.

————. 1959a. Patterns of Trade and Development: Wicksell Lectures. Stockholm: Amqvist and Wiksell.

————. 1957. 'Balanced and Unbalanced Growth.' In Haberler and Stern (eds), 1961. 241–281.

————. 'International Investment today in the Light of Nineteenth Century Experience.' In Haberler and Stern (eds) 1961, 134–150.

————. 'Period Analysis and Inventory Cycles.' In Haberler and Stern (eds) 1961, 104–133.

————. 1953a. Problems of Capital Formation in Underdeveloped Countries. New York: Oxford University Press.

————. 1953b. 'Notas sobre o trabalho do Sr. Furtado relativo a 'Formação de capital e desenvolvimento ecônomico'.' Revista Brasilera de Economia 7 (1), 67-86. Republished in Centro Internacional Celso Furtado 2007, 231–244.

————. 1947. 'Domestic and International Equilibrium.' In Haberler and Stern (eds). 1961. 41–71.

————. 1935. 'The Schematic Representation of the Structure of Production.' Review of Economic Studies June 1935. Reprinted in Haberler and Stern (eds). 1961. 22–40.

Peres, W. 2006. 'El lento retorno de las políticas industriales en América Latina y el Caribe.' Revista de la CEPAL 88, 71–88.

Peres, W. and A. Primi. 2008. Theory and Practice of Industrial Policy: Evidence from Latin America. Santiago, Chile: ECLAC, Unit of Industrial and Technological Development.

Pérez, C. and L. Soete. 1988. 'Catching up in Technology: Entry Barriers and Windows of Opportunity.' In G. Dosi et al. (eds). Technical Change and Economic Theory. London: Francis Pinter, 38–66. Reprinted in H. Hanusch (ed.). 1998. The Economic Legacy of Joseph Schumpeter. London: Elgar , 458–479.

Pinto, A. 1976. 'Naturaleza e implicaciones de la heterogeneidad estructural de América Latina.' El Trimestre Económico 37 (145), 83–100.

————. 1971. 'El modelo de desarrollo reciente de la América Latina.' El Trimestre Económico 38 (150), 477–498.

————. 1970. Heterogeneidad estructural y modelo de desarrollo reciente de América Latina, Inflación: raíces estructurales. México, DF: Fondo de Cultura Económica.

Pisano, G. 2006. Science Business: The Promise, the Reality and the Future of Biotech. Harvard Business School.

Prebisch, R. 1981. 'Diálogo acerca de Freeman y Hayek desde el punto de vista de la periferia.' Revista de la CEPAL 15, 161–182.

————. 1964. Hacia una nueva política comercial en pro del desarrollo: Informe del Secretario General de la Conferencia de las Naciones Unidas sobre Comercio y Desarrollo (E/Conf.46/3). New York: United Nations. Selected pages republised in CEPAL 1998, 349–398.

————. 1950. The Economic Development of Latin America and its Principal Problems. New York: ECLA, United Nations.

Reinert, E. 2007. How Rich Countries Got Rich…and Why Poor Countries Stay Poor. London: Constable and Robinson.

Rodríguez, O. 2006. El estructuralismo latinoamericano. Santiago, Chile, PLACE: CEPAL, Naciones Unidas.

————. 2001. 'Prebisch: The Continuing Validity of its Basic Ideas.' ECLAC Review 75 (Tribute to Raul Prebisch), 39–50.

Schumpeter, J. A. 1934. *The Theory of Economic Development*. Cambridge: Harvard University Press.

Stallings, B. and W. Péres. 2000. *Growth, Employment and Equity: The Impact of Structural Reforms in Latin America and the Carribean*. Santiago, Chile: ECLAC United Nations.

Tsuru, S. 'Economic fluctuations in Japan 1868–93.' *Review of Economic Statistics*. 1941.

UNCTAD. 2007. *Knowledge, Technological Learning and Innovation for Development: Least Developed Countries Report*. Geneva: UNCTAD.

_____. 2006. *Developing Productive Capacities: Least Developing Countries Report*, Geneva: UNCTAD.

Wiliamson, J. 1990. 'What Washington Means by Policy Reform.' in J. Williamson (ed.). *Latin American Adjustment: How Much Has Happened?* Washington, DC: Peterson Institute for International Economics.

World Bank. 1991. *World Development Report*. Oxford: Oxford University Press.

Chapter Seven:

LEWIS, THE LONG WAVE AND INDUSTRIALIZATION IN THE PERIPHERY

Keith Nurse

Introduction

W. Arthur Lewis is a canonical figure in economics and can be considered as one of the key thinkers in twentieth-century development thought. His output over more than a half century was voluminous and varied in subject matter. By the time of his Nobel Prize lecture, Lewis had authored ten books and 80 scholarly articles on topics as wide ranging as industrial economics, world trade, development planning, agricultural economics, race and economic development, education, politics, economic integration and economic history (Tignor 2006).

Lewis was a contemporary of Nurske. Both men were among a small group of theorists and analysts working on the problem of economic development in the 1950s. Strangely, there are little or no references to each other's work, even though there are clear areas of contention and synergy. For example, under what became known as the Lewis model of 'industrialization by invitation', the modernization of the peripheral economy would tend to favour the interest of foreign firms and the local elite whose tastes and ideologies are aligned to foreign consumption. On the other hand, Nurske's (1952) balanced growth thesis is critical of the view that productivity gains and increased savings can accrue to peripheral economies through external sources, for example, foreign investment. Indeed, Nurske argues that the problem is not just one of production, but of the widening gap between developed and developing countries and the problem of emulation of lifestyle and consumption. What Nurske is outlining is that development is a relational construct; it is always about invidious comparisons and it is always about filling gaps and catching up with the 'leaders'. Similarly, the Plantation Economy School in the Caribbean argued that Lewis placed too much faith in the dynamics of industrialization coming from external sources as compared to the indigenous or residentiary sector (Best 1974; Figueroa 1998; Girvan 2005).

Lewis (1978a) did appreciate that 'industrialization by invitation' was difficult to execute for a number of reasons. The first is the lack of an 'internal drive towards an industrial revolution' on account of a shortage of local entrepreneurs who could rise to the challenge of international competition. This is compounded by the absence of government policies to facilitate industrial development. Colonization and its legacies of domination by foreign merchants and other tendencies are viewed as a major obstacle, too. He cites the entrenched power of the groups that benefit from commodity exports as an obstacle to peripheral countries making the transition to manufacturing and industrial development. He argues as well that the tendency in such a context is a strong orientation towards 'the enjoyment of foreign-produced goods, ideas and institutions' (200–201).

Another key contribution of Lewis is in his explanation of why so few countries have been able to close the income and technology gaps. Much of the development literature analyzes the problem at the nation-state level and often from an ahistorical standpoint. Lewis's (1978a) magnum opus, *Growth and Fluctuations 1870–1913* provides a useful corrective because it argues that long-wave cyclical shifts in growth rates affect core-periphery relations. Lewis (1980), in his Nobel Laureate lecture, made the point that the 'engine of growth' had slowed since the early 1970s and, as a consequence, peripheral economies were experiencing a secular decline in their terms of trade and having trouble with their balance of payments. Lewis argues that this is not a singular experience and that the periphery had gone through a similar depressionary phase after the 1870s. From this standpoint, Lewis is among a small group of analysts (Perez 2002; Tylecote 1992; Wallerstein 1980) who use long-wave theory and the cyclical shifts in core-periphery relations to explain the widening gap between the two groups of countries.

This aspect of Lewis's work has received less attention. In this regard, the aim of this paper is to examine and extend the theoretical contribution of W. Arthur Lewis to the field of development economics and specifically to the issue of industrialization in peripheral economies. The principal focus is on elaborating a theoretical framework to understand the impact on peripheral industrialization of long-wave changes in the world economy.

The Lewis Thesis on Peripheral Industrialization

Lewis is probably best known and internationally recognized for his article *Economic Development with Unlimited Supplies of Labour*, which was published in

1954. It is in this article that Lewis articulates the 'dual economy model', outlines the terms of trade problem between industrial and primary producers and explains the international division of labour between temperate and tropical zones. It is here he makes his seminal contribution to the field of economics. Indeed, it is argued that 'the article galvanized the new field of development economics, providing it with a legitimacy that it had not previously enjoyed' (Tignor 2006, 79).

In a recent paper on the contribution of Lewis to development thinking and policy, Gustav Ranis (2004, 11) concludes that Lewis's 'notion of dualism, especially that focused on the labor market dimension, rural and urban, continues to offer a theoretically valid, empirically relevant and practically useful framework for dealing with some fundamental real world issues of development.'

The key insight that Lewis offered in the 1954 article was that international trade based on the factoral terms of trade embedded in the classical international division of labour had limited prospects for commodity producing countries once the conditions of unlimited supplies of labour, both nationally and internationally, persisted. In this seminal article he argues,

> The contribution of the temperate world to the tropical world, whether in capital or knowledge, has in the main been confined to the commercial crops for export, where the benefit mainly accrues to the temperate world in lower prices. The prices of tropical commercial crops will always permit only susbsistence wages until, for a change, capital and knowledge are put at the disposal of the subsistence producers to increase the productivity of tropical food production for home consumption. (183)

Based on the empirical evidence, Lewis asserts, 'given the difference in the factoral terms of trade, the opportunity which international trade presented to the temperate settlements was very different from the opportunity presented to the tropics' (1978a, 192). In short, Lewis rejected the neoclassical framework, thus he argued, 'the solution does not depend on accepting the old view that the comparative advantage of the temperate world is in manufactures and of the tropical world in agriculture ...' (1969, 27). Instead, he argued,

> If the tropics could produce a wider range of manufactures, this same propensity to invest would generate a higher level of industrial employment ... For it is only greater industrialization that will eliminate the difficulties; will provide a pool of trained supervisors who eliminate expatriates; will make markets big enough to justify local production of machinery; will raise the productive skills of workers; and will increase domestic savings, so that profits no longer go abroad. (1969, 33)

He argues further that the industrialization of the core countries since the nineteenth century presents two options to the peripheral areas: (1) 'to follow the example of the core' and engage in industrial deepening and upgrading, or (2) to rely on international trade with the core and 'develop by selling to expanding core markets' raw materials and commodities (1978a, 158–159). The second option is viewed not as a stand-alone strategy but potentially a catalyst for the first through graduating from commodity production to import substitution and ultimately export-oriented manufacturing.

The first option, Lewis argues, is only open to countries that 'already had sizable industrial sectors' like India and China or the settler colonies like the US, Canada and Australia. The latter group, although originally commodity exporters, enjoyed significant economic surpluses on account of productivity improvements. Thus, Lewis shows that when commodity prices in 1913 are compared with prices in 1883, the temperate countries enjoyed far superior factoral terms of trade in commodities than tropical countries. He notes, 'with the exception of sugar, all the commodities whose price was lower in 1913 than in 1883 were commodities produced almost wholly in the tropics. All the commodities whose prices rose over this thirty-year period were commodities in which the temperate countries produced a substantial part of total supplies' (1978a, 189). Lewis prescribes that if economic growth and development are not to be constrained by these factors, then developing countries must employ one or more of the following strategies:

a. Sell more non-traditional exports to developed countries
b. Become individually more self-sufficient
c. Sell more to each other (1972, 418)

Lewis, Peripheral Industrialization and the Long Wave

Long-wave theory suggests that price fluctuations and economic development are correlated in a broad sense. Kondratieff (1984), the Russian economist credited with the discovery of long wave-like patterns in the world economy, estimated that these long waves last some 48–55 years, his calculations and empirical work dating from the 1780s, the beginning of the Industrial Revolution. Kondratieff documented that the world economy experiences cyclical rhythms of upswings (periods of growth) and downturns (periods of stagnation) and argued that this pattern was a response to the contradictions inherent in global capitalism, most evident during downturns when the world economy faces 'crises' in accumulation. It is these periods of tension that give global capitalism its dynamic, its 'changingness', or what Schumpeter has described so lucidly as the paradox of 'creative destruction' (Schumpeter 1939).

In many respects, contemporary transformations in global economic restructuring have remained unexplained by neoclassical growth theories, and by short-term and intermediate-term cycle theories (e.g., Juglar, Kitchin). This has stimulated renewed interest in theories of long-term, large-scale cycles, or waves of capitalist development (Mandel 1984). Causality is a major concern in the literature on long waves. For instance, there are innovation theories (Schumpeter. Mensch. Van Duijin) relating long waves to the clustering of innovations; capital accumulation theories (Kondratiev; Mandel), considering changes in capital accumulation as the causal dynamic; the labour theory (Freeman) relating technical change to levels of employment; and, the terms of trade approach (Rostow), whose main focus is on the movement of relative prices of raw materials and foodstuffs (Delbeke 1984). In many respects Lewis's work falls into the last category, although he gives strong consideration to the wide range of causal factors. As he puts it,

> The mechanisms which cause these long Kondratiev swings in the world agricultural prices is controversial. The Victorians thought that it was changes in gold supply; Schumpeter that it was changes in the level of investment in major industrial innovations; others, including myself, that it is primarily changes in the relative growth of world demand and supply of foodstuffs. Whatever the cause may be, the effect seems to be that the terms of trade move in the same direction as agricultural prices. (Lewis 1978b, 37)

In the book *Growth and Fluctuations 1870–1913*, Lewis examines the long-term and cyclical trends in the world-economy utilizing the Kondratiev price swing as the key methodological approach to explain the changes in core-periphery relations. He specifically focuses on the Kondratiev price swing to explain: (a) the dynamics of growth in the core economies, what he calls the 'engine of growth', (b) the change in the terms of trade between agriculture and industry and, (c) the consequent changes in core-periphery relations (1978a, 27).

Lewis's thesis is that the 'engine of growth' in the world economy results from the process of innovation and technological change in the core countries that generates growth, creates demand for inputs and pulls raw material and food imports from the peripheral areas. The 'engine of growth' thesis is premised on 'the proposition that the upward movement of those already on the escalator helps to pull more and more countries into the moving company' (1978a, 16). This does not mean that all countries will benefit equally or will seize the opportunity. Lewis notes, for example, that:

> New technology has its own backwash; those sugar plantations which failed to keep up with new varieties and large-scale milling in the last quarter

of the nineteenth century simply found themselves in bankruptcy – as in Jamaica and Mauritius, in contrast to Java and Cuba. (1978a, 191)

In summary, his argument is that the core countries contributed to the development of the countries at the periphery in three ways:

1. They offered a new and highly productive technology.
2. The core countries contributed resources – specifically, capital and people.
3. The core contributed its own markets (1978a, 29–30).

There is a cyclical dimension to this, however. What is described above relates specifically to the upswing phase where innovations emerge forging the new techno-economic paradigm that leads to increased investment in the core with expanding demand for inputs from the periphery. Prosperity generated in the core diffuses to the periphery through trade. However, much of the benefits of the new innovations that are applied to peripheral exports accrue to consumers and specifically to the traders in the core. Consequently, when the downswing in the core economies arrives international demand for peripheral exports declines, the terms of trade deteriorate, the balance of payments become unfavourable and ultimately an outflow of capital to the core is effected through external debt and other mechanisms.

  Lewis maps the effect of the downswing phase on the periphery by relating tropical agricultural exports and total tropical exports to industrial production in the core countries over the period 1883–1965. Figure 7.1 shows industrial production in the core dipping first and having a knock-on effect on tropical exports and agricultural exports. It also shows that the decline in growth rates for the latter was more significant than that for industrial production and total tropical exports. The figure also shows that the recovery of growth for core industrial production was faster with a twelve- to fifteen-year lag for the peripheral exports. However, after 1937, peripheral exports jump rapidly to catch up with the growth rate for core industrial production. In short, agricultural exports proved to be more vulnerable to the slump in global demand compared to core industrial production. As Lewis (1978a) puts it:

> The intervening three and a half decades were for the tropics a period of disaster. First there was the First World War, culminating in the great slump of 1920. Then in the 1920s the terms of trade moved against tropical products. Then came the great depression of the 1930s with sharp curtailment of demand and even more adverse terms off trade. Finally there came the Second World War. (225)

  By the middle 1930s tropical development had come to a standstill. Private investment had ceased. Governments had cut back their budgets

Figure 7.1. Rates of Growth for Core Industrial Production, Tropical Exports and Agricultural Exports

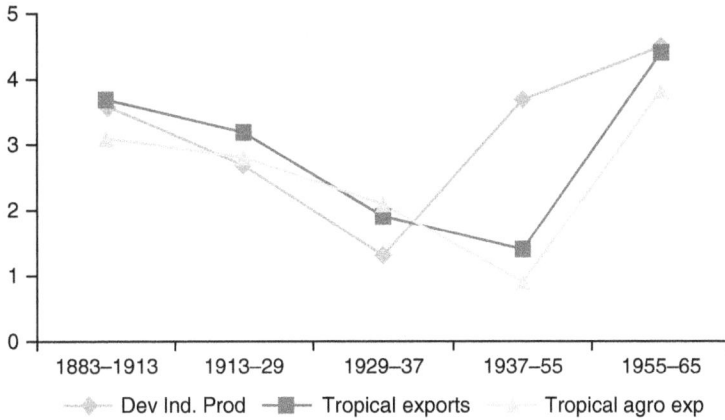

Source: *Growth and Fluctuations 1870–1913* (Lewis 1978a, 226).

on education and welfare services, and with international investment paralysed, infrastructure could not be expanded. (227)

What Lewis has illustrated in Figure 7.1 is a pattern of stagnation and rejuvenation for the periphery over the Kondratieff long wave. The old adage that 'every dark cloud has its silver lining' applies here. The key benefit to peripheral areas was the spurt in indigenous industrial production when imports were expensive and inaccessible . Lewis is not alone in pointing to the surge in industrialization, particularly in Latin America, in this period of economic strife. Hirschman (1978), for example, links the growth in industries to the war, and balance of payments problems. However, what is not often captured in the analysis is the extent to which what is counted as national industrial production is actually the result of the migration or relocation of foreign firms.

Peripheral Industrialization as Relocation

What the above historical analysis suggests is that we should be looking at both shifts in the core and the periphery during a downturn in the Kondratieff long wave. The impact of the downturn on firms and sectors in the core of the world economy is a critical feature of the industrialization process in the periphery. This is on account of the fact that one of the key ways in which the periphery factors into the long wave is as a profitable destination for the relocation of mature industries and technologies coming from the core. As Carlota Perez (2002) notes:

> This outspreading of infrastructures and mature processes has been one of the forces diffusing capitalism throughout the world and widening its potential markets, at the same time it is one of the mechanisms fuelling the catching-up efforts of lagging countries. (83)

Relocation involves the migration of firms and, or the redeployment of technologies from relatively more-advanced to relatively less-advanced areas where the organic composition of capital is lower, labour power is cheaper and the exploitation of labour is less regulated. Over time, relocation has expanded from being an intranational and intraregional (for example, within continental Europe or within the United States) phenomenon to become a transnational process in which cheaper sources of labour power from developing countries are integrated into the declining sectors of the industrial production cycle. The development of this trend is reflected in the migration of industrial production to peripheral countries during the 1930s under import substitution industrialization (ISI) and through export oriented industrialization (EOI) and export oriented services (EOS) from the late 1960s, early 1970s (Nurse 1998; see appendix A).

The long-wave thesis is that during a downturn when markets become saturated in the core economies, and the innovation potential and profit rates have declined, it impels relocation. Ranjit Sau (1978a, 75), focusing more narrowly on the migration of technology from the core to the periphery, argues in a similar vein that 'it is the possibility of selling the near-obsolete machinery to the capitalists in the Third World that helps stabilize the profit rate in the metropolis; it also paves the way for continuous technological advancement there, which again keeps the rate of profit from tumbling down.' He elaborates further that:

> In the Third World, the wage rate is much lower and the profit rate considerably higher in comparison with the advanced capitalist countries; besides, technical progress and rising wages in the latter are continuously taking their toll on obsolescence. Under such circumstances, the class interests of the bourgeoisie of the advanced capitalist countries neatly converge with those of the bourgeoisie of the Third World. The metropolitan bourgeoisie is eager to dispose of its old, obsolete plant and equipment, and its counterpart in the outer periphery of world capitalism is equally interested in welcoming the outmoded, second-hand stuff. (81–82)

Sau concludes his hypothesis by noting, 'it appears that technology tends to filter down across layers of economies, beginning at the top, then into less- and less-developed economies in descending order' (83). The historical record suggests that with each successive downturn, there have been spurts in capital exports and the parallel integration of new zones into the product cycle (see appendix B). Take the case of Latin America during the 1930s: For example, it is estimated that US FDI in Latin America increased by 28.4 per cent between 1929 and 1950 (UNECLAC 1965, 33). The production relocated by US capital to Latin America was primarily in food processing (mostly meat packaging), light industry (phonographs and radios), petroleum, automobiles and tires, construction materials (including cement) and pharmaceuticals. A 1930s study by D. M. Phelps (1969) on American investments in Argentina, Brazil, Uruguay, and Chile provides information on the value of these industrial investments. Of the 66 subsidiaries listed, 75 per cent of these operations were relocated after 1921. However, before 1920, there were 16 branch plants in operation, nine of them meatpacking plants (14).

The extent of the relocation phenomenon in Latin American industrialization can be estimated by the level of foreign participation in industry. Jenkins (1984, 23–26) estimates that foreign capital accounted for 18 per cent of total manufacturing capital in Brazil and 25 per cent in Chile. Estimates by Baklanoff (1966, 112) for Brazil, indicate a higher level of foreign participation, 40 per cent in 1940. For Argentina, an estimate is that half of all industrial capital was foreign. Similarly, Corradi (1974, 353) points out that the Argentinean Industrial Census of 1935 'indicates that 60 per cent of all industrial entrepreneurs in Argentina were foreign born'.

These observations contradict the conventional view that ISI was a nationalist development strategy. After World War II, ISI became more of a nationalist state strategy through tariffs and quantitative restrictions on manufactured imports and managed foreign exchange regimes, but even then it was largely externally propelled. It has been revealed that ISI was sponsored to a large extent by the US administration; US technical aid missions were sent to most developing countries to help draft and implement ISI development plans. The rationale behind the sponsorship is related to Cold War concerns but also to the interests of the powerful internationalist bloc of US business. Maxfield and Holt (1990) argue that:

> Subsidized branch plant investment behind ISI trade barriers was an acceptable alternative to freer trade. Thus US sponsorship of ISI was necessarily linked to vigorous efforts to secure favourable conditions for US FDI. This ensured that ISI protectionism stimulated the internationalization of large US firms rather than the loss of these foreign markets. (50)

These observations highlight that much of what has passed for national production in the literature, particularly under ISI, needs to be reinterpreted as transnational operations in a globalized world market. This argument is also applicable to export-oriented industrialization given the high level of TNC participation in the industrialization efforts of most countries. Both modes of industrialization perpetuate inorganic and extraverted production and social structures.

Peripheral Industrialization as 'Seizing the Chance'

As indicated in the above analysis, the long-wave shifts in the world economy have a direct impact on the fortunes of the peripheries. For example, the arrival of a downturn results in reduced demand in the core economies for commodity and natural resource based exports from the periphery. This is the main mechanism by which the 'crisis' of accumulation is transmitted to the periphery of the world economy (Pamuk 1982). Reduced export earnings result in adverse terms of trade, balance of payments problems and debt crises, particularly among semi-peripheral countries. Ultimately, it results in economic decline manifested by increased unemployment and declining standards of living for peripheral populations.

During the downturn, the tendency is for semi-peripheral and core states (except the hegemon) to erect tariff restrictions and protectionist policies so as to foster domestic industry along the infant-industry argument lines. This mercantilist response to periods of crisis or downturn equates with what Wallerstein (1979, 76–77) describes as the strategy of 'seizing the chance': an aggressive state response to the contraction in the world market that takes advantage of the weakened political position of core countries and the weakened economic position of domestic opponents to such policies. This strategy, however, is limited to those peripheral countries that are relatively strong politically and have some industrial base on which to expand when the opportunity presents itself.

This strategy is very different from the 'industrialization by invitation' model adopted by most of Latin America and the Caribbean (Lewis 1950). Historically, the countries that have been able to move from peripheral to semi-peripheral status or from semi-peripheral to core status are those that have been able to amass the requisite human and technological resources to capture global market shares in key industries. What we know is that there tends to be a window of opportunity when this is easier to effect. It occurs when there is a downturn in the economic growth of the world economy. As Wallerstein (1980) notes:

What needs to be underlined most of all is that a downturn is a slowdown of activity, not a stoppage. It represents, in economic terms, a set of obstacles in the search for profit that, if you will, weeds out the capitalist sheep from the goats. The strong not only survive; they frequently thrive. For the peripheries, therefore, a downturn in the world-economy occasions both involution and evolution; both a seeming decline in the monetarization of economic activity and the emergence of new enterprises; both abandonment and restructuring or relocation; both a decline in their specialized role in the world-economy and a deepening of it. (129)

Wallerstein (1979), in an essay entitled 'The Limited Possibilities For Transformation Within The Capitalist World-Economy' argues that this strategy accounts for the industrial development of a few countries: Italy and Russia in the late nineteenth century and Brazil, Mexico and South Africa during the period of the Great Depression of the 1930s. This strategy also applies to the ascent of countries like the United States (Chase-Dunn 1980), Germany (Rubinson 1982; Tylecote 1982) and Japan (Moulder 1977) in the mid to latter part of the nineteenth century, Turkey (Pamuk 1982) during the 1930s and South Korea and Taiwan since the late 1960s. In the period after the Korean War until 1962 South Korea and Taiwan enjoyed significant amounts of economic, military and food aid from the US, as well as technical assistance programmes, and non-reciprocal access to the US market. Thus, South Korean and Taiwanese ascent can be more accurately described as a combination of two strategies: 'promotion by invitation' via hegemonic sponsorship (1952–1962) and 'seizing the chance' through assertive state intervention after 1962.

One of the main effects of these mercantilist strategies has been to stimulate relocation or foreign direct investments in protectionist countries. Relocation into these protected markets affords transnational firms the ability to segment markets and gain monopolistic rents. Under these circumstances the erection of tariff barriers and other protectionist measures are a means to eliminate competition and secure market shares. This illustrates the point that import-substitution industrialization, if it involves technological dependence, does not necessarily equate with a successful strategy of 'seizing the chance'.

Success here has historically required the 'possession' as well as the 'promotion' of emerging leading sectors (high technology) through a developmentalist-oriented entrepreneurial class with strong state intervention. 'Possession' in this case requires that the combination of complex techno-economic structures needed for the emerging leading sectors be resident within the country and operated, controlled and owned by the country's people. 'Promotion', on the other hand, requires the adoption of strategies by firms and policies by the state that would expropriate rents from internal sources (e.g., through subsidies, transfers and monopolies) or externally through tariffs, quotas, devaluations and dumping (Tylecote and Lonsdale-Brown 1982).

Extending the Lewis Thesis

Lewis's framework for understanding how the periphery is incorporated into the long wave provides a useful framework to explain and predict core-periphery relations. By focusing on the terms of trade, for example, between agriculture and industry, Lewis is able to identify the key impacts for the periphery of cyclical shifts (i.e., upswings and downswings) in the world economy. His main argument is that the demand for peripheral exports are reliant on industrial production in the core and that this is subject to cyclical swings of prosperity and stagnation. This pattern repeats itself in long-wave patterns because the international division of labour has continued as obtained in the sixteenth century. This is the case even though some developing countries have moved into services or light manufacturing. The key point is that whether it is tourism, call centres or electronics manufacturing, most developing countries continue to provide basic inputs and services and consequently operate at the low value-added end of global production chains. These inputs function like commodities in the sense that there is no brand identity or market control for the producers in peripheral countries. The term 'tropical trade' that is used by Lewis (1950; 1969; 1981) to typify such production can be broadened to apply to a wide range of peripheral exports.

Another key insight that emerges from Lewis's analysis is the uneven nature of global development. He clearly shows that for most peripheral economies, the arrival of a downswing in the long wave stalls development and may even reverse some of the gains of the prior period of growth and prosperity. The only countries that have been able to avoid severe economic impact have been those countries that have been able to build industrial capabilities and win global market shares (Reinert 2007). In this regard he is very critical of those countries that rely principally on trade as a mechanism for development, especially where the factoral terms are low. In short, he argues, 'the tropics could not really hope to 'take off' until technological change became embedded in their way of life' (1978a, 202).

Lewis highlights the unequal nature of global development and that the division of labour is not rooted in the products themselves but in the productivity, labour regimes and the social structure of accumulation in the respective economies. For example, he makes the point that 'if tea had been a temperate instead of a tropical crop, its price would have been perhaps four times as high as it actually was. And if wool had been a tropical instead of a temperate ... it would have been had for perhaps one-fourth of the ruling price' (1978a, 189).

Lewis's long-wave framework is largely restricted to the terms of trade elements, although he does link it to international investment and international migration (1978a, 176–188). It can be argued that the integration of the periphery into the long wave of the world economy is critical to its functioning and not just a negative feedback effect. In short, the synergistic relationship between core and peripheral economies in the long-wave movement is a critical feature of the Lewis thesis.

A useful approach suggests that the role of the periphery in the long wave is cyclical and can be captured in an appreciation of the upswing and downswing tendencies (Stewart 1993; see appendix C). In the first phase, the application of new technologies generates investment and growth in the core with intercore trade and core-periphery trade in raw materials or low value-added inputs. By the second phase, the periphery emerges as a market for the new products as the markets of the core begin to saturate. In the third phase, the periphery becomes a destination for the new technologies and industries through the migration or relocation of firms on account of intense competition and falling profit rates. The fourth phase leads to the debt crisis in the periphery as the investments in the prior phase generate low returns on investment, tend to be foreign exchange consuming and consequently dependent on earnings from the declining export oriented primary sector. In the fifth phase, the peripheral economies are subject to increased governance through debt administration by the core economies and through international financial organizations. The final phase sees the massive outflow of resources from the periphery being utilized to finance the core's restructuring and facilitating the rise of the next techno-economic paradigm.

What this diagram illustrates is that the peripheral economies play multiple roles at different phases in the evolution of the long wave: in the upswing, the periphery first plays the role as supplier of raw material and basic inputs, then as a market for the new products and services, and lastly as a destination for mature technologies and industries. In the downswing, the failure of this mode of peripheral industrialization becomes evident and sets up the conditions for high levels of leakage of capital to the core. This pattern repeats itself in the next long wave, except for those peripheral countries that restructured their economies for global competitiveness.

Lewis (1978a), like neo-Schumpeterians, argues, 'the long-run engine of growth is technological change' and not trade 'except in the initial period of laying development foundations' (245). However, there is no broad theorizing on how the periphery is incorporated in the dynamics of long-wave change. What is elaborated below suggests that the process is more a matter of how the three key impulses of innovation, rationalization and relocation by global capital plays out in the world economy and reshapes the international division of labour during the downswing (see Table 7.1).

A cyclical shift in the techno-economic paradigm on account of innovation generally results in the adaptation and adjustment of peripheral economies

***Table 7.1.* Long Wave Downturns and Changes in Core-Periphery Relations**

Transformations in the Core Countries	Role of the Periphery

• Innovation:
  ○ New production processes
  ○ New products
  ○ New trade regimes
  ○ New labour regimes
• Rationalization:
  ○ Concentration of capital
  ○ Convergence of sectors
• Relocation:
  ○ Migration of mature industries and technologies
  ○ Immigration of labour in key sectors
	• Adaptation/Adjustment:
	  ○ New inputs/exports
	  ○ New terms of trade
	  ○ End of preference
	  ○ External indebtedness
	• Fragmentation:
	  ○ Reduced bargaining power in key sectors
	  ○ Privatization of key state assets
	• Respecialization:
	  ○ New modes of FDI and technology/ capital imports
	  ○ Labour exportation and brain drain

(see Table 7.1). Traditional exports lose their market power (e.g., declining terms of trade). New raw materials and industrial exports are required and new demands are made on the economy. New trading regimes emerge, resulting in the end of preference for peripheral exporters (Nurse 2005). The rationalization of industrial sectors through concentration and convergence spells weaker bargaining power for peripheral producers/exporters in world markets, increased dependence on imported technology and management, and a substantial transfer of capital to the core through cheap food, raw materials, manufactures and the privatization of state assets. The third key transformation occurs with the relocation or migration of the new industries and technologies to the periphery as the techno-economic paradigm matures. The low or negative return on these investments and industrialization strategies trigger a debt cycle that further intensifies the peripheralization process (Nurse 1998). In the current long wave, the emigration of labour from the periphery to the core has emerged as a new feature of peripheral respecialization, particularly for those industries that cannot migrate, for example, health, education, tourism, farming. While remittances and other flows have emerged as important contributors to the balance of payments problem they do not offset the losses from the brain drain in all cases (Nurse 2004).

In conclusion, it is important to note that Lewis (1978a) elaborated on, or at least hinted at, many of these issues and trends. He also cautions, 'after one has studied worldwide trends and opportunities, the response of any particular country cannot be fully understood without detailed analysis of its particular circumstances' (167). This is a good caveat to end on because the key benefit of the long-wave methodology is to discern long-term and large-scale patterns and trends in the world system. The advantage of this approach is that one can track the evolution of phenomena, all the time being conscious of the 'continuity' within the 'discontinuity' and so avoid the conceptual trap of 'newness' attached to so many analyses of the prospects for the periphery of the world economy when a new techno-economic paradigm emerges. Lewis was a pioneer in this regard and needs to be celebrated accordingly.

References

Baklanoff, E. (ed.). 1966. *Foreign Private Investment and Industrialization in Brazil: New Perspectives of Brazil*. Nashville: Vanderbilt UP.

Bergesen, A. and R. Schoenberg. 1980. 'Long Waves of Colonial Expansion and Contraction, 1415–1969.' In A. Bergesen (ed.). *Studies of the Modern World-System*. New York: Academic Press, 231–277.

Best, L. 1974. 'Independent Thought and Caribbean Freedom.' In N. Girvan and O. Jefferson (eds). *Readings in the Political Economy of the Caribbean*. Kingston: New World, 7–26.

Chase-Dunn, C. 1980. 'The Development of Core Capitalism in the Antebellum United States: Tariff Politics and Class Struggles in an Upwardly Mobile Semiperiphery.' In A. Bergesen (ed.). *Studies of Modern World-System*. New York: Academic Press, 189–203.

_____. 1978. 'Core-Periphery Relations: The Effects of Core Competition.' In B. Kaplan (ed.). *Social Change in the Capitalist World Economy*. London: Sage, 159–176.

Corradi, J. E. 1974. 'Argentina.' In R. H. Chilcote and J. C. Edelstein (eds). *Latin America: The Struggle with Dependency and Beyond*. New York: Wiley, 309–407.

Delbeke, Jos. 1984. 'Recent Long-Wave Theories: A Critical Survey.' In C. Freeman (ed.). *Long Waves in the World Economy*. London: Frances Pinter, 1–10.

Figueroa, Mark. 1998. 'The Plantation School and Lewis: Contradictions, Continuities and Continued Caribbean Relevance.' *Marronage* 1 (1), 98–123.

Freeman, C. and C. Perez. 1988. 'Structural Crises of Adjustment, Business Cycles and Investment Behaviour.' In G. Dosi, C. Freeman and R. Nelson (eds). *Technical Change and Economic Theory*. New York: Pinter Publishers, 38–66.

Freeman, C. et al. 1984. *Long Waves in the World Economy*. London: Frances Pinter.

Girvan, Norman. 2005. 'W. A. Lewis, The Plantation School and Dependency: An Interpretation.' *Social and Economic Studies* 54 (3), 198–221.

Hirschman, A. 1978. 'The Political Economy of Import-Substitution Industrialization in Latin America.' In S. P. Singh (ed.). *Underdevelopment to Developing Economies*. New York: Oxford UP, 340–74.

Jenkins, Rhys. 1984. *Transnational Corporations and Industrial Transformation in Latin America*. New York: St. Martin's Press.

Kondratiev, N. 1984. *The Long Wave Cycle*. Trans. Guy Daniels. New York: Richardson and Snyder.

Lewis, Arthur. 1981. 'The Rate of Growth of World Trade, 1830–1973.' In S. Grassman and E. Lundberg (eds). *The World Economic Order: Past and Prospects*. London: Macmillan, 11–26.

————. 1980. 'The Slowing Down of the Engine of Growth' [The Nobel Lecture]. *American Economic Review* 70 (4), 555–564.

————. 1978a. *Growth and Fluctuations 1870–1913*. London: Allen & Unwin.

————. 1978b. *The Less Developed Countries and Stable Exchange Rates* (Per Jacobsson Lecture). Washington, DC: IMF, 33–48.

————. 1972. 'Objectives and Prognostications.' In G. Ranis (ed.). *The Gap Between Rich and Poor Nations*. London: Macmillan, 411–420.

————. 1969. *Aspects of Tropical Trade 1883–1965* (The Wicksell Lectures). Stockholm: Almqvist & Wicksell.

————. 1954. 'Economic Development with Unlimited Supplies of Labour.' *The Manchester School* 22 (2), 139–191.

————. 1950. 'The Industrialization of the British West Indies.' *Caribbean Economic Review* 2 (1), 1–51.

Mandel, Ernest. 1984. 'Explaining Long Waves of Capitalist Development.' In C. Freeman (ed.). *Long Waves in the World Economy*. London: Frances Pinter, 195–201.

Maxfield, S. and J. Holt. 1990. 'Protectionism and the Internationalization of Capital: U. S. Sponsorship of Import Substitution Industrialization in the Philippines, Turkey and Argentina.' *International Studies Quarterly* 34, 49–81.

Moulder, Frances. 1977. *Japan, China and the Modern World Economy*. Cambridge: Cambridge University Press.

Nurkse, Ragnar. 1952. 'Growth in Underdeveloped Countries: Some International Aspects of the Problem of Economic Development.' *American Economic Review* 42 (2), 571–583.

Nurse, Keith. 2005. 'Hegemonic Rivalry and the Periphery: The Case of the Transatlantic 'Banana Wars.'' In Faruk Tabak (ed.). *Allies as Rivals: The U. S., Europe, and Japan in a Changing World-System*. New York: Paradigm Publishers, 165–186.

————. 2004. 'Migration, Diaspora and Development in Latin America and the Caribbean.' *International Politics and Society* 2, 107–126.

————. 1998. 'Third World Industrialization and the Reproduction of Underdevelopment.' *Marronnage* 1 (1), 69–97.

Pamuk, Sevket. 1982. 'World Economic Crises and the Periphery: The Case of Turkey.' In E. Friedman (ed.). *Ascent and Decline in the World-System*. Beverly Hills: Sage, 147–161.

Perez, Carlota. 2002. *Technological Revolutions and Financial Capital: The Dynamics of Bubbles and Golden Ages*. Cheltenham: Edward Elgar.

Phelps, D. 1969. *The Migration of Industry to South America*. York, PA: Maple Press.

Sau, R. 1978. *Unequal Exchange, Imperialism and Underdevelopment: An Essay on the Political Economy of World Capitalism*. Calcutta: Oxford UP.

Ranis, G. 2004. Arthur Lewis' Contribution to Development Thinking and Policy. *Manchester School* 72.6: 712–723.

Reinert, Erik. 2007. *How Rich Countries Got Rich … and Why Poor Countries Stay Poor*. London: Constable.

Rubinson, Richard. 1978. 'Political Transformation in Germany and the United States.' In B. Kaplan (ed.). *Social Change in the Capitalist World Economy*. London: Sage, 139–174.

Schumpeter, Joseph. 1939. *Business Cycles* 2 vols. New York: Mc Graw-Hill.

Stewart, Taimoon. 1993. 'The Third World Debt Crisis: A Long Waves Perspective.' *Review* 16 (2), 117–171.

Tignor, Robert. 2006. *W. Arthur Lewis and the Birth of Development Economics*. Princeton, New Jersey: Princeton University Press.

Tylecote, Andrew. 1992. The Long Wave in the World Economy: The Present Crisis in Historical Perspective (London: Routledge.)

Tylecote, Andrew. 1982. 'German Ascent and British Decline, 1870–1980: The Role of Upper-Class Structure and Values.' In Edward Friedman (ed.). *Ascent and Decline in the World-System*. Beverly Hills: Sage, 41–68.

Tylecote, Andrew and Marian Lonsdale-Brown. 1982. 'State Socialism and Development: Why Russian and Chinese Ascent Halted.' In Edward Friedman (ed.). *Ascent and Decline in the World-System*. Beverly Hills: Sage, 255–288.

UNECLAC. 1965. *External Financing in Latin America*. New York: United Nations.

Wallerstein, I. 1980. *The Modern World-System II: Mercantilism and the Consolidation of the European World-Economy, 1600–1750*. New York: Academic Press.

———. 1979. *The Capitalist World-Economy*. Cambridge: Cambridge UP.

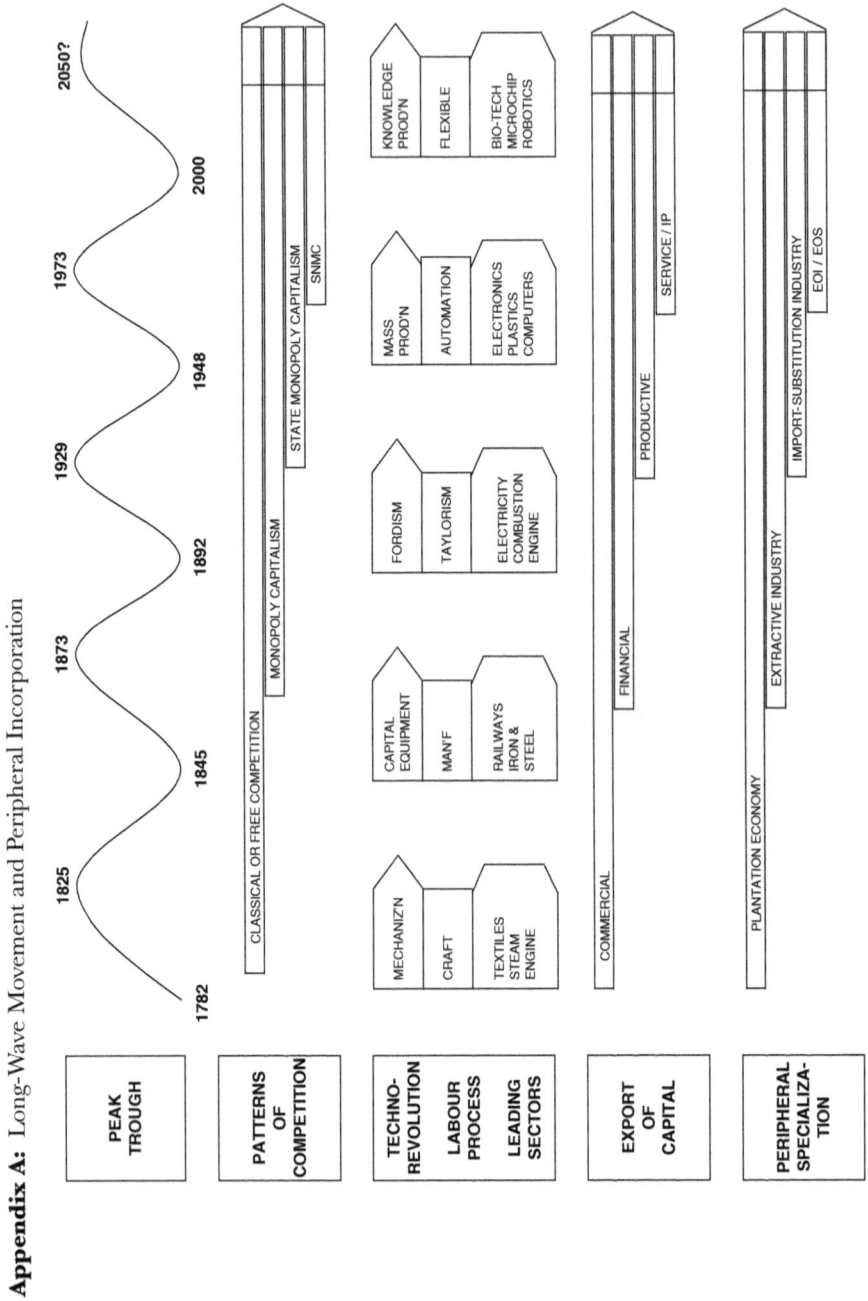

Appendix A: Long-Wave Movement and Peripheral Incorporation

	1782	1825	1845	1873	1892	1929	1948	1973	2000	2050?
PEAK TROUGH										
PATTERNS OF COMPETITION	CLASSICAL OR FREE COMPETITION			MONOPOLY CAPITALISM			STATE MONOPOLY CAPITALISM SNMC			
TECHNO-REVOLUTION										
LABOUR PROCESS	MECHANIZN CRAFT		CAPITAL EQUIPMENT MANF		FORDISM TAYLORISM		MASS PROD'N AUTOMATION		KNOWLEDGE PROD'N FLEXIBLE	
LEADING SECTORS	TEXTILES STEAM ENGINE		RAILWAYS IRON & STEEL		ELECTRICITY COMBUSTION ENGINE		ELECTRONICS PLASTICS COMPUTERS		BIO-TECH MICROCHIP ROBOTICS	
EXPORT OF CAPITAL	COMMERCIAL			FINANCIAL			PRODUCTIVE		SERVICE / IP	
PERIPHERAL SPECIALIZA-TION	PLANTATION ECONOMY			EXTRACTIVE INDUSTRY			IMPORT-SUBSTITUTION INDUSTRY		EOI / EOS	

Appendix B: Long-Wave Movement, Technological Diffusion and the Periphery

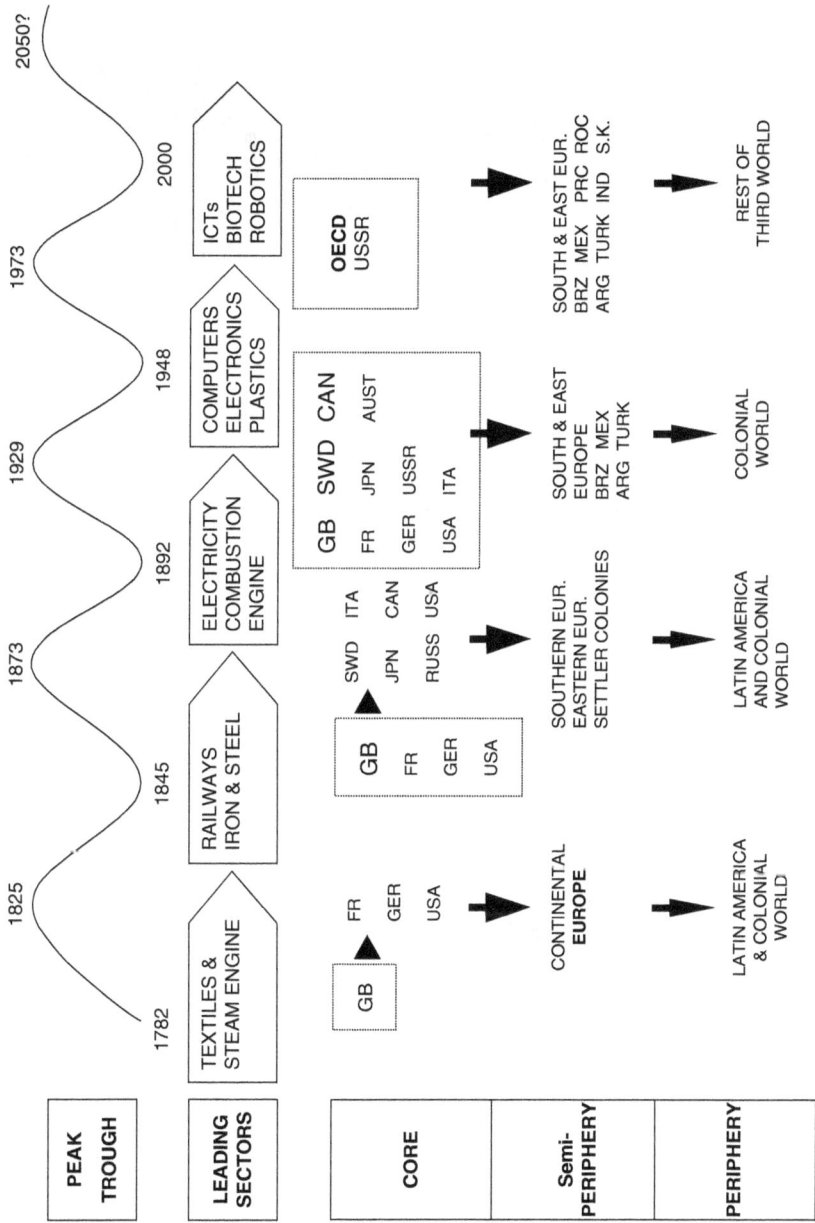

Appendix C: Peripheral Integration and Long-Wave Theory (Source: Stewart 1993)

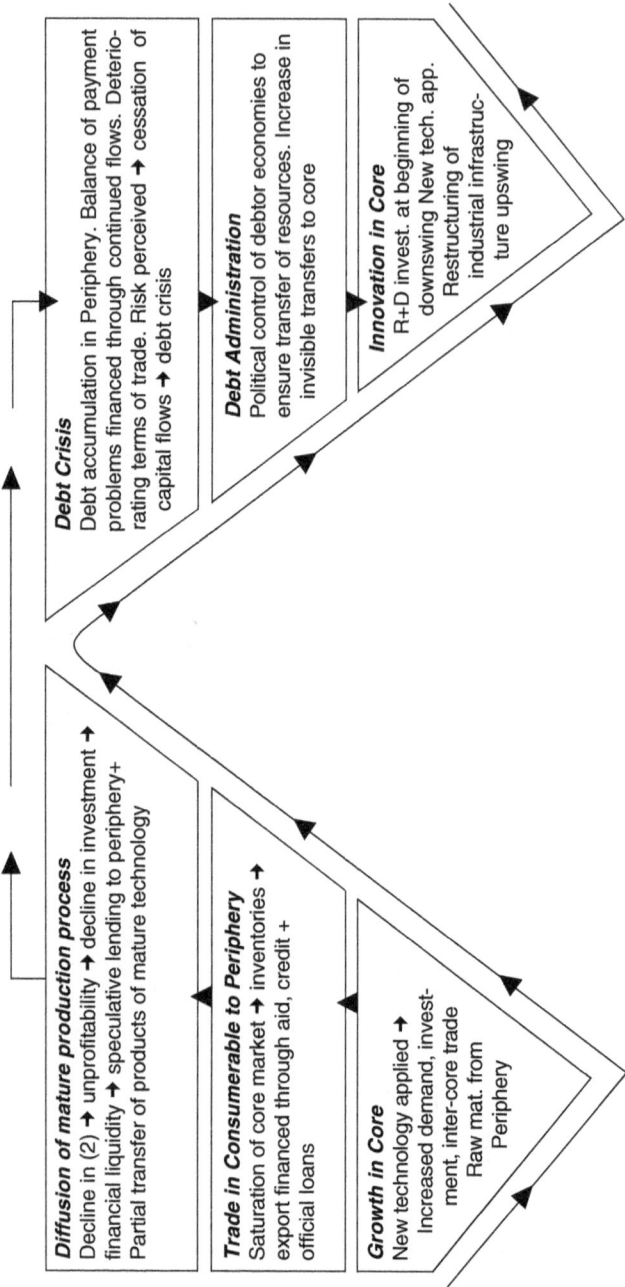

Chapter Eight:

RAGNAR NURKSE AND THE LAW & ECONOMICS OF DEVELOPMENT

Wolfgang Drechsler[*]

We economists should always be ready to adapt the framework of our thinking if our work is to have relevance to the changing real world. (Nurkse 1959, 283)

Introduction

Ragnar Nurkse (1907–1959) is one of the founding fathers of classic development economics (also called classical economic development theory, or early development economics) as it emerged during the times after World War II. His work on capital formation, balanced growth and international capital flow was highly important, and his influence as an academic teacher at Columbia University was significant. In several respects, Nurkse is quite easily applicable today, not least because his ideas of globalization and governance are largely the ones used currently (see Nurkse 1952a, 576) – even down to the importance of tourism (1935a, 21).

The purpose of this essay is first, to show that Nurkse can also be classified as a Law & Economics thinker. Given the recent interest in the Law & Economics of Development, showing how a classic figure in the field successfully used such

[*] This essay was originally delivered, in a different form that included a biographical part and a larger survey of Nurkse's œuvre, at the 20th Consecutive Law & Economics Workshop in Erfurt on 5 April 2007. I would like to thank Rainer Kattel and Erik S. Reinert for their help and criticism; Ingbert Edenhofer for proofreading the essay; and the participants of the Erfurt and Tallinn workshops, especially Jan Kregel, Gerrit Meijer and Robert M. Stern, for a lively and helpful discussion. Research for this essay has been funded by ETF grant no. 6703, on 'Ragnar Nurkse and Development Policy', 2006–2009.

an approach might be of considerable interest, especially because development economics is an emotional field that may well profit from the 'objectivizing' the function of Law & Economics. Nurkse's classic contribution underlines that, and how development economics can be done *sine ira et studio*, and perhaps to a greater effect, via, or at least including, such an approach. Nurkse's focus on what effect a program really has, rather than is supposed to have, and on what a policy can steer or change and what not, based on a typically Stiglerian attention to aggregate welfare (Stigler 1992), seem especially productive. Second, based on extrapolations from Nurkse, the attempt is made to present a tentative description of what the Law & Economics of Development could look like.

Nurkse's Work

Balanced Growth

Nurkse is probably best known for his advocacy for balanced growth (see especially 1957b), i.e., the idea that developing economies should grow in all sectors so that people there can become each other's domestic customers (1957b, 247 def.). This aspect was not invented by Nurkse alone, but emerged in discussions with Rosenstein-Rodan and C. Furtado. It is, in short, based on 'the important idea that though each commodity may find an expansion unprofitable because of limitations of the market, a coordinated expansion of all productive activities could be profitable for all producers' (Basu 1987, 687 – though, as Nurkse says, not 'all' but 'some').

Although often seen as the counter-view to comparative advantage, for Nurkse (1957b, 244), this was not an antagonism; he intended balanced growth to supplement comparative advantage, and in any case, 'even 'unbalanced' and unsteady growth through foreign trade is surely much better than no growth at all.' But the question would be whether limited means 'should be used to promote comparative advantage' or 'diversified so as to provide markets for each other locally' (1957b, 241). Still, in his opinion, the entire 'theory of international specialization as such is a static analysis' (1957b, 254), and comparative advantage, especially in raw materials and for the poorest countries, was also heavily diminishing when he wrote (1959, 294–297).

For Nurkse, balanced growth is about getting out of the mess, not a panacea (1957b, 248), and the point was not having at home, in the developing countries, 'a little bit of everything', but 'establishing a pattern of mutually supportive investments over a range of industries' (1957b, 252). This means that 'external resources, even if they become available in the most desirable forms, are not enough. They do not automatically provide a solution to the problem of capital accumulation in underdeveloped areas. No solution is possible without strenuous domestic efforts, particularly in the field of public finance' (1952a, 582; 1964, 140). From today's perspective, we would emphasize what is certainly in Nurkse's argument but not stressed as much as the inner development aspect of balanced growth, that it also significantly improves the external balance (current account).

Following Singer, Nurkse (1956, 144; see 1959, 289 would also say that Foreign Direct Investment might create a dual economy, heightening the tensions. In fact, foreign financing in developing countries may subsidize, and has often ended up subsidizing, the wealthy strata of society and the like, often actually ensuring their lock-in of the domestic economy and preventing any serious development. For the well-known reasons, such as cheap exports of raw materials, it may also aid the wealthy countries more than the receiving ones (Kregel 2004, 1–4). 'The upshot is that large-scale foreign aid had better not be relied upon; countries should use their own resources to the utmost. This conclusion again is a platitude... Domestic effort is the first prerequisite. Without it even the most lavish outside aid could not ensure progress' (Nurkse 1958, 77).

Capital Formation

The sister concept to balanced growth is capital formation, which is only possible if, in a given developing country, there is a large enough overall capacity to save. However, the capacity to save is dependent on the relative, not on the absolute level of real income, and this is influenced by the modern information mechanisms that spread 'Western' lifestyles all around the globe (Nurkse 1952a, 577–580). According to this very classic, indeed Puritan-seeming view (which Nurkse manages to discuss without any reference to Max Weber), following J. S. Duesenberry,[1] capital formation is marred in its execution by the 'desire for social emulation through conspicuous consumption' (1956, 58), but also by the fact that, simply, people are exposed to new and good devices, see what is possible, and want them (1956, 58–59; generally, 58–81). It is the gap between countries that matters, not absolute growth of income (1956, 63), and developing countries 'now accept the same standards of economic welfare. They therefore *feel* poorer than others, and that is what matters' (1958, 75). These countries were once set apart and had their own values; since then, American ones 'have conquered the world' (1958, 75). Key here are 'American movies, the radio, and aviation' (1956, 64) and American advertising (62). All this does not create, but increases the problems of the worst-developed countries (1956, 70).

In this context, Nurkse (1947, 148, incl. note 2) chides Keynes for the latter's proclivity against saving and for spending, mostly on aesthetic, anti-Victorian grounds – this is 'pernicious when transplanted to the conditions in which underdeveloped countries find themselves' (1964, 148). Rather, the 'two components of capital formation, saving and investment, depend on thrift and enterprise' (1964, 151), and 'Nothing matters so much as the quality of the people,' featuring optimally 'initiative, prudence, ingenuity and foresightedness' (1964, 155), the 'human qualities of enterprise and initiative', hallmarks of the middle class (1964, 17). The policy consequences are that 'it is well for the state to leave scope for the exercise of these qualities and to reduce barriers to their development. The state might withdraw from areas where individual enterprise has learned to stand on its own feet and turn its attention to other fields where its powers are needed to clear the way' (1964, 156).

Governance

In all of this, Nurkse strongly promotes good governance, not remaining on the static level of institutions, but, in a very timely and relevant way, on working structures, action and administrative capacity (On governance, esp. Nurkse 1964, 95, 140–141). In this, he prefigures the current 'Good Governance' discourse without the latter's impositional pitfalls, such as telling the developing countries to adopt certain precise institutions and policies the donor countries only established after getting off the ground, if ever at all.[2] In acknowledging that for administrative capacity (as in many respects), one needs good institutions as well as good people, he would have been very unpopular in scholarly circles dealing with these issues until very recently, but by 2007 his thoughts are again 'state of the art' in this respect as well (Ottmann 2005, 24).

Key for development along Nurkse's lines is 'domestic action in the receiving countries' (Nurkse 1956, 150), because once governance capacity is there for outside investment control, then also internally things can be done (1956, 150). If a country has a hold over its domestic economy – a capacity question (1956, 141) – then all looks better, but this is too rarely the case; capacity is weak for fiscal policy exactly in the countries that need it the most (1952c, 151, 264–265).

Still, development policy cannot end with this recognition – 'we yield to the vicious circle of poverty' is the worst attitude, because exactly here, 'there may be some hope of breaking the circle' (1964, 143). The task is to increase domestic capacity, not to be defeatist about it (1952c, 264–265). And it is the task of the economists to push for that (1952c, 265), although, of course, the issue is one of governance.

Law & Economics

Before we now look at whether and how Nurkse qualifies as a Law & Economics thinker, one first must define what Law & Economics is. My definition (Drechsler 2005a, 2005b, 2005c, 2003, 2002, 2001, 2000a, 1998) is a rather larger and more all-encompassing one than perhaps usual.[3]

Generally speaking, Law & Economics refers to the economic analysis of the law, or – the other side of the coin – to the study of the influence of the law, widely understood and including institutions generally, on the economy. The first aspect of Law & Economics is a form of legal realism, i.e., the concern with what effect a law really has, rather than with what effect it is supposed to have or addresses. The basis of this kind of Law & Economics, thus, lies in Plato's sentence, 'This is what the law-maker must often ask himself: What is my purpose? Do I indeed achieve this or rather miss my goal?' (*Nomoi* 744a; on Plato and Law & Economics, see Drechsler 2005a, 2003, 2002). Key here is a differentiation between the simple goal of a law and its *telos*, i.e., the final purpose it is supposed to achieve, which might be quite different from the goal. In fact, the realization that a given law fulfills its goal but not its *telos* is sometimes one of the most helpful insights of a Law & Economics analysis.

The same holds true, *mutatis mutandis*, for the second aspect of Law & Economics, the 'institutionalist' one, as well. This aspect, which for the context of nineteenth century Germany (and particularly well explained by Grossekettler 2005, 690–692), goes back to the 'natural' and traditional interweaving of legal and economic problems, as well as those of governance generally, i.e., the integrated 'State Sciences' or *Staatswissenschaften* approach since the days of Christian Wolff (see Backhaus 2005, 1–2), neglected during most of the twentieth century until their rebirth in the form of concept of governance.

Of course, all definition, or at least much of it, is a matter of power, or at least of dominance, and this is *a fortiori* true with areas, fields, or research programs such as Law & Economics, which are more 'constructed' than 'found'. However, I would say that such a rather wide approach as the one outlined above is certainly at least viable, as the publication and reception of J. G. Backhaus' *Elgar Companion to Law and Economics* (2005, which is the second edition, and there was a paperback edition of the first as well) indicate. The standard to which we shall hold Nurkse is the standard used (implicitly) for the *Elgar Companion*, and specifically, there in Part IX, the 'Classical Authors in Law and Economics' section (Backhaus 2005, 475–749).

Another question is whether in Law & Economics analysis, one has to focus on neoclassical/mathematical economics. I would argue that the opposite is the case, because realism is systemic for Law & Economics, while neoclassical/ mathematical economics is marked by a systemic lack thereof (see Drechsler 2000b), but in the Nurksean context, this is less important, as he is certainly no modeler or formalizer, but is still generally acceptable in approach and execution to most mainstream economists as well, and frequently even called neo-classical (Ros 2005, 82, 88). His work on money and currency policy certainly is, and is also so displayed; he has, thus, a certain 'neo-classical street credibility'.[4]

Nurkse's Law & Economics: Cases

Nurkse, understandably, never was connected to the Law & Economics school as it emerged in Chicago in 1959, which was the year of his death, nor does he seem to have been in touch with its founders, who were active within a very different paradigm from that of development economics. To establish Nurkse as a Law & Economics thinker, then, first just a few anecdotal examples from the development context, all along the lines that economic dynamics find their way around the attempts of policy and legislation.

Luxury Import Restrictions

One of the key aspects of Nurkse's programme of capital formation is that the money of developing nations is not wasted on importing luxury items, the tendency for which being very strong. The obvious answer to this by governments who have understood the problem, and one often carried out, is luxury import restrictions, something one would think Nurkse to be strongly in favour of. However, in a rather classical Law & Economics manner, his treatment of this issue (1964, 110–119; also 1952a, 580) makes clear that this is not so easy, because luxury import restrictions might be purely performative. What matters is what people actually do, once there are restrictions imposed, with the money they used to spend on imported luxury items. They could indeed save it, but, as Nurkse (1964, 112) points out, they could also spend it on domestic luxury items instead. And this might be more likely, because the spending pattern would still be the same, rather than shift to different behaviour.[5]

In order for luxury import restrictions to work, therefore, there would have to be restrictions on domestic luxury consumption as well (Nurkse 1964, 116). This, in turn, could for instance lead to building luxury real estate, as happened in some countries of Latin America – not necessarily a desirable effect (117). So, luxury import restrictions as a policy tool 'attack ... only the surface of the problem' (118). Taxation of luxury imports would be better, but this is politically difficult to implement, especially in poor countries, for capacity and popularity reasons (118). 'Commercial policy is easier' (118). It is 'the line of least resistance in all these cases, not the most effective or equitable line' (119).

A classic Law & Economics argument, then: A law that would theoretically have a desirable effect is marred by the likelihood that people would behave differently than the law had intended, and it is even potentially counterproductive if the changed economic behaviour would be detrimental to the *telos* of the law. The alternative, more effective way to achieve that *telos* is likely blocked though because of exogenous (political) reasons that, however, one must consider when dealing with the problem.

The Matching Principle

Another excellent Law & Economics example concerns the matching principle in foreign aid (1957b, 276–277). The issue here is infrastructure investments in developing countries that are co-financed by international organizations. Nurkse points out that while this is basically a good idea – such as creating ownership and responsibility on the part of the receiver – and while infrastructure investments are the main beneficial foreign investments in developing countries, as the lack of infrastructure is one of the main obstacles to development, there are several problems with this, of which at least one is a Law & Economics issue: If matching costs divert scarce local funding away from direct investments, local growth is easily slowed down, and thus the amortization of the infrastructure investment is actually slower, perhaps too slow to be still viable. Matching as such is a good idea, then, but if the *telos* of the principle – not the goal – is economic growth, then that idea might be detrimental to the *telos* if it were more effective to have infrastructure investments paid from foreign sources alone and direct investments by the receiving country.

The Vienna Opera

Finally, there is the case of the Vienna Opera (the "Staatsoper"; Nurkse 1964, 95–96), the reconstruction of which after the devastations of World War II was supposed to be funded by means of the Economic Cooperation Administration (ECA), the agency to implement the Marshall Plan. However, according to ECA rules, an opera was not something that could be funded, because it was not part of the infrastructure of economic development. Perhaps it is worth mentioning here that from today's development perspective, especially if we think about innovative cities, this is too short a view, because it is precisely an institution like an opera, let alone one on the scale of the Viennese one, which will not only send a message about successful recovery, but which as such will attract both entrepreneurs and representatives of production capital and which can certainly be crucial in economic development.[6] In any case, in order to circumvent this problem, one of the classical moves in such situations was exercised by the Austrian government: An electric power plant for which the state was planning to pay for anyway was submitted to be financed by the ECA, which it did, and so the government's money was free to be spent on the opera. Nurkse tells this story with the clear slant to show that earmarkings are not effective if one does not include and attend to the entire context. Yet, in the end, one would have to say anyway that the circumvention of the ECA rules actually led to the *telos* of the ECA as an institution, viz. the economic recovery of Austria after the War, being better achieved than if the idea of the rules had been honored.

Nurkse's Law & Economics: Overall

General

Moving from the anecdotal to the methodological and systematical, we can say that Ragnar Nurkse was what is today seen as a classical economist in the sense that he tried to focus on economics and economic issues only; he was not fond of either ethical or political reasoning within the economic sphere. He explicitly shunned away from 'matters relating to cultural, social and demographic conditions' (1964, 2), partially because he was not an expert in them. He was certainly not of the opinion that these spheres did not matter, but he tried to isolate the economic perspectives, and very insistingly so. This is the opposite of the *Staatswissenschaften* approach; however – and, for many people, because of it – it has a distinct Law & Economics ring to it in its attempts to keep the 'dirty world' of politics and ethics out and to isolate what the economic connections are – without relegating the political to the allegedly unimportant.[7] In the application of Law and Economics by and for public policy and public administration and management, this perspective is actually the decisive one, because it isolates and thus often makes visible the political 'manipulation' of, or at least impact on, the measures and institutions in question.

In fact, as Nurkse (1952c, 151–152) says, 'It is too easy for an economist to dump all unsolved problems on the shoulders of 'the government.' Who are '"the government"?' The framework given needs to be accepted: 'The economist as such cannot object to a goal set on non-economic grounds' (1957a, 230; see 1952c, 151, 164). Thus, in his first book, national borders are called 'from an economic perspective accidental and arbitrary' (1935a, 10, 11; 1947, 42), but the political facts are, even here, considered as well (1935a, 13). In the end, for Nurkse, if things matter, they need to be considered, be they political or sociological, or economic (1964, 68), to which he can contribute the analysis of the latter.

As an illustration: On economic grounds, Nurkse would have strongly objected to Sir H. Campbell-Bannerman's famous dictum that 'self-government is better than good government,'[8] because economically, what matters is the 'good', whereas self-rule is entirely exogenous to economic considerations. That does not mean that one cannot, or even should not, prioritize self-government, and economic analysis then needs to accept and live with this and look for optimal outcomes, but the realm of the economist within development policy is development economics, and for effective development economics as such, one needs good government.

Nurkse's work, from the beginning, is therefore strongly geared towards realism and against appearances (1935a, 3) – there is strong empiricism and a strong focus on the 'factually given' matters (1935a, 7), something not self-understood at all, and a very clear Law & Economics feature. Nurkse points out that a theory, if held too harshly, makes one neglect phenomena as they exist (1935a, 7, 10–11). And certainly, with Nurkse, a model, a picture has to be 'a representation of reality' (1935b, 22). Typical is an entire essay on the question of whether a schematic scheme (by Böhm-Bawerk) genuinely reflects reality, with an alternative provided (1935b, esp. 36: 'It is quite possible to imagine a world where the productive system of society works in the "linear" manner as shown by the triangular *tableau économique*, but it is not the world in which we live').

To this, one must add Nurkse's attention to multicausal relations, of which, for instance, he is covering one aspect, capital formation, which is a *conditio sine qua non* of development but, as everything else, not sufficient: 'Economic development has much to do with human endowments, social attitudes, political conditions – and historical accidents. Capital is a necessary but not a sufficient condition of progress' (Nurkse 1964, 1; see 1958, 72). This is an argument of Nurkse's throughout. Another example: 'This is accepting ... the common view that an import surplus is a depressive influence to be avoided at all costs. Needless to say any depressive effect of an import surplus can be offset by appropriate domestic fiscal and monetary policies' (1964, 133).

Along the same lines, there is also an emphasis on space and time (Nurkse 1935a, 10) and thus, on specificity, which alone would qualify as a serious step towards Law & Economics, rightly understood. Usually, the railroad was a key infrastructure investment (1964, 141), usually it worked, but sometimes, as in India, it did not (1964, 141 note 7). Countries are different, and things happen differently (1957b, 252; 1958, 71); 'different countries all have their special circumstances' (1964, 1). Contrary to Lewis, Nurkse does differentiate carefully between types of developing countries, such as between over- and underpopulated areas, as in the former, which are the real problem, 'a large part of the population engaged in agriculture could be removed without reducing agricultural output' (1964, 32). In the 'regions of recent settlement' (1956, 135 et passim), one had a complementary move of labour and capital; in the twentieth century, capital moved 'as a *substitute*' for people (1956, 136).

The Role of the State

So, when and how does the state come into play? State intervention is 'to a great extent an outcome of the failure of nations under laissez-faire conditions to accumulate capital rapidly enough for the desired rate of growth' (Nurkse 1956, 144). Nurkse is basically of the opinion that the state can make a difference, but that, for economic reasons, there will be side effects, or better: effects that may be more harmful than the problem that was to be ameliorated. It is not that the state cannot make a difference, nor that it should not – in specific circumstances. And Nurkse is unideologic and empirically based enough to realize that to asume a general and a priori failure of state acitivity in the economic sphere is yet another form of faith, or superstition.

Regarding this issue, there is development in Nurkse's thought. Especially in his first book, the primacy of economics is clear, and following political lines of thought is seen as basically dangerous (Nurkse 1935a, 243–245). Here, he takes an antistate and pro-economics stand – that in a country, loans by an enemy in a war could be placed and were purchased is something that Nurkse likes (1935a, 245). The segment in which he defends Keynes against the charge of economic nationalism (1947, 62–64, 70–71) makes clear how much he is against it – but it also shows his global vision: 'in the modern world nothing but a multilateral system would do' (70). So, one could almost argue that at least part of Nurkse's critical view of the state is based on his recognition of the nation-state's obsolete role in historical development.

A key Law & Economics example in this context is that Nurkse clearly sees that the liberal trading system of the nineteenth century was time-specific and only in the interest of some countries, especially Great Britain (1959, 351; 1952b, 361). Haberler's claim that Nurkse 'did not draw protectionist conclusions from his theory and did not say that 'balanced growth' requires central planning' (1961, xi) is not really correct – one should rather say that for Nurkse, as for Laspeyres or Roscher, free trade is not right or wrong as such, but dependent on country, context and circumstances (Drechsler 2000a, 239; Streissler 2005, 650; most clearly in Nurkse 1952b, 361). 'A relatively wealthy and powerful nation, as England was in the middle decades of the last century, can do things that weaker countries – with low reserves, with external deficits, with the terms of trade to worry about or infant industries to protect – cannot so easily do' (1952b, 361; cf. Reinert 1998, 2007).

Specifically, for instance, Nurkse (1957b, 256–257; 1964, 104–105) argues that infant industry protection may be sensible in some cases, but that infant creation is more important – however, capital must be there to develop the infant (1964, 105). 'To put it bluntly: tariff protection, if it can help at all, can only help the strong – it cannot help the weak' countries. (106) It could be 'quite effective' where one had a capital and labour inflow (109); so, Brazil could gain from it, for instance, but others not (107). But here, as always, realism 'gets' to Nurkse – with Bentham, he makes state intervention dependent on circumstances and specifically on the capacities of the peoples involved. (1964, 16)

Development

But if Nurkse is so hesitant to talk about goals, what reason do we have for development economics at all? Nurkse (1952a, 576) starts from an assumption of aggregate global welfare: 'World income is a more basic criterion of world prosperity than the volume of international trade' Nurkse likens international income transfers to progressive income taxation: 'Both are based on political value judgments, and both arise from pressures having to do with the coexistence and increasingly close association of people at widely different levels of material welfare' (1952a, 582). But even more so: In the end, he says early on, 'Any deviance from the optimal distribution of economic means across the earth is not only detrimental to the concerned national economies, but in the long term, it must have harmful repercussions to the state of economic supply of all mankind' (1935a, 247).

Note that it is not important to differentiate between 'what is best for the greatest number of people' and economic benefit, because, at least in a tacit context, both should actually be the same.[9] In any case, it is important to see that development of the developing countries, especially the poorest ones, is in the economic interest of the developed ones, and this is Nurkse's basis.

On the country level as well, Nurkse (1947, 58–59, 62–63) makes clear that going against neighbouring countries economically is not a viable option because it leads to conflict. 'Could the alternative be for the richer countries to provide, to some extent, for the needs of the poorer? The desirability of such transfers need not be questioned, at least so long as they are compatible with the maintenance or, better still, expansion of world income' (1964, 77).

The more the world comes together, the more income transfers are logical, just as within a single country (Nurkse 1964, 80). This not being the case, and private initiative not being enough, noneconomic means and motivations must be sought (80). They are, then, based on political value judgments (80). But, 'If we are realists, we can hardly expect a pure, automatic and non-political mechanism of international income transfers to come into existence' (81). Yet, Nurkse cautions that those transfers are unstable, just as private ones (81). Still, 'A transfer of consumable resources from the rich to the poor may increase the world total of human happiness' (93). So, exactly because of his economic focus that largely excludes ethics and politics, Nurkse arrives at a model of development economics that is not based on morals, ethics, responsibility or guilt, but rather on rational behaviour and aggregate welfare. It may be argued that the context being what it is, it is all the stronger for that.

Finally, one of Nurkse's key arguments for development economics is that he downplays, from an economic perspective, the negative role of colonialism, especially of the British nineteenth-century one.[10] He claims that exploitation did precisely not characterize colony-time investment, at least not in the later nineteenth century and beyond (Nurkse 1952a, 574–575). British 'colonial' investment was only a fraction of general investment abroad, i.e., in extraction, less than 25 per cent (1956, 138), and most of it was not in the poor countries, but rather in those of recent settlement (1957b, 242–244; 1959, 289–290, *pace* J. A. Hobson). Additionally, this investment was primarily in infrastructure and capital goods, which were needed the most to begin with. Particularly needed is investment in infrastructure: 'Lack of basic services, such as transport, power, and water supply, is a particularly serious bottleneck in the poor countries' (1956, 145–146; generally on infrastructure investment, 1957b, 259–270; 1957a, 233–235). Contrary to J. Robinson and the (neo-)Marxist view, Nurkse argues that the colonial powers did in fact not conquer existing markets, but that 'Markets were created there by labor, enterprise and capital all drawn from Europe' (1956, 142–143).

Nurkse (1952a, 573) also claims that in his time, 'the reluctance of private business capital to work for domestic markets in underdeveloped countries' has an 'obvious economic explanation.' He emphasizes the 'vicious circle of poverty' – 'a country is poor because it is poor' (1964, 4). '*The inducement to invest is limited by the size of the market*' (6), smallness meaning volume – 'The main trouble ... is not that countries are too small but they are too poor to provide markets for local industries' (1964, 19; it is this that is primarily meant by Nurkse's famous statement that 'a country is poor because it is poor,' 1964, 4). But 'International investment on private business account is attracted by markets' (1964, 29). Therefore, foreign money goes for exports of primary products to advanced countries because it makes economic sense. This 'does not reflect any sinister conspiracy or deliberate policy, still less any concerted attempt of the rich countries to exploit the poor. ... This pattern can be readily accounted for on obvious economic reasons. There is nothing sinister about it' (1964, 25).

Towards a Law & Economics of Development?

The Nurkse-based Law & Economics of Development, in principle and approach, could then perhaps be, based on the previously cited work, summed up and systematized as follows:

Goals

- The goal of development economics is Global Aggregate Welfare.
- Although there are socio-political and/or ethical reasons for development aid, which, if politically decided, need to be implemented by optimal economic means, there is also an economic rationale for development as being in the interest of everyone upon which development economics should be primarily based.
- There needs to be an incentives-based approach for all stakeholders.
- Thus, the interest of the wealthy countries, as donors as well as economic partners, needs to be made explicit, it must be clear and convincing.

- Balanced growth, specifically adjusted, is the goal – not as a panacea, but as the overall strategy under limited means.

Means

- This is achieved by genuine results orientation – no grandstanding, but realism.
- From the economic side, an almost exclusive focus on economic reasoning is necessary, but all relevant factors have to be factored in for realistic results.
- Differentiation according to country and circumstances – specificity – is crucial.
- What can be explained economically, should be.
- Economic phenomena have multiple causes and policies multiple effects – one must always think of side effects, spillovers, and repercussions.
- Therefore, there needs to be a cohesive strategy of development from the country in question, no piecemeal approach.

Governance

- For all this, domestic capacity is the key; where it is lacking, this should not be bemoaned, but it should be developed (governance capacity).
- Institutions, especially fiscal ones, and public administration and management are the key features of capacity.
- The state has, thus, an important role to play, but it is context- , capacity- and issue-dependent.
- It can and sometimes has to be strong, but in other cases the state should retrench entirely. When what is the case depends on the judgment of the three features in question.

It is open to debate whether this list could be called a serious basis for a Law & Economics of Development. It is, as was said, a set of principles, not a proto-handbook. Especially for a more comprehensive approach to such a concept, a more careful comparison and perhaps integration of Nurkse's work with that of his colleagues in Classical Development Economics, especially Lewis (1956), would very likely be necessary as well. One may say at this point already, however, that development economics being particularly divided over the question of the possibilities and powers of the state and over what purpose economics has, Nurkse is a particularly suitable starting point for a Law & Economics of Development with:

- his undogmatic approach that is not the hallmark of 'wishy-washy' but rather of attention to realism and specificity

- an approach to the state that grudgingly, but in the end pragmatically, admits to its power, potential, and sometimes necessary role in development
- a Law & Economics that is halfway between Berlin and Chicago and thus potentially acceptable to all sides of the political spectrum.

Conclusion

Fashions come and go, in development economics as much as anywhere else; the problems Nurkse addressed, in spite of the changes in time and circumstance that he was always first to acknowledge, have in several respects stayed the same, and so have, to some extent and suitably updated, his questions and even some of his answers. Twenty years ago, it was said that the 'potential of his branch of development economics remains large' (Basu 1987, 687), and today, this is not different (see, e.g., Cimoli et al. 2006). As B.-Å. Lundvall (2007) has suggested very recently, when focusing on the role of higher education and innovation systems within the less developed countries,

> In order to break out of vicious circles there is a need for a comprehensive national strategy rooted in a strong common engagement to change .... . Such a strategy needs to give much attention to human resources in general, not only higher education, but also including for instance labour market institutions. It also needs to include an industrial policy aiming at developing economic activities matching domestic competences but with positive learning curves. Studying innovation systems in Latin America, Africa and Asia we have found little evidence .... . that market forces spontaneously will establish the necessary prerequisites for catching up (36–37).

It seems that Nurkse is indeed still relevant and, as I have argued *supra*, potentially so for all wings of the spectrum of development economics.

That the latter point is quite weak, because the two sides of the discourse can also reject Nurkse's approach for the same reasons they could like it – his being positioned, as I said, halfway between Berlin and Chicago – is, however, also true. For the one side, he can be too soft on the possibilities of the state and of interventionism; for the other, he can be too much of a defender of the status quo, of 'structural violence' and of the dominance of the 'West'. What seems to be clear, to me in any case, however, is that on the one hand, from the perspective of Law & Economics, if it is not too dogmatically Chicagoesque, Nurkse provides an inroad of Law & Economics to development economics that allows for the specificities of both paradigms, and that on the other hand, a Nurksean Law & Economics so fashioned can still enrich and improve the development economics discourse, and based on the latter's foundations at that. Not, as Nurkse would have probably said, as a panacea, but as one possible way to deal with the real problems and issues at hand, now and in the times to come.

References

Backhaus, J. G. (ed.). 2005. *The Elgar Companion to Law and Economics*. 2nd edn. Cheltenham: Elgar.

Backhaus, J. G. and W. Drechsler (eds). 2006. *Friedrich Nietzsche (1844–1900): Economy and Society*. New York: Springer.

Basu, Kaushik. 1987. 'Ragnar Nurkse (1907–1959).' In *The New Palgrave* 3. London: Macmillan, 687–688.

Cimoli, M. et al. 2006. 'Institutions and Policies Shaping Industrial Development: An Introductory Note.' LEM Working Paper Series 2006/2. Pisa: Laboratory of Economics and Management, Sant'Anna School of Advanced Studies.

Drechsler, W. 2005a. 'Plato.' In Backhaus 2005, 635–641.

_____. 2005b. 'Christian Wolff'. In Backhaus 2005, 745–749.

_____. 2005c. 'Etienne Laspeyres.' In Backhaus 2005, 585–589.

_____. 2004. 'Governance, Good Governance, and Government: The Case for Estonian Administrative Capacity.' *Trames* 8 (4), 388–396.

_____. 'Plato's *Nomoi* as the Basis of Law & Economics.' In S. Scolnicov and L. Brisson (eds). *Plato's Laws: From Theory into Practice*. St. Augustin: Academia, 215–220.

_____. 2002. 'Les *Lois* de Platon, fondement de l'Économie du droit.' *Revue Française d'Histoire des Idées Politiques* 16, 399–410.

_____. 2001. 'On the Viability of the Concept of *Staatswissenschaften*.' *European Journal of Law and Economics* 12 (2), 105–111.

_____. 2000a. 'Etienne Laspeyres' *History of the Economic Thought of the Netherlanders*: A Law & Economics Classic?' *European Journal of Law and Economics* 10 (3), 235–242.

_____. 2000b. 'On the Possibility of Quantitative-Mathematical Social Science, Chiefly Economics: Some Preliminary Considerations.' *Journal of Economic Studies* 27 (4/5), 246–259.

_____. 1998. 'Christian Wolff, Law & Economics, and the Heilbronn Symposia in Economics and the Social Sciences: An Introduction.' In J. G. Backhaus (ed.). *Christian Wolff and Law & Economics: The Heilbronn Symposium* = Ch. Wolff. *Gesammelte Werke* III 45. Hildesheim: Olms, v–x.

Dutt, A. K. 2005. 'International Trade in Early Development Economics.' In Jomo and Reinert 2005, 99–127.

Ellis, H. S. 1960. Review of Nurkse 1959. *American Economic Review* 50 (1), 201–203.

Grossekettler, H. 2005. 'Lorenz von Stein.' In Backhaus 2005, 689–699.

Haberler, G. 1961. 'Introduction.' In Nurkse 1961, vii–xiii.

Jomo, K. S. and E.S. Reinert (eds). 2005. *The Origins of Development Economics: How Schools of Economic Thought Have Addressed Development*. New Delhi/London: Tulika/Zed.

Kregel, J. A. 2004. 'External Financing for Development and International Financial Instability.' G-24 Discussion Paper 32. New York: United Nations/UNCTAD.

Lewis, W. A. 1956. *The Theory of Economic Growth*. London: Allen & Unwin.

Lundberg, E. 1959. 'Introduction.' In Nurkse 1959 (book version only), 7–8.

Lundvall, B.-Å. 2007. 'Higher Education, Innovation and Economic Development.' Paper presented at the World Bank's Regional Bank Conference on Development Economics, Beijing, 16–17 January.

Nurkse, R. 1964 [1953]. *Problems of Capital Formation in Underdeveloped Countries.* 9th impr. Oxford: Basil Blackwell.

———. 1961. *Equilibrium and Growth in the World Economy.* Edited by G. Haberler and R. M. Stern. Cambridge, MA: Harvard University Press.

———. 1959. *Patterns of Trade and Development.* Wicksell Lectures 1959. Stockholm: Almqvist & Wiksell. Also in, and cited according to, 1961, 282–336.

———. 1958. Contribution to 'The Discussion of Professor Viner's Paper.' In D. Hague (ed.). *Stability and Progress in the World Economy: The First Congress of the International Economic Association.* London: Macmillan, 69–77.

———. 1957a. 'Reflections on India's Development Plan.' In 1961, 221–240.

———. 1957b. 'Balanced and Unbalanced Growth.' In 1961, 241–281.

———. 1956. 'International Investment Today in the Light of Nineteenth-Century Experience.' In 1961, 135–150.

———. 1955. Review of L. Robbins, *The Economist in the Twentieth Century. American Economic Review* 45 (3), 437–438.

———. 1952a. 'Growth in Underdeveloped Countries: Some International Aspects of the Problem of Economic Development.' *American Economic Review*, Papers and Proceedings 62 (May), 571–583.

———. 1952b. Review of J. Viner, *International Economics – Studies.* In 1961, 348–351.

———. 1952c. 'Trade Fluctuations and Buffer Policies of Low-Income Countries.' *Kyklos* 12 (3), 141–154; 'Epilogue', 244–265.

———. 1947. 'Domestic and International Equilibrium.' In 1961, 41–71.

———. 1935a. *Internationale Kapitalbewegungen.* Beiträge zur Konjunkturforschung 8. Vienna: Julius Springer.

———. 1935b. 'The Schematic Representation of the Structure of Production.' In 1961, 22–40.

Ottmann, H. 2005. *Platon, Aristoteles und die neoklassische Philosophie der Gegenwart.* Baden-Baden: Nomos.

The Oxford Dictionary of Modern Quotations. 1993. New York: Oxford University Press.

Peukert, H. 1999. 'Gustav von Schmoller.' In Backhaus 2005, 662–671.

Reinert, E. S. 2007. *How Rich Countries Got Rich ... And Why Poor Countries Stay Poor.* London: Constable & Robinson.

———. 1998. 'Raw Materials in the History of Economic Policy; or, Why List (the Protectionist) and Cobden (the Free Trader) Both Agreed on Free Trade in Corn.' In G. Cook (ed.). *The Economics and Politics of International Trade: Freedom and Trade Volume II.* London: Routledge, 275–300.

Ros, J. 2005. 'The Pioneers of Development Economics and Modern Growth Theory.' In Jomo and Reinert 2005, 81–98.

Rosenstein-Rodan, P. N. 1943. 'Problems of Industrialization of Eastern and South-Eastern Europe.' *Economic Journal* 53, 202–213.

Stigler, G. J. 1992. 'Law or Economics?' *Journal of Law and Economics* 35, 455–468.

Streissler, E. 2005. 'Wilhelm Roscher.' In Backhaus 2005, 642–651.

Webster, A. 2006. *The Debate on the Rise of the British Empire.* Manchester: Manchester University Press.

Chapter Nine:

RAGNAR NURKSE'S DEVELOPMENT THEORY: INFLUENCES AND PERCEPTIONS

Hans H. Bass*

Introduction

The present discussion on a 'rebirth' of systematic development economics (Herrera 2006) renders it appropriate to look more closely at its theoretical foundations before it became absorbed in an ad-hoc reasoning vis-à-vis the increasingly complex reality of (many) falling-behind and (few) catching-up processes, eventually falling into near oblivion for three decades (Krugman 1994). Undoubtedly, Ragnar Nurkse, the great Estonian-American economist, was undoubtedly one of the most rigorous theoreticians and therefore his contribution to the sub-discipline of development economics deserves special attention when discussing the relevance of classical development economics for today.

Ragnar Nurkse's contribution to economics was in three areas, the later being an extension of the previous ones (for details on the bio-bibliographical background see Basu 1987, Kukk 2004, Bass 2007): The first period of his work (in the 1930s) was dedicated to research on international capital movements. In the middle period (in the 1930s/1940s), he additionally covered issues of international trade and finance. Finally (from the mid-1940s to his death in 1959), he considered the international commodity and factor

---

* The author is grateful for a grant by *Konrektorat Forschung* of Bremen University of Applied Sciences, which allowed research in Princeton University Library. The author also gratefully acknowledges valuable comments on a previous version of this paper by J. Krishnamurty and Hans Martin Niemeier. The usual disclaimer applies.

movements and their financial framework as merely one aspect of a broader issue in the world economy, to which he then turned his attention: the overcoming of structural underdevelopment. His three most eminent publications are hallmarks of these three phases: *Internationale Kapitalbewegungen* (in German, 1935), *International Currency Experience* (1944) and *Problems of Capital Formation in Underdeveloped Countries* (1953).

The founding fathers of development economics, from Rosenstein-Rodan in his ground-breaking essay of 1943 to Hirschman's 1958 publication considered 'development' as tantamount to *output growth by industrialization*. Contrary to the static idea of realizing welfare gains by adhering to absolute or comparative advantages of a country – be it in agriculture, in minerals, or in labour – development economists thus promoted a dynamic *diversification* of an economy. This still appropriate, albeit already then somewhat 'heterodox' approach implied an active role of the state in changing the economic structure by generating and re-allocating rents (i.e., gains that the non-interfered market would not create).

On the other hand, early development economists shared some 'orthodox' views, which would soon prove to be shortcomings, when applied to development politics. The main issue was probably that the pioneers of development economics regarded the relation of the macro-economic aggregates (employment, consumption, saving and investment) as the main or even sole determinant of underdevelopment or development. More than a decade was to pass before development economists became aware of other and equally important aspects of development, such as access to food, health and education, or issues of economic vulnerability, income distribution and spatial agglomeration. Dudley Seers' (1967) emphasis on *social* issues represented as a turning point in development thinking: development economics became more specific. Eventually, the differentiation of the developing world – most prominently the emergence of newly industrializing countries and least developed countries respectively – triggered focussing on *cultural* country-specific factors as relevant determinants of development (Hofstede 1980). Finally, the Brundtland Report (WCED 1987) made clear that development had to be defined and approached on a global and inter-generational level, taking into account the long-term *environmental* balances. At about the same time Amartya K. Sen pointed to *normative* issues such as empowerment, freedom for people to lead the kind of life they value, and justice as integral elements of the development process (Sen 1999, with antecedents in the 1980s).

The development of the development doctrine (Thorbecke 2007, Nafziger 2007) finally culminated in such complex definitions of development as those underlying the 'Millennium Development Goals' (for a critical view of the arbitrary proliferation of the development goals, see Vandemoortele 2007).

Without doubt, all the above-mentioned considerations – social, cultural, environmental, value-related – were important amendments in framing development processes. Nevertheless, in spite of the enlargement of the development idea, the notion of diversifying economic growth – by increasing the division of labour, i.e., by moving from subsistence agriculture to a diversified industrial society and by sacrificing today's consumption for tomorrow's, i.e., by saving and investment – remains at the core of all development concepts, other aspects forming additional layers (the only exception being the 'zero growth' school (Daly 1996): here the core of the model remains hollow).

Under these circumstances the present author finds it most appropriate to aim at a *diachronical* 'historical reconstruction' (Blaug 2001, 150–151) of Nurkse's development theory rather than at an *anachronical* 'rational reconstruction'. This paper therefore does not aspire to the 'almost irresistible' temptation to reconstruct in the light of all we now know. It rather wishes to reconstruct one of the classical theories, Nurkse's idea of the circular causation of a lack of real capital in poor countries, 'as faithfully as possible to the times in which they were written' (Blaug 2001, 151).

It is in this attempt that we look at how contemporaries perceived the main ideas of Ragnar Nurkse in the field of development economics. This approach will also include a study of 'the previous generation of thinkers in order to understand the context in which the economists in question were writing' (Blaug 2001, 151). In particular, the paper will trace the relation of Keynes and Schumpeter to Nurkse. Finally, it will look into Nurkse-inspired present thinking on the causes of persistent poverty in developing countries.

The Nurkse Model in the View of its Contemporaries

A Disciplinary Classification of the Nurkse Model

Given today's increasing awareness of development thinkers and practitioners regarding the necessity of interdisciplinary approaches to their subject, it should be emphasized that Ragnar Nurkse's diagnosis of 'underdevelopment'[1] and his policy suggestions are strictly confined to economics. Contemporary book reviews already criticized Nurkse's 1953 opus for neglecting non-economic factors in development, such as his failure to consider capital formation in education, skills and health (Richmond 1953, 467, thus anticipating ideas of the human capital theory), even for 'economic myopia.' (Hagen 1955, 233) At various instances, however, Nurkse had commented on 'educational investments' as one of the basic targets for capital formation (such as Nurkse 1957, 199). But why did Nurkse not make such factors of development explicit in his model?

Nurkse's concentration on the formation of capital in the explanation of poverty and in the formulation of policies to overcome this was not so much because he was not aware of social and cultural determinants of poverty. He rather intended to deliberately confine himself to a problem, to the solution of which he as an economist could contribute most. This becomes apparent in the introduction to his 1953 book: 'Economic development has much to do with human endowments, social attitudes, political conditions – and historical accidents. Capital is a necessary but not a sufficient condition of progress' (Nurkse 1953, 1).

As an economist, Nurkse had been trained in Edinburgh and in Vienna in the tradition of the Anglo-American 'formal' school rather than in the tradition of the then still important German Historical School.[2] Consequently, in development economics he refrained from subscribing to 'substantivist' approaches.[3] This contributed to an abstraction from real-world societies to a degree that nearly no allowance was made for country-specific institutional factors in the 'typical' developing country as analyzed in his studies – although he was definitely aware of such factors, particularly when it came to policies. However, 'the question of method [of development] must be decided on the ground of broader considerations; on the ground, especially, of the human qualities and motive forces existing in any particular society. The economist, as an economist, has no categorical imperatives to issue on this subject' (Nurkse 1953, 16). In an unpublished note on 'excess population,' Nurkse even amended this argument: 'Low productivity is the problem.... The econ.[omic] remedy for the problem is capital creation (though I [...] readily agreed that non-economic remedies may be more important)' (Nurkse unpublished n.d. a).

Nurkse's Poverty Trap Model

From the idea that in poor countries poverty as under-*consumption* results from under-*production* of material commodities (which in the light of A. K. Sen's 'entitlement' theory is not at all trivial), Nurkse identifies the lack of real capital as the main bottleneck in economic development. Lack of real capital is both the starting point and the end of a causal chain.

Nurkse analyzes the deficiency of real capital both from the supply side and from the demand side. The supply of capital is determined by the ability and the desire to save. In poor countries saving is restricted due to low income, which mainly has to be used for consumption ('Engels' Law'). In addition, low income countries save little because of the *demonstration effect*,[4] not only valid inside a country, but also between countries: higher standards of living elsewhere encourage levels of consumption that are higher than feasible. Low income, on the other hand, results from low labour productivity, which again is a result of deficient capital. Thus the circle is closed on this side. The demand for capital depends on the propensity of enterprises to invest. They invest little in a country with low purchasing power, which is the case, as the real income is low – thus closing this part of the circle.

The system's condition thus described has two characteristics: the economy is in a state of stable equilibrium, and the equilibrium is sub-optimal. Nurkse chose the term *underdevelopment equilibrium*, analogous to the *underemployment equilibrium* analyzed by Keynes. We may also call it a 'poverty trap' (see Bowles, Durlauf and Hoff 2007), as no endogenous forces exist to overcome poverty. Consequently, Nurkse rejected the market optimism of the liberal school: 'Economic progress is not a spontaneous or automatic affair' (Nurkse 1953, 10). According to Nurkse, nor could monetary and fiscal policy measures alone, such as those advised by Keynes to increase monetary demand in a state of cyclical economic stagnation, overcome the vicious circle of deficient real capital and poverty in developing countries. What would rather be necessary would be an extraordinary effort, aiming directly at the provision of real capital – the *big push*.

As investment for an individual entrepreneur is ruled out due to the small size of markets, it becomes necessary that enterprises all at once create demand for all others. Only by 'a wave of capital investments' (Nurkse 1953, 13) would it be possible to overcome the stationary equilibrium, to get a self-enforcing growth process off the ground and to turn the *vicious circle* into a *virtuous circle*.

The process should be sustained by private investment, encouraged by growing markets. To initiate this process, Nurkse thought that governmental mobilization of 'virtual' domestic saving, especially in the form of disguised rural unemployment, could be feasible, such as the use of rural surplus labour for the construction of capital goods, especially infrastructure. A further source of initial capital was seen in the form of credit provided by international organizations. If there were enough initial investment, an avalanche of private investment would be set in motion.

It is interesting to note that Nurkse thus did not consider the developing countries as poor in resources, forever dependent on the development aid flow of rich countries to overcome their development bottleneck. He rather stressed that the mobilization of their own resources would have to be the starting point for development.

With regard to the industries this avalanche should be directed towards, Nurkse (1962, 247) argued for 'a balanced pattern of investment in a number of different industries, so that people working more productively, with more capital and improved techniques, become each other's customers.' While Paul N. Rosenstein-Rodan, W. Arthur Lewis and others shared this idea, Nurkse was undoubtedly its most influential advocate.

Critical Debates on the Nurkse Model

Contemporary critical debates on the Nurkse model refer to various issues, including the industrialization strategy (balanced vs. unbalanced growth), the coordination agency (state vs. markets) and the international implications (free trade vs. import substitution):

A major debate in early development economics was on the subject of balanced vs. unbalanced growth. Contrary to the Balanced Growth adherents, contemporaries such as Albert O. Hirschman, Paul Streeten and others argued that due to the lack of capital in developing countries investment projects had to be selected according to the strength of their backward and forward linkages ('unbalanced growth'). The empirical fact of sectoral and/or regional polarization in economic development rather than presuming equalization has a long history in (heterodox) economic thinking: probably commencing with the ideas of Joseph Schumpeter and continuing to Paul Romer's New Growth Theory, in which knowledge as a factor of production with increasing marginal productivity is responsible for cluster generation, and to the Gravity Theory of International Trade. Why was it that Nurkse not only showed no awareness of this thinking, but actually argued for a strategy counter to the factual development? Basically, he was afraid that the Hirschman approach would only allow for progress at a snail's pace. According to Nurkse, the vertical transmission of growth impulses along the value chain would take longer than a strategy starting from the demand for a multitude of consumer products, thus the argument for a horizontally oriented approach to finally achieve 'diversification'. Some of Nurkse's remarks show that he became obsessively involved in a rather sterile debate on 'balanced vs. unbalanced growth' strategy in his later years. In fact, 'the similarities between the balanced and unbalanced growth theses are more important than their apparently different prescriptions' (Thorbecke 2007, 9).

Another issue discussed among contemporaries concerned the role of markets or the state as possible coordination mechanisms. As Nurkse considered a balanced pattern to be one where investment would be according to the income elasticity of demand for the final products, he did not want to rule out market forces in determining the growth pattern of an economy – but rather assist their realization (for different understandings of balanced growth, see Scitovsky (1987)).

There are, of course, specific demands of the balanced-growth model regarding planning. Nurkse even stated: 'From the technical viewpoint of capital theory, the case for socialism is that it cuts the connection between investment activity and consumption change; all investment becomes autonomous' (Nurkse 1959, 297). Nevertheless, Nurkse should not be considered as an unconditional follower of central planning methods: 'as regards the mechanics I am inclined to be 'liberal', accepting as alternative possibilities: central planning; [...] spontaneous advance on a wide front; or the 'disequilibrium' method of zigzag growth' (Nurkse 1962, 80). Actually, Nurkse can be best addressed as an advocate of a 'mixed' economic system: 'To rely merely on the price system for the structural changes that constitute development may not be enough. But mere 'programming' [...] is probably not enough either. In the last resort we must rely on the acts of faith that spring from enterprise private or public, or both' (Nurkse 1957, 2).

The propagation of a mixed economic system did not only refer to the coordination mechanisms, but also to property rights. Nurkse considered independent collective bodies to be the main agents for the accumulation of overhead capital: 'some independent and continuous body, unaffected, if possible, by shifting cabinets and parliamentary fortunes' (Nurkse 1953, 154).

Overall, this is a non-dogmatic approach (see also Hancock 1954, 315). Nevertheless it is obvious that an application of this model in reality could not have abstained from complex planning techniques, the adherence to which was much in accordance with what Stiglitz (1998) had called the first (state-optimistic) phase of development thinking on the relation between state and markets with India as a role model – but which, as von Hayek argued, is an effort in principle doomed to failure due to the unpredictability of consumer decisions.

It is interesting to note that Eugenio Gudin, a Brazilian, i.e., an economist with first-hand experience of the actual situation of a developing country, was particularly critical of Nurkse's state-optimism:

> The big-push model cannot very well avoid a bias toward Government action. It is not quite conceivable as a joint and simultaneous procedure of a group of entrepreneurs. And in countries of a precarious level of political education such as these Government's intervention in the private economic sector has proved very harmful indeed. On the other hand I do not think that the spirit of enterprise and private initiative lacks in these countries. What lacks is 'know-how' and what is excessive is 'industrial protection', these two factors together being largely responsible for the comparatively slow pace of development. (Gudin unpublished n.d., 5)

Another much-debated issue was the presumed consequences of balanced growth on the international division of labour. Would it demand dissociation from the world economy to carry out investments in such a planned manner?

And would horizontal diversification of production run contrary to specialization in absolute and comparative advantages and thus abstain from urgently needed efficiency gains?

The issue was targeted by balanced growth adherents by pointing to the fact that classical trade theory is static; welfare effects will originate from specialization only once and cannot be replicated if there is no change in the production structure – or economic development. According to Nurkse, a balanced-growth model could best produce such dynamics of superseding cost advantages: 'Balanced growth is the best friend that international trade can have' (Nurkse 1961, 257). Nurkse definitely did not see trade as an engine of growth – but probably as an additional device. A successful integration of developing countries into the world economy, however, demands security in the planning framework: this would be the case when following a further model, to the temporary realization of which Ragnar Nurkse had contributed substantially: an international regime of fixed exchange rates.

From these contemporary discussions one might conclude that the Nurkse model was remarkably coherent, albeit not a completely convincing concept. Some blind spots may be seen with hindsight and misdirections taken by development policies in the following decades seem to have been inherent in the views of the early development economists, including Nurkse: the alleged direct link between growth and poverty reduction (which was rejuvenated only recently by the 'revisionist' school, cf. Dollar and Kraay 2001) and, closely connected, a disregard of 'pre-modern' forms of production (small-scale family-based agriculture, rural industry) partly due to an imperturbable belief in the ubiquitous existence of increasing economies of scale and of utility-maximizing behaviour of economic agents. This becomes particularly clear when reading Nurkse's comments on the Indian Development Plan (Nurkse 1957), arguing in favour of a concentration of land holdings, in favour of urban agglomeration and against cottage industry. There are also scattered comments on Russia and China in his work pointing in the same direction.

Yet it has to be noted that the disasters of the Stalinist and Maoist collectivizing of agriculture had not yet surfaced: Nurkse commented on Russia before historians began to unearth the truth about the Ukrainian famine of 1932–33 and other results of collectivizing in agriculture, before China had even set out on the Great Leap Forward (1958–59), before state-owned enterprises around the world had collapsed – but also before the dynamics of the informal sector had been discovered (Hart, ILO, de Soto) and agriculture-led industrialization had been discussed as an option (Adelman). However, an early hint on the neglect of agriculture connected with the Nurksean assumption that peasant livelihoods should be limited in order to direct 'virtual' saving (in the form of disguised unemployment) to capital construction projects can already be found in Condliffe (1954).

Looking Back: Theories Influencing Nurkse's Circular Model

The general idea of a circular causation of poverty, a vicious circle, does not originate with Nurkse, for whom it was already 'a phrase that crops up frequently' (Nurkse 1953, 5) – the idea that in a precarious situation everything is blocked by everything is obvious. However, Nurkse did not intend to create a formula covering all aspects of poverty generation, but to analyze the circular causation of a lack of real capital. Here, particularly, influences by Keynes and by Schumpeter can be discerned.

Schumpeter and Keynes are, to a considerable extent, antipodes (for a comparison of Keynes and Schumpeter published during Nurkse's lifetime see: Smithies 1951). Keynes argued that abstaining from consumption could not only lead to decreasing demand for consumption goods but also to a decrease in demand for investment goods. Saving could thus set a depression spiral in motion. Schumpeter on the other hand argues that saving provides capital for innovation (although only of secondary importance after creation of money by bank credit). Innovations provide new production opportunities, which set off an expansive process. And while Schumpeter's interest is in the advantages in the long run (i.e. techniques of production changing), Keynes argues with the problems of the present (i.e. techniques of production unchanged). How can such differences be reconciled by Nurkse? The answer lies in his holistic view of the underdevelopment situation.

Furthermore, Nurkse could build on similarities in Keynes' and Schumpeter's approach. Both deviate from the (neo-) classical view of equilibria: Keynes analyzes the fact that an equilibrium can exist without the clearance of markets, Schumpeter defines the disequilibrium as the normal situation of capitalism. As a consequence for Nurkse, in view of the problems of the developing world, scepticism toward market forces and optimism regarding central planning seemed to be in place. 'Balanced Growth' was therefore the correct answer in terms of economic policies to what had been analyzed in terms of economic theory.

Nurkse and Keynes

Nurkse was well acquainted with various aspects of Keynes' (1883–1946) oeuvre: during his student days in Edinburgh (1929–32) Nurkse had already been introduced to the work of Keynes and had carefully read, as proven by his exercise books (Ragnar Nurkse Papers, Box 3, Public Policy Papers, Department of Rare Books and Special Collections, Princeton University Library), books such as 'Indian Currency and Finance' (1913) and 'A Treatise on Probability' (1921). Nurkse seems to have met Keynes personally during the Bretton Woods conference and took a great interest in the publishing process of Seymour E. Harris' 'The New Economics' (1947) – the first book to provide a complete picture of 'Keynesianism' immediately after the death of its hero in 1946.

In the second phase of his own work, Nurkse made *explicit* implications of Keynesian theory for international economic relations, while he *enlarged* Keynesian theory in the formation period of development economics, to which Nurkse contributed in the third phase of his own oeuvre.

Nurkse elaborated on Keynes' theory in his 1947 contribution on 'Domestic and International Equilibrium' to the book edited by S. E. Harris. While Nurkse considered the (neo-) classical theory of international economic relations to be concerned with the *compositional* or *allocation* aspects of international trade only, Nurkse applied Keynesian macroeconomics ('Keynes gave us no positive and systematic account of international relationships in his system' Nurkse 1947, 284) to the results of imports and exports on the *volume* of national income (Nurkse 1947, 268) and aimed at providing links between international trade theory and business cycle theory (Nurkse 1947, 264).

The international division of labour – rather than being at the centre of economic analysis and economic policy to realize (static) welfare gains – became instrumental in Nurkse's view of how to generate employment: 'Just as free trade by itself cannot ensure full employment, so the suppression of trade, though it might increase employment numerically, can never bring real prosperity. It is utterly senseless to create employment by reducing the level of economic efficiency. There are other ways of solving the employment problem' (Nurkse 1947, 276). This already foreshadowed Nurkse's idea that the balanced-growth strategy is supplemented rather than questioned by the specialization of regions and nations according to comparative advantages.

Another interesting foreshadowing of Nurkse's later ideas can be seen in the idea of *simultaneity*, which is also used as a reference to Keynes in his assessment of Keynes's contribution to the problems of international economics. Keynes is quoted by Nurkse regarding the notion that policies to overcome national equilibria-cum-unemployment should be safeguarded by a simultaneous proceeding of many countries in order to avoid pressure from outside:

> We should attach great importance to the simultaneity of the movement towards increased expenditure. For the pressure on its foreign balance

which each country fears as the result of increasing its own loan-expenditure, will cancel out if other countries are pursuing the same policy at the same time. (Keynes, *The Means to Prosperity* 1933; quoted in Nurkse 1947, 281)

This idea becomes juxtaposed in Nurkse's later writing to overcome the international problem of (relative) underdevelopment by balanced growth. Nurkse's 1947 article can therefore be understood as an important step in his deviation from the subject of international economics to the emerging subject of development economics.

Undeniably, Nurkse appreciated Keynesian economics: 'Keynesian economics is a powerful and flexible tool of analysis. At any rate formally, it can be adapted to all kinds of different situations' (Nurkse 1953a, 148). However, in spite of being labelled as a 'Keynesian,' as Haberler for instance can be understood ('like most economists of his generation, Nurkse was quickly drawn into the stream of Keynesian thought' (Haberler 1962, p. viii)), a somewhat anti-Keynesian position in terms of criticizing the Keynesian 'bias against saving and in favour of spending' by Nurkse was discovered by book critics of Condliffe (1954, 454) and particularly Bronfenbrenner (1954, 176).

In my opinion, Nurkse actually stood aloof from Keynesian economics and in fact there are various arguments in his development theory that are not in accordance, if not in contrast, to Keynes' argumentation – Nurkse either elaborating on differences between the monetary sphere and the real sphere, considering different time frames, seeking a middle way between classical and Keynesian views, or classing Keynesian arguments as biased or peripheral:

(1) In contrast to a crisis in industrial countries when mass unemployment and overcapacities exist but cannot be overcome by the market forces, Nurkse argues that the underdevelopment equilibrium is structural and that it is caused by deficiency of real capital and real demand and not just by a deficiency of monetary demand ('effective demand'), which is shown by the fact that inflation in underdeveloped countries is the rule rather than the exception. There is a lack of *real demand* ('purchasing power'), as there is too little to be offered in exchange – resulting from low productivity, which in turn results from the lack of real capital, i.e. the reverse side of the vicious circle (cf. Nurkse 1953a, 17). On the international level, Nurkse's argumentation runs along the same lines: although he agrees with the view that the volume of international trade *in the short run* is a function of employment and thus the effective demand in the main trading countries, he argues that *in the long run* supply-side conditions are more fundamental: the level of productivity and (thus) the size of the market (Nurkse 1953a, 21).

(2) In the underdeveloped countries of the 1950s, Nurkse considered consumption and investment *neither* in a (classical) trade-off *nor* in a (Keynesian) synergetic relationship, but as isolated from each other. That Nurkse did not agree with either view (neither classical nor Keynesian) can best be explained by the fact that in spite of Nurkse's mostly theoretical reasoning he was implicitly aware of the historic limitations of both theories: 'Neither the economics of business enterprise nor the Keynesian theory of employment nor the Anglo-centric views developed a hundred years ago by Marx were designed to take account of India's overcrowded peasant economy' (Nurkse 1957, 203).

The (British) classical economists wrote after the near completion of the seventeenth- to eighteenth-century agricultural revolution, when such means as the enclosures of commons had not only allowed for productivity gains in agriculture but had also reduced the basis for gaining a livelihood for the rural poor, thus turning them into 'surplus' population. In this situation, *industrial* capital formation seemed only possible by exploiting this cheap labour, i.e., by keeping their consumption to a bare minimum. Thus the theory that industrial investment was only possible by forced saving (i.e., forced limitation of labourer consumption) sprang into the minds of the classical economists. On the other hand, during the Great Depression of the 1930s, idle factors of production – both already existing industrial capital and experienced and skilled industrial labour – provided the material basis for the idea of the possibility of simultaneously expanding both (additional) capital formation and consumption.

In the underdeveloped countries of the 1950s, however, Nurkse seems to have seen a situation that was similar to the one *prior* to the seventeenth- to eighteenth-century agricultural revolution in Britain: the marginal productivity of agricultural labour was (around) zero. Keeping the consumption of the labour population (both agricultural and newly industrial) more or less constant would allow the use of labour directly to build up capital goods – thus more or less forcibly turning 'virtual' saving by disguised (rural) unemployment immediately into (industrial) investment.[5] Of course, in the present day perspective this is a rather limited view, as this is only possible in terms of very specific projects, such as the Chinese-type building of dams and irrigation systems in the 1950s by mere manual work (which is not possible of course with more complex capital goods).[6]

With regard to policy instruments, Nurkse, contrary to, for instance, W. Arthur Lewis, considered instruments in the 'real' sphere of the economy rather than 'monetary' instruments to be feasible for actualizing the saving potential of the rural sector:

I referred to the Japanese land tax, to the Russian collective farms, to some form of requisitioning (where I had in mind the Sudan's wartime experience [...]). [...] I would agree with the view that it cannot be done without some inflation [...] which is not the same as saying that it can be done only by inflation); I would accept inflation as a necessary evil, not as the prime instrument of forced saving. (Nurkse 1952, 1–2)

(3) Given a sceptical view of Keynes on perspectives of investment opportunities in industrial economies, Keynesians saw investment abroad as a means to reducing the capacity effect of investment while at the same time making use of its income effect. Nurkse, however, considered this problem from the much more pressing point of view of a capital-lacking underdeveloped world as important:

> The employment effect of foreign investment, which Keynesian economists tended to stress, is an incidental and unimportant effect; unimportant because, as Keynesian economics itself showed, it could be equally well achieved by domestic policies. Concern with employment tended to obscure the much more important developmental aspects of international investment. (Nurkse unpublished 1951; see also Nurkse 1953a, 129)

Obviously, the reason for Nurkse's distance in development theory to the Keynesian approach is rooted in the holistic approach of his circular theory.

Nurkse and Schumpeter

Ragnar Nurkse was well versed in Schumpeter's (1883–1950) ideas. Excerpts can already be found in Nurkse's University notes from Edinburgh, for example on Schumpeter's business cycle theory (such as Ragnar Nurkse Papers, Box 4, Public Policy Papers, Department of Rare Books and Special Collections, Princeton University Library). While Nurkse to a certain extent had borrowed the demand-orientation of his model from Keynes ('the money-income effect'), he focused on the supply side along with Schumpeter: 'this *real-income effect* [...] is indeed the sum and substance of long-run economic progress' (Nurkse 1953a, 13, emphasis added). When it comes to Schumpeter's influence on Nurkse, the issue of the *big push* is also a focal point.

The notion of Schumpeter as being relevant for development economics has long been rejected (exceptions are Hans W. Singer and Tsuru Shigeto); Developing countries were (and often still are) considered as a 'non-Schumpeterian world' (a term used by Singer (1953), albeit a Schumpeter disciple himself) – economically characterized by stagnation and the passive adoption of technical and commercial achievements from outside. The main reasons are said to be the lack of entrepreneurial potential and the lack of innovation opportunities (see for instance Rimmer 1961; only recently have there been more differentiating opinions particularly under the consideration of abundant entrepreneurial activities in the 'informal sector' economy and under the impression of neo-Schumpeterian studies of the East Asian innovation systems, which in the catching-up process focussed on the dynamics of accumulation of incremental innovations (Reinert 1994a, 1994b; Bass 1999, 2003).

Ragnar Nurkse was also in accordance with the first objection against the application of Schumpeterian theories to underdeveloped countries: 'We can never take it for granted that the human qualities of enterprise and initiative, with which the American economy has been so amply supplied, are present in the same degree elsewhere' (Nurkse unpublished n.d. b, 4; similar: Nurkse 1953, 17). More specifically, he argues, 'In communities afflicted with mass poverty the qualities of enterprise and initiative are usually in short supply' (Nurkse 1953, 10). However, Nurkse also writes, 'Schumpeter's theory seems to me to provide the mould which we must use, although we may use it with slightly different ingredients' (Nurkse 1953a, 12). What does this mean and what are the differences?

First, Nurkse – in contrast to other contemporary economists – refers to what he called the 'real' Schumpeter, i.e. Schumpeterian theory with regard to the long-term development rather than to the short-term theory of business cycles along the development trend.

Second, while Schumpeter's main concern is with the individual entrepreneur who starts a 'new wave,' Nurkse's main concern is with the wave, or – the (various) Big Pushes in economic history:

> Schumpeter's creative entrepreneurs achieved a process of Balanced Growth, albeit with cyclical setbacks, through the spontaneous action of private initiative in the past, by carrying out waves of new investment on a wide front. [Celso] Furtado is sceptical about the usefulness of Schumpeter's theory for the underdeveloped countries of the present day – and here I entirely agree with him. [...] I suggested, by contrast, that the problem is, at least in theory, capable of solution through Balanced Growth [...] in the domestic economy. [...] This is, conceptually, a process whereby capital is applied more or less simultaneously to a wide range of complementary industries, so that increased productivity in each of these industries creates an expanding market for the others. (Nurkse unpublished n.d. b, 4–4a)

Third, while Schumpeter allegedly sees only the entrepreneur as the agent of economic change and growth, according to Nurkse, 'It may be that in other types of society [other than Western capitalism] the forces that are to defeat the grip of economic stagnation have to be deliberately organized to some extent, at any rate initially' (Nurkse 1953a, 15). Japan is – referring to the work of Schumpeter's Japanese disciple Shigeto Tsuru – quoted as a case in point: 'In the early industrial development of Japan … the state was the great innovator and the industrial pioneer on a wide front' (Nurkse 1953a, 15). In particular, in a letter to François Perroux on his book on Schumpeter (Perroux 1951), Nurkse commented on 'Schumpeter's failure to consider the springs of innovation in a socialist economy' (Nurkse 1953b). Most probably, however, Nurkse was wrong in this respect as Schumpeter had already provided for this case: 'Every social environment has its own ways of filling the entrepreneurial function' (Schumpeter 1951, 255) – and only restored the 'real' Schumpeter.

Beyond Keynes and Schumpeter

As a development economist, Nurkse, as most of the first generation (Toye 2007), is often understood to have argued in the footsteps of John Maynard Keynes. This is true at least as far as Nurkse explains what he regards as the central factor in underdevelopment, the lack of capital, not only from the supply side but also from the demand side. In this way, Nurkse avoids the one-eyed view of neoclassical thinking. He also gives due consideration to the role of expectations and the time-consuming nature of adjustment processes. Nurkse's contribution to development economics, however, exceeds the borders of conventional Keynesian theory in at least two respects: first, the analysis of suboptimal equilibria is transferred from short-term to long-term analysis (i.e., from unemployment to underdevelopment equilibrium). Second, while Keynes was a market-pessimist with regard to the short-term adjustment task, as a consequence of the shift of focus, Nurkse was a central-planning optimist regarding the long-term task: the balanced-growth approach.

Interestingly, Nurkse also made positive notion of the second 'giant' in the field of economics in the twentieth century, Joseph A. Schumpeter. In contrast to Keynes, Schumpeter is widely considered to have overstressed supply-side factors in economic development as well as market forces in the adjustment process. Thus, Schumpeter's view of disequilibria as the 'normal' situation in capitalist development seems incompatible with Nurkse's balanced-growth concept. There are, however, good reasons for Nurkse's stance: the long-term perspective and the focus on big-push development processes (as materialized in the upswing phase of the Kondratieff waves) turned Schumpeter the ideal King's evidence against the noninterventionists and the gradualists in development thinking.

By analyzing the influence of Keynes and Schumpeter on Nurkse's contribution to development thinking it becomes clear that Nurkse's approach abounds with originality and individuality.

Looking Ahead: Nurkse's Circular Model Influencing Modern Poverty Theories

As argued in the first section, the heyday of 'classical' development economics as a consistent theoretical body had ceased by the late 1950s and a period of diversified approaches came into being. In the field of international organizations, however, after a state-optimistic view of development policy in the 1950s and the 1960s, the neo-liberal turn in the 1970s to 1980s became the most influential, probably best summarized in the Washington Consensus formula.

Shortcomings of the neo-liberal approach have led development thinkers to a more complex view of the issue in recent years. It is no wonder that under these circumstances circles of mutual and cumulative causation of persistent poverty have come to the fore. The World Development Report of 2000/2001 ('Attacking Poverty') set up a model where in one circle extreme levels of material poverty lead to poor risk management capacity and vulnerability, which then leads to limited savings, investments and livelihood opportunities from self-employment, in turn leading to extreme levels of material poverty – while other parts of the model refer to the circular causation of poor health and poverty, or social exclusion and poverty (World Bank 2000a).

To provide one more of a number of examples, The World Bank and other international organizations in their important document on the perspectives for Sub-Saharan Africa (World Bank 2000 b) proposed a model consisting of four circles of mutual and cumulative causation of development: 'improving governance and resolving conflict; investing in people; increasing competitiveness and diversifying economies; reducing aid dependence and debt and strengthening partnerships' (World Bank 2000b, 39).

Based on this model, the publication identified various areas of policy intervention to spur the catching-up process of economies in sub-Saharan Africa and to provide the level of per capita growth in output necessary to overcome poverty. The authors argued for improved governance; a directly targeted reduction of poverty and inequality; better education; enhanced physical, financial and informational infrastructure; rural development; diversified external economic relations; and strengthened external partnership. The central message of the document is that only when *simultaneously* succeeding in these tasks, will Africa be able to claim the new century and 'to overcome the development traps that kept it confined to a vicious cycle of underdevelopment, conflict, and untold human suffering for most of the 20th century' (World Bank 2000b, x).

Causal connections and points of intervention in some of the above-mentioned policy areas have recently been discussed in development economics on a particularly controversial level, especially the growth-to-poverty transmission. Beyond all doubt, sustained economic growth is considered essential to overcome poverty in Africa, as there is only a small basis for re-distributive efforts. An important factor in generating economic growth, however, is seen in the formation of human capital, which in turn depends on better health care and schooling. Also the financing of physical capital accumulation by domestic saving is seen as based on social conditions, such as an accelerated demographic transition by lower child mortality and higher female education. These causality chains provide a strong argument for direct anti-poverty policies: 'reducing poverty and improving social conditions are not simply consequences of development – they are essential components of any viable development strategy' (World Bank 2000b, 84). In addition, economic growth is considered to be less effective for poverty alleviation in the face of massive inequality. As according to the sceptical view of the authors of this document, the macroeconomic reforms of the 1990s did not benefit all poor groups to the same degree, targeted public services and public spending are considered necessary: 'Growth that translates into rising consumption is thus essential for poverty reduction. But growth is not sufficient, given Africa's low incomes and high inequality and exclusion' (World Bank 2000b, 91). Key ingredients of the proposed poverty reduction strategy are a growth rate of output of more than 7 per cent per year (a *big push?*) as well as funds allocation directed at geographically marginalized areas.

In spite of the much more complex nature of these models, partly reflecting a better understanding of the subject, partly a more complex reality, a certain inspiration of this approach by Nurksean thought cannot be overlooked.

References

Unpublished Sources

Gudin, Eugenio. Unpublished. (RNP, 1957), Comments on Professor Nurkse's Paper on 'International Trade and Development Policy.' Roundtable of the International Economic Association, Rio de Janeiro, 19–28 August 1957. Ragnar Nurkse Papers, Box 9, Folder 10; Public Policy Papers, Department of Rare Books and Special Collections, Princeton University Library.

———. Unpublished. (RNP, 1941), Letter to Mary Rankin, 30 March 1941. Ragnar Nurkse Papers, Box 12, Folder 3; Public Policy Papers, Department of Rare Books and Special Collections, Princeton University Library.

———. Unpublished. (RNP, 1945), Letter to Mary Rankin, 20 August 1945. Ragnar Nurkse Papers, Box 12, Folder 3; Public Policy Papers, Department of Rare Books and Special Collections, Princeton University Library.

———. Unpublished. (RNP, 1951), Letter to Norman S. Buchanan, 27 June 1951. Ragnar Nurkse Papers, Box 8, Folder 4; Public Policy Papers, Department of Rare Books and Special Collections, Princeton University Library.

————. Unpublished. (RNP, 1952), Letter to W. Arthur Lewis, 24 December 1952. Ragnar Nurkse Papers, Box 11, Folder 6; Public Policy Papers, Department of Rare Books and Special Collections, Princeton University Library.

————. Unpublished. (RNP, 1953), Letter to François Perroux, 17 January 1953. Ragnar Nurkse Papers, Box 11, Folder 6; Public Policy Papers, Department of Rare Books and Special Collections, Princeton University Library.

————. Unpublished. (RNP, 1955), To the Columbia University Council for Research in the Social Sciences: An application for a Summer Grant in Aid of Research, 29 October 1955. Ragnar Nurkse Papers, Box 5, Folder 6; Public Policy Papers, Department of Rare Books and Special Collections, Princeton University Library.

————. Unpublished. (RNP, 1956), Letter to Jacob Viner, 7 May 1956. Ragnar Nurkse Papers, Box 7, Folder 4; Public Policy Papers, Department of Rare Books and Special Collections, Princeton University Library.

————. Unpublished. (RNP, 1957), Comments on the paper by N. Rosenstein-Rodan on Notes on the Theory of the 'Big Push.' Roundtable of the International Economic Association, Rio de Janeiro, 19–28 August 1957. Ragnar Nurkse Papers, Box 9, Folder 10; Public Policy Papers, Department of Rare Books and Special Collections, Princeton University Library.

————. Unpublished. (RNP, n.d. a), Excess population [note]. Ragnar Nurkse Papers, Box 7, Folder 4; Public Policy Papers, Department of Rare Books and Special Collections, Princeton University Library.

————. Unpublished. (RNP, n.d. b), A note on investment incentives in underdeveloped countries. Ragnar Nurkse Papers, Box 13, Folder 9; Public Policy Papers, Department of Rare Books and Special Collections, Princeton University Library.

Published Sources

Bass, Hans H. 2007. 'Entwicklungstheorie. Wer ist wer? – Ragnar Nurkse (1907–1959). Balanced Growth und die Rolle der Kapitalbildung im Entwicklungsprozess.' *Entwicklungspolitik, Information Nord-Süd* 11 (2–3), 58–60.

————. 2003. 'Relevanz und Implikationen Neo-Schumpeterscher Theorien für die KMU-Förderung in Entwicklungsländern.' In Robert Kappel et al. (eds.). *Klein- und Mittelunternehmen in Entwicklungsländern. Die Herausforderungen der Globalisierung.* Hamburg: Deutsches Übersee-Institut, 25–42.

————. 1999. 'Entwicklungstheorie. Wer ist wer? – Joseph A. Schumpeter (1883–1950). Innovation und schöpferische Zerstörung: der Unternehmer als Motor der Entwicklung.' *Entwicklung und Zusammenarbeit* 40 (7), 215–218.

Basu, K. 1987. 'Ragnar Nurkse.' In *The New Palgrave. A Dictionary of Economics*, Vol. 3. London: Macmillan, 687.

Blaug, Marc. 2001. 'No History of Ideas, Please, We're Economists.' *The Journal of Economic Perspectives* 15 (1), 145–164.

Bowles, Samuel, Steven N. Durlauf and Karla Hoff (eds). 2007. *Poverty Traps*. Princeton: Princeton University Press.

Bronfenbrenner, M. 1954. Review of Nurkse 1953. *The Journal of Political Economy* 62 (2), 175–176.

Condliffe, J. B. 1954. Review of Nurkse 1953. *The American Economic Review* 44 (3), 451–454.

Daly, Herman E. 1996. *Beyond Growth: The Economics of Sustainable Development*. Boston: Beacon Press.

Dollar, David and Aart Kraay. 2001. 'Growth *Is* Good for the Poor.' Washington D. C.: The World Bank, Working Paper No. 2587.

Haberler, Gottfried. 1962. 'Introduction.' In Haberler and Stern 1962, vii-xiii.

Haberler, Gottfried and Robert M. Stern (eds). 1962. *Ragnar Nurkse. Equilibrium and Growth in the World Economy. Economic Essays.* Cambridge, MA: Harvard University Press.

Hagen, Everett E. 1955. Review of Nurkse 1953. *Econometrica* 23 (2), 232–234.

Hancock, W. K. 1954. 'The Under-Developed Economies [includes Review of Nurkse 1953].' *The Economic History Review* 6 (3), 310–315.

Herrera, Rémy. 2006. 'The Neoliberal 'Rebirth' of Development Economics.' *Monthly Review* 58 (1), 38–50.

Hirschman, Albert O. 1958. *The Strategy of Economic Development.* New Haven, Conn.: Yale University Press.

Hofstede, Geert H. 1980. *Culture's Consequences: International Differences in Work-Related Values.* Beverly Hills: Sage.

Keynes, J. M. 1933. *The Means to Prosperity.* London: Macmillan.

Krugman, Paul. 1994. 'The Fall and Rise of Development Economics.' At http://web.mit. edu/krugman/www/.

Kukk, Kalev. 2004. '(Re) Discovering Ragnar Nurkse.' *Kroon & Economy* 1, 45–51.

Makower, Helen. 1953. Review of Nurkse 1953. *The Economic Journal* 63 (252), 897–899.

Mavrotas, George and Anthony Shorrocks (eds). 2007. *Advancing Development: Core Themes in Global Economics.* Houndsmill: Palgrave Macmillan.

Nafziger, E. Wayne. 2007. 'From Seers to Sen: The Meaning of Economic Development.' In Mavrotas and Shorrocks 2007, 50–62.

Nurkse, Ragnar. 1959. 'Notes on Unbalanced Growth.' *Oxford Economic Papers N. S.* 11 (3), 295–297.

_____. 1953. *Problems of Capital Formation in Underdeveloped Countries.* Oxford: Oxford University Press.

_____. 1947. 'Domestic and International Equilibrium.' In Seymour E. Harris (ed.) *The New Economics.* New York: Alfred A. Knopf, 264–292.

_____. 1944. *League of Nations: International Currency Experience. Lessons of the Inter-War Period.* Princeton: League of Nations.

_____. 1935. *Internationale Kapitalbewegungen.* Wien: Springer.

Olano, Francis G. 1954. 'Views of Economic Development [Review of Nurkse 1953].' *World Politics* 6 (3), 413–420.

Perroux, François. 1951. 'Les trois analyses de l'évolution chez J. Schumpeter.' Reprinted in François Perroux. 1993. *Œuvres completes: VI. Théorie et histoire de la pensée économique. Marx, Schumpeter, Keynes.* Grenoble: Presses Universitaires de Grenoble, 261–338.

Polanyi, Karl, 1944. *The Great Transformation.* New York and Toronto: Farrar and Rinehart.

Reinert, Erik S. 1994a. 'Symptoms and Causes of Poverty: Underdevelopment in a Schumpeterian System.' *Forum for Development Studies* 21 (1–2), 73–109.

_____. 1994b. 'A Schumpeterian Theory of Underdevelopment: A Contradiction in Terms?' *STEP Report* 15/94.

Richmond, F. E. 1953. Review of Nurkse 1953. *Journal of the Royal Statistical Society*, Series A 116 (4), 467–469.

Rimmer, Douglas. 1961. 'Schumpeter and the Underdeveloped Countries.' *The Quarterly Journal of Economics* 75 (3), 422–450.

Robinson, Joan. 1936. 'Disguised Unemployment.' *The Economic Journal* 46 (182), 225–237.

Rosenstein-Rodan, Paul N. 1943. 'Problems of Industrialization of Eastern and South-Eastern Europe.' *The Economic Journal* 53 (210/211), 202–211.

Schumpeter, Joseph A. 1951. *Essays on Economic Topics.* Port Washington NY: Kennikat Press.

Scitovsky, Tibor. 1987. 'Balanced Growth.' In *The New Palgrave. A Dictionary of Economics,* Vol. 3. London: Macmillan, 177–179.

Seers, Dudley. 1967. *The Meaning of Development.* Brighton, England: Institute of Development Studies Brighton. IDS Communication No. 44.

Sen, Amartya K. 1999. *Development as Freedom.* New York: Alfred A. Knopf.

Singer, Hans W. 1953. 'Obstacles to Economic Development.' *Social Research* 20, 19–31.

Smithies, Arthur. 1951. 'Schumpeter and Keynes.' *The Review of Economics and Statistics* 33 (2), 163–169.

Stiglitz, Joseph. 1998. 'Staat und Entwicklung: Die Überwindung des Konzeptes vom minimalistischen Staat.' *Entwicklung und Zusammenarbeit* 39 (4), 101–104.

Streeten, Paul. 1959. 'Unbalanced Growth.' *Oxford Economic Papers,* N. S. 11 (2), 167–190.

Sutcliffe, Robert B. 1964. 'Balanced and Unbalanced Growth.' *The Quarterly Journal of Economics* 78 (4), 621–640.

Thorbecke, Erik. 2007. 'The Evolution of the Development Doctrine, 1950-2005.' In Mavrotas and Shorrocks 2007, 3–36.

Toye, John. 2007. The Significance of Keynes for Development Economics, mimeo.

University of Edinburgh, The. 2007. *Complete History of Economics at Edinburgh.* At http://www. econ.ed.ac.uk/history.html.

Vandemoortele, Jan. 2007. 'The MDGs: 'M' for Misunderstood?' *Wider Angle* (1), 6–7.

WCED 1987. *Our Common Future.* Oxford etc.: Oxford University Press.

Weyforth, William O. 1955. Review of Nurkse 1953. *The Journal of Finance* 10 (1), 91–92.

World Bank, The. 2000a. *World Development Report 2000/2001: Attacking Poverty.* Washington D. C.: The World Bank.

———. 2000b. *Can Africa Claim the 21st Century?* Washington D.C: The World Bank.

Chapter Ten:

NURKSE MEETS SCHUMPETER: IS MICROFINANCE A 'SILVER BULLET' TO ECONOMIC DEVELOPMENT?

Cord Siemon

Economic development has much to do with human endowments, social attitudes, political conditions – and historical accidents. Capital is a necessary but not sufficient condition of progress.

Ragnar Nurkse (1960, 1)

Introduction

It's only very recently that the field of economics (and policy) has rediscovered development and/or evolutionary economics as an important area of research. According to the pioneering work of Schumpeter, innovation can be seen as a driving force for economic development and growth. Schumpeter's second important (and often neglected) cornerstone is financial capital. The innovator needs financial capital for the new combination of given resources from the outside, made available from the bank system in the form of credit. Schumpeter uses the static equilibrium as a reference point. To move beyond static equilibrium, dynamic skills in the sphere of financial and monetary systems as well as in the realm of public and private goods are necessary. Therefore the credit-drawing bank system and the value-drawing entrepreneur system must be counterparts. In addition, Schumpeter used the term capital– in contrast to the dominant neoclassical opinion – in a balance sheet-oriented sense as 'financial capital'. Interestingly enough, Ragnar Nurkse, the best known Estonian economist, dedicated his scientific work (e.g., his books, *Problems of Capital Formation in Underdeveloped* ([1953] 1960) and *Countries* and *Equilibrium and Growth in the World Economy* (1962)) to very similar topics by referring to Schumpeter partly. Astonishingly, his contribution to development economics (innovation and capital) hasn't been analyzed thoroughly yet. This paper intends to elaborate a comparison between Nurkse and Schumpeter by analyzing similarities and differences based on a very current topic: The problem of financing innovations and start-ups in developed and underdeveloped countries. By referring to the theoretical insights of Ragnar Nurkse and Joseph Alois Schumpeter, this paper dedicates itself to the question of whether and to what extent money, financial technologies (credit, venture capital) and financial entrepreneurs (bootstrapper, business angels, banks, venture capital firms) have a significant influence on real economic activity. The goal of this paper is to shed light on the context between economic development, financial capital and entrepreneurial activity by referring to a very popular financial issue: Microfinance.

Schumpeter's 'Theory of Economic Development'

Innovation and Finance

The financing of innovations is consulted as one starting point for a political offensive to support economic growth and development, since Schumpeter supplies a theoretical basis by the complementary pillars of innovation and financial capital. Schumpeter marked innovation as an endogenous driving force of economic development. His ideas shaped the development of the neoclassical growth theory as well as the theory of evolutionary economics. Therefore, the credit-drawing bank system and the value-drawing entrepreneurial system must be counterparts.

> Capitalism is that of private property economy in which innovations are carried out by means of borrowed money … that is credit creation … Most of the features … of capitalism would be absent from the economic and … cultural process of a society without credit creation. (Schumpeter 1939, 223–4)

In addition, Schumpeter used the term capital– in contrast to the dominant neoclassical opinion – in a balance sheet-oriented sense as 'financial capital':

> Capital is nothing but the lever by which the entrepreneur subjects to his control the concrete goods which he needs, nothing but a means of diverting the factors of production to new uses, or of dictating a new direction of production. (Schumpeter [1934] 2002, 116)

Schumpeter believed it was possible for genuine bankers to steer economic surplus units into innovation-conditioned deficit units. Thereby, he attributes special financial business abilities to them:

> Even if he confines himself to the most regular of commodity bills and looks with aversion on any paper that displays a suspiciously round figure, the banker must not only know what the transaction is which he is asked to finance and how it is likely to turn out, but he must also know the customer, his business and even his private habits, and get by frequently 'talking things over with him', a clear picture of his situation. *But if banks, whether technically so called or not, finance innovation, all this becomes immeasurably more important. It has been denied that such knowledge is possible. The reply is that all bankers who at all answer to type have it and act upon it.* The giant banking concerns of England have their organs or subsidiaries which enable them to carry on that old tradition: However, at the same time *it is clear that this is not only highly skilled work, proficiency in which cannot be acquired in any school except that of experience, but also work which requires intellectual and moral qualities not present in all people who take the banking profession.* (Schumpeter 1939, 116–7; emphasis added)[1]

The main hypothesis of Schumpeter's work is the strong conjecture that money has impact on economic development and growth. This endogenous meaning of money in terms of economic growth has been discussed controversially until today, especially because of the multiplicity of Keynesian and monetary economists.[2] Some empirical work has been done supporting the endogeneity of money in the context of economic growth.[3] However, the crucial question has not been brought up for discussion: The empirical facts do not support the existence of 'genuine bankers' who finance innovation and/or new firms at early stages. The question arises: Which mechanism of money transmission do we find?

In industrialized countries, there is informal financing ('bootstrapping' and 'business angels'), which is responsible for the bulk of innovation financing in its critical seed-/start-up-stages. Eighty to ninety-five per cent of all innovative start-ups are financed, more or less, by bootstrapping in order to cover their liquidity requirements (Bhidé 1992; Winborg and Landström 2001). This astonishing phenomenon is observable for well-developed financial markets as well as for low-industrialized countries; founders do not want and/or are not able to fulfil the requirements of a bank credit (collateral) or venture capital financing (high lot sizes, large and realizable growth potentials on short notice).[4] Bootstrapping actually contains the investment of one's own money, sophisticated use of favourable purchase possibilities, payment and customer goals and/or the long-term deference of payment to the entrepreneur himself/herself (muscle capital), in order to mobilize sufficient liquidity ('resource-oriented bootstrapping'). This form of bootstrapping can be regarded as unconventional forms of internal financing using one's own savings and producing short-term cash flow to cover the need for liquidity. 'For the great majority of would-be founders, the biggest challenge is not raising money but having the wits and hustle to do without it' (Bhidé 1992, 110). Furthermore, friend and family relationships play an important role in financing innovations and start-ups. This confidence-intensive social network is known as 'relationship-oriented bootstrapping'.[5] This form of external financing differs in interests in the organization and control of the capital service modalities that are atypical for banks or venture capital firms ('love money'). The three f-components of bootstrapping – founder, family, friends – contradict the Schumpeter argument. This alternative allows them to operate without input and/or beyond the social capability of the founder by using 'highly creative ways of acquiring the use of resources without borrowing money or raising equity financing from traditional sources' (Freear, Sohl and Wetzel 1995, 395).

Since the 1980s, the theoretical and empirical basis of so-called 'business angels' has become more widely accepted. Business angels invest financial capital as innovation-relevant input, removing the middleman. Successful business angels typically have been successful entrepreneurs themselves and have been dependent on bootstrapping methods and business angels support (money and advice). They have created their wealth by partially investing in new enterprises *by* entrepreneurship. This investment is usually provided as equity capital ('informal venture capital market'). Estimations in the literature even assume that the informal market for venture capital is exponentially larger than that of formal venture capital markets. Furthermore, several studies show that these findings do not constitute a region-specific phenomenon.[6] Business angels are characterized by t heir preference for investing smaller amounts of capital into seed and start-up stages: Angels not only exist, they tend to invest into precisely those areas that are perceived as gaps in the capital markets for entrepreneurs. There are business angels who make available up to €500,000 ('seraphine angels'); in addition, smaller financing needs of up to €5,000 make it possible for other firms to take off ('cherubim angels'). Furthermore, it is interesting to note that so-called 'virgin angels' with different investment preferences exist. They are interested in investing in new enterprises in principle. However, there is still a lack of theoretical support to explain the role of business angels in the process of economic development. The roots of financial intermediaries (banks, venture capital firms) can be referred strongly to financial entrepreneurship of business angels. Even nowadays, business angels often unite to form a syndicate if there is need for larger capital requirements, thereby acting in the grey area between formal and informal markets. Empirically, there is a provable and theoretically important complement between the informal and formal venture capital market (Harrison and Mason 2000; Freear, Sohl and Wetzel 1995):

Figure 10.1 illustrates the relationship of information problems, profitability and different sources of financing in early and later stages of development by means of a typical financing life cycle of an innovator.[7] Seed and start-up stages are often characterized by low profitability and are dominated by informal financing systems. Their active role in these early stages is replaced and/or supplemented by formal financing systems in later stages, where the demands between established entrepreneurs and financial intermediaries match each other. Financial investments by banks and venture capital firms often rely on a combination of bootstrapping and/or business angels. Trustworthy signals are created (Prasad, Bruton and Vozikis 2000), which then support reliable communication in a decisionmaking situation typically marked by special seed and start-up risks (uncertainty and asymmetrical information). From an

Figure 10.1. Financing Cycle of Innovative Firms

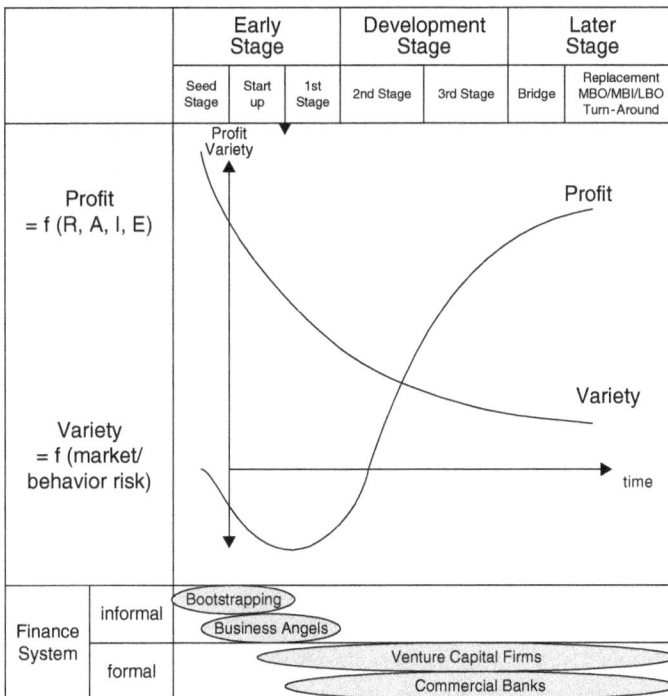

evolutionary standpoint, referring to a term of Ashby's system theory, this situation can be characterized by high 'variety'. According to traditional theory of finance, variety can be characterized by a combination of market and behaviour risks (see next chapter). Thus, with regard to the empirical picture and the feeder function of the informal financing market, Schumpeter's thesis can be viewed as an error.

According to nostalgic Schumpeter's prime example – financial business work of the brothers Pereire – there are some historical references that in former times, innovative ventures were largely informally financed, i.e., from the free cash flow of industrial enterprises and of wealthy industrial magnates (business angels). It cannot be denied that banks in particular seized the initiative during the founding years with the establishment of industrial corporations. The industrial revolution in the mid-nineteenth century revealed the efficiency of the bank system in financing innovations and establishments. Schumpeter interpreted the financial business circumstances (action-legal liberties, business abilities, etc.) correctly and brought these matters up for discussion.[8] Nowadays, it seems to be a general (but of course provable) law that the demand of a public good to protect investors' (and/or depositors') interests arises across the world, and at any time when a financial crisis shows the X-inefficiencies, problems and irrationalities of a free, i.e., non-regulated, capital market system. Banks (and in general all intermediaries) *must* invest other people's money (Benjamin and Margulis 2000) and thereby *have to* (and *had to*) change to later-stage businesses in order to fulfil the carried interests of their fiduciary capital. Particularly, if these interests represent entrepreneurial non-innovative skills (see later: 'routine,' 'arbitrage'), all the well-known problems of market uncertainty and asymmetric information lead to regulations between funds investors and the intermediary diminishing innovation-related variety. An intermediary that allows capital – representing entrepreneurial routine and arbitrage interests – to flow into the capital funds leads to a problem caused by input logic; because of this capital input, the demand for a special breed of funds managers arise. The management has to invest its fiduciary money by observing funds-specific rules and laws (Burlamaqui and Kregel 2005).

It is interesting to note that the venture capital industry followed a similar path of involution.[9] Similar to the controversy of the role of banks during the industrial revolution, it is still difficult to assess whether the formal venture capital market has ever had an important impact on the process of financing innovations at early stages. But the first venture capital intermediaries were, of course, more focused on seed and start-upstages than current intermediaries. According to initial success stories, formal venture capital became a target for public policy in order to support the process of economic development by mobilizing more money flowing into venture capital funds. This political standpoint is widespread even today and refers to an (intuitively logical) input-logic interpretation of economic growth (Siemon 2006a, 2006b). But astonishingly, there is empirical support that these initiatives were restricting rather than successful. Today, the fundraising of venture capital firms is dominated worldwide by other intermediaries (pension funds, banks). Their money represents 50 to 75 per cent of the entire market; their influence on strategic decisions and allocation of resources within the venture capital industry increased progressively (van Osnabrugge and Robinson 2000). The more the quantitative dimension of the formal venture capital industry increased, the more their investment behaviour moved significantly away from early stage to large-scale investments.[10]

Schumpeter's Error

Interestingly enough, Schumpeter's theory of economic development is closely related to input logic in an elementary point:[11] The innovator needs financial capital for the new combination of given resources from the outside, made available from the bank system in the form of credit. In addition, he supplies a theoretical reason; Schumpeter uses static equilibrium as a reference point. To move beyond static equilibrium, dynamic skills in the sphere of financial and monetary systems as well as in the realm of public and private goods are necessary. The static remainder of Schumpeter's theory is his idea of an entrepreneur, who combines given production factors, in a new way, *with given competencies*. This is the innovation function that makes Schumpeter's entrepreneur different from the bulk of routine entrepreneurs ('Wirte') who act in the state of equilibrium. Kirzner (1992, 1997) added – referring to theoretical insights of Austrian Economists' analysis of market processes (von Mises, von Hayek, Lachman) – an arbitrage function to this perspective. Thereby, entrepreneurial 'alertness' leads the economic system from the state of disequilibrium to equilibrium, i.e., the use of different prices at one point of time ('spatial arbitrage') or of different prices at different points of time ('temporal arbitrage').[12] The disequilibrium caused by innovation and characterized by pure uncertainty (in the sense of Knight and Shackle), is the soil for Kirzner's arbitrage entrepreneur. The arbitrage function of entrepreneurship is connected with entrepreneurial alertness that leads the system by tracing all opportunities back to a situation of neoclassical equilibrium – characterized by certainty and human behaviour's focus on adaptation. Thereby, the routine function of entrepreneurship is strongly linked to successful arbitrage. Routine, arbitrage and innovation are the bearers of the evolutionary function (Röpke 2002, 2005; Siemon 2006a, 2006b). Their energy of action relies on given competencies that can be lost by diffusion of knowledge during the market process. They reflect different solutions to overcome economic scarcity over time. Evolutionary logic is focused, however, on the creation of that capability, i.e., the evolution of new competencies, which are important for maintaining the function of innovation and they are necessary for the survival and success of routine and arbitrage functions as well. An evolutionary entrepreneur is a learning entrepreneur who has (and gains) the capability to reflect (on visions, weaknesses and strengths) and on 'getting things done' (Schumpeter). Thereby he brings *inter-* and *intra*functional stability into the routine, arbitrage and innovation functions.[13] Figure 10.2 shows the relationship between these different entrepreneurial functions.

The economic system reproduces itself inputlessly by an autopoietic process of payments between different entrepreneurial functions in the social system, thus money represents an implemented medium and mechanism of communication within the subsystems of the economy.[14] Thus, there is an intuitive link to Schumpeter's opinion of financial capital as a driving force for the entrepreneurial (autopoietic and structurally linked) functions routine, arbitrage and innovation and the idea of connecting these fields to a broader view of financial entrepreneurship. The explanation of impact would thereby refer to the evolution (and involution) of financial entrepreneurship (and its functions) within the process of economic development causing (as a vehicle of

Figure 10.2. Relationship Between Evolution, Innovation, Arbitrage and Routine

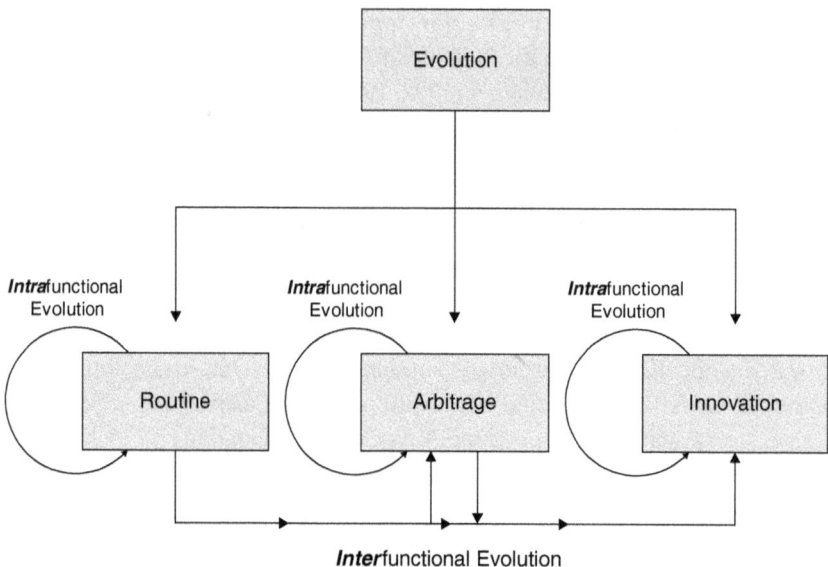

Source: Based on the framework developed by Jochen Röpke (2002).

entrepreneurial communication) the transmission of monetary impulse for development and – as a by-product – economic growth (Siemon 2006b). A (financial) innovator, who wants to stay in the field of innovation needs evolutionary capabilities (gained by self-evolution), otherwise, he becomes a victim of 'creative destruction' and loses his innovative function of entrepreneurship ('involution'). A routine entrepreneur who wants to survive and be successful in the sphere of innovation needs variety, as gained by *inter*functional self-evolution. If he wants to survive as a 'mere manager' to reproduce his routine function, he needs variety as well (gained by *intra*functional evolution). Otherwise, he would have problems being successful, due to a lack of variety to be able and willing to operate lastingly and successfully. This evolutionary standpoint is strongly connected with questions of a chance to 'produce' entrepreneurs consciously and based on scientific insights from learning and teaching entrepreneurship. Thereby, we refer to a Schumpeterian model of entrepreneurial energy that combines three elements of successful entrepreneurial action (Röpke 1977): *rights* (law, culture, business charta, etc.), *competencies* (evolutionary skills, knowledge, 'variety') and *motivation* (intrinsic motivation, internal locus of control, 'need for achievement').[15] Figure 10.3

Figure 10.3. Input, Development and Evolutionary Logic

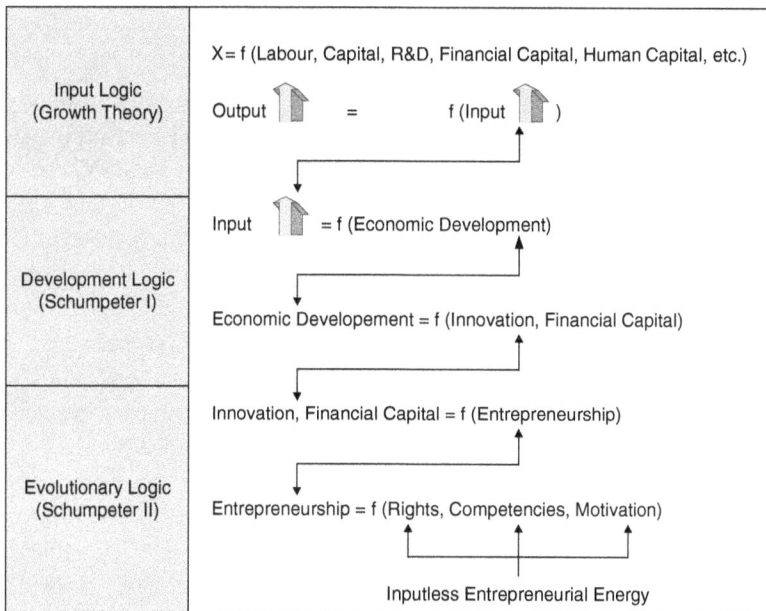

Source: Based on the framework developed by Jochen Röpke (1977, 2002).

illustrates this relationship between input, development and evolutionary approach based on Schumpeter's pillars of economic development.

The evolutionary function of entrepreneurship is the (re)production of variety (competencies) that can (and has to!) be used commercially by functions of routine, arbitrage and innovation; otherwise, it is threatened with losing its basis of survival and success. The key factor of evolutionary entrepreneurship is evolutionary learning, because the production of knowledge itself cannot be a factor causing economic growth. The focus has to be on the demand of knowledge by entrepreneurs who have gathered enough entrepreneurial energy to require resources for their major goal ('vision'). The operator for acquiring these resources (capital, knowledge, financial capital, etc.) is communication. Can these skills be learnt (and taught)? Maybe. For our discussion it is first of all beneficial to compartmentalize the evolutionary process of learning into four different, but (chaotically) connected stages (see Röpke 2005, 9):

- Optimizing of given factors, adaptation under given circumstances *(learning 0)*
- Acquisition of professional skills and knowledge (*learning 1*)
- Acquisition of competencies in order to follow the vision (*learning 2: communication, time management, mind mapping etc.*)
- Acquisition of the ability to find out: What are a person's strengths and weaknesses? What is the 'vision'? Impact of 'values,' 'ethics', etc.? (*learning 3: learning to reflect*).

The key competence to be learnt (at the second level of learning) by innovative entrepreneurs seems to be communication capabilities, and therefore, they have to challenge themselves by reflecting on vision, comparative (dis)advantages, etc. To act and to stay in a successful (and economically important) field of innovation, you have to be successful in the realm of the evolutionary function (learning 2 and 3), because learning is like swimming upstream; if you stop, you will fall back. An entrepreneur loses his innovative capabilities by involution and becomes a victim of other people's evolutionary competencies and their 'creative destruction' by innovation. Entrepreneurial energy has to be (re)produced by an entrepreneur again and again. Evolutionary capabilities (and their lack) are the key to understanding entrepreneurial success (and their problems of staying in the market for long-term periods). Evolutionary skills are needed in order to gain sustainable comparative advantages that are responsible for entrepreneurial success factors in the sense of John Kay (1993) (architecture, reputation, innovation, strategic assets) or John B. Miner (1997), who worked out a typology of entrepreneurial characteristics.

For the development and evolutionary logic, the interaction of business capabilities is considered to be as elementary in the financial sphere as in the realm of public and private goods. This is the starting point of Schumpeter's and Evolutionary Economics' social-technological explanation. Schumpeter's view for the causality of money is subject, however, to an erroneousness that is based on the fact that investors' entrepreneurial skills of innovation can be present within the sphere of financial intermediaries, but there are evolution-logical reasons, however, that such capabilities can be almost lost irrevocably ('involution' within the banking system) and managed without input by the credit creation/procurement of capital, i.e., by the founder him-/herself (bootstrapping). An important input-feeding function for financing innovation can only be reported beyond the sphere of financial intermediaries (business angels). It is possible to argue that Schumpeter's thoughts are essential for evolutionary theory if we take his opinion of the relevance of financial capital (and entrepreneurship) seriously in terms of real growth processes. But there is still a missing link to overcoming his financing error, because a theoretical approach is needed to overcome input logic in order to integrate financial entrepreneurship (and transmission-process-causing multipliers) as well as traditional entrepreneurship for explaining phenomena of economic development (Siemon 2006b). How can investors and entrepreneurs overcome 'market risks' and 'behaviour risks'? Why can the informal financing system reproduce entrepreneurial energy, needed especially in the context of financing innovations by evolution? Why do financial intermediaries have tremendous problems to sustain (and to implement) the innovation function by interfunctional evolution? Which factors have led (and always lead) to a loss of entrepreneurial energy by involution when financial intermediaries enter the formal market? What is the concrete underlying transmission process behind the endogeneity of money?

Recently, some effort has been made to further the development of a theory of financial intermediation and the analysis of dynamic competition processes of capital market actors.[16] Some economists illustrate that there are entrepreneurial ways for the banking system, such as gaining comparative advantages toward capital market investors (Burlamaqui 2000; Perez 2003). There is no empirical support for a general trend of disintermediation in the form of capital markets (Schmidt, Hackethal and Tyrell 1999) as long as banks and other intermediaries are still able to evolve their intrafunctional skills of arbitrage. Accordingly, the oft-articulated claim that banking systems are close to death loses its validity. Seen from an evolutionary approach, it is clear that the banking system has not evolved interfunctionally from entrepreneurial arbitrage to innovation as proffered by Schumpeter.[17] Banks lost their innovative perspective by acting as an intermediary for their depositors and shareholders. In the course of time, banks have been forced to be price-competitive and faced with typical problems of institutional economics when assessing and selecting 'good' and 'bad' innovative enterprises.[18]

Particularly, the phenomenon of bootstrapping represents the necessity of certain evolutionary capabilities – especially for the innovators – to bite the bullet during the financial hell of their early stage (Prasad, Bruton and Vozikis 2000; Coveney and Moore 1998).[19] But why do business angels – compared with formal intermediaries like venture capitalists and banks – have advantages in financing early stages of innovation processes?[20] Business angels are both evolutionary teachers and learners. Even if they are officially retired, they still see themselves as entrepreneurs and allow their entrepreneurial skills to permanently flow into the innovation system. Most active and successful angels have an entrepreneurial background; 'It is worth noting that they never consider themselves as ex-entrepreneurs, but still as entrepreneurs'. (Aernoudt 1999, 188). As a result, the mechanism of autopoietic reproduction is secured between the financial system and the realm of goods and services. A business angel relies on certain property rights that financial intermediaries cannot depend on due to their dependence on input from their investors. The business angel despises the idea of an open invitation forum for presenting business plans. He prefers to remain behind the scenes and relies on his trusted network contacts to control his deal flow. The informal process of making contacts is reasonably successful in overcoming the typical market and behavioural risks of financing a seed or start-up enterprise. Business angels preselect certain founders for their deal flow who – in addition to their promising ideas – demonstrate the willingness to cooperate and the promise of evolutionary work, rather than one innovative idea that could be obsolete after one or two months. Founders in search of capital, who reach the limit of bootstrapping, can often enter the financial circle of a business angel and thereby profit from their experiences, network contacts, etc. For the founder skilled in evolutionary entrepreneurship, the path to funding by a business angel syndicate or corporation with venture capital firms and banks in the latter financing phases is no longer unreachable. But he has to reflect on the need to search for and convince an angel investor that suits his entrepreneurial enterprise. Evolutionary logic is the key to overcoming the problems of trust rooted in problems of asymetrically distributed information (institutional economics) and/or problems of cash-flow forecasts and pricing (neoclassical capital market theory). Since the seed and start-up investor is investing predominantly in the entrepreneur and this asset is a very mobile commodity, the vision of the entrepreneur must be in congruence with the investment objective of the business angel (Sohl 1999, 111–12). Thus, it is noteworthy to analyze the investment behaviour of business angels regarding their personal motivation, their entrepreneurial background and their integrated investment career phase (Politis and Landström 2002, 93–94; Steier and Greenwood 2000). According to well-known theories of entrepreneurial motivation ('need for achievement,' 'internal locus of control', etc.), there seems to be a strong difference between their motivation of their efforts in early stage investments and venture capital firm ones (Duxbury, Haines and Riding 1996, 53). Due to the fact that the venture capital market has received more and more money from banks, pension funds and other formal investors, they are forced to invest according to the interests of the depositors. Venture capital firms would never be able to act on intrinsic motivation in the realm of seed and start-up phases as business angels can:

> [V]enture capital fund managers raise their finance predominantly from larger financial institutions such as pension funds, banks, and insurance companies, and have a duty of care when investing this money. Their investment decisions are therefore based *on purely economic considerations.* Business Angels, in contrast, are investing their own money and so are not responsible to anyone else for how it is invested and for what reasons. (Mason and Harrison 2002, 220; emphasis added)

In contrast to this process of involution within the financial network of business angels, an additional co-evolutionary reproduction mechanism exists to secure innovation variety: On the one hand, they act as an evolutionary sounding board by hands-on/off interaction; on the other hand, active business angels teach potential investors ('latent' and 'virgin' angels) and help each other with their initial step into the business angel sphere (Steier and Greenwood 1999, 159). But a founder searching for angel capital has to be careful as well. Otherwise, he is endangered to select a business devil respectively a business angel who does not fulfil his needs for capital and complementary know-how. There are different types of angels, which can be distinguished by their investment behaviour (size and frequency of investment, hands-on/hands-off strategy, etc.). The informal market for venture capital is thereby clearly characterized by a higher variety of investor types. 'The private investor does not have to invest. Therefore, unlike the institutional investor and the money manager, the private investor market cannot be approached as some monolithic block' (Benjamin and Margulis 2000, 93). An important approach in this field is the business angels typology of Coveney and Moore. Based on empirical research by questioning about 500 angels, they identify the 'Entrepreneur Angel' as the most relevant angel type responsible for Schumpeterian financings in seed and start-up phases:

Particularly, Coveney and Moore stress the coevolutionary function of 'Entrepreneur Angels'. Even after their financial investment, there is a process of social interaction with entrepreneurs:

> For a new entrepreneur without a great deal of experience in a particular industry or in start-ups in general Angels can potentially provide a valuable

source of advice. Given the typical backgrounds of Entrepreneur Angels, a wise entrepreneur will use their Angel and consult with them on major decisions: how effectively to run the business, negotiations, marketing, and other key business tasks. Used judiciously, Entrepreneur Angels can provide an excellent source of inexpensive but first-class management consulting. (Coveney and Moore 1998, 39)

A problem arises within the process of economic development when the financial intermediary takes the responsibility of fiduciary money (in conjunction with the rise of financial assets of all economic classes). This is an input logic problem that leads to the loss of relevant variety of innovation. Financial intermediaries who operate with the traditional invitation system for selecting investors and are thus open to the input of routine and arbitrage-entrepreneurial functions can only (and have to) transform these liabilities within the restrictions of property rights. The intermediary's main source of funding (e.g., pension funds, banks or private investors) is faced with the information problem regarding the capability and integrity of the financial intermediary who claims to be specialized in innovation financing. This is especially true when the funding sources hold a general interest in arbitrage and routine strategies. While business angels, due to their innovative business chartas, are capable of containing externalities informally within their syndicates, the acceptance of fiduciary funds, however, increases the demand of investor protection rules as a public good and influencing the business charta. For a financial intermediary, this necessity accompanies the unfolding demand for appropriate factors of production and for the development of appropriate concepts for the strategy adjustment. They are usually (and *have* to be) oriented towards diversification and minimizing risk strategies, university-based knowledge (learning 0 and 1), but not on evolutionary entrepreneurial competencies (learning 2 and 3), so they are not able to fulfil the need of variety requirements typical of innovations and the necessity for a holistic viewpoint of innovation projects. Their investment decisions have to rely on verifiable data to justify themselves to their depositors and shareholders, so 'formal investors emphasise more the objective aspects of the decision, while business angels are more driven by the subjective aspects' (Aernoudt 1999, 190). Directly in the course of governmental initiatives motivated by input logic, this entrepreneurial gap between business angels and formal Venture Capitalists is strengthened, particularly by the process of erosion of variety needed for assessing innovations. The interests of the higher liabilities, and the requirement *of having to act* as functionary of arbitrage and routine,[21] have removed formal Venture Capitalists' investment focus away from the 'innovation' pole to the 'imitation/arbitrage/routine' pole (Siemon 2006b).

Let us summarize our evolutionary explanation of removing the innovation inclination of financial intermediaries. Figure 10.4 illustrates the process of involution. The roots of financial intermediation can be seen in the realm of financial entrepreneurship. The problem of involution is strongly connected with input logic. An entrepreneurial business angel fund, which takes money

Figure 10.4. 'Dutch Disease' of Financial Intermediaries

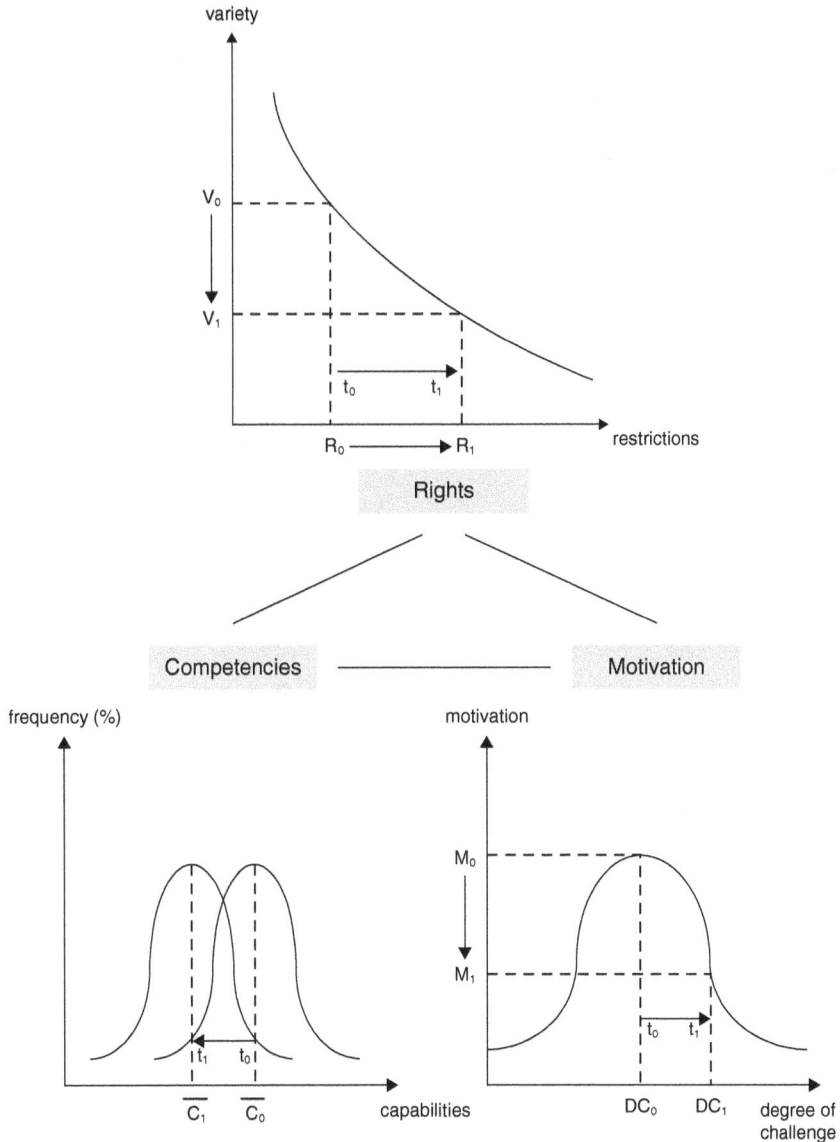

from non-innovative outsiders in t_0 loses entrepreneurial variety that is needed to secure autopoietic reproduction of innovative skills during the period t_0 to t_1. He now has to fulfil somebody else's interests or certain protection rules, etc. These restrictions increase from R_0 to R_1 so that financial intermediaries are constrained to act innovatively more and more. Entrepreneurial variety decreases from V_0 to V_1. An intermediary is part of the formal capital sector and its basis of success is the reproduction of money flow into the fund, whilst business angels (and business angels funds respectively syndicates) avoid this formal mechanism. Instead, they use (and need) their informal structure for pre-selecting their deal flow of ongoing entrepreneurs and prefer to act anonymously and independently from outside investors. As a result, they remain able to secure variety that is needed for further investments in innovations. On the other hand, the now more formal financial intermediary is not able to control market and behaviour risks connected with financing innovations anymore. The loss of innovative competencies can be seen as a movement aside from the *average* amount of innovative capabilities. Also, the motivational basis for successful entrepreneurship in the field of innovation changes from t_0 to t_1. In terms of McClelland's 'Need for achievement', the degree of challenge ('task difficulty') in t_0 (DC_0) is moving to t_1 (DC_1). Motivation declines from M_0 to M_1.[22] The financial intermediary loses his innovation identity during the period t_0 to t_1. The entrepreneurial paradigm has changed and the intermediary is now allowed, able and willing to control typical challenges of arbitrage, imitation and/or routine enterprises.

But this orientation to later stages of financing could nevertheless be seen as an effective way to realize the 'division of labour' principle,[23] at least as long as innovators and their corresponding informal financial resources play a vital role in feeding those financial intermediaries and their arbitrage and routine perspective. Thus, the explanation of empirical results of complementary informal and formal venture capital markets could be referred to their different, but structurally linked entrepreneurial standpoints. The endogenous meaning of an input-spending, credit-drawing bank system relies on the endogenous force of informal financing systems reproducing their evolutionary capabilities (that are needed to dominate variety-innovative enterprises) autopoietically. Within this transmission process, several components of co-evolutionary learning is embedded.[24]

Nurkse's *Problems of Capital Formation in Underdeveloped Countries*

Gottfried Haberler has given an illustrative overview about the life and work of Ragnar Nurkse by an introduction to a collection of Nurkse's essays (*Equilibrium and Growth in the World Economy* 1962) that has been edited by Haberler and Stern. Ragnar Nurkse (1907–1954) was an international, reputable economist from Estonia who specialized in the fields of international economics, international finance and economic development. Nurkse was an early backer of the 'balanced growth' doctrine and continued to build on the Rostenstein-Rodan theory ('Big Push') as well. Furthermore, he was a forerunner of the Lewis doctrine by stressing the role of savings and capital formation in economic development. For our topic, of utmost importance is his work, *Problems of Capital Formation in Underdeveloped Countries*, first published in 1953 (our edition: 1960). Nurkse focused the problem of financing within the process of economic development on underdeveloped countries and their strong difficulties to get into a path where they can participate on Kondratieff-dynamics and where they can compete with developed countries in order to catch up to their standard of living and technology. Even today there are controversial opinions regarding the 'optimal' path of development. Are their any parallels and differences between Schumpeter's *Theory of Economic Development* and our evolutionary standpoint regarding the endogeneity of money?

Vicious Circle of Poverty

It is interesting to note that the theory of economic development and the theory of international trade are often discussed in isolation. From our point of view, it is necessary to integrate Schumpeter's pillars of economic development (innovation and finance) into the logic of comparative advantages (in the sense of Ricardo), because from a Schumpeterian perspective, the role of dynamic comparative advantages are responsible for the bulk of international trade fluxes. So a policy of international trade should be integrated into a Schumpeterian policy of economic development described by Hirschman:

> Development theory and policy therefore face the task of examining under what conditions development decisions can be called forth in spite of these imperfections, through pacing devices or inducement mechanisms. (Hirschman 1958, 26)

To integrate those elements we have to break out of the dominating input logic paradigm in order to focus on the entrepreneurial process of combining input factors,[25] e.g., '…capital or technical education are scarce or the banking system is inadequate because the country has found it difficult to take the steps necessary to create, direct, or to procure capital, to spread education, and to introduce the proper financial institutions' (Hirschman 1958, 25).

While traditional theory of international trade is supporting the free trade doctrine, apostatical economists favour a critical point of view by endorsing the protection of infant and important domestic industries. Following the equilibrium doctrine of the neoclassical growth and international trade theory, free trade can lead a country (using a term of Theodore Schultz) into a state of 'efficient poverty' (Röpke 1981). They ask how to get out of the paradigm of static allocative efficiency and how to create comparative dynamic advantages (in the sense of Schumpeter) by leaving the field of X-Inefficiency (using the well-known term of H. Leibenstein). For example, the political and entrepreneurial focus on routine products and/or natural goods (Ricardo goods) can hinder the economic system in mobilizing enough resources and (entrepreneurial) energy in to combine given resources in a new way and to enter into Kondratieff dynamics. Those nations are (especially in the case of a country that already possesses dynamic comparative advantages, or at least has received the status of a Heckscher-Ohlin country) threatened to stick in a Dutch Disease by exploiting natural resources that have been suddenly detected.[26] In case of an underdeveloped, poor country, it probably sticks in a situation that Nurkse (1960, 4) has described as a 'Vicious Circle of Poverty' (see figure 10.5):

> For example, a poor man may not have enough to eat; being under-fed, his health may be weak; being physically weak, his working capacity is low, which means that he is poor, which in turn means that he will not have enough to eat; and so on. A situation of this sort, relating to a country as a whole, can be summed up in the trite proposition: 'a country is poor because it is poor.'

Generally, in such a situation there seems to be not enough endogenous power to get out of this vicious circle by Schumpeterian entrepreneurship, because there are not enough financial engines to start up entrepreneurial enterprises by bootstrapping, business angels, etc. This case seems to be the classical one where Schumpeter was right with his thesis of a credit-drawing bank system that has to spend money ('input') in order to move the system beyond the state of equilibrium. Hirschman (1958) has shown in his book *The Strategy of Economic Development* that entrepreneurial energy (and a underlying efficient financial system) is the main source to get out of a state of equilibrium, poverty and backwardness. 'If backwardness is due to insufficient number and speed of development tasks, then the fundamental problem of development consists in generating and energizing human action in a certain direction' (Hirschman 1958, 25). Furthermore, 'We have identified the ability to make such decisions as the scarce resource which conditions all the other

Figure 10.5. Nurkse's 'Vicious Circle of Poverty'

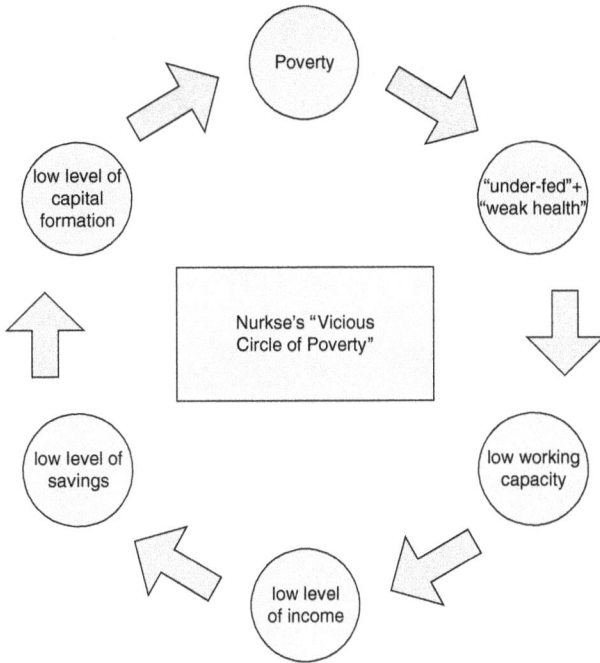

Source: Based on Nurkse (1960 [1953]).

scarcities and difficulties in underdeveloped countries' (Hirschman 1958, 27). From our evolutionary perspective, (see chapter 2) the rise and decline of evolutionary and innovative capabilities within an economy is responsible for a process of catching up, forging ahead or falling behind (to use the well known terms of Moses Abramowitz 1986).[27]

How does the 'Vicous Circle of Poverty' affect the process of fund raising and capital accumulation? Nurkse's answer (1960, 5):

> On the supply side, there is the small capacity to save, resulting from the low level of real income. The low real income is a reflection of low productivity, which in turn is due largely to the lack of capital. The lack of capital is a result of the small capacity to save, and so the circle is perfect.
>
> On the demand side, the inducement to invest may be low because of the small buying power of the people, which is due to their small real income, which again is due to the low productivity. The low level of productivity, however, is a result of the small amount of capital used in production, which in turn may be caused at least partly by the small inducement to invest.

According to Adam Smith, Nurkse argues that the inducement to invest is limited by the size of the market and the crucial determinant of the size of the market is productivity (Nurkse 1960, 6–11). He called a constellation of circumstances tending to preserve any backward economy in a stationary condition 'underdevelopment equilibrium' (ibid., 10), e.g., what nowadays can be called 'efficient poverty' in a state of X-Efficieny. Thus, the main question arises: How to get out of this state? Nurkse refers to several theories of economic developement in the context of 'balanced growth' and he asks, 'But how do we get balanced growth?' He then refers to Schumpeter and states that 'rapid growth was achieved through the action of individual entrepreneurs, producing recurrent waves of industrial progress. ... Schumpeter's work, properly understood, is just what its title says it is: a theory of economic development. Business cycles appear in it only as a form in which economic progress takes place' (ibid., 12). Nurkse states that Schumpeter's Theory of Economic Development is a suitable starting point in order to figure out the meaning of innovations and capital, carried out by entrepreneurs and financiers within a process of leaving poverty, equilibrium and backwardness:

> Schumpeter's theory seems to me to provide the mould which we must use, although we may use it with slightly different ingredients. As everyone knows, this theory assigns a central role to the creative entrepreneur, or rather to the action of considerable numbers of such entrepreneurs and their imitators, carrying out innovations, putting out new commodities and devising new combinations of productive factors. Even if an innovation tends each time to originate in one particular industry, the monetary effects of the initial investment – and other circumstances as well – are such as to promote a wave of new applications of capital over a range of industries. (Nurkse 1960, 12–13)

With regard to our main topic, 'microfinance', he states that for underdeveloped countries the main question is how to receive and mobilize the money to enter the next innovation wave:

> In our present context it seems to me that the main point is to recognize how a frontal attack of this sort – a wave of capital investments in a number of different industries – can economically succeed while any substantial application or capital by any individual entrepreneur in any particular industry may be blocked or discouraged by the limitation of the pre-existing market. (Nurkse 1960, 13)

Schumpeter's Theory is primarily a theoretical reference system that can explain and be applied for the rise and fall of western, industrialized countries.

In a state of poverty and/or equilibrium, the 'eyes of innovators' are not there; innovators have to be born or – using evolutionary economics' line of thought – to be created:

> In the early dawn of industrial development, it takes the eye of faith to see the potential markets. Schumpeter's creative entrepreneurs seem to have what it takes, and as they move forward on a broad front, their act of faith is crowned with commercial success.
>
> Schumpeter's theory of economic development was intended to apply primarily to the rise and growth of Western capitalism. It is not necessarily applicable in the same way to other types of society. It may be that in other types of society the forces that are to defeat the grip of economic stagnation have to be deliberately organized to some extend, at any rate initially. In the early industrial development of Japan, for instance, the state was the great innovator and the industrial pioneer on a wide front.[28] (Nurkse 1960, 15)

Interestingly enough, he refers to the doctrine of 'balanced growth' by referring strongly to Schumpeterian arguments of development economists that defeat the equilibrium orientation or view it as a byproduct of an evolutionary process.[29] He claims for a system of interventions by implementing important industries simultaneously, and is thereby in line with Keynes. Interestingly, he comes to the same conclusion as modern evolutionary economists do: 'Yet the case which the poor countries advance in favour of the 'balanced growth' and 'diversification' of their domestic economies is not always well received. Does it not mean turning away from the principle of [static] comparative advantage?'[30]

Nurkse saw that there is a very strong relationship between aspects of economic development and of international trade,[31] and he refers to Ricardo's theorem of comparative costs. This theorem mainly shows that it is impossible to outcompete a country totally. Due to the logic of opportunity costs, every country can make use of a certain comparative advantage and enables every country to participate in international trade. But what kinds of goods are embedded, allowing them to make use of their comparative advantage? Innovative Kondratieff-goods (nanotechnology/biotechnology) or goods of routine/nature capital (Ricardo goods)? An underdeveloped country that is focused on static comparative advantages like routine products or primary production (Ricardo goods: oil, fruits, etc.) is threatened to stick in a development trap and the Dutch Disease.[32]

In his work *Patterns of Trade and Development* (1961), Nurkse states that 'it may be that nothing can be done about the quantity of natural resources … But physical permanence need not be economically relevant. What matters is the amount of *useful* natural resources. This depends on human knowledge. And knowledge is variable' (Nurkse 1961, 56). Here we find a strong theoretical relationship we figured out when talking about the necessity of entrepreneurs and their evolutionary capabilities to make use of the huge amount of knowledge nowadays (see chapter 2). An underdeveloped country that is going to catch up has to be endowed with a setting of innovative entrepreneurs paving the way for all other kinds of entrepreneurs. These innovators – they could be imitators as well, perceiving their task as innovative and supplying 'me too' goods – have to be allowed, to be able and willing to adapt and transform their resources ('input': knowledge, capital, natural resources, etc.) within their domestic markets in order to induce positive linkages (in the meaning of A. Hirschman) to all kind of industry sectors. We have shown (see chapter 2) that an evolutionary process of entrepreneurial learning (in the real and financial sphere) is the key to climbing up the ladder to economic development. And, according to Nurkse, the search for dynamic aspects of trade theory becomes essential as well (Nurkse 1961, 51–62).[33] Therefore, a microeconomic analysis is needed. In his paper 'Period Analysis and Inventory Cycles' (1954), Nurkse figures out that one should 'doubtless be aware of the limitations of macroeconomic analysis'. Thus, his main concern 'is not simply to present a stylized model, but to relate it to individual business motives and to the observed facts' (Nurkse 1962, 105–106). Furthermore, he states:

> The classical theory of trade shows that at least up to a point a country can benefit by concentrating its effort and resources along lines of international comparative advantage. This is an important and familiar truth which no country that is seeking development can afford to ignore. But once a country has adopted an optimal pattern and optimum degree of specialization along these lines, how is it to achieve *continued* further growth if external demand conditions do not induce it? There is no doubt that the opening up the trade can bring very sizable gains to a primitive economy, but is there any guarantee that trade alone will thereafter cause a rate of growth that can be regarded as satisfactory in the light, for instance, of population increase at home or of the living levels prevailing abroad? ... Granted all the advantages of international specialization, there remains a possibility of deadlock and comparative stagnation. (Nurkse 1962, 253)

From a development perspective, an entrepreneurial approach to a dynamic form of X-Efficency is clearly needed in order to gain dynamic comparative advantages. Therefore, time and the absence of allocative efficiency is necessary in order to create a milieu where evolutionary and innovative skills can be learnt. Nurkse points out 'that the case for specialization as such is just as strong as ever, but that the forces making for the transmission of growth from advanced to less developed countries may not be as powerful as they were a hundred years ago' (Nurkse 1962, 254). Of course, this is not necessarily an argument for autarky,[34] but as Röpke (1981) states, the gap of entrepreneurial capabilities between two countries might be accompanied with the problem of task difficulties (in the sense of McClelland; see chapter 2) regarded as too high for underdeveloped countries, thus they have to focus on goods with low added value where their comparative advantage is embedded. Seemingly, Nurkse refers implicitly to List's argument of protection in order to bring the domestic industry of underdeveloped countries incrementally up to the level of industrialized regions.[35] But, of course, protection may lead to negative effects even in case of an underdeveloped country that wants to support an infant industry instead of sticking in the vicious circle of poverty or in a state of Dutch Disease. Nurkse points out what kind of problems can arise if a policy approach of protection is not combined with an innovation approach:

> It is not to be denied that import restrictions can help a policy of balanced domestic investment, but their unfavourable effect on real income and hence possibly on saving should always be remembered. They should therefore be used sparingly. Import restrictions enforced in spite of such unfavourable effects can be justified only on the ground of the greater future benefit; which is the infant industry argument for protection. On this point I'm still inclined to maintain that infant creation is far more important than infant protection. (Nurkse 1962, 256–257)

Furthermore, the question of finance arises when talking about integration of people in underdeveloped countries into an entrepreneurial doctrine. Similarly to Schumpeter, the question of financing entrepreneurial enterprises rises again:

> Let us consider more closely the possibility of taking the surplus people off the land and setting them to work on capital projects – irrigation, drainage, roads, railways, houses, factories, training schemes and so on. The question arises now: how are these various forms of capital formation to be financed? In real terms, how are people to be fed when they are set to work on projects of this sort? (Nurkse 1960, 37)

In case of financing entrepreneurial action in infant industries, the problem of finance arises beyond the problem of vicious circles of poverty, as Nurkse states: 'The gap in the infancy stage arises therefore chiefly from inability to earn enough to meet the fixed interest charges, though for a time there my be a difficulty even in covering operating costs from current earnings' (Nurkse 1962, 261). Furthermore, 'Default occurred when any resources obtained through additional borrowing or government subsidies ran out, or the gap turned out to be longer than expected. ... In the early development stage there simply is not enough traffic, or else what traffic there is will not bear charges high enough to make the project pay' (ibid., 263). Thus, with regard to our theoretical discussion and the empirical picture the question arises, whether bootstrapping and angel capital can be mobilized in a region that is stuck in a vicious circle of poverty. How can a financial intermediary, faced with involutionary processes due to being responsible for investing fiduciary resources, be involved in order to back the need of money to get out of the vicious circle and leave the state of underdevelopment? Is saving a relevant aspect of capital mobilization and a necessary component at all? Is there within the vicious circle still enough space for self-financing in form of 'bootstrapping'? Nurkse emphasizes that the problem of financing underdeveloped countries' need for capital can be compartmentalized in two distinct fields: 'First and foremost is the necessity of feeding the new investment workers, keeping them supplied with the consumption goods they need in order to work on the capital project. ... Secondly, there is the financing which consists in giving the new investment workers tools to work with' (Nurkse 1960, 44). As alternatives for external sources of capital he discusses direct business investments and international loans and grants (Nurkse 1960, 82–103). But what we want is to combine some ideas of Nurkse and Schumpeter by referring to an important and strongly discussed topic nowadays, microfinance. Is microfinance the key to combine the ideas of these famous development economists? Is microfinance a silver bullet to economic development and to leave the vicious circle of poverty?

Concept and History of Microfinance

Today, about 1.2 billion people live on less than US$1 (and about 50 per cent on less than $2 a day);[36] 70 to 75 per cent of these people are women. Poverty reigns, despite the fact that since World War II organizations such as the World Bank have poured resources and money into hundreds of schemes in order to stop poverty. The World Bank alone has dispersed more than $550 billion since its founding in the 1940s. Microcredit and microfinance, more broadly, are seen as important tools for eradicating poverty and hunger – one of the United Nations 'Millennium Development Goals' – and for empowering poor people. Microcredit is helping millions of poor people, especially poor rural women, with tiny loans in order to enable them to start small enterprises, create self-employment and improve their lives. Microfinance programmes also provide clients with other basic financial services that they need to grow the money they earn. They provide savings accounts, so that clients can safely store their money and earn interest over time. They also offer insurance so that sudden mishaps do not mean family ruin. Some also provide 'consumption loans'. Additionally, they cover a sudden expense like a child's tuition. One of the most innovative aspects of microfinance is that it engages communities, not just individuals. The World Bank estimated in 2004 that there were over 7,000 microfinance institutions worldwide, serving over 16 million poor people. The combined turnover of these institutions was estimated at $2.5 billion. The experience of microfinance institutions shows that women are a good credit risk, and that they invest their income for the well-being of their families. At the same time, they benefit from the higher social status they achieve through being able to provide income. The Grameen Bank of Bangladesh, with origins in 1976, has loans currently in the hands of borrowers totalling over $300 million, with deposits of a similar amount. Over 95 per cent of the Grameen Bank's 3.8 million members are women. No wonder that the United Nations declared 2005 as the 'International Year of Microcredit'.

Microcredit loan cycles are usually shorter than traditional commercial loans – typically six months to a year, with payments plus interest weekly. Shorter loan cycles and weekly payments help the borrowers stay current and not become overwhelmed by large payments. Clearly the transaction-intense nature of weekly payment collections, often in rural areas, is more expensive than running a bank branch that provides large loans to economically secure borrowers in a metropolitan area. As a result, microfinance institutions must charge interest rates that might sound high – the average global rate is about 35 per cent annually – to cover their costs. This reflects the relatively high cost of providing a large number of very small loans.[37] Further, traditional banks are not generally interested in issuing small loans – $50 to $150 – as the interest benefits do not exceed the transaction costs. One should note that although microfinance institutions may charge rates of 20 to 70 per cent to cover their costs, these interest rates are still significantly lower than the 300 per cent to 3,000 per cent annual rates that many borrowers were previously paying to moneylenders ('credit sharks'), and that are typical of the local credit card interest rates.[38]

According to Nurkse's 'Vicious Circle of Poverty', its worst attribute is that poverty breeds poverty; it is virtually impossible to break free from its grasp. If one cannot afford appropriate nutrition or health care for one's family, children grow up at greater risk. Thus, they are potentially threatened by disabling diseases. If one cannot afford to buy one's own land or home or livestock, there remain only a few opportunities to build assets that will last over time. A microfinance institution is an innovative solution for the problem of poverty by giving the poor the tools they need to *lift themselves* out of poverty, providing opportunity through microfinance. Thereby, tiny loans and financial services help 'micro-entrepreneurs' to reap the rewards of their own labour. These tiny loans are enough to start or expand small businesses such as weaving baskets, raising chickens, or buying wholesale products to sell in a market. Income from these businesses provides better food, housing, healthcare and education for entire families, and most important, additional income provides hope for a better future. In addition, the poor, like all of us, need a secure place to save their money and access to insurance for their homes, businesses and health (Clogherty 2006; Morduch 1999a, 1999b; Armendariz and Morduch 2004).

The traditional banking system requires that a borrower have collateral to receive a loan. The world's poorest people have no such collateral. Thus, many microfinance institutions organize small 'solidarity groups' of about five people searching for capital, while others have groups as large as up to fifty people. The main rule of all these programmes: Individuals receive their loans, but the whole group is responsible for repayment. Thus, microfinance institutions generally use social collateral in the form of peer groups to ensure loan repayment. Borrowers take out loans in groups and if a borrower defaults on the loan, the entire group typically is penalized and sometimes barred altogether from taking further loans. This peer pressure encourages borrowers to be very selective about their peer group members and to repay loans in full and on time, resulting in the higher than 95 per cent repayment rates industrywide. Sharing the responsibility gives the bank assurance that the loan will be repaid without the need for collateral, which people living in poverty simply do not have (Clogherty 2006; Morduch 1999a, 1999b; Armendariz and Morduch 2004).

Microfinance institutions exist in many forms – credit unions, commercial banks and, most often, non-governmental organizations. However, the concept of microfinance is not new.[39] In the 1800s, various types of larger and more formal savings and credit institutions began to emerge in Europe, organized primarily among the rural and urban poor. These institutions were known as People's Banks, Credit Unions and Savings and Credit Cooperatives.[40] In the early 1900s, various adaptations of these models began to appear in parts of rural Latin America.[41] Between the 1950s and 1970s, governments and donors focused on providing agricultural credit to small farmers, in hopes of raising their level of productivity and income. These efforts to expand access to agricultural credit emphasized supply-led government interventions in the form of targeted credit through state-owned development-finance institutions that offered concessional loans to customers at below-market interest rates. These subsidized schemes were rarely successful, because rural development banks suffered massive erosion of their capital base due to subsidized lending rates and poor repayment discipline, and the funds did not always reach the poor.

To summarize: Over the years, these institutions became inefficient and at times, abusive and from an evolutionary standpoint, we can refer – to more or less extending and by adding some modifications – to our given explanation of the inherent involutionary processes of financial intermediaries (see chapter 2). Meanwhile, starting in the 1970s, experimental programmes in Bangladesh, Brazil and a few other countries extended tiny loans to groups of poor women to invest in microbusinesses. This type of microenterprise credit was based on solidarity-group lending in which every member of a group guaranteed the repayment of all members as already mentioned. These 'microenterprise lending' programmes had an almost exclusive focus on credit for income generating activities (in some cases accompanied by forced savings schemes) targeting very poor (often women[42]) borrowers. Most famous has become the case of the Grameen Bank. In Bangladesh, Professor Muhammad Yunus addressed the banking problem faced by the poor through a programme of action-research. With his graduate students in Chittagong University in 1976, he designed an experimental credit programme and tested an important hypothesis: *If financial resources are made available to the poor at reasonable terms and conditions, the poor could generate productive self-employment without additional external assistance.* After much persuasion, he convinced a bank to provide a loan – *without collateral.* The pilot experiment turning out successfully, the Grameen Bank ('Grameen' = 'rural', 'countryside') project was launched in 1979 (Clogherty 2006; Morduch 1999a, 1999b; Armendariz and Morduch 2004). Within a year, 24 branches were set, ultimately spreading rapidly to hundreds of villages. Through a special relationship with rural banks, Yunus disbursed and recovered thousands of loans, but the bankers refused to take over the project at the end of the pilot phase. They feared that it was too expensive and risky in spite of his success. What nobody besides Yunus believed turned into reality again: in the new branches, a 98 per cent recovery of loans was achieved. Through the support of donors, the Grameen Bank was founded in 1983 and now serves about four million borrowers. The initial success of Grameen Bank also stimulated the establishment of several other giant microfinance institutions like BRAC, ASA, Proshika, etc. The 1990s saw growing enthusiasm for promoting microfinance as a strategy for poverty alleviation. The microfinance sector blossomed in many countries, leading to multiple financial services firms serving the needs of microentrepreneurs and poor households. These gains, however, tended to concentrate in urban and densely populated rural areas.

Schumpeter Meets Nurkse? An Entrepreneurial View on Microfinance

Microfinance institutions need both capital and internal operating capacity to achieve scale. Most microfinance institutions lack the capital to grow. Even though the industry has demonstrated that microfinance institutions can be self-sustaining businesses, most still rely on a limited pool of donor dollars. Without access to capital, growth traditionally stops once initial grant money is distributed as microcredit loans. To scale rapidly, microfinance institutions must access large amounts of capital to expand their operations and provide loans and other financial products to dramatically more clients. These large amounts of capital are accessible only through the formal capital markets, and currently most microfinance institutions have neither the track record nor the clearly articulated business plan to attract this funding. Most microfinance institutions lack large-scale internal operating capacity; without sufficient internal operating capacity, growth stops once a programme reaches several thousand clients. Adequate internal operating capacity includes improvements in areas such as information technology infrastructure, internal controls, new product development and human resources. When microfinance institutions rely on donor dollars, there is rarely enough money to make the necessary investments in these key areas to create an operation that is well run and has the ability to grow on a sustainable basis. Thus, most microfinance institutions are small and stay small. Grameen Foundation, however, provides funding for microfinance institutions through direct loans, grants, loan guarantees and other innovative financing techniques. Other funding comes from individuals, philanthropists, foundations and governments and international institutions such as the World Bank. Microfinance institutions also borrow funds from traditional banks to loan to their clients. In addition, the interest paid by clients on microfinance loans goes back into the programme to cover costs and fund more loans.[43] One of the most attractive features of microfinance is the goal of self-sufficiency for both microentrepreneurs and microfinance institutions. Grameen Foundation is spearheading several initiatives to give microfinance institutions access to the private market financing options available to traditional banks. By combining access to private market financing with more efficient management and technology, microfinance institutions can begin to move from reliance on philanthropy to self-sufficiency. Grameen Bank in Bangladesh has proven that this can be accomplished. It is totally self-supporting and accepts no grants or donations.

Nowadays, the Grameen Bank is an exciting object of theoretical research. Yunus received the Nobel Prize for Peace in 2006 and hundreds of articles and a dozen books have looked into the causes of the Bank's apparent success. Despite extensive research, a sufficient explanation of the Bank's success has remained a challenge. It seems every researcher reconstructs the Bank's development path with his own theory and sometimes prejudices, resulting in widely divergent explanations. Furthermore, Grameen Bank's practice has been brought up for some critical discussion due to its nontransparent and inefficient mien. Our own theory being based on entrepreneurship and innovation theory (see chapter 2), is no exception to this selective construction of the Grameen

Bank. Our main focus in this section is not primarily the success of the Bank as a viable financial organization, but, more narrowly, the impact of the credit policies on the reduction of poverty among microfinance institution's beneficiaries. Does Schumpeter meet Nurkse via microfinance?

Nurkse meets Schumpeter means to face a hopeless situation of poverty and to instrumentalize a concept of finance in order to break out of the vicious circle by following a path of economic development. Thus, to overcome a state of poverty we have not only to destroy the vicious circle, but we have to enter into a system of innovation (innovation not necessarily meant as basic innovations in the sense of Kondratieff). Our hypothesis is: Microfinance could be a starting point if we combine the Grameen concept with evolutionary logic in order to extend the entrepreneurial paradigm of traditional microfinace intermediaries. This would be an evolutionary 'silver bullet' to melt Nurke's and Schumpeter's ideas.

We defined economic development by reference to innovation (the cause of development), entrepreneurs (as the carriers of development) and financial capital, especially credit (the means of development). Does Grameen contribute to innovation of its clients/members? If the answer is 'no', Grameen Bank fails in an important sense, and Grameen's contribution to a long-term alleviation of poverty beyond a crucial ('survival'), but low level of poverty, is questionable. There can be no question; a person who would be a successful borrower must first live. But a bank's mission can reach out beyond survival of clients. How far financial intermediaries promote innovation of its clients is the crucial development test of dynamic or Schumpeterian efficiency. The basic idea of the Grameen Bank and other microloan providers has now to be critically evaluated. Does a microloan trigger a change in the system (borrower) strong enough to move out of poverty – *given* the systems cognitive and emotional competences and the sociocultural constraints in which it operates and interacts with the environment and other systems? Can credit help poor people to 'mutate' into innovative entrepreneurs, or does it serve to conserve their present organization. Let us therefore return to Grameen Banks success story in order to characterize how Schumpeter and Nurkse are combined by microfinance and what kind of limitations can be stated.

Credit has been the entry point for Grameen., Now the bank is active in many other fields such as housing, sanitation, children's education and, most recently, telecommunications services. Reasons for the apparant success of the Grameen Bank model are not so difficult to understand: (1) The bank has come up, through a process of trial and error, with a mode of operation that provided strong incentives for repayment; (2) the bank is catering to poor people *exclusively*, avoiding what Yunus called the 'good old Gresham law' of poverty, that the non-poor drive out the poor if one mixes both within the format of a single programme (Yunus 1993, 8); and (3) the bank was led by an exceptional entrepreneur in the person of Muhammad Yunus. For microfinance institutions, the same questions arise (especially in case of financing innovations respectively Schumpeterian entrepreneurs) as for any financial intermediary (see chapter 2): How to cope with information problems in terms of asymetrical distributed information and true uncertainty? How to overcome the involutionary process of many financial intermediaries infected by a financial Dutch Disease (see chapter 2) and thereby disabled to back entrepreneurs' financial needs during their seed and start-up phase?

The incentive system employed by Grameen bank makes use of many of the 'motivators' responsible for credit discipline: Lending is group-oriented; interested persons are asked to form groups of five people. Why groups of five? Initially, loans were given to individuals, but that proved uncontrollable for the staff. Then groups of 10 or more were organized, hoping that peer monitoring and social pressure would guarantee loan repayment. But that size turned out to be too large and the effectiveness of monitoring was impaired; members became economically too heterogeneous and thus required more information for mutual control; the well-known free-rider problem emerged.[44] So the bank finally settled on a group of five. Effective peer pressure seems, indeed, to work so well that credit default is no problem with Grameen and other institutions using similar methods (as BRAC and TRDEP in Bangladesh) – but often at the cost of substantial cost to defaulters as the 'forced acquisition of defaulters' assets ... and their sale in order to raise the necessary repayments' (Hulme and Mosley 1996, 154).

What are Grameen members doing with their loans?[45] The empirical accounts give answers like this: Borrowers contract loans for activities with which they 'are *already familiar*, such as paddy husking, cattle fattening' (MacIsaac and Wahid 1993, 193). Erhard Kropp, who was involved for many years with the Grameen Bank on behalf of the German goverment's promotional efforts, has observed a paucity of investment ideas among borrowers. The focus of Grameen to lend for familiar activities is not accidental, but an explicit part of the strategy. Yunus has referred to the Bank's approach as – more or less (Khandker 2005) – 'antitraining'. Grameen Bank did not offer training and credit for members simultaneously for a long time, but believed that borrowers *possessed all the relevant skills* to use credit productively. This was a *strategic* assumption of the Bank, making it operate differently from competing organizations. Thus, Grameen Bank can concentrate on credit to finance activities with which borrowers are already familiar (MacIsaac and Wahid 1993, 196). The low default rate and rather modest transaction costs (which keeps interest rates low and hence, allows for decent profit margins for the borrowers operating in traditional market segments) depend on – what may be termed an implicit – anti-innovation bias. Grameen and the replicators must focus, so it seems, on self-employed people or microenterprises operating in the 'economic core' (low growth, low innovation), routine or 'adaptive response' entrepreneurs. The strategic focus on noninnovators is critical, since it makes possible the survival and expansion of the Bank itself, especially the low default rate. Default has been the nemesis of conventional antipoverty schemes.

Despite a focus on familiar activities, the impact on income, as reported in some studies, seems surprisingly high, sometimes reaching several hundred per cent. How is this possible? The answer can be inferred from Leibenstein's concept of X-Inefficiency: (a) The markets in which the poor operate are imperfect. Those who get access to financial capital can correct 'market failure' and earn, for the time being, above-average returns. If market coordination improves, these returns will normalize, ie., turn towards zero; (b) In labour-surplus economies, in which the poor operate, capital, especially for the poor is exceedingly scarce; many an opportunity remains unexploited for lack of financial capital; if finance becomes available, these opportunities can now be taken up very fast by poor entrepreneurs, allowing the pioneers to capture above-normal profits again. But also, here we have to expect that, as time goes on, profit opportunities will disappear ('law of diminishing returns'). These aspects are rooted strongly to a search for more allocative (static) than dynamic efficiency. The crucial question that follows from this analysis: Is the positive *initial* impact on the poor's income from opening market opportunities through credit enduring enough to bring and keep the poor decisively above the poverty line? Our argument in the following tries to show that this cannot be ruled out, but we cannot assume or imply this to be a normal outcome. If the poor stick to their routine, do not venture into the unfamiliar, do not innovate, many of them will not make it. First, they cannibalize themselves; the more of them that enter into a given market, the more they will crowd each other out, mutually ruining their investment returns. This effect may become more pronounced in the future for two reasons: First, Grameen's success created imitators – the largest being BRAC and TREDP – both catering to similar target groups.[46] Second, there is a gradual shift from loans used for working capital to fixed capital (Hulme and Mosley 1996, 132), meaning an increasing 'capacity effect' resulting in increasing output. Thirdly, they get killed off by the forces of creative destruction: The circular flow of the routine economy, in which the poor operate, is destroyed by the introduction of innovation. Moreover, when innovation gets underway, the co-innovative and co-evolutionary processes initiated by innovation, result in contionuous destruction of those unable or unwilling – including previous innovators – to participate in new rounds of innovation. As far as we see, the supply of financial capital to *non*-innovating entrepreneurs will only contribute to their dismal fate. Creative destruction is entering Bangladesh's villages, whether Grameen has initiated and fostered innovation or not. Grameen may indeed promote these Schumpeterian forces through new ventures that bring handphones and the internet into village economy, that may undermine the very foundation on which the financial operations of Grameen have been built. The very success of the non-financial initiatives taken by Grameen, will produce factors that are inconsistent with it.

What is the problem with such activities? They make obvious sense for poor people. They are low-risk, allow a steady cash flow, are easily to understand, screened and evaluated by other members of the credit group who have to agree to the loan proposal. The two main difficulties are quite well overcome: asymmetrical information and uncertainty (see chapter II.2). But they have one drawback: they do not bring very much in additional income. The latter, because new recombinations implying radical uncertainty are weeded out. Borrowers with Grameen and adopter organizations engage in relatively low-return but steady income producing projects. People living at the subsistence level do not engage in innovations. The occupations they prefer consist typically of 'me too' activities: easy entry, easy exit. These make for intensive competition, bringing down profits to zero and leaving the entrepreneurs not more than wage income, often below subsistence. Loss minimization rather than profit maximization is the dominant concern. As routine entrepreneurs, they construct the world as a closed opportunity space: there are entrepreneurial opportunities, since the system in which they operate is characterized by imperfections in factor and product markets (low-income economies being, 'obstructed, incomplete and 'relatively dark' economic systems,' as Leibenstein 1968, 77 notes) and arbitrage opportunities emerge continuously also in a stationary economy.

Microfinance programmes may enable poor people to improve their situation, but they do not eliminate the need for other basic social and infrastructure services. Microfinance can help poor households to reduce their vulnerability to economic shocks, but they do not eliminate such shocks. It helps the poor to take advantage of economic opportunities, but it does not create such opportunities. Microfinance can only ever be one part of a broader process of social and economic development. The type of income-generating projects favoured by Grameen and other microlending institutions takes a long time to achieve a dramatic poverty impact. That is the difference between routine allocation and the creative emergence of new opportunities of transcending from routine to innovative (creative) entrepreneurship.[47] Ten years is a long time, even in the life of poor people. Quite some may have died before reaching a decent living standard.

Given Grameen's mixed record on promoting innovation among its members, it remains an open question of how far the Bank succeeds in alleviating poverty beyond a basic level of basic needs satisfaction (in itself a big achievement). Have these difficulties something to do with the way Grameen operates? We believe this to be the case. Grameen's model of credit delivery is built around groups of five self-selecting persons. But do jointly liable group members really want innovators to become members? What happens with loan access if a member mutates into an innovator? Since all members are jointly liable for any loan, risk aversion – already very pronounced among poor people – will likely prevent selection or promotion of innnovators. An architecture that works extremely well for routine business becomes a drawback if *new* combinations need finance secured by social collateral.[48] By externalizing the problem of assessment to the real sphere of an entrepreneurial group – representing possibly different entrepreneurial functions – a strong impact on each business charta (and strategy) may arise, possibly accompanied by negative effects on innovative enterprises.

The above factors together may contribute to unravelling the morale of repayment, that is, destruct the very social and cultural core responsible for the success of the Grameen Bank model. The Bank's (more or less) 'antitraining' approach created an anti-innovation bias in lending. Indeed, co-evolution, the symbiotic creation of new capabilities in processes of mutual learning, becomes negated. This is the rule among common banks, and a reason why they face difficulties with innovators and why innovation finance remains the comparative advantage of informal financiers (see chapter 2).[49] A training approach should not be focussed only on entrepreneurial learning at different stages; it is important to include gender training as an important part of the microfinance programme.[50] Actually, there is growing consciousness that a training approach may help to support entrepreneurial efforts more effectively, as Karlan and Valdivia (2006) state:

> Can one teach entrepreneurship, or is it a fixed personal characteristic? Most academic and policy discussion on microentrepreneurs in developing countries focuses on their access to credit, and assumes their human capital to be fixed. However, a growing number of microfinance organizations are attempting to build the human capital of microentrepreneurs in order to improve the livelihood of their clients and help further their mission of poverty alleviation.

The challenge ahead for the Grameen Bank and similar organizations is clear enough: how to self-mutate into a bank able and willing to promote non-routine entrepreneurs without self-destruction. This requires new competencies among the bank's leadership, probably a new architecture (within the bank and in its relationship with the members) in order to implement a more Schumpeterian, i.e., innovation-orientated strategy. This requires self- and co-evolution, i.e., evolutionary learning: higher competence to financial interactions allowing for innovation. To promote innovators is a tremendous task.[51] The problem is what the bank can do to promote innovation among its own (women) membership. Just to maintain that every woman is or could become an innovator is idealistic, if not surrealistic. We have no information about the distribution of innovators among Grameen's membership. Based on estimates from developed countries, about one in ten entrepreneurs could be considered an innovator. Transferring this percentage to Bangladesh, it would mean one innovator in every other compartment of the five-person credit groups. It could be less (if potential innovators do not become group members), or more (if innovators have strong incentives to enter). How it looks in reality, we do not know. What we do know is that if innovation enters, the credit delivery mechanism of any bank must become much more complex. Grameen would have to change in many ways, with substantial risk for institutional survival. Most banks have given up catering to innovative entrepreneurs (see chapter 2). Grameen is in a good neighbourhood. An outcome like this is no problem as long as noninnovative borrowers live well above the poverty line or can easily find jobs with sufficient incomes.

Given the difficulties of promoting poor innovators with financial capital, Grameen seems to have followed another strategy: *Grameen innovates on behalf of the poor.* Grameen ventures into fisheries, tubewell irrigation, agricultural irrigation, telecommunications, personal computers, etc.. There is no future without creative destruction. Yunus has said that 'poverty does not belong in a civilized human society. It belongs in museums' (cited in Clark 1997, 5). Grameen Bank is considered *the* ultimate success story in the development community. It has received academic attention and public awareness as no other Third World institution. In general public and the academic literature alike, there is little critical assessment and evaluation of this success. And a lack of critical awareness has contributed to many attempts worldwide to 'replicate' the Grameen Bank model seen by many as a miracle cure for poverty and by others a sure bet on donor funds. Thomas Dichter states that recent experience and the economic history of rich countries, however, suggest that those expectations are unrealistic. Most people, poor or otherwise, are not entrepreneurs, so there is little reason to think that mass credit would, in general, lead to viable business start-ups.[52] Today as in the past, business start-ups in the advanced countries depend predominantly on savings and informal sources of credit; past forms of microcredit never played a role in small business development, and much microcredit is actually used for consumption rather than investment. In the history of today's rich countries, moreover, economic growth occurred first, then came credit for the masses.

Conclusion vs. Confusion: Microfinance as a 'Silver Bullet'?

In his book *Protectionism*, Bhagwati (1988, 130) states, 'Let me conclude by reasserting my guarded optimism in regard to the long-run prospects for keeping protectionism at bay. My mind turns back to Ragnar Nurkse, whose pessimism about the prospects for world trade was invalidated by the glorious 1950s and 1960s. I hope that my optimism encounters a more indulgent future.' Actually, the role of Ricardo's comparative advantage doctrine and the necessity of a free trade or protectionism paradigm for an effective policy approach is discussed controversially even today. In this context, the role of money has become an important starting point for an economic policy in industrialized *and* underdeveloped countries. Thus, (how) can Schumpeter's and Nurkse's ideas be combined? Can microfinance be a tool to achieve dynamic comparative advantages to overcome poverty lastingly and to enter into a path of economic development?

If our expectations concerning poverty alleviation remain modest, Grameen and imitators have achieved a lot. Grameen Bank has succeeded where others failed: bringing basic financial services, especially credit, to poor people. Regular salaried or wage-paying jobs are scarce in many developing countries. Most of their citizens instead make their living through self-employment in the informal sector. But without access to the quality, affordable financial services they need to fuel their productivity and reduce their vulnerabilities to external shocks, the poor majority can never grow their microenterprises into businesses that can help them escape poverty. They can never escape survival mode and according to Nurkse, they are stuck in a vicious circle of poverty. By providing credit to self-employed and underemployed poor people, the microfinance institutions have laid the foundation to help them achieve survival income. The bank has contributed to self-reliant behaviours of the poor and created hope and competences in their children, which in the future may create new, growing enterprises that will create employment and income for others. The poor can achieve upward mobility and thus break out of the vicious circle of self-perpetuating poverty, characteristic of poor and stationary economies, where negative feedback rules and evolutionary learning is absent. Can we expect more?

From a Schumpeterian perspective, most of microfinance's work remains to be done. Best estimates indicate that there are hundreds of millions of self-employed poor, worldwide, who could benefit from, but do not yet have, access to financial services. Microfinance institutions are currently reaching only an estimated 4 per cent of them. One can claim that we have to go further. The very success of the Grameen Bank may block future progress. To some extent,

Grameen seems aware of this. It is diversifying into fields not related to banking, becoming a champion of innovation for the poor via financial services. Having liberated the poor – to some extent – it follows through with a paternalistic approach: innovation for the poor, not by the poor. Helping the poor to do something new via financial services is a new frontier. Commercial banks anywhere have been *unable* to provide innovation finance, especially for new firms. Innovation finance has remained, also in highly developed capitalist states, the birthright and comparative advantage of informal agents. Karlan and Valdivia (2006) have shown that an entrepreneurial training can have strong impact on their clients' efforts:

> We find that the treatment led to improved business knowledge, practices and revenues. The microfinance institution also had direct benefits through higher repayment and client retention rates. Larger effects found for those that expressed less interest in training in a baseline survey have important implications for implementing similar market-based interventions with a goal of recovering costs.

Thus, the Nurkse-Schumpeter challenge for microfinance institutions is a dual one: provide finance to the poor (Nurkse), and help the poor to become innnovators (Schumpeter). What Grameen has achieved with finance for the poor – extending the frontier of formal finance where hitherto informal transactions were dominating – has now to be repeated with innovation finance for the poor. This requires incorporating spheres of informal transactions into formal banking procedures. It needs managerial and entrepreneurial competences far superior to the ones now necessary to deliver financial services to clients who, engaged in routine and arbitrage business, mainly self-enforce credit discipline and internalize transaction costs. Grameen would need to learn, step by step, to live with transactions far away from equilibrium and central control. It needs to create and maintain zones of creativity at the edge of organization and formality, and this implies moving away from a hierachical structure into a network institution that is neither market nor hierarchy – at least for those transactions that are part of the innovation system. To help members innovate and self-evolve, the microfinance bank needs to entertain innovation and evolution within itself. Otherwise, mutually satisfactory interactions with members remain difficult. The bank would further be called on to integrate the new activities and business units into the economic lives of its members. This again requires experiments in financial services, including venture capital for the poor and microenterprises. As any financial intermediary that wants to be allowed, able and willing to play an active role in the sense of Nurkse and Schumpeter, microfinance institutions have to establish and keep an innovation-related business charta and entrepreneurial spirit despite the fact that the money gathered from outside overwhemingly represents routine and arbitrage functions, and may influence the portfolio strategy and leading the financial intermediary astray.

We doubt all this can be achieved with a minimalist approach that actually assumes learning (evolutionary learning, i.e., beyond learning on level 0 and 1) does not matter, especially evolutionary learning. Mastering this challenges and future tasks means evolving into a hybrid organization to a much larger degree than is the case now (where only the five-person credit groups have elements of a quasi-cooperative nature). Grameen Bank as a hierarchy is too cumbersome and inflexible to cope with the turbulences and uncertainty of an innovation-richer internal and external environment. Entrepreneurship will need to be shared with lower levels of the hierarchy, requiring entrepreneurial freedom. Grameen Bank could no longer function as a pyramid of power, led by a charismatic entrepreneur, but resemble more a web of units with higher autonomy, bonded together by their collective ability to assist one another and the poor (innovating entrepreneurs). The bank would thus have to re-architect internal and external interactions, create internal markets or become more market-like. Hybrid governance replaces hierarchical control. New structural couplings with the members then allows for more internal and external (member) innovation, presently made difficult by internal credit procedures and the culture of poverty of the members. In other words, Grameen, as any other financial institution with a mission to cater for innovation among its clients, must evolve capabilities allowing the construction of a reality in which the poor can innovate; competences that permit the increase of more complex constructions of reality (higher internal complexity), allow more complex actions by the organization's members (the poor) and consequently open up possibilities for creative responses for clients.

Donor support for traditional microfinance models has helped provide basic financial services to millions of poor people. But in order to build dynamic competitive economies in developing countries, the time has come to pay greater attention to the potential of small and medium-sized commercial firms to promote economic growth. The areas and structures of collaboration between the state and microfinance institutes still have to be explored more thoroughly (Sriram 2005). Thus, it is important to combine Nurkse and Schumpeter by a structurally linkage between microfinance as one tool to overcome poverty on the one side and the informal forces of bootstrapping and angel capital benefits in order to enter on a path of economic development and growth. Microfinance institutions are threatened to be infected by the involutionary process that many financial intermediaries have experienced when opening their funds to money from outside, representing entrepreneurial paradigms and thereby hindering an innovative portfolio strategy. Beside the integration of philanthropists, etc., the integration of experienced business angels – their flow of money and their know-how – into the microfinance business charta may be a solution to help ongoing entrepreneurs to step into a learning process on different levels. Innovation might be a byproduct of (self-) evolution if angels act as a coevolutionary sounding board and as a doorkeeper to relevant networks.

Evolution, according to Schumpeter, is spontaneous, disharmonious and discontinous change, not a smooth, gradual process of doing more of what always has been done (learning 0: the neoclassical world). Development cannot proceed slowly and gradually: '... the new cannot be reached from the old one by infinitesimal steps. Add successively as many mail coaches as you please, you will never get a railway thereby' (Schumpeter [1934] 2002, 64). Add successively as many loans as you please, your will never get an end to poverty. Grameen will not succeed to eradicate the disease of poverty (Yunus 1993, 9: 'Poverty is a chronic disease') by sticking with proceedures successful in the past. Path dependency is a powerful constraint on innovation. It has been built into the culture, hierarchy and the procedural routines of the bank. To a large degree, Grameen stands with one foot in the stationary economy, where innovation and creative destruction are absent. With the second foot, it entered new territory, outside the financial system (telecom services and the like). It has used its prestige and reputation to build up nonfinancial businesses, leaving the members well implanted in a culture of poverty characteristic of stationary economies. But in this traditional field of transactions with the members, the bank is running more and more into the constraints of the law of diminishing returns of poverty alleviation, pursuing to the bitter end a product cycle created by itself.

Microfinance also appeals to the Western appetite for market solutions to social problems. Microlending is, after all, a financial innovation that harnesses market forces, and the resulting social benefits of poverty reduction and community investment can be seen as positive externalities. Grameen Bank boasts a 98 per cent repayment rate on loans that often carry high interest rates, indicating that microfinance is not a form of charity. The borrowers use their loans to produce a marketable product and make enough profit on the sale to pay back their lender in full. Microfinance, it seems, is good business. Like all good ideas, microfinance will have to prove itself in the unforgiving arena of scientific rigor and evidentiary proof. Will it survive? The spotlight provided by the Nobel Committee suggests that now is the opportune time to find out. Microfinance is maturing into a transparent and regulated industry. Regulators, well-known business auditors and rating agencies pay significantly closer attention to leading microfinance institutions, given their growing importance in national capital markets. Their involvement provides a solid legal, financial and political framework to sustain the growth of the industry. This evolution does not mean necessarily that microfinance is shifting away from its focus on poverty alleviation; on the contrary, commercialization, expertise and regulation are the means to improving the scale and quality of impact on the socioeconomic situation of the microentrepreneurs and their families. Sustainability is the key to this long-term effort, and this, in turn, is based on the economic longevity of the microfinance institutions themselves. But, microfinance institutions have encountered the necessity of gaining and keeping evolutionary and innovative competencies in order to avoid the problem of many financial intermediaries' problems of involution. And only innovation and, hence, innovative capabilities in the real and financial sphere are responsible for a path towards economic development and growth. Thus, according to Nurkse *and* Schumpeter, innovative and evolutionary competencies in both areas are needed and have to be integrated into a microfinance-based policy approach of economic development in underdeveloped countries. Thus, microfinance is not a silver bullet. It will not defeat global poverty by itself. But, it is an important part of the solution. Microfinance provides a stable and sustainable source of income, mostly in the real sphere of routine (and arbitrage) based on entrepreneurial activity that enables clients to climb steadily out of poverty, while providing better living conditions and opportunities for their families. But to meet Schumpeter, an evolutionary path to innovation and economic development has to be followed. This is, of course, not a request to bring people living in poverty up to enter into a system of basic innovations. But it means to help them to catch, up step by step, by integrating some Kondratieff paradigms into their entrepreneurial efforts by imitation and/or arbitrage. Thereby, financial structures needed for economic development can be created and the autopietic process of a complemetary interplay between informal and formal financial systems (bootstrapping, business angels, venture capital firms and banks) can be initiated. Ultimately, we can finish our conclusion with an important statement of Ragnar Nurkse (1960, 1): 'Economic development has much to do with human endowments, social attitudes, political conditions – and historical accidents. Capital is a necessary but not sufficient condition of progress.'

References

Abramovitz, Moses. 1986. 'Catching Up, Forging Ahead, and Falling Behind.' *The Journal of Economic History* 46 (2), 385–406.

Aernoudt, Rudy. 1999. 'Business Angels: Should they Fly on their own Wings?' *Venture Capital: An international Journal of Entrepreneurial Finance* 1 (2), 187–195.

Allen, Franklin and Anthony M. Santomero. 2001. 'What Do Financial Intermediaries Do?' *Journal of Banking and Finance* 25 (2), 271–294.

Armendariz, Beatrice and Jonathan Morduch. 2004. 'Microfinance: Where do we Stand?' In Charles Goodhart (ed.). *Financial Development and Economic Growth: Explaining the Links*. London: Palgrave Macmillan, 135–149.

Benjamin, Geral A. and Joel Margulis. 2000. *Angel Financing – How to Find and Invest Private Equity*. New York: John Wiley & Sons.

Bhagwati, Jagdish. 1988. *Protectionism*. Cambridge, MA: MIT Press.

Bhidé, Amar. 1992. 'Bootstrap Finance: The Art of Start-Ups.' *Harvard Business Review* 70 (November/December), 109–117.

Burlamaqui, Leonardo. 2000. 'Schumpeterian Competition, Financial Innovation and Financial Fragillity: An Exercise in Blending Evolutionary Economics with Minsky's Macrofinance.' Conference paper for the '8th International J. A. Schumpeter Conference', Manchester.

Burlamaqui, Leonardo and Jan Kregel. 2005. 'Innovation, Competition and Financial Vulnerability in Economic Development.' *Revista de Economia Politica* 25 (2), 5–22.

Bygrave, William D. and Jeffrey A. Timmons. 1992. *Venture Capital at the Crossroads*. Boston, MA: Harvard Business School Press.

Caves, Richard and Ronald Jones. 1981. *World Trade Payments: An Introduction*. Boston: Little Brown & Company.

Clark, B. 1997. 'Big Role for the Small Loan.' *Financial Times*, 6 February, 5.

Clogherty, Tom (ed.). 2006. *Microfinance: Harnessing Enterprise to Fight Poverty*. London: Globalisation Institute Research Ltd.

Coveney, Patrick and Karl Moore. 1998. *Business Angels: Securing Start Up Finance*, Chichester: John Wiley.

Diamond, Douglas. 1984. 'Financial Intermediation and Delegated Monitoring.' *Review of Economic Studies* 51 (3), 393–414.

Dichter, Thomas. 2003. *Despite Good Intentions: Why Development Assistance to the Third World Has Failed*. Amherst and Boston: University of Massachusetts Press.

Duxbury, Linda, George Haines and Allan Riding. 1996. 'A Personality Profile of Canadian Informal Investors.' *Journal of Small Business Management* 34 (2), 44–55.

Fama, Eugen. 1980. 'Banking in the Theory of Finance.' *Journal of Monetary Economics* 6 (1), 39–57.

Fiet, James. 1995. 'Risk Avoidance Strategies in the Venture Capital Markets.' *Journal of Management Studies* 32 (4), 551–574.

Freear, John, Jeffrey Sohl and William Wetzel. 1995. 'Angels: Personal Investors in the Venture Capital Market.' *Entrepreneurship & Regional Development* 7 (1), 85–94.

Gompers, Paul. 1998. 'Venture Capital Growing Pains: Should the Market Diet?' *Journal of Banking & Finance* 22 (6), 1089–1104.

Harrison, Richard and Colin Mason. 2000. 'Venture Capital Market Complementarities: The Link between Business Angels and Venture Capital Funds in the United Kingdom.' *Venture Capital: An international Journal of Entrepreneurial Finance*, 2 (3), 223–242.

————. 1992. 'International Perspectives on the Supply of Informal Venture Capital.' *Journal of Business Venturing* 7 (6), 459–475.

Hirschman, Albert. 1958. *The Strategy of Economic Development*. New Haven: Yale University Press.

Hossain, Mahabub and Binayak Sen. 1992. 'Rural Poverty in Bangladesh: Trends and Determinants.' *Asian Development Review* 10 (1), 1–34.

Hulme, David and Paul Mosley. 1996. *Finance against Poverty*, vol. 1 and 2. London: Routledge.

Karlan, Dean S. and Martin Valdivia. 2006. 'Teaching Entrepreneurship: Impact of Business Training on Microfinance Clients and Institutions.' Yale University Economic Growth Center. Discussion Paper No. 941.

Kay, John. 1993. *The Foundations of Corporate Success*. Oxford: Oxford University Press.

Khandker, Shahidur. 2005. 'Microfinance and Poverty: Evidence Using Panel Data from Bangladesh.' *World Bank Economic Review* 19 (2), 263–286.

King, Robert G. and Ross Levine. 1993. 'Finance and Growth: Schumpeter Might Be Right.' *Quarterly Journal of Economics* 108 (3), 717–737.

Kirzner, Israel. 1997. 'Entrepreneurial Discovery and the Competitive Market Process: An Austrian Approacch.' *Journal of Economic Literature* 35 (1), 60–85.

————. 1992. *The Meaning of Market Process: Essays in the Development of Modern Austrian Economics* (Foundations of the Market Economy Series). Routledge Chapman & Hall.

Leibenstein, Harvey. 1968. 'Entrepreneurship and Development.' *American Economic Review (Papers and Proceedings)* 58 (2), 72–83.

Luhmann, Niklas. 1999. Die Wirtschaft der Gesellschaft. 3rd edition. Frankfurt (Main): Suhrkamp Verlag.

Lewis, David. 1996. 'Appropriating Technology? Tractor Owners, Brokers, Artisans and Farmers in Rural Bangladesh.' *Journal of International Development* 8 (1), 21–38.

MacIsaac, Norm and Abu N. M. Wahid. 1993. 'The Grameen Bank: Its Institutional Lessons for Rural Financing.' In Abu N. M. Wahid (ed.). *The Grameen Bank. Poverty Relief in Bangladesh*. Boulder/San Francisco/Oxford: Westview Press, 191–209.

Mason, Colin and Richard Harrison. 2002. 'Is it Worth it? The Rates of Return from Informal Venture Capital Investments', *Journal of Business Venturing*. 17 (3). 211–236.

Miner, John. 1997. 'A Psychological Typology and its Relationship to Entrepreneurial Success.' *Entrepreneurship & Regional Development* 9 (3), 319–334.

Morduch, Jonathan. 1999a. 'The Microfinance Promise.' *Journal of Economic Literature* 37 (4), 1569–1614.

————. 1999b. 'The Role of Subsidies in Microfinance: Evidence from The Grameen Bank.' *Journal of Development Economics* 60 (1), 229–248.

Murray, Gordon. 1999. 'Early-Stage Venture Capital Funds, Scale Economies and Public Support.' *Venture Capital: An International Journal of Entrepreneurial Finance* 1 (4), 351–384.

Nurkse, Ragnar. 1962. *Equilibrium and Growth in the World Economy*. Ed. by Gottfried Haberler and Robert M. Stern. Cambridge, MA: Harvard University Press.

————. 1961. *Patterns of Trade and Development*. New York: Oxford University Press.

————. 1960 [1953]. *Problems of Capital Formation in Underdeveloped Countries*. Oxford: Blackwell.

Perez, Carlotta. 2003. *Technological Revolutions and Financial Capital: The Dynamics of Bubbles and Golden Ages*. Cheltenham: Edward Elgar.

Politis, Diamanto and Hans Landström. 2002. 'Informal Investors as Entrepreneurs: The Development of an Entrepreneurial Career.' *Venture Capital: An International Journal of Entrepreneurial Finance* 4 (2), 78–102.

Prasad, Dev, Garry D. Bruton and George S. Vozikis. 2000. 'Signalling Value to Business Angels: The Proportion of the Entrepreneur's Net Worth Invested in a New Venture as a Decision Signal.' *Venture Capital: An International Journal of Entrepreneurial Finance* 2 (3), 167–182.

Röpke, Jochen. 2005. 'The Construction of Entrepreneurship: Theoretical Foundation and Practical Problems.' Paper presented at Workshop 'Entrepreneurship and Higher Education,' The University of Tehran, 26–28 September 2004, this version: 18 September 2005.

_____. 2002. *Der lernende Unternehmer: Zur Evolution und Konstruktion unternehmerischer Kompetenz.* Marburg/Norderstedt: Books on Demand.

_____. 1981. 'Free Trade, Protection and Economic Development.' *Intereconomics* 16 (January/February), 26–30.

_____. 1977. *Die Strategie der Innovation. Eine systemtheoretische Untersuchung der Interaktion von Individuum, Organisation und Markt im Neuerungsprozeß*, Tübingen: Mohr-Siebeck.

Schmidt, Reinhard H., Andreas Hackethal and Marcel Tyrell. 1999. 'Disintermediation and the Role of Banks in Europe: An International Comparison.' *Journal of Financial Intermediation* 8 (1), 36–67.

Scholtens, Bert and Dick van Wensveen. 2000. 'A Critique on the Theory of Financial Intermediation.' *Journal of Banking & Finance* 24 (8), 1243–1251.

Schumpeter, Joseph. [1934] 2002. *The Theory of Economic Development: An Inquiry into Profits, Capital, Credit, Interest and the Business Cycle.* Cambridge, MA: Harvard University Press.

_____. 1939. *Business Cycles: A Theoretical, Historical, and Statistical Analysis of the Capitalist Process.* New York, Toronto, London: McGraw-Hill Book Company.

Siemon, Cord. 2006a. 'Financing 6th Kondratief's Start-ups: Evolutionary Economics and Financial Entrepreneurship.' Paper for Conference 'Neo-Schumpeterian Economics: An Agenda for the 21st Century.' Trest, Czech Republic, 27–29 June 2006.

_____. 2006b. *Unternehmertum in der Finanzwirtschaft: Ein evolutionsökonomischer Beitrag zur Theorie der Finanzintermediation.* Marburg/Norderstedt: Books on Demand.

Sohl, Jeffrey. 1999. 'The Early-Stage Equity Market in the USA.' *Venture Capital: An International Journal of Entrepreneurial Finance* 1 (2), 101–120.

Sriram, Mankal. 2005. 'Microfinance and the State: Exploring Areas and Structures of Collaboration.' *Economic and Political Weekly* 40 (7), 1699–1703.

Steier, Lloyd and Royston Greenwood. 1999. 'Newly Created Firms and Informal Angel Investors: A Four-Stage Model and Network Development.' *Venture Capital: An International Journal of Entrepreneurial Finance* 1 (2), 147–168.

Stiglitz, Joseph. 1990. 'Peer Monitoring and Credit Markets.' *World Bank Economic Review* 4 (3), 351–66.

van Osnabrugge, Mark. 2000. 'A Comparison of Business Angel and Venture Capitalist Investment Procedures: An Agency Theory-Based Analysis.' *Venture Capital: An International Journal of Entrepreneurial Finance* 2 (2), 91–110.

van Osnabrugge, Mark and Robert Robinson. 2000. *Angel Investing: Matching Start-up Funds with Start-up Companies – The Guide for Entrepreneurs, Individual Investors, and Venture Capitalists.* San Francisco: Jossey-Bass.

Winborg, Joakim and Hans Landström. 2001. 'Financial Bootstrapping in Small Businesses: Examining Small Business Managers' Resource Acquisition Behaviors.' *Journal of Business Venturing* 16 (3), 235–254.

Yunus, Muhammad. 1993. 'On Reaching the Poor.' In Ismael P. Jr. Getubig, Mohol Y. Johari and Angela M. Kuga Thas (eds). *Overcoming Poverty through Credit: The Asian Experience in Replicating the Grameen Bank Approach.* Kuala Lumpur: Asian and Pacific Development Center, 3–12.

Chapter Eleven:

STOCKPILING OF INTERNATIONAL RESERVES AND DEVELOPMENT: A MISGUIDED LINK

Moritz Cruz and Bernard Walters

Introduction

The economic policy response to prevent the cycle of speculative attack-capital, flight-financial crisis, adopted by both crisis-affected and other non-affected emerging economies since Mexico's 1994–95 financial crisis, but particularly since the 1997–98 East Asian crisis, has been simply to increase liquidity through the accumulation of international reserves. Developing countries' international reserves 'have risen from 6–8 per cent of GDP during the 1970s and 1980s to almost 30 per cent of GDP by 2004' (Rodrik, 2006, 255). Furthermore, today, around two-thirds of international reserves are held by developing countries (Aizenman, 2007).

   The dominant explanation for the build-up of reserves is that it simply represents precautionary behaviour designed to provide insurance against the high output and other costs associated with earlier crises. Countries following this strategy are evidently hoping to emulate those economies that escaped speculative attacks and/or capital flight (e.g., Chile, Columbia, China and India) and maintained policy autonomy, thereby providing 'a way of reducing the risks of future crises and of minimizing the need to turn to the IMF if crises occurred' (Bird and Mandilaras, 2005, 85). A second, alternative but not exclusive, explanation for reserves accumulation identifies it with an active policy of export-led industrialization characteristic of several countries in East Asia (especially China). This is the mercantilist interpretation of reserve accumulation, in which increased reserves are a by-product of maintaining a competitive exchange rate designed to expand tradeable production (see Aizenman and Riera-Critchton, 2006).

However, there has been little concern in the literature to evaluate the trade-offs involved in the stockpiling of international reserves; the factors that predispose an economy to financial crisis; and finally, whether there are policies better suited to the promotion of financial stability and policy autonomy that also allow sufficient space to promote development in the sense of aiding the process of industrialization.

Those studies that have attempted to estimate the cost of holding precautionary reserves have typically done so on the basis of the difference between a market rate of interest and the much lower rate available on holding reserves. These studies suggest the excess of international reserves has a cost of around 1 per cent of GDP (Rodrik, 2000, 2006; Bird and Rajan, 2003). However, such an approach does not address the logic of accumulating large reserves when a country is most in the need of them for alternative productive projects. In addition, other studies have implied that this strategy can have detrimental effects on the financial sector through the creation of either moral hazard problems, due to very liquid banking systems channelling excess credit to overheated asset markets and/or domestic macroeconomic risks such as inflation, high intervention costs and monetary imbalances (García and Soto, 2004; Mohanthy and Turner, 2006; Schiller, 2007).

In addition, the empirical significance of the alternative, mercantilist strategy is contested, that is, as Aizenman (2006, 2) observes, 'the mercantilist case for hoarding international reserves, as an ingredient of an export led growth strategy, is lacking empirical evidence'.

An important point that needs highlighting is that some of the issues that the phenomenon of reserves accumulation brings under scrutiny, like industrialization and financing development, were the key concern of Ragnar Nurkse. In his studies (Nurkse 1954, 1962), for example, he actually discussed the relevance of necessarily finance-productive projects from domestic resources, avoiding, in this sense, the constraint of supply finance. The fact that developing countries are forgoing productive resources when accumulating foreign exchange or, to put it differently, that are not effectively using available funds, set parallels with some of Nurkse's concerns.

The aim of this paper is to argue that the accumulation of international reserves is misguided and overly pessimistic. There are alternative policies that are feasible, have proved effective during earlier periods of financial instability (such as capital controls and restrictions on currency convertibility) and therefore provide an alternative route to financial stability while maintaining policy autonomy and allowing a more effective focus on developmental goals. The paper is set out as follows: The second section explains why international reserves around the world have substantially increased. The third section argues that at least three important issues need to be considered when deciding whether or not to adopt a stockpiling reserves strategy: (1) what factors predispose an economy to financial crisis; (2) whether reserve accumulation can contribute to broader developmental objectives as well as offering some form of self-insurance against crises; and finally, (3) whether there are feasible alternative policies that can provide financial stability and successfully promote development without sacrificing policy autonomy. The fourth section presents policy alternatives to achieve and maintain financial stability and contribute to development in a variety of different ways. The final section presents the concluding remarks.

International Reserves: What Explains Their Recent Accumulation?

Since the mid-'90s, because of the emergence – indeed, the boom – in financial crises in the developing world, notably in Mexico, Thailand, Korea, Malaysia, Philippines, Indonesia, Brazil, Turkey, Russia and Argentina, the issue of the accumulation of international reserves has regained relevance and interest (see Aizenman, et al 2004; Aizenman and Marion, 2002; Bird and Rajan 2003; Mendoza, 2004; Wijnholds and Kapteyn, 2001).[1] The majority of these were associated with the adoption of the neoliberal financial liberalization strategy of free mobility of capital (see, inter alia, Allen, 2004; Arestis and Glickman, 2002; Cruz, Amman and Walters, 2006; Grabel, 1996; Palma, 2003; Singh, 2003), which increased the vulnerability of the balance of payments emanating from the capital account, a source ignored during the earlier era of capital controls.

The observed increased vulnerability to crises in the modern era of financial liberalization has meant that stockpiling international reserves has been seen as the central policy option that a country could pursue to avoid a financial crisis and its high economic costs (Bird and Rajan, 2003). This choice is reflected in the evolution of world international reserves. As can be seen from Figure 11.1, the accumulation of international reserves has constantly increased since the early 1990s. In fact, worldwide accumulation registered one marked break in 1994–1945, just in the aftermath the Mexico's financial crisis. Furthermore, if high income OECD countries are eliminated from our sample, given that they liberalized their financial markets only after the early stages of development were long completed, the pattern described becomes more marked. Interestingly, after the South East Asian financial crisis of 1997–1998 and the crises in Brazil (1998) and Argentina (2001), the growth of international reserves shows a further acceleration. As a proportion of GDP, international reserves have increased almost 10 per cent since the late 1990s, going from around 15 per cent in 1999 to nearly 25 per cent in 2005. This suggests, as

Figure 11.1. Evolution of international reserves (expressed as per cent of GDP), 1990–2005

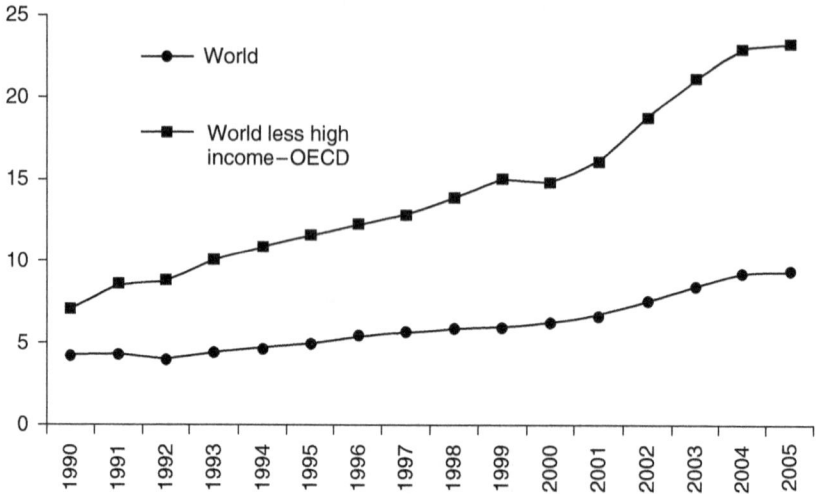

Source: WDI (2007).

Rodrik (2006) stresses, that developing economies are deeply involved in international reserves accumulation.

From this evidence, it can be argued that the accumulation of international reserves was seen initially as a source of protection or insurance, and more recently as a permanent buffer stock against the *total* or overall vulnerability of the balance of payments, defined as the vulnerability arising from both the capital and the current accounts. In other words, large stocks of reserves provide financial stability by decreasing the likelihood of financial crises and their associated costs (or from another perspective, international reserve accumulation prevents, or at least reduces, the likelihood of a speculative attack).[2]

Of course, in the current era of free mobility of capital, much more attention has been placed on the vulnerability arising from the capital account. That is, a 'developing country's reserves are related to changes not in *real* quantities (such as imports or output) but in *financial* magnitudes' (Rodrik, 2006, 257, emphasis in the original).

In fact, the results reported by Mendoza (2004), for a sample of 65 developing economies, are consistent with the hypothesis that since the boom in financial crises, the strategy of reserve accumulation has been linked to the idea of financial stability. In addition, the econometric work of Aizenman and

Lee (2005) confirms that developing countries mainly demand and accumulate foreign exchange for precautionary reasons, that is, against the possibility of costly output contractions induced by sudden halts in capital inflows or capital flight.

The evolution of international reserves just described seems unrelated to any clear notion of what might constitute an optimal level of reserves. The so-called Guidotti-Greenspan rule,[3] which proposes 'the maintenance of reserves equivalent to 12 months of a country's total foreign obligation, which includes but is not limited to imports' (Mendoza, 2004, p. 76), does not adequately explain the trend. This is unsurprising as this sort of criteria is based on a rule of thumb,[4] rather than any formal theory.[5] Nevertheless, as we have already stressed, there are clear precautionary reasons to hold reserves, but 'quantifying optimum reserves is … not straightforward since it is difficult to estimate the adjustment costs and output losses that reserves may enable a country to avoid' (Bird and Mandilaras, 2005, 86). In the absence of consensus about the optimal level of reserves, the data is best characterized as following what has come to be called Mrs. Machlup's wardrobe theory (Machlup, 1966). According to Bird and Rajan (2003, 877), this suggests that the 'acquisitive characteristics of monetary authorities in terms of adding to their reserves resembled those of Mr. Machlup's wife in terms of clothes. According to this idea no level of reserves was ever enough.'

Developing countries have also seen that the adoption of international reserves holdings can have other, non-precautionary purposes. Some economies have recently pursued the mercantilist strategy of maintaining a competitive real exchange rate (RER) to promote (and maintain) a high export growth rate (see Aizenman and Lee, 2005, Aizenman, 2006). The mechanism is explained in a recent study of Frenkel and Ros (2006, 636). They argue that if the rate of accumulation in the tradable goods sector is a positive function of profitability, and profitability in that sector is a positive function of the RER, then a competitive RER will lead to faster growth of the traded goods sector. And they further note that a competitive RER operates as an industrial policy designed to distort relative prices in favour of tradable-goods activities (like any industrial policy, such as export promotion industrialization). In this sense, a more depreciated domestic currency is equivalent to a uniform tariff on imports, with the advantage that a depreciated domestic currency does not distort relative prices against exports because it simultaneously implies a 'subsidy' (an income transfer) of the same size. Thus, by maintaining a competitive RER as a result of reserve accumulation, the profitability of the tradable sector can be promoted and, in turn, firms will invest and expand production.

Finally, developing countries have seen additional benefits related to the accumulation of international reserves. For example, large stocks of reserves may reduce the volatility of the foreign exchange rate (see Aizenman, 2006; Aizenman and Riera-Critchton, 2006; Cady and Gonzalez-Garcia, 2006). In addition, the cost of foreign borrowing may be reduced. Furthermore, countries can gain policy sovereignty, but only in the sense of avoiding turning to the IMF and its conditionality packages in the case that a financial crisis occurs (see Bird and Mandilaras, 2005).

Is Reserve Accumulation Worthwhile?

What is striking in the literature discussing the strategy of holding international reserves is that it has not attempted to evaluate all of the possible consequences and potential costs and benefits involved in this policy choice. This is particularly relevant as developing countries try to emulate economies that avoided speculative attacks and/or capital flight (e.g., Chile, Colombia, China and India) and others that have experienced impressive growth (namely, China and India), while simultaneously stockpiling international reserves.

In the first place, it is clear that following Mrs. Machlup's theory comes with considerable costs. First, holding reserves incurs an opportunity cost, which is the difference between what the reserves could have earned and what they actually earn (Ramachandran, 2004, 365). This opportunity cost has been estimated for the Report of the High-Level Panel on Financing for Development to the United Nations in 2001 to be of the order of 8 per cent, which represents the differential between the yield on the reserves and the marginal cost of borrowing.

In addition to establishing the differential, estimating the cost also requires identifying the size of the excess holdings relative to some optimum level, which, as we have stressed, is difficult to establish in the first place. Rodrik (2000) and Bird and Rajan (2003), for example, have estimated that the excess of reserves holdings above the level defined by the conventional ratio R/M, to be around 1 per cent of GDP. In this line, Mendoza (2004), estimates that the quarterly cost of reserves accumulation, for a sample of 65 developing economies during the 1998–2001 period, was approximately US$450 million.[6]

Very few studies have gone one step further and estimated the cost of the excess of reserves accumulation relative to an alternative criterion, such as the Guidotti-Greenspan rule, which reflects how much a country has to pay to protect the balance of payments from its overall vulnerability.[7] Rodrik (2006), for example, estimates the cost of the excess of holding reserves at around 1 per cent of GDP. Cruz and Walters (2007), applying the notion of a maximum sustainable external threshold,[8] estimate this cost at around 0.19 per cent of GDP for the Mexican economy during the 1996–2004 period. In any case, these costs are 'a large number by any standard. It is a multiple of the budgetary cost of even the most aggressive anti-poverty programs implemented in developing countries' (Rodrik, 2006, 262). In summary, it is clear that based even on a narrow criteria defining excess and cost, as Rodrik (2006, 261) observes, 'developing countries are paying a very high price to play by the rules of financial globalization.'

Furthermore, the logic of accumulating large amounts of any resource, like reserves, when the country is most in the need of them for alternative productive projects, is questionable.[9, 10] The broadest interpretation of the opportunity cost of holding excess reserves allows the cost of reserves to be considered in terms of foregone developmental projects.[11] Although the approach is contentious,[12] in a recent study, Cruz (2006) estimates that had the excess of international reserves been absorbed by the Mexican economy during the 1996–2004 period (either through investments in infrastructure or in sectors with a high rate of return), the upper bound of Mexico's growth would have been 4.3 per cent per year instead of the 3.7 per cent observed.

In addition to these direct costs, it is important to note that reserve accumulation can actually be counterproductive: 'large reserves stocks may create moral hazard problems that could weaken the financial system of a country. This, in turn, could make crises to be deeper...' (García and Soto, 2004, 17–18). This is because currency intervention injects liquidity into domestic money markets producing very liquid market systems that can spill over into overheated assets markets and perhaps distort the banking system (see Schiller, 2007). In addition, according to Mohanty and Turner (2006, 40), large and prolonged reserve accumulation aimed at resisting or delaying currency appreciation can create a range of domestic macroeconomic risks through its effects on the balance sheets of the central bank and the private sector. These risks include near-term inflation, high intervention costs and monetary imbalances. In their study, the authors argue that these potential risks have been controlled so far, because many countries accumulating reserves over the past few years have faced conditions of substantial excess capacity and low inflation, which has meant that policy could be eased in the face of upward pressure on the currency. In these conditions, reserve accumulation has not created the dilemma for policymakers of choosing between their inflation and their exchange rate objectives.

On the other hand, the empirical significance of using international reserves to promote growth (the mercantilist view) is challenged. According to Polterovich and Popov (2002), there are a number of economies that have been using their large reserve holdings to maintain a competitive RER in order to boost export growth and thus economic growth. The results of their cross-country econometric analysis suggest that countries with growing foreign exchange reserve ratios to GDP, other things being equal, exhibit higher investment/GDP ratios, higher trade/GDP ratios, higher capital productivity, and higher rates of growth. By contrast, the results of Aizenman and Lee (2004) indicate that despite the variables associated with the mercantilist motive being statistically significant, their economic importance in accounting for reserves hoarding is close to zero and is dwarfed by other variables. In a similar vein Aizenman (2006), concludes that the management of international reserves should not be seen as a panacea, particularly for an export-led growth strategy. Furthermore, as previously highlighted, large and prolonged reserve accumulation aimed at delaying currency appreciation can create a range of domestic macroeconomic risks.[13] It is also important to emphasize that if it is to promote growth and development effectively, a policy of maintaining a competitive RER through reserves accumulation needs to be coupled with appropriate long-run supply—side policies, while a competitive RER can only be a short-term policy. Japan, Korea, Singapore and China (according to Polterovich and Popov (2002), examples of successful development strategies using growing foreign exchange reserves), are manufacturing high-value added-export leaders. However, this is an outcome that has involved much more than a non-appreciated currency strategy. They have, in fact, long since developed an export structure that allows them to enjoy the benefits of trade. Their superb export performance is not something recent that has occurred since the boom of financial crises. It is, rather, the story of East Asian economies during the last fifty years. The corollary is that adopting a large reserves holdings strategy will not, on its own, deliver the benefits of export-led growth from a developmental point of view.[14] Thus, it is not appropriate to embark on reserves accumulation and its effects on the foreign exchange rate and export promotion, especially in the long term, without other complementary policies aimed at creating the supply-side structures that are needed for (high value added) export growth.

The balance of this discussion suggests that, even while it can be argued that 'prevailing patterns of reserve holdings are far from crazy in view of the significant costs of being less liquid' (Rodrik, 2006, 10), at least two further questions should be considered before deciding to embark on a strategy of stockpiling reserve holdings.

In the first place, the factors that open the door to financial crises or, in other words, to a rapid drain of liquidity, should be considered. The empirical evidence indicates that there are mainly two routes by which an economy can suffer a financial crisis. Directly, by opening the capital account of the balance of payments and simultaneously deregulating domestically, that is, by implementing the neoliberal strategy of financial liberalization. And indirectly, via contagion, which is, however, to a considerable extent, an inevitable consequence of the increasingly tight commercial and financial links between countries.[15] The implication, therefore, is that it is only if policymakers are planning to implement (or reinforce) the neoliberal financial integration strategy,[16] will it be worthwhile to think about the accumulation of international reserves in the sense of Mrs. Machlup's rule. As we have stressed, however, a large literature suggests that, among other things, financial liberalization has preceded financial crises with the associated huge costs, and that it has reduced significantly the space for and the autonomy to formulate policies in the pursuit of national development objectives. In this sense, neoliberal financial liberalization it is not supportive of industrialization, does not provide more space for policy manoeuvre and sharply increases financial instability.[17] Furthermore, it is important to stress that 'even an emerging-market economy with an idealized external position would remain highly exposed to the punishing vicissitudes of liberalized financial flows' (D'Arista, 2000, 3). In other words, there is no guarantee for a poor economy that even holding large amounts of international reserves will completely eliminate the risks that emanate from hot money. This is because it has not been possible thus far to identify either exactly what moves international liquidity holders to attack a currency or what determines their timing. International reserves holdings can be seen therefore as simply an *ad hoc* protection against speculative attacks. The assessment that needs to be done, from this perspective, is not whether large reserve holdings might be less costly than undergoing a financial crisis, but whether it is necessary to implement the policy that open the door to financial crises.

The second question that needs to be asked when considering a strategy of reserve accumulation is whether there are feasible policy alternatives that can provide not only financial stability and policy autonomy, but also promote industrialization. Fortunately, the historical evidence of both developed and newly industrialized economies shows that there are indeed several alternatives that have proven to be effective in these common aims. Within the variety of alternative strategies are restrictions on currency convertibility, the famous (Chilean) management-of-capital controls and the recently proposed tripwires and speed bumps approach (see Grabel, 2003).

Table 11.1 summarizes the costs and benefits of the strategy of international reserve accumulation with respect to development purposes, policy autonomy and financial stability. As can be seen, the benefits of this strategy are very attractive but, as we have argued, they can only be enjoyed on a short-term basis: as soon as the neoliberal strategy of financial liberalization is applied, financial stability is subject to the vicissitudes of hot money, and policy autonomy for development purposes disappears. Also, the competitive RER policy can only be sustained as long as monetary and macroeconomic imbalances can be managed and, in the same vein, long-term export promotion depends on supply-side policies. In this sense, the costs, especially the long term costs, outweigh the benefits of the reserves accumulation strategy. Finally,

Table 11.1. **Costs and Benefits of the International Reserve Accumulation Strategy**

	Benefits	Costs
Development purposes	– Foreign exchange stability. – Export growth (through a competitive RER). – Increased creditworthiness.	– Forgone resources for developmental purposes. – Moral hazard problems – Macroeconomic risks (inflation, high intervention costs, monetary imbalances).
Policy autonomy	– Avoid reliance on the IMF in the case of a crisis occurring.	– No room for industrialization and growth policies.
Financial stability	– Prevents speculative attacks.	– The economy remains highly exposed to hot money, particularly from capital outflows.

the need for policy autonomy, financial stability and industrialization through excessive accumulation of international reserves can be reduced substantially if alternative policies that can provide these goals are implemented. These alternative strategies will be the focus of the next section.

Financial Stability and Development: The Alternative Strategies

As we have already stressed, many studies have shown that recent financial crises can be identified with the degree of freedom with which foreign capital flows are able to leave the country, given an economic or political change. This suggests that any strategy that aims at reducing financial vulnerability without trying to reduce agents' financial freedom to transfer funds across borders is likely to fail. As Keynes (quoted by Davidson, 2002, 214) warned, 'loose funds may sweep round the world disorganising all steady business. Nothing is more certain than that the movement of capital funds must be regulated.' Moreover, 'it is easy to forget that the Golden Age was, among other things, an era of effective national economic regulation' (Crotty and Epstein, 1996, 118). From here, it is clear that only financial stability strategies aimed at controlling the flow of capital and thus the behaviour of agents, provide options that are likely to offer better results. Additionally, by reducing the freedom of capital, policy autonomy can be increased because 'freedom to [move money across the borders] is one of the main sources of capitalist political power' (Crotty and Epstein, 1996, 120).

Policy autonomy cannot be trimmed to avoid the IMF support when collapses occur; it needs to be broader and should imply, among other things, the capacity of the authorities to address monetary and fiscal policy towards industrialization and growth goals and also be able to smooth business cycles. In other words, "… countries must be allowed to impose capital controls in the interest of demand management" (Badhuri, 2002, 45). Furthermore, there is evidence that these sorts of strategies have contributed in the process of development: through subsidising imports, stabilizing the exchange rate, improving the allocation of investments and so on. For these reasons, we focus here on presenting and analysing the feasible alternative proposals, summarized by Grabel (2003), that can be applied by domestic policymakers to achieve financial stability. They include the management of capital flows (à la Chile), restrictions on currency convertibility and the tripwires and speed bump approaches.

Before discussing these options, it is important to make two important observations. First, conclusions from the large literature arguing both for and against these strategies, particularly the management of capital controls and the restrictions on currency convertibility, always involve trade-offs. Thus, the issue is not whether the policies have costs but whether policymakers can ensure that these costs do not offset the benefits. If these strategies have proved to offer financial stability (by practically eliminating the risk of speculative attacks and capital flight) and support the process of development in the past, it may be worthwhile considering readopting them. But this need not imply that they operate as they were originally applied; they need to be adjusted to the present context of globalization. This raises the question of which strategy is most appropriate; evidently, this depends on the particular circumstances of the economy (such as the level of development) and the prevailing external conditions.

Second, a growing literature has suggested alternative policies to achieve financial stability, and thus promote development, through the involvement of the international community (see for example Eichengreen, 1999 and Davidson, 2002, for a proposed changes in the international financial architecture; Mendoza, 2004, and Bird and Rajan, 2003, for strategies that involve measures to redefine and readjust international financial instruments (like the SDRs) to the needs of emerging economies; Bird and Mandaliras, 2005, for mechanisms to achieve global balance of payments equilibrium; see also Griffith-Jones, 2003, for a review about why global financial stability has not been achieved and what needs to be done). These proposals are essentially based on the assumption that financial stability can be seen as a global public good (see Kaul et al. 1999, for a definition of global public good). The idea is that poor people may lack income and barely participate in financial markets. Yet financial crises, through multiple transmission channels, can hurt them badly. Thus international financial stability is important for all people (Griffith-Jones, 2003). Notwithstanding the remarkable value of this approach, our emphasis in this paper, however, is on policies that are feasible in the sense that they can be applied by domestic authorities. If developing countries really want to protect themselves and accelerate industrialization, they need to apply, sooner rather than later, policies that are effective, but which are under their control. In this sense, they cannot depend on "… international organizations nor expect that a new financial international architecture that will make the world less dangerous" (Feldstein, 1999, 1). This does not mean, of course, that they should stop the search for mechanisms to attain global financial stability.

The Management of Capital Flows (the Chilean Model)

The so-called management of capital flows is one of the strategies that have been shown to be effective in reducing speculative attacks and capital flight and provide policy autonomy whilst contributing to development goals. This is because, as Thirlwall (2003, 95) points out, "capital controls, in whatever form… allow countries to manage their exchange rate effectively and provide a greater degree of monetary independence" (cf. Joshi, 2003, for the case of India). In this regard, he emphasizes that for a country with a liberalized capital account, it will be difficult, if not impossible, to pursue an exchange rate target and operate an independent monetary policy at the same time. He further adds that the only way to reconcile internal and external equilibrium is either to control capital movements or to allow the exchange rate to float.

This strategy was applied successfully in countries like Chile and Colombia during the 90s (see Agosin and Ffrench-Davis, 1996; De Gregorio et al., 2000; Edwards, 1999, 2003; and Palma, 2002), India, China and, during the East Asian crisis, for a short period in Malaysia (see Doraisami, 2004; Joshi, 2003; and Athukorala, 2003). The strategy allowed these economies to pass through the era of financial crises with low levels of financial and macro instability (see Ocampo, 2002 and David, 2007). Also in the early postwar years, capital controls for macroeconomic reasons were generally imposed as part of policies dealing with balance of payments difficulties so as to avoid and reduce devaluations. Rich and poor countries alike used controls on capital inflows for long-term development reasons. When freer capital movements were allowed from the 1960s onward, large capital inflows posed problems for rich countries such as Germany, Holland and Switzerland. They, then, imposed controls such as limits on nonresidents' purchases of local securities and on bank deposits of nonresidents (Khor, 2001).

Although there may be some national differences in design, capital controls promote development and financial stability essentially by seeking to 'lengthen the maturity structure and stabilize capital inflows, mitigate the effect of large volumes of inflows on the exchange rate and exports, and protect the economy from the instability associated with speculative excess and the sudden withdrawal of external finance' (Grabel, 2003, 326). Moreover, capital controls insulate a country's financial system from the contagion effects of financial crises and enhance the autonomy of pro-growth and social policy (Epstein, Grabel and Jomo, 2003). They also promote development by attracting favoured forms of foreign investment and by maintaining foreign exchange stability, which is crucial to subsidize capital imports. In other words, the risk of currency collapse is reduced through the adoption of a crawling band exchange rate regime coupled with capital inflows control,[18] and the probability of a sudden exit of investors is reduced by allocating investment towards longer-term activities. Edwards (1999) provides evidence that these goals were achieved in the case of Chile, and Ocampo (2002) illustrates their successful application in Colombia and other emerging economies. Importantly, Feldstein (1999) highlights this policy as a means of increasing liquidity, thus further improving policy autonomy.

In summary, the management of capital flows has proved to be a highly effective strategy to mitigate speculative attacks and capital flight and to enhance policy autonomy for pro-growth goals (see Epstein et al., 2003 and David, 2007). Furthermore, it is evident that those economies that have managed capital inflows and outflows have recorded very stable growth and a marked move towards further industrialization.

The main cost of capital controls, as stressed by its critics, is that their adoption could inhibit access to financial resources as well as investment, thereby reducing economic growth. However, it must be stressed that, first of all, there is no evidence supporting the view that portfolio investment encourages productive investment (through financing productive projects) and growth (there is also empirical evidence showing that foreign direct investment doesn't necessarily promote growth; it is not, as Chang and Grabel (2004) point out, the *Mother Theresa* of capital flows).[19] And secondly, there is evidence suggesting that the volume of capital inflows does not necessarily decrease in the face of capital controls; in fact, there is evidence that the only change is a positive one, with a larger share of capital going to longer-term activities (see Chang and Grabel 2004 and Epstein et al. 2003, for evidence in the case of Chile, Colombia, Taiwan, Singapore, Malaysia in 1998, India and China). This suggests that resources can indeed be efficiently allocated. Other emerging economies recently seem to have realized the benefits of this strategy and have adopted it. This is the case in respect of Argentina, which in June 2005 decided to apply measures to retain 30 per cent of portfolio capital inflows with the specific aim of stabilizing the exchange rate. Moreover, capital management should represent a developmental option for developing economies as it did in the past for today's industrialized ones; it cannot be accepted, as Chang (2002) stresses, that in the name of market efficiency, the same state action could be considered an 'intervention' in one society and not in another.

Finally, many criticisms of capital management arise from their potential microeconomic costs. The argument is that capital controls have the potential to harm medium-sized enterprises because the strategy forces domestic lenders to raise domestic costs during the economic boom (see Forbes, 2003, 2004). However, severe limitations on data availability in these studies suggest that the results should be treated cautiously; nor do they present their analysis in the necessary comparative context. Finally, neither study shows clear evidence that the microeconomic costs are likely to offset the macroeconomic benefits of capital management.

Restrictions on Currency Convertibility

Another feasible policy measure to attain financial stability, increase policy autonomy and support development goals is for the government to manage foreign exchange currency transactions. With free currency convertibility, that is, with investors' ability to move their money freely from one financial centre to another by converting capital from one currency into another regardless of the purpose of the conversion or the identity of the holder, it is likely that investors can easily put the domestic currency under pressure, further decrease the value of assets and cause a financial crisis.

However, currencies that cannot be exchanged freely for other currencies or assets denominated in them cannot be put under pressure because there are restrictions in acquiring them in the first place (Chang and Grabel, 2004). Thus, the greater the restrictions on exchanging the currency, for both national and foreign residents, the lower the chance of the currency being put under pressure, reducing the risk of suffering a speculative attack. Furthermore, capital flight is also reduced because currency convertibility can effectively discourage investors from acquiring the kind of domestic assets that are more prone to flight, because they cannot be converted to their own currency (particularly portfolio assets). These effects translate into a reduction in foreign exchange pressures, thus increasing policy autonomy and the ability of the authorities to pursue development goals.

It is worthwhile noting that as with the management of capital flows, there is enough evidence to show that restrictions on currency convertibility are capable of providing financial stability and improving policy autonomy. There is also evidence that they support the process of industrialization by allowing the subsidy of capital imports, implementing countercyclical fiscal and monetary policies and directing resources towards the development of a productive structure. The experiences of Taiwan, China and India support this. On the other hand, and equally important, is the fact that many of today's industrialized economies removed restrictions on capital movements only very recently; the United States, Canada, Germany and Switzerland in 1973, while Britain and Japan only did so in 1979 and 1980 respectively, and France and Italy made the transition as late as 1990 (Nayyar, 2003, 66). Importantly, these economies not only made this transition when they considered that their currencies (and their economies) were strong enough to resist foreign exchange pressures, but also only after this strategy had fulfilled its function within the development process.

Among the mechanisms that a government can apply are restrictions on capital account transactions, in particular, restrictions on both domestic residents and foreigners, on the form of foreign direct or portfolio investment in national assets. This measure can decrease abrupt capital flight.[20] The authorities can also authorize currency convertibility for trade transactions, repayment of loans or profits repatriation previously authorized. This mechanism is similar to the adoption of a dual exchange-rate system, where a specific exchange rate is set up for capital account transactions and another, cheaper exchange rate, is set up for the current account. Multiple exchange rate systems, of which the dual is a special case, imply different exchange rates for different transactions on either the current or financial account (see Thirlwall 2003 and Mikesell 2001). Importantly, according to the IMF Articles of Agreement (specifically, Article 8), this kind of selective exchange rate convertibility is allowed (Chang and Grabel, 2004).[21] Moreover, the government could manage convertibility by requiring that investors apply for a licence that entitles them to exchange currency for a particular reason. This mechanism would allow the government to influence the pace of currency exchanges.

Despite the likely effectiveness of this policy measure, it is important to notice that the Achilles' heel of restrictions on currency convertibility has been leakages between the commercial and the financial rate, after a dual exchange-rate system has been set up. According to Eichengreen and Wyplosz (1996), experience suggests that dual exchange rates work well when the gap between the commercial and financial rates is small meaning that they work least well during crises. Furthermore, the IMF has traditionally been hostile to these sorts of exchange rate practices, seeing them as an interference with the free market in goods and capital. This view is consistent with studies suggesting that low levels of restriction on currency convertibility (and capital controls) are associated with higher levels of economic development, efficiency and integration of the financial sector (see Johnston, 1999).[22] Edwards (1999, 69), points out that these types of outflow controls have been largely ineffective, particularly because the market finds ways of evading them; he also stresses that evidence shows that in almost 70 per cent of the cases where controls on outflows have been used as a preventive measure, a significant *increase* in 'capital flight' has been detected after the controls had been put in place. Finally Eichengreen (2000, 1110) has also stressed that "not too much should be expected of outflows controls in times of crisis, given the strong incentives that then exist for avoidance".

However, Chang and Grabel (2004, 173) stress that critics of this type of policy generally focus on their high costs, "[B]ut they overlook the fact that the resources devoted to these wasteful activities are generally dwarfed by the resources wasted in the currency speculation that frequently occurs in liberal financial environments. Moreover, the economic and social costs of financial instability and crisis tend to be much greater than the economic costs of convertibility restrictions."

The Tripwires and Speed Bumps Approach

Finally, a policy alternative that can offer financial stability and aid the attainment of development goals is the tripwires and speed bumps approach proposed by Grabel (2003, 2004).23 The idea consists in providing policymakers (and investors) with measurable variables that can indicate if the country is approaching dangerous levels of risk of suffering capital flight or a speculative attack, and tools to reduce such risks. To achieve financial stability, the central idea is that if the tripwires indicate (through the establishment of specific thresholds) that the economy is reaching risky levels of capital flight and/or speculative risks, 'policymakers could immediately take steps to prevent a crisis by activating what we might think of as speed bumps. Speed bumps would target the type of risk that is emerging with a graduated series of mitigation measures' (Grabel, 2003, 323) through any mechanism related to the management of capital flows or currency convertibility previously described. It is important to note that the threshold risk should be defined on the basis of the particular characteristics of the economy. Moreover, the thresholds must be very sensitive to changes in the environment, and adjustable. In a sense, this approach represents the dynamic version of the policies previously outlined.

Grabel (2003) proposes a number of possible tripwires that could continuously reflect the levels of financial (in)stability. The ratio of foreign international reserves to private and public foreign-currency-denominated debt (with short-term obligations receiving a greater weight in the calculation) could be an indicator of (lender) flight risk. As an indicator of currency risk, she proposes the ratio of official reserves to the current account deficit.[24, 25] In the event that tripwires indicate approaching trouble, the speed bumps will include, inter alia, measures to decrease the pace of imports or foreign borrowing, limit the convertibility of the currency and control the exit and entrance of portfolio investment (Grabel 2003).

It may be that applying these regulatory devices will result in some slowdown in economic activity. Nevertheless, it seems preferable to maintain financial stability by acting accordingly, rather than face the costs of leaving the market to eliminate imbalances, with the likely occurrence of sudden, large falls in growth and other welfare indicators (as demonstrated in the large number of financial crises in emerging economies). In addition, achieving financial stability will make it easier to promote industrialization and raise the long-run sustainable growth rate. Lower pressures on the exchange rate will allow capital imports to be subsidized. Resources can be also be diverted to support the development of specific industries, build productive human and physical capital, promote R&D, and so on. Moreover, fiscal and monetary policies are freed to smooth business cycles and maintain robust domestic demand.

The tripwires-speed bumps approach depends essentially on policymakers' will; administrative costs and technical requirements are manageable. More generally, Grabel (2004) has evaluated its feasibility positively by anticipating and responding to a number of likely concerns raised by sceptics of this approach. Particularly, she argues that the tripwires-speed bumps approach will not trigger the risk they are trying to avoid (she rejects the Lucas critique), as this approach "entails moderate and graduated responses to small changes and conditions. The activation of speed bumps is therefore not apt to trigger market anxiety..." (Grabel, 2004, 20). However, it is dangerous to predict that agents will react passively to a major policy change.

In summary, this policy combination is a mix of the policies previously discussed with the added tool of the tripwires. It represents a viable alternative (to reserve accumulation) for preventing financial instability and, in that sense, support the process of development.

Conclusions

This paper has considered whether the widespread policy among developing economies of amassing foreign exchange reserves is, in any sense, optimal from the perspective of supporting the process of industrialization, achieving financial stability and extending policy autonomy. It argues that this policy cannot be justified in these terms, particularly in the long term.

In the first place, the policy of international reserves accumulation has been defended as a mechanism to deter speculative attacks and thus, is legitimate relative to the enormous costs associated with financial crises and their aftermath. Although clearly persuasive. this defence fails to take account a number of issues. First, it accepts, albeit reluctantly, the necessity and indeed inevitability of neoliberal financial liberalization of both domestic and capital markets. The paper points out that this is contestable and that the evidence shows that the neoliberal financial liberalization strategy is deeply implicated in precipitating such crises (and their associated output costs) and reducing policy autonomy. Second, it is possible to defend such a strategy as a reflection of an active export growth policy of maintaining a competitive exchange rate. However, it was argued that the empirical evidence does not unambiguously support this conclusion, and even in situations where this strategy appears to have worked, this has been because it has been accompanied by a range of complementary, supply-side policies to promote the long-run expansion of exports. In addition, in these cases it has also been applied during a period when its inherent difficulties have been muted. It was concluded that no general endorsement of the policy was provided by these examples. Finally, it might be argued that the costs of such a reserve accumulation strategy would be acceptable if there were no feasible alternatives available to governments. However, it was argued that both current and historical evidence suggested that a range of policies based on controlling the free flow of capital were, as a matter of fact, both feasible and effective. Against a counterfactual of an effective set of capital and currency management controls, the real cost of excess reserves was the opportunity cost of developmental projects.

A set of alternative policies than was discussed. These included: the management of capital flows according to the Chilean model; restrictions on currency convertibility; and the tripwires and speed bumps approach. It was accepted that these policies were not without cost and would need to be consistent with the new context of increasing globalization. However, it was argued that they provided an effective alternative to holding excess reserves while providing financial stability, increasing policy autonomy and supporting the industrialization process.

In conclusion, this paper has argued that the policy of amassing large foreign exchange reserves is not consistent with developmental goals. Countries seeking financial stability and an autonomous development strategy should resist full capital account liberalization and impose restrictions on the ability of capital holders to liquidate their positions without cost or delay. In the context of globalization, the speed bumps and tripwires approach deserves active consideration. Finally, it is important to observe that although financial stability can be seen as a global public good and, as such, is the responsibility of the international financial community, developing countries cannot wait indefinitely for a new financial architecture to make the world less dangerous. Developing countries need the freedom of action that developed countries allowed themselves when they were in their early stages of development.

References

Agosin, D. and Ffrench-Davis, R. 1996. 'Managing Capital Inflows in Latin America.' In M. Haq, I. Kaul, and I. Grunberg, eds. *The Tobin Tax: Coping with Financial Volatility*. New York: Oxford University Press, 161–191.

Aizenman, J. 2007. 'Large Hoarding of International Reserves and the Emerging Global Economic Architecture.' *NBER Working Paper*, no. 13277, 1–21.

———. 2006. 'International Reserves Management and the Current Account.' *NBER Working Paper*, no. 12734, 1–52.

Aizenman, J. and J. Lee. 2005. 'International Reserves: Precautionary Versus Mercantilist Views, Theory and Evidence.' *NBER Working Paper*, no. 11366, 1–28.

Aizenman, J., Y. Lee and Y. Rhee. 2004. 'International Reserves Management and Capital Mobility in a Volatile World: Policy Consideration and a Case Study of Korea.' *NBER Working Papers Series*, no. 10534, 1–27.

Aizenman, J. and N. Marion. 2002. 'The High Demand for International Reserves in the Far East: What's Going On?' *NBER Working Papers Series*, no. 9266,1–44.

Aizenman, J. and D. Riera-Critchton. 2006. 'Real Exchange Rate and International Reserves in the Era of Growing Trade and Financial Integration.' *NBER Working Paper*, no. 12363, 1–36.

Allen, R. 2004. (Ed.). *The Political Economy of Financial Crises*. Cheltenham: Edward Elgar.

Arestis, P. and M. Glickman. 2002. 'Financial Crisis in Southeast Asia: Dispelling Illusion in the Minskyan Way.' *Cambridge Journal of Economics*, vol. 26, 237–60.

Athukorala, P. 2003. *Crisis and Recovery in Malaysia: The Role of Capital Controls*. Cheltenham: Edward Elgar.

Bhaduri, A. 2002. 'Nationalism and Economic Policy in the Era of Globalization.' In D. Nayyar, ed. *Governing Globalization*, Oxford; New York: Oxford University Press, 19–49.

Ben-Bassat, A. and D. Gottlieb.1992. 'Optimal International Reserves and Sovereign Risk.' *Journal of International Economics*, vol. 33, 345–362.

Bird, G. and A. Mandilaras. 2005. 'Reserve Accumulation in Asia.' *Wold Economics* vol. 6, no. 1, 85–99.

Bird, G. and R. Rajan. 2003. 'Too Much of a Good Thing? The Adequacy of International Reserves in the Aftermath of Crises.' *World Economy*, vol. 26, no. 6, 873–891.

Cady, J. and J. Gonzalez-Garcia. 2006. 'The IMF Reserves Template and Nominal Exchange Rate Volatility.' *IMF Working Paper*, no. 627, 1–24.

Chang, H-J. 2002. 'Breaking the Mould: An Institutionalist Political Economy Alternative to the Neo-Liberal Theory of the Market and the State.' *Cambridge Journal of Economics*, vol. 26, 539–559.

Chang, H. and I. Grabel. 2004. *Reclaiming Development. An Alternative Policy Manual,*.London: Zed Books.

Chui, M., S. Hall and A. Taylor. 2004. "Crises Spillovers in Emerging Market Economies: Interlinkages, Vulnerabilities and Investor Behaviour.' *Working Paper 212*, The Bank of England, 1–44.

Cruz, M. 2006. 'Pueden las Reservas Internacionales Contribuir al Crecimiento Mexicano?' *Economía UNAM*, vol. 3, no. 8, 115–124.

Cruz, M., E. Amann and B. Walters. 2006. 'Expectations, the Business Cycle and the Mexican Peso Crisis.' *Cambridge Journal of Economics*, vol. 30, 701–722.

Cruz, M. and B. Walters. 2007. 'Acumulación de Reservas Internacionales: Costos y Alternativas para la Economía Mexicana Durante el Periodo 1995–2004.'

In J. L. Calva (ed.), *Macroeconomía del Crecimiento Sostenido. Agenda para el Desarrollo*, vol. 4, Porrúa, México, 77–94.

Crotty, J. and G. Epstein. 1996. 'In Defence of Capital Controls.' In L. Panitch (ed.). *Are There Alternatives?* London: Social Register, 118–149.

D'Arista, J. 2000. 'International Foreign Exchange Reserves: An Update' *Capital Flows Monitor*, June, 1–4.

David, A. 2007. 'Controls on Capital Inflows and External Shocks.' *World Bank Policy Research Working Paper*, no. 4176, 1–26.

Davidson, P. 2002. *Financial Markets, Money and the Real World*. London: Edward Elgar.

De Gregorio, J., S. Edwards and R. Valdés. 2000. 'Controls on Capital Inflows: Do They Work?' *Journal of Development Economics*, vol. 63, 59–83.

Doraisami, A. 2004. 'From Crisis to Recovery: The Motivations for and the Effects of Malaysian Capital Controls.' *Journal of International Development*, vol. 16, 241–254.

ECLAC (1998) 'Impacto de la Crisis Asiática en América Latina.' [available at: www.eclac.cl/publicaciones].

Edwards, S. 1983. 'The Demand for International Reserves and Exchange Rate Adjustments: The Case of LDCs, 1946–1972.' *Economica*, vol. 50, 269–280.

———. 1999. 'How Effective are Capital Controls?' *Journal of Economic Perspectives*, vol. 13, no. 14, 65–84.

———. 2003. 'Financial Instability in Latin America.' *Journal of International Money and Finance*, vol. 22, 1095–1106.

Eichengreen, B. 2000. 'Taming Capital Flows.' *World Development*, vol. 28, no. 6, 1105–1116.

———. 1999. *Towards a New Financial Architecture: A Practical Post-Asian Agenda*, Washington, DC: Institute for International Economics.

Eichengreen, B. and C. Wyplosz. 1996. 'Taxing International Financial Transactions.' In M. Haq, I. Kaul and I. Grunberg (eds.). *The Tobin Tax: Coping with Financial Volatility*, New York: Oxford University Press, 15–39.

Epstein, G., I. Grabel and K. S. Jomo. 2003. 'Capital Management Techniques in Developing Countries: An Assessment of Experiences from the '90s and Lessons for the Future.' Paper prepared for the XVIth Technical Group Meeting of the G-24 in Port Spain, Trinidad and Tobago, 1–43.

Feldstein, M. 1999. 'Self-Protection for Emerging Market Economies.' *NBER Working Papers*, 1999, 1–23.

Forbes, K. 2003. 'On Cost of the Chilean Capital Controls: Increased Financial Constraints for Smaller Trade Firms.' *NBER Working Papers*, no. 9777, 1–51.

———. 2004. 'Mud in the Wheels of Market Discipline.' *NBER Working Papers*, no. 10284, 1–24.

Fry, M. 1997. 'In Favour of Financial Liberalization.' *Economic Journal*, vol. 107, no. 442.

Frenkel and Ros. 2006. 'Unemployment and the Real Exchange Rate in Latin America.' *World Development*, vol. 34, no. 4, 631–646.

García, P. and C. Soto. 2004. 'Large Hoardings of International Reserves: Are They Worthy?' *Central Bank of Chile Working Papers*, no. 299, 1–39.

Grabel. I. 2004. 'Tripwires and Speed Bumps: Managing Financial Risks and Reducing the Potential for Financial Crises in Developing Economies.' *Intergovernmental Group of Twenty-Four (G-24) Research Papers*, 1–30.

———. 2003. 'Averting crisis? Assessing Measures to Manage Financial Integration in Emerging Economies.' *Cambridge Journal of Economics*, vol. 27, 2003, 317–36.

————. 1996. 'Marketing the Third World: The Contradictions of Portfolio Investment in the Global Economy.' *World Development*, vol. 24, no. 11, 1761–1776.

————. 1995. 'Speculative-led Economic Development: A Post-Keynesian Interpretation of Financial Liberalization Programmes in the Third World.' *International Review of Applied Economics*, vol. 9, 127–147.

Griffith-Jones, S. 2003. 'International Financial Stability and Market Efficiency as a Global Public Good. In K. Inge, P. Conceição, K. Le Goulven and R. Mendoza (eds.). *Providing Global Public Goods*. New York: Oxford University Press, 435–454.

Johnston, R. 1999. *Exchange Rate Arrangements and Currency Convertibility: Development and Issues*, Washington, DC: International Monetary Found.

Joshi, V. 2003. 'India and the Impossible Trinity' *World Economy*, vol. 26, no. 4, 555–583.

Kaul, I., I. Grunberg and M. Stern. 1999. 'Defining Global Public Goods.' In K. Inge, I. Grunberg and M. Stern (eds.). *Global Public Goods*. New York: Oxford University Press, 2–19.

Khor, M. 2001. *Rethinking Globalisation*. London: Zed Books,.

Kose, M., E. Prasad, K. Rogoff and S-J. Wei. 2006. 'Financial Globalization: A Reappraisal.' *IMF Working Paper*, 1–94.

Machlup, F. 1966. 'The Need for Monetary Reserves.' *Banca Nazionale del Lavoro Quarterly Review*, Sept, 58–75.

Mendoza, R. 2004. 'International Reserve-Holding in the Developing World: Self Insurance in a Crisis-Prone Era.' *Emerging Markets Review*, vol. 5, 61–82.

Mikesell, R. 2001. 'Dual Exchange Markets for Countries Facing Financial Crises.' *World Development*, vol. 29, no. 6, 1035–1041.

Mohanty, M. and P. Turner. 2006. 'Foreign Exchange Reserve Accumulation in Emerging Markets: What are the Domestic Implications?' *BIS Quarterly Review*, September, 39–52.

Nayyar, D. 2003. 'Globalization and Development.' In H-J Chang (ed.). *Rethinking Development Economics*, London: Anthem Press, 61–82.

Nurkse, R. 1954. 'International Investment Today in the Light of Nineteenth-Century Experience.' *Economic Journal*, vol. 64, no. 256, 744–758.

————. 1962. *Problems of Capital Formation in Underdeveloped Countries*. Oxford: Blackwell.

Ocampo, J. 2002. 'Capital-Account and Counter-Cyclical Prudential Regulations in Developing Countries.' *WIDER Discussion Papers*, no. 82, 1–25.

Palma. G. 2002. 'The Three Routes to Financial Crises: The Need for Capital Controls.' In J. Eatwell and L. Taylor (eds.). *International Capital Markets: Systems in Transition*. Oxford; New York: Oxford University Press, 297–338.

————. 2003, 'The ' "Three Routes" to Financial Crises: Chile, Mexico, and Argentina [1], Brazil [2]; and Korea, Malaysia and Thailand [3].' In H-J. Chang (ed.). *Rethinking Development Economics*, London: Anthem Press, 347–376.

Polterovich, V and V. Popov. 2002. *Accumulation of Foreign Exchange Reserves and Long-Term Growth*. Moscow: New Economic School.

Ramachandran, M. 2004. 'The Optimal Level of International Reserves: evidence for India.' *Economics Letters*, 2004, 365–370.

Rodrik, D. 2000. 'Exchange Rate Regimes and Institutional Arrangements in the Shadows of Capital Flows.' Unpublished working paper. Harvard University Mimeo, Sept. 2000, 1–19. [http://ksghome.harvard.edu/~drodrik/Malaysia%20conference%20paper.PDF]

————. 2006. 'The Social Cost of Foreign Exchange Reserves.' *International Economic Journal*, vol. 30, no. 3, 253–266.

Singh, A. 2003. 'Capital Account Liberalization, Free Long-Term Capital Flows, Financial Crises and Economic Development.' *Eastern Economic Journal*, vol. 29, no. 2, 191–216.

Singh, C. 2006. 'Should India Use Foreign Exchange Reserves to Finance Infrastructure?' *Economic and Political Weekly*, vol. 43, 517–525.

Schiller, T. 2007. 'How Asia Could Have Vibrant Capital Markets.' *Financial Times*, April 25.

Thirlwall, A. 2003. *Trade, the Balance of Payments and Exchange Rate Policy in Developing Countries.* Cheltenham, UK; Northampton, MA: Edward Elgar.

Tornell, A., F. Westermann and L. Martinez. 2004. 'The Positive Link between Financial Liberalization, Growth and Crisis.' *NBER Working Paper*, 10293, 1–53.

Wheatley, J. 2007. 'A Real Problem? How Brazil Risks Becoming a Victim of Its Own Success.' *Financial Times*, September 3.

Wijnholds, J. and A. Kaptey. 2001. 'Reserve Adequacy in Emerging Market Economies.' *IMF Working Paper*, no. 143, 1–48.

Chapter Twelve:

INTERNATIONAL CURRENCY EXPERIENCE AND THE BRETTON WOODS SYSTEM: RAGNAR NURKSE AS ARCHITECT

Scott Urban

Introduction

'Bretton Woods' is many things. Superficially, it is the New Hampshire resort where the globe's soon-to-be victorious nations agreed in principle to a new postwar order. It is also the 'Bretton Woods institutions', which gave rise to the World Bank, the International Monetary Fund and, with some delay, the World Trade Organization. And it is the most ambitious international monetary experiment in human history: the 'Bretton Woods system.'[1] Governments of most of the world's main trading nations agreed to guarantee the price of dollars in their local currency. To appreciate this brio, imagine a government agreeing internationally to guarantee the price of any asset: a home, a share, a bond. As one of the foremost monetary law experts at the time commented, 'The new plans are of a complication entirely unprecedented in the history of international law' (Nussbaum 1944, 256).

How was this possible? One answer is Ragnar Nurkse. His *International Currency Experience: Lessons of the Inter-war Period* perfectly supported the case made by Keynes and White for an audacious codification of international finance.[2] Nurkse's book sought to uncover the sources of interwar economic implosion; its villain is the international monetary system. The account is so thorough, so accessible and so compelling that its basic premises were considered axiomatic well into the second half of the twentieth century.[3] His book was distributed to delegates meeting for the preparatory sessions for Bretton Woods; it may have been required reading for parliamentarians debating the merits of the Bretton Woods plan subsequently laid before them. With time, it constituted an intellectual and historical bulwark for the Bretton Woods system as difficulties in its implementation fuelled debate over its merits. Such influence makes Nurkse an underappreciated 'architect' of Bretton Woods.

The second section of this paper (Background) reviews Bretton Woods' genesis. The third section details the portions of *International Currency Experience* that directly support the Bretton Woods plan. The fourth section considers Nurkse's book from a modern perspective. The fifth section concludes.

Background

By 1941, Allied powers were already turning their minds to the postwar reality. John Maynard Keynes was uniquely suited to the task. Not only had he witnessed the previous postwar transition following the First World War, he took an active part in it. Moreover, time proved him prescient. He had warned that an unrealistic reparations bill for Germany would undo liberal currents in that country (Keynes 1919, 133). He had warned that tying the pound sterling to the same quantity of gold as it held before the war would doom Britain to high unemployment (Keynes 1925).

Now, in the throes of the Second World War, Keynes focused on humankind's second opportunity to establish a new world order. He was Honorary Advisor to the British Treasury. Yet, it was not the travails of the early twenties that preoccupied him. Very much apiece of his times, he focused on the 1930s. After all, the twenties saw an economic boom and restoration of the international gold standard. By contrast, the thirties brought economic collapse and a crumbling of that very same international standard. It brought fascism, civil war, aggressive military expansionism, deflation and implacable unemployment.

To Keynes and other minds focusing on the new order, the key to a better international system lay in learning the lessons of the thirties. What were they?

Contemporary opinion was divided. Some theories lost credibility with the unfolding of events. Devaluations in the 'gold bloc' in 1935–1936 undermined notions that trade and activity could be restored if only credit were withdrawn and domestic wages and prices driven down.[4] Comparatively strong economies in the 'sterling bloc' reinforced the appeal of that group's characteristics: exchange-rate fixity, a centre currency and freedom of transactions on current account, i.e., for trade and other current transactions such as travel and services.[5]

Keynes' thinking is elucidated in his *General Theory* and in the vast literature written on him since. Written for economists, the book would not have been accessible to policy makers and opinion leaders from other disciplines. For these audiences, Keynes wrote frequently in the *Times*. Keynes' US counterpart was

Harry Dexter White, who did not vie for public opinion. White, a PhD economist from Harvard, was head of the Treasury Department's monetary research section.[6]

In addition to academia, one could turn to the League of Nations for prolific analysis. Discredited for its inability to deliver on political initiatives, the League at this time focused on analytical and technical research on world problems. Its Economic and Financial Office (EFO) busily drew together what would become the definitive accounting of the interwar monetary system. The work was carried out in Princeton, USA, where the EFO had relocated from Geneva in the summer of 1940 (Clavin and Wessels 2005, 476). Nurkse was one of several bright lights among the EFO economists.

It is tempting to assert that *International Currency Experience* directly contributed to the negotiations at Bretton Woods or to its immediate antecedents. The book was distributed to delegates convening for the Bretton Woods preparatory working sessions in Atlantic City only weeks before the 1 July 1944 Bretton Woods conclave (Bordo and James 2001, 8). According to Clavin and Wessels, 'inter-governmental connections' put the EFO in 'a strong position to shape post-war reconstruction' (Clavin and Wessels 2005, 492).

More generally, Pauly (1996, 31) argues that studies, including Nurkse's, 'contributed to a new consensus that ultimately found its authoritative expression in the 1944 Bretton Woods Agreement.' Yet Anglo-American discussions had been in train since mid-1942.[7] They culminated in the Joint Statement of Principles in April 1943, long before the release of *International Currency Experience*.[8]

One might argue that Nurkse's contribution came through his membership in an epistemic community with shared opinions on the interwar problems. According to Clavin and Wessels (2005, 492), '... the inter-governmental committees of the EFO and the Secretariat which supported them generated a network of men, publications, experience and ideas that was to inform and shape the economic internationalism that reshaped the world after 1945.' This is the correct channel between Nurkse and Bretton Woods, according to Pauly (1996, 36), who asks: 'Precisely how was the experience of the League transmitted to the IMF?' Its lessons 'seemed simply to be in the air when the IMF began its institutional journey.'

Ikenberry (1992, 293) rejects this notion. 'The group of economists and policy specialists involved in the postwar settlement ... did not constitute an epistemic community.... The community of experts in this case was not an independently existing scientific community; rather, it was a community created by the process of Anglo-American negotiations.'

In fact, Nurkse's contribution is more subtle, but no less important. Since *International Currency Experience* was published in time for the Bretton Woods deliberations and the subsequent parliamentary debates that preceded national ratifications, the book was ideally situated to support or undermine whatever recommendations came from the Bretton Woods meeting. As it happens, those recommendations meshed extremely well with the analysis and prescription laid down in *International Currency Experience*. Such overlap made the book a powerful catalyst for wider public and official acceptance of the radical proposals contained in the Articles of Agreement of the new International Monetary Fund.

Nurkse's influence does not stop there. Unsurprisingly, with the experience of hindsight, implementation of the Articles of Agreement proved exceptionally difficult. Why did national governments remain committed to it? One answer is, again, *International Currency Experience*. This book suggested that, despite its difficulties, the Bretton Woods system was worth the effort. *International Currency Experience* was uniquely positioned to lend such credibility to the Bretton Woods plan. The book was exclusively dedicated to monetary lessons from the interwar period; Bretton Woods was foremost a monetary compact. Indeed, success at the Bretton Woods meeting owed much to the fact that the main protagonists turned the issue away from trade and toward monetary matters, avoiding a potentially irreconcilable conflict between America's staunchly pro-free trade State Department and a British cabinet sold on the merits of imperial privilege (Ikenberry 1992, 291).

International Currency Experience: Lessons of the Inter-war Period

To pinpoint the overlap between Bretton Woods' Articles of Agreement and Nurkse's *International Currency Experience*, the starting place is the international monetary system. Economies are differentiated with respect to performance, vulnerability to shocks, adaptability to changing conditions and many other phenomena. As a result, their currencies undergo varying levels of demand and supply vis-à-vis the rest of the world's currencies. The international monetary system makes the exchange of these currencies possible. But more important, it also facilitates resolution to any discrepancies in such demand. What distinguishes an international monetary system is its mechanism of resolution, or 'adjustment'.

Amid the Second World War, architects of the new order sought a system with the most acceptable method of international adjustment. What they agreed at Bretton Woods was in most respects perfectly reflected in *International Currency Experience*. The main overlaps between the two follow, illustrated by relevant extracts drawn from *International Currency Experience* and the IMF's original Articles of Agreement.

Internationally Agreed and Fixed Exchange Rates

Contemporary opinion on exchange-rate policy is well represented in *International Currency Experience*. An entire chapter of the book dismisses the exchange rate as a viable means of adjustment to discrepancies in the foreign exchange market. (Nurkse 1944, 113) The first basis of objection is the immediate post-World War One period, in which monetary authorities had no choice but to float the currency, such was the deficiency in their reserves. According to *International Currency Experience*, the experience was totally unsatisfactory; private speculators ruined currencies through caprice.[9] More damning, in *International Currency Experience*'s judgement, was the use of exchange-rate adjustment in the decade that followed; it was the 'devaluation cycle of the thirties' (Nurkse 1944, 19).

A network of exchange rates set up by simultaneous and coordinated international action would have a better chance of avoiding major initial strains and would serve as a better starting-point from which, in case of need, moderate readjustments could be made from time to time. It may be that the initial establishment of a workable system of exchange rates would in future be less hampered by rigid preconceived notions as to the parities to which currencies should return. (Nurkse 1944, 117)

The way in which exchanges were eventually stabilized during the years 1922–1928 led us to stress the importance of establishing an initial system of exchange rates by coordinated and, as far as possible simultaneous international action (Nurkse 1944, 137).

Articles of Agreement:
Article I. Purposes
The purposes of the International Monetary Fund are:
  iii. To promote exchange stability, to maintain orderly exchange arrangements among members, and to avoid competitive exchange depreciation.
Article IV. Par Values of Currencies
  SEC. 3. Foreign exchange dealings based on parity.
The maximum and the minimum rates for exchange transactions between the currencies of members taking place within their territories shall not differ from parity
  i. in the case of spot exchange transactions, by more than one per cent; and
  ii. in the case of other exchange transactions, by a margin which exceeds the margin for spot exchange transactions by more than the Fund considers reasonable.

Domestic Policy Autonomy

The 1930s had shown definitively that governments and their monetary authorities were no longer free to subvert domestic conditions to the needs of maintaining a fixed exchange rate amid mobile capital. The increasingly enfranchised electorate would not tolerate the declines in wages needed to establish external equilibrium in the face of a balance of payments deficit. Governments therefore could not be expected blindly to follow, or 'synchronize' with, a policy of deflation elsewhere.

> [Policy coordination] could scarcely be expected in a world in which many governments have become conscious of a greater responsibility for maintaining economic stability and social security. A synchronisation involving each country in booms and depressions originating elsewhere has therefore tended to become less and less acceptable. (Nurkse 1944, 15)
>
> Emphasis has shifted to the broader criterion of employment and productive activity, and to policies acting on income and effective demand to maintain a satisfactory level of employment. (Nurkse 1944, 106)

Articles of Agreement:

Article I. Purposes

The purposes of the International Monetary Fund are:

ii. To facilitate the expansion and balanced growth of international trade, and to contribute thereby to the promotion and maintenance of high levels of employment and real income and to the development of the productive resources of all members as primary objectives of economic policy.

Article IV. Par Values of Currencies

SEC. 5. Changes in par values.

f. In particular, provided it is so satisfied, [the IMF] shall not object to a proposed change because of the domestic social or political policies of the member proposing the change.

Capital Controls

To help governments combine domestic policy autonomy with a fixed exchange rate, capital flows would have to be restricted. In the view of contemporaries, short-term capital movements continually undermined the international monetary system; restricting them would be uncontroversial after the 1930s. It was an incredible turnaround of the standard orthodoxy.[10]

Even if changes in exchange rates were in future ruled out as a normal method of international adjustment, the mere memory of the interwar period – the period of uncoordinated business cycle policies and flexible exchange rates – may keep the disequilibriating tendencies alive, and may consequently necessitate restrictions on the international flow of funds. (Nurkse 1944, 141)

Articles of Agreement:
  Article VI. Capital Transfers
    SEC. 3. Controls of capital transfers.

Members may exercise such controls as are necessary to regulate international capital movements, but no member may exercise these controls in a manner which will restrict payments for current transactions or which will unduly delay transfers of funds in settlement of commitments, except as provided in Article VII, Section 3 (b) and in Article XIV, Section 2.

Adjustable Peg

To Keynes' great frustration, many portrayed his post-war 'clearing union' plan, and the subsequent Bretton Woods plan, as a return to the gold standard. As the Bank of England's champion in the Cabinet warned, 'THIS is the Gold Standard all over again.'[11] In response, the Bretton Woods protagonists cited the plan's 'adjustable peg' as the differentiator with the gold standard. Whereas the latter held the gold parity as sacrosanct, the former explicitly countenanced changes of parity under conditions of 'fundamental disequilibrium'. The rationale for doing so was consciousness of the alternative: difficulty maintaining parity in the 1930s led some countries to unsavoury ends, including clearing arrangements, exchange controls and exclusive trading arrangements. Far better to grant a devaluation – with the imprimatur of an official arbiter.

Persistent ... disequilibria ... must be dealt with by a readjustment of exchange rates. (Nurkse 1944, 112)
  As a general rule, such exchange adjustments as prove necessary after the establishment of an initial system should be made by mutual consultation and agreement. It ought to be an elementary principle of international monetary relations that exchange rates should not be altered by arbitrary unilateral action. (Nurkse 1944, 141)
  ... the difficulty of fixing appropriate exchange rates in the first instance is so great that there should be a reasonable willingness to adjust them in the

light of experience and a reasonable latitude should be afforded to governments under any international system to make some adjustment unilaterally. Refusal to allow necessary adaptations may result in the country which finds its balance of payments out of gear imposing unilaterally restrictions on imports or subsidizing exports. To afford an incentive to such unilateral action regarding international trade by refusing any latitude as regards monetary relations is to the advantage of no one. (Nurkse 1944, 141)

Articles of Agreement:
Article IV. Par Values of Currencies
SEC. 5. Changes in par values.

a. A member shall not propose a change in the par value of its currency except to correct a fundamental disequilibrium.
b. A change in the par value of a member's currency may be made only on the proposal of the member and only after consultation with the Fund.
c. When a change is proposed, the Fund shall first take into account the changes, if any, which have already taken place in the initial par value of the member's currency as determined under Article XX, Section 4. If the proposed change, together with all previous changes, whether increases or decreases,
    i. does not exceed ten per cent of the initial par value, the Fund shall raise no objection;
    ii. does not exceed a further ten per cent of the initial par value, the Fund may either concur or object, but shall declare its attitude within seventy-two hours if the member so requests;
    iii. is not within (i) or (ii) above, the Fund may either concur or object, but shall be entitled to a longer period in which to declare its attitude.
f. The Fund shall concur in a proposed change which is within the terms of (c) (ii) or (c) (iii) above if it is satisfied that the change is necessary to correct a fundamental disequilibrium. In particular, provided it is so satisfied, it shall not object to a proposed change because of the domestic social or political policies of the member proposing the change.

Liquidity Provision / Currency Swap

The 1937 US recession had shown that a depression could quickly be turned around, releasing the rest of the world from payments pressures at existing exchange rates. That recession was so quickly reversed that, for much of the world, recourse to international reserves was sufficient to bridge the gap (Urban 2006). Since reserves would play the vital 'buffer' role in the new system, it was important to augment national supplies with a store of lendable official reserves or officially coordinated lendable reserves.

> If there are grounds for believing, however, that a balance of payments deficit has arisen for manifestly temporary or exceptional reasons, a country whose currency reserve is not sufficient to tide it over the emergency may well prefer exchange control to exchange depreciation. These are, of course, the conditions for which foreign credit operations constitute the obvious solution, and resort to exchange control would represent a failure not only of the monetary mechanism but also of the capital market to function. (Nurkse 1944, 223)

Articles of Agreement:
Article V. Transactions with the Fund
   SEC. 3. Conditions governing use of the Fund's resources.

a. A member shall be entitled to buy the currency of another member from the Fund in exchange for its own currency subject to the following conditions:
   i. The member desiring to purchase the currency represents that it is presently needed for making in that currency payments which are consistent with the provisions of this Agreement;
   ii. The Fund has not given notice under Article VII, Section 3, that its holdings of the currency desired have become scarce;
   iii. The proposed purchase would not cause the Fund's holdings of the purchasing member's currency to increase by more than twenty-five per cent of its quota during the period of twelve months ending on the date of the purchase nor to exceed two hundred per cent of its quota, but the twenty-five per cent limitation shall apply only to the extent that the Fund's holdings of the member's currency have been brought above seventy-five per cent of its quota if they had been below that amount;
   iv. The Fund has not previously declared under Section 5 of this Article, Article IV, Section 6, Article VI, Section 1, or Article XV, Section 2 (a), that the member desiring to purchase is ineligible to use the resources of the Fund.
b. A member shall not be entitled without the permission of the Fund to use the Fund's resources to acquire currency to hold against forward exchange transactions.

Scarce Currency/Surplus Disincentive

A key source of friction in the interwar monetary system, particularly in its second decade, was the persistent external surplus generated by the US economy. This made it difficult for other countries to acquire dollars; all the more so when US lending practically collapsed after the Great Depression. Keynes may have been motivated by this experience more than any other in his design of a new world system. His preference was to ensure that any such serial accumulations would be available for international settlement – if not by the accumulator, then by someone else. The US Treasury disagreed. But Harry Dexter White, its representative, offered a compromise: the 'scarce currency' clause. If any member of the international monetary system accumulated serial surpluses, other members would have the right to ration access to that member's currency.

> It would be natural in such circumstances [of serial accumulations] to apply exchange rationing, if at all, to the centre of the disturbance....
> Rationing of the surplus country's scarce currency by an international agency might be a means for preventing the surplus country from draining away the liquid reserves of other countries and for preventing the spread of depression to other countries. (Nurkse 1944, 223-224)

Articles of Agreement:
Article VII. Scarce Currencies
　SECTION. 1. General scarcity of currency.
If the Fund finds that a general scarcity of a particular currency is developing, the Fund may so inform members and may issue a report setting forth the causes of the scarcity and containing recommendations designed to bring it to an end. A representative of the member whose currency is involved shall participate in the preparation of the report.
　SEC. 2. Measures to replenish the Fund's holdings of scarce currencies. The Fund may, if it deems such action appropriate to replenish its holdings of any member's currency, take either or both of the following steps:

　i. Propose to the member that, on terms and conditions agreed between the Fund and the member, the latter lend its currency to the Fund or that, with the approval of the member, the Fund borrow such currency from some other source either within or outside the territories of the member, but no member shall be under any obligation to make such loans to the Fund or to approve the borrowing of its currency by the Fund from any other source.
　ii. Require the member to sell its currency to the Fund for gold.

International Currency Experience and the Case for Fiat Currency

As much as *International Currency Experience* is a plea for negotiated exchange rates and pegged currencies, it is also an impassioned criticism of collateralized currency; 'collateralized' in the sense that central bank statutes required the monetary authority to hold a minimum ratio of gold and/or foreign assets to central bank sight liabilities. Only Germany and Italy eliminated such statutes in the interwar period, notwithstanding the fact that almost everyone had suspended convertibility (Nurkse 1944, 12). The overriding message of *International Currency Experience* is the inherent destructiveness of maintaining such a cover function for scarce international reserves. The effect is to tie up reserves that otherwise would have been available to settle payments discrepancies – a 'buffer' function as distinct from a 'collateral' function.

The Articles of Agreement make no mention of the cover ratio nor suggest steps to banish the practice. And the practice was not banished. The IMF reported reserve statutes of its members' central banks in volumes published in 1961 and 1967 (International Monetary Fund 1961/1967). These show the widespread legal requirement of maintaining a fixed proportion of foreign exchange or gold to central bank sight liabilities (see Table 12.1). Bretton Woods, from a modern perspective, was not as far from a gold standard as its founders had believed. It neither highlighted nor banned the practice of 'backing' the central bank's liabilities with precious assets. Nurkse must have been disappointed with this omission.

Cover ratios, or 'statutory reserve requirements', have not received much attention in the literature.[12] Bordo and Eichengreen (1998, 83–88) report cover requirements for some 21 countries in three gold-linked periods: 1880–1914 (the 'classical gold standard'), 1925–1931 (the 'interwar gold-exchange standard') and 1944–1972 (the Bretton Woods system). These they use to test econometrically for a source of gold demand and find significant and positive coefficients. But they overlook cover ratios in the 1930s.

Bernanke highlighted the restrictive impact of the cover ratio on international liquidity, through a notional 'world money multiplier': global broad money (currency in circulation plus the public's sight deposits, i.e., M1) over world monetary gold. It adds to the standard money multiplier (term a) terms for fractional currency backing (term b) and fractional fx reserves (term c, the 'gold-exchange standard') (Bernanke 1993, 251–267).

World money multiplier $= (M1/M0) * (M0/\text{reserves}) * (\text{fx reserves}/\text{gold})$
                                    (a)   (b)   (c)

Table 12.1. **Statutory Requirements on Minimum Assets of the Central Bank as of 1960**

	Gold only	Gold or fx	Notes	Other Liabilities	Asset Requirement May be Suspended by:
Rhodesia and Nyasaland		25%		Liabilities to public	Minister of Finance
South Africa	25%		Note issue	Other liabilities to public	Minister of Finance
UK	1/		Bank of England note issue 1/		
Burma		25%	Currency in circulation	Bank's liability on account of deposits	The Bank with prior approval of president of the union
India	1,150 million rupees 2/	850 million rupees 2/	Currency notes Government of India and bank notes in circulation.		The Bank with prior approval of central government.
Indonesia		20%	Bank notes	Balances on current account and other demand liabilities	
Pakistan		30%	Bank notes in circulation		The Bank with previous sanction of central government
Cuba	$16\frac{2}{3}$%	25%	Bank notes in circulation	Deposits	
Dominican Republic	$12\frac{1}{2}$%	50% of monetary issue	Notes	Deposits	
El Salvador	25%		Notes in circulation	Sight liabilities	
Mexico		25%	Notes in circulation	Sight liabilities	

1/ Under Sec. 2(1) of the Currency and Bank Notes Act, 1954, gold coin and gold bullion for the time being in the Issue Department of the Bank of England form part of the statutory note cover. In accordance with Sec. 2(7) of the same Act, the period during which the fiduciary issue may stand at amounts continuously exceeding £1,575 million has been extended for two years from 14 March 1960 by virtue of the Fiduciary Note Issue (Extension of Period) Order, 1960, No. 327.

2/ The minimum statutory assets requirement of Sec. 33(2) of the Reserve Bank India Act, 1934, has been amended under Sec. 2 of the Reserve Bank of India (Amendment) Ordinance, 1957, of 31 October 1957, subsequently enacted as the Reserve Bank of India (Second Amendment) Act, 1957, so that the aggregate value of gold coin, gold bullion and foreign securities held in the Issue Department at any time should not be less than Rs200 crores; of this cover the value of gold (bullion plus coin) should not be less than Rs115 crores in value. One crore equals 10 million.

Source: Aufricht, H., *Central Banking Legislation* Vol. 1 (Washington DC 1961, 998–1000).

As Bernanke notes, his 'World money supply multiplier' collapsed between 1928 and 1936. Among modern academics, he seems nearly alone in joining Nurkse in emphasizing this pernicious influence of 1930s currency cover requirements (see Table 12.2).

Fiat currency earned a poor reputation from early times, partly because its issuers lacked a commitment device to keep from debasing the currency.[13] With the birth of 'modern' monetary syste ms in the eighteenth and nineteenth centuries (i.e., those in which the note issue was monopolized by the state and given explicit legal tender status), governments were keen to differentiate their notes from the inflationary currencies that had provided so many unhappy episodes in monetary history. The new currencies, though paper, would not be 'fiat'; they would be backed by a legally mandated amount of foreign assets or gold.

World War One necessitated a temporary escape from such backing requirements. But the postwar inflations led governments to make cover requirements even more onerous in the interwar period. As Nurkse pointed out, this 'meant that the cover reserves were really not international currency at all'.[14] They could provide international liquidity only insofar as the central bank could reduce sight liabilities. This is deflation. Nurkse cited Britain's MacMillan Committee, which in 1931 noted that enforcing the fiduciary limit forbade the Bank of England from using 'by far the greater part of its gold for the only purpose for which it is held or could be used'. According to the Committee, 'the sole purpose of gold [is] to enable a country to meet deficits in its international balance of payments.'[15] The MacMillan Committee was not alone. The League of Nation's Gold Delegation in 1929 had recommended a universal cut in the cover ratio. The London World Monetary Conference in 1933 did likewise.[16]

Table 12.2. **Interwar Reduction in Currency Cover Ratios. Gold and/or Foreign Exchange as Per cent of the Note Issue**

	Changed From	To	Date
Argentina	100	40	Dec 1929
Australia	25	15	June 1930
Denmark	50	33–1/3	Oct 1931
Germany		suspended	July 1931
Greece		suspended	April 1932
Bulgaria	33–1/2	25	'Later'
Latvia	50	30	'Later'
Ecuador	50	40	'Later'
South Africa	40	30	'Later'

Source: Nurkse *International Currency Experience* (1944, 97).

Indeed, the collapse of the gold-exchange standard around 1931 had a paradoxical effect. Foreign exchange was demonstrably liable to devaluation. Hence, central banks sought to convert their foreign reserve balances into gold.

Legislatures understood the constrictions that cover ratios entailed for the money supply, and in the 1930s reduced statutory backing requirements. In 1929, combined reserves of 41 countries (excluding Germany and Italy) dedicated to currency cover were 3.1 times the amount of reserves available for international settlement. By 1936, this ratio was almost balanced, with 6.018 billion dollars of reserves dedicated to note cover and 7.109 billion dollars of reserves for balance of payments settlement.[17] Nurkse's injunction was to free those seven billion dollars for international liquidity.

Uncollateralized, or true 'fiat' currency, came only with the end of Bretton Woods after 1971. It is one of the features that distinguishes today's international monetary system from all that came before.[18] The great irony is that, to modern eyes, fiat currencies go hand in hand with floating exchange rates – an anathema for Nurkse, who conceived of fiat currencies only in the context of pegged exchange rates. Nurkse got the postwar formula only half right.

Conclusion

Ragnar Nurkse wrote the most influential study on the interwar currency system, *International Currency Experience*. The book's strongly normative passages constitute an intellectual bulwark for the Bretton Woods agreement. This should have proven vital to the Bretton Woods plan's acceptance among national parliaments, in the first instance during the year-long or longer ratification process, and years later as the plan proved exceptionally difficult to implement.

The overlap between *International Currency Experience* and the IMF Articles of Agreement is uncanny. In *International Currency Experience*, Nurkse advocated a system reconciling fixed exchange rates with income and employment stability. Discrepancies in international payments would not be reconciled by domestic price adjustment, as sought in the interwar gold standard. Nor would it be achieved by floating exchange rates, as was practiced in the early interwar period. It would be accomplished through purchase and sale of official reserves, and it would be sustained by limitations on short-term capital flows. Temporary deficiency in reserves would not crash the system; a central authority would make liquidity available in small amounts as needed, so that a member country would not have cause to resort to trade restriction, exchange control or devaluation. Similarly, 'fundamental disequilibrium' would not be allowed to wreck the system; if an exchange-rate peg had drifted too far from underlying equilibrium, the central authority would condone a peg change, rather than exhaust its own reserves.

These qualities are all clearly detailed in *International Currency Experience* and are all present in the original IMF Articles of Agreement. As calls arose for a fundamental rethink of the Bretton Woods system, policymakers could turn to the lessons outlined in Nurkse's book for a reminder of why they had endorsed the Bretton Woods plan in the first place. For this contribution, Nurkse's name should be as closely associated with the Bretton Woods system, as are the names John Maynard Keynes and Harry Dexter White.

References

Bernanke, B. 1993. 'The World on a Cross of Gold.' *Journal of Monetary Economics* 31, 251–267.

Bordo, M. and B. Eichengreen. 1998. 'The Rise and Fall of a Barbarous Relic: The Role of Gold in the International Monetary System.' *NBER Working Paper* 6436.

Bordo, M. and H. James. 2001. 'The Adam Klug Memorial Lecture: Haberler versus Nurkse: The Case for Floating Exchange Rates as an Alternative to Bretton Woods?' *NBER Working Paper* 8545.

Clavin, P. and J. W. Wessels. 2005. 'Transnationalism and the League of Nations: Understanding the Work of its Economic and Financial Organisation.' *Contemporary European History* 14, 465–492.

Dormael, A. 1978. *Bretton Woods: Birth of a Monetary System*. London: Macmillan.

Haberler, F. 1964. *Prosperity and Depression*. 5th edn. London: Allen and Unwin.

Ikenberry, G. J. 1992. 'A World Economy Restored: Expert Consensus and the Anglo-American Postwar Settlement.' *International Organization* 46 (1), 289–321.

International Monetary Fund. 1961/1967. *Central Banking Legislation*. Washington DC: International Monetary Fund.

Keynes, J. M. 1925. *The Economic Consequences of Mr Churchill*. London: Hogarth.

———. 1919. *The Economic Consequences of the Peace*. London: Macmillan.

Nurkse, R. 1944. *International Currency Experience*. Geneva: League of Nations.

Nussbaum, A. 1950. *Money in the Law: National and International*. New York: Foundation Press.

———. 1944. 'International Monetary Agreements.' *The American Journal of International Law* 38 (2), 242–257.

Pauly, L. O. 1996. *The League of Nations and the Foreshadowing of the International Monetary Fund*. Essays in International Finance, No. 201. Princeton, New Jersey: Internat. Finance Sect., Dep. of Economics, Princeton Univ.

Strigl, R. 2000. *Capital and Production*. Auburn: Ludwig von Mises Institute.

Urban, S. 2006. 'Revisiting the Inter-War Monetary System: The Sterling Bloc and the 1937 Shock.' Unpublished MSc thesis, St. Antony's College, Oxford.

Chapter Thirteen:

SOME REFLECTIONS ON NURKSE'S *PATTERNS OF TRADE AND DEVELOPMENT*

Alan V. Deardorff and Robert M. Stern

Introduction

In his Introduction to *Equilibrium and Growth in the World Economy: Economic Essays by Ragnar Nurkse*, Gottfried Haberler concluded that:

> The Wicksell Lectures (7 and 10 April 1959) were Ragnar Nurkse's last words on trade and development. He had evidently spent much care on their preparation. But he was fully aware that he left many loose ends, and he was full of plans for further work. He intended to write a comprehensive volume on trade and development and had started to draft parts. His untimely death (in May 1959) at the age of fifty-two has deprived us of any further help from his fertile mind and wise counsel; it was a grievous loss for economic science as a whole, to say nothing of his many friends. Let us hope, however, that the present collection will stimulate many others to follow the leads which he has given and to explore the lands which his researches have opened. (Haberler and Stern 1961, xii)

We will never know how Nurkse's views of trade and development would have evolved, had he been able to observe the contrasting experiences of developing countries over subsequent years. However, with the benefit of hindsight, we can ask how well the policies and the performances of developing countries corresponded to the expectations that Nurkse laid out in his essay.

In this paper we will review the theory of trade and development that Nurkse suggested, interpreting it in the light of subsequent advances in the theories and empirics of trade and growth. We will then examine the extent to which developing countries' growth experiences during the second half of the twentieth century have matched Nurkse's expectations, and also the extent to which his policy advice was followed and, where followed, successful. Perhaps not surprisingly, given the limited information he had available when he wrote, the growth performance of countries following various development strategies has turned out to differ rather markedly from Nurkse's expectations. But his expectations for the policies that would be used, both by the majority of developing countries in the first decades after he wrote and by developed countries in response to those few who followed a more export oriented path, were remarkably prescient.

Contrasting Trends in World Trade from the Nineteenth Century to the Late 1950s

In his Wicksell Lectures, Nurkse reviewed at length 'Contrasting Trends in the Nineteenth and Twentieth Century World Trade'. He noted that, in the nineteenth century (1815–1914), trade was an engine of growth transmission as well as a means of improved allocation of existing resources. This was a period in which Great Britain was the focal center of economic expansion that resulted in a very substantial increase in the demand for primary commodities from the so-called Regions of Recent Settlement (RRS) located in the temperate zones of North and South America, Australia and New Zealand. Great Britain was also the source of the very large movements of financial capital that were instrumental (especially) in building the railway infrastructure in the RRS that facilitated the movement of their exports to Great Britain. This period in time was truly the first great movement of globalization that served to integrate what are now many of the world's high-income, industrialized countries.

From World War I to the end years of the 1950s, once the postwar recovery took hold, the production and trade of the major industrialized countries rose significantly. But in contrast to the nineteenth-century experience, Nurkse noted there was a marked slowdown in the rate of expansion in the primary exports, excluding oil, of the poorer countries. He attributed this slowdown to a number of factors: (1) the shift in the industrial countries from industries with a high raw-material content to industries with a low material content; (2) the rising shares of services that did not depend on significant material inputs; (3) the low income elasticity of demand for many agricultural products; (4) increased agricultural protectionism; (5) substantial economies in industrial uses of natural materials; and (6) development of synthetic and other man-made substitutes for many staple commodities.

The question that Nurkse then raised was, what are the less developed countries to do? Given the pessimistic outlook for expanding production of agricultural products and other raw materials, the issue was whether and how industrialization could be pursued. The choices appeared to be production for export and production mainly for the domestic markets. Nurkse was inclined to favor industrialization for export, especially in developing countries that were relatively labor abundant. But he expressed some concern about supply-side difficulties arising from the comparative lack of social and physical infrastructure in many poor countries, and, on the demand side, the possible protectionist reactions in the industrialized countries if their high-cost suppliers especially of labor-intensive manufactures were to be injured and displaced by imports. Nurkse considered at some length the difficulties that might arise in promoting industrialization to serve the home market. The concerns here related to the interactions of agricultural and industrial development in relation to the patterns of expansion of domestic demand and the pitfalls of following policies of import substitution.

From his vantage point in the late 1950s, Nurkse noted (323):

Manufacturing for export to more advanced countries ... is being tried to some extent, in some places with success, and there are experts who predict great things for it in the near future. But it can hardly be described as a major factor at present. ... More is happening along the lines of ... the pattern of home-market expansion. ... Industrialization for home markets is undoubtedly spreading.

Developments in World Trade and Growth from the Late 1950s to the Present

In the preceding section, we have reviewed the essentials of Nurkse's views and analysis of the factors that shaped the patterns of trade and development from the nineteenth century to the late 1950s. We now consider the major developments in world trade since Nurkse presented his Wicksell Lectures in 1959. It is obvious that Nurkse did not foresee the truly remarkable expansion of world production and trade that has occurred in the past half century and that has encompassed the major industrialized countries and many developing countries. There has literally been a 'second coming' of globalization that makes the nineteenth century look to be a pale comparison.

To address the developments that Nurkse did not fully anticipate, we shall focus attention analytically on the determinants of trade and growth that may help to further the understanding of how the global trading system has been transformed.

We will first review the policy choices that developing countries made in the 1950s and 1960s, confirming the preponderance that he noted above of countries choosing 'home-market expansion', or what came to be called 'import substitution', as their strategy for economic growth. At the same time, as he also noted, a handful of countries opted for 'manufacture for export', or 'export promotion', as their strategy.

Nurkse anticipated correctly that the latter countries would face increasing barriers to their exports, especially in the labor-intensive textile and apparel sectors where their relative labor abundance gave them comparative advantage. He did not anticipate, however, how well such countries would nonetheless succeed in growing, or that their success would gradually attract converts from the first group of countries.

Nurkse fully understood that the home-market expansion strategy was only second best, and he suggested it only because of the barriers that he thought developed countries would place in the way of export expansion. We will review the growth performance of countries that chose the different strategies.

Theoretical Insights: Nurkse's Model of Trade and Growth, in Retrospect

In his Wicksell Lectures, Nurkse laid out three strategies for growth and trade. In this he was primarily interested in the prospects for success of these three strategies and thus their policy implications, and he was therefore not explicit as to what economic model he had in mind. In fact, it is not likely that he would have claimed to be working with an explicit model of the sort that was only then coming into fashion with the works of Samuelson and others. Indeed, he was sufficiently attuned to the complexities of the economy that he might have renounced any such explicit model as being too simplistic.

But he was definitely thinking within the general framework of the Heckscher-Ohlin model of trade, and his reasoning reflected that. Here we will ask what particular variant and extension of that model might have most closely corresponded with his thinking. Then, in the context of that model, we will ask how his theoretical ideas about trade and growth look today, with fifty more years of experience in both economic theory and the experiences of developing countries.

The Strategies

Nurkse described three strategies of trade and growth, distinguished by the portions of the economy in which that growth was to be concentrated. The first strategy – what we will here call Strategy I – is to grow by producing and exporting primary products. This is the mechanism he described in his first lecture as having successfully achieved the growth of the RRS during the nineteenth century. At that time, countries such as the United States provided primary inputs to the rapidly expanding industrial complexes of Europe, especially the UK.

The RRS themselves therefore remained relatively unindustrialized under Strategy I. This worked well during the nineteenth century, but for reasons we will mention later, was inadequate during the twentieth. Therefore, his other two strategies were directed toward industrialization.

Strategy II is also export-based, but instead of exporting raw materials, this exploits another comparative advantage of many developing countries: their relative abundance of unskilled labor. Thus, this strategy rests on the exports of labor-intensive consumer goods, such as textiles and apparel.

Strategy III, introduced for reasons to be discussed in a moment, is not based on exports at all, but rather on producing for the domestic market of the developing country itself, or perhaps for itself and other developing countries in its region. Because the domestic market for any good is rather small, and because without substantial exports demands for other consumer goods could not be satisfied through imports, Strategy III requires production not just in a few sectors, but in nearly all, including both a broad range of consumer manufactures and also food. Nurkse did allow this strategy to include imports of capital goods, which he regarded the developing countries as least capable of producing themselves. Thus, there had to be a certain amount of exports of something, perhaps again primary products, but in smaller volume than in Strategy I.

Nurkse saw substantial limitations to each of these strategies, and it was the limitations on Strategies I and II that led him to consider the third in spite of its obvious economic inefficiency. The limitation on Strategy I, exporting primary products, was the now-familiar expectation that world prices of primary products tend to fall over time. This evidently was either not true or not a problem during the nineteenth century, but Nurkse was in good company during the 1950s in perceiving it to be a problem then, and in expecting the problem to continue. Therefore, he dismissed Strategy I as inadequate for the developing countries of his day.

The limitation that he saw for the Strategy II was not nearly as commonly perceived in the 1950s, and indeed, one can marvel at his prescience. This was that as developing countries expand their exports of labor-intensive goods, they would encounter increasing trade barriers for these products in their developed-country markets. He well understood that labor-intensive sectors in the developed world would have to contract for this strategy to succeed, and that political forces in those countries would resist that contraction. Thus, the access into these markets by developing countries would be limited by tariffs or other trade barriers, as a direct result of any success that they began to achieve. Thus, the strategy of growth through manufactured exports would be undermined.

It was the limitations on the first two strategies that led him to consider the third, for which he also saw limitations – several of them, in fact – but also at least one positive effect that bears mentioning. The most obvious limitation, of course, is that countries would be denying themselves most of the benefits of pursuing their comparative advantage. By allowing them, under this strategy, to continue importing capital goods, he did not deny them that benefit completely. But by having them produce a full range of consumer manufactured goods, he more or less assured that consumers in developing countries, to the extent that their incomes rose enough to afford these goods, would be poorly served. It seems clear that he was well aware of that, but as already noted, he found the alternatives nonviable.

The more severe limitation of Strategy III, and one he stressed, was that it depended on countries being able to feed themselves. Without exports to pay for imported food, countries would have no choice but to be essentially self-sufficient, and yet it was not obvious to him that they could do it. Resources would have to continue to be devoted to agriculture and to improving productivity there, or there would be no surplus labor available to produce other goods for the domestic market. He saw this as the most binding constraint on economic development, given his pessimism about the other two strategies, and he seemed rather pessimistic about this as well.

He also discussed one other important limitation on this strategy of producing for the domestic market; that the domestic market would be very small in many countries, often too small to support efficient production. Thus, he acknowledged the existence of economies of scale in manufacturing production, and thus, that producing for only a small domestic market would be very costly, with or without comparative advantage. His solution to this, mentioned only in passing, was that developing countries should not eschew exports entirely, but that they should export to each other, and that they presumably should specialize within their developing-country regions to the extent needed to support minimally efficient plants.

This essentially completes the description of Strategy III, although it includes one additional implication that if successful, bears mentioning. To the extent that a developing country succeeds in growing its productive capacity in a broad range of manufactures, not just labor-intensive ones, it will eventually be able to export some non-labor-intensive goods to the rich world. The advantage of this is that by steering clear of the overstressed labor-intensive industries of the developed world, it will avoid the protectionist backlash that he forecast to be stimulated by labor-intensive exports. Instead, developing-country exports of more capital-intensive goods would feed into the nexus of trade within more advanced industries that already goes on among developed countries, and the new additions from the developed counties would be accepted without complaint.

Nurkse's Growth Model

It may be noticed that these strategies do not really address how to make economic growth happen in the first place. Rather, they simply assume such growth, and they are concerned instead with how to accommodate that growth within the world economy. Nurkse did not, at least in these Wicksell Lectures, pretend to have anything new to say about the causes of growth or how to achieve it.

Instead, he simply accepted that growth requires saving. He did not discuss how this saving was to be achieved, although he seemed to see it as coming from within the developing economies rather than from abroad. And he did not discuss the mechanisms by which savings are to be transformed into investment of one sort or another, and the associated difficulties with that transformation.

In particular, he did not really address how each of his three strategies for trade and growth might be implemented. He simply spoke of countries as choosing one or another. We can infer that his Strategy III would have to be implemented with trade barriers of some sort, to prevent imports of manufactured goods, but there is no implication here that such trade policies would themselves cause growth to occur. His lectures were about accommodating a country's growth within or outside of world markets, given that the growth occurs. They were not about how to achieve that growth.

His first lecture seems to be explaining the growth that occurred in the nineteenth century as being a result of the exports of primary products, but it seems unlikely that Nurkse believed that such exports, in and of themselves, would have produced growth. Rather, when these exports took place in a growing world market, they added nicely to the incomes of the countries, and thus provided a source from which savings and investment could be extracted. But presumably, he would have agreed that additional ingredients are needed to prompt that savings, even out of a higher income, and that some countries undoubtedly participated in the nineteenth-century export boom without translating it into savings and growth. Indeed, it is to some extent those countries who remained underdeveloped, and thus were the subject of his strategies when he wrote.

As for implementing the strategies, aside from using trade barriers for Strategy III, it is not clear what Nurkse had in mind for directing an exporting economy into either raw materials or manufactures. He tends to speak of these choices as though policy makers might control them directly, which of course may have been true in some developing countries of his day.

Alternatively, one could argue that the world market would determine this specialization. If a developing country does have an abundance of raw materials, then absent any policy to prevent it happening, exports of these will occur, with implications for income that depend on their price. However, if prices decline as Nurkse expected, and if in addition the country's labor force is expanding beyond the capacity of the resource sector to employ it, then again, in the absence of policy to prevent it, labor-intensive production and exports will occur.

In other words, unless a country deliberately implements Strategy III by restricting trade, the choice between Strategies I and II will be made for it by world markets. In each case, whether these will lead to growth will depend both on the returns that a country is able to derive from its specialization, which Nurkse discusses, and on whether it is able to turn income into savings and investment, which Nurkse leaves aside.

Nurkse's Trade Model

In order to accommodate many of Nurkse's ideas within an economic model, that model must include, at a minimum, more than one manufacturing sector as well as a primary product or agricultural sector. These sectors must employ labor, of course, some sort of capital, and presumably land and/or natural resources for the primary-product sector. In addition, to capture the role of scale economies that play a small role in his discussion, it would be desirable to have increasing returns to scale in at least some manufacturing. Finally, the model may treat a small country for which prices in trade are given, except that it must also include the feedback from exports to rest-of-world protection that Nurkse expected in labor-intensive manufactures.

To capture these elements, the model would have to be a hybrid of other models, and one might fear that it would be too cumbersome to be of use. That is not the case, however, as we will suggest.

Start with the model that Anne Krueger (1977) presented of trade and development in her Graham Lecture thirty years ago. This was itself a hybrid of a two-factor (labor and capital), many-sector Heckscher-Ohlin (HO) model combined with a three-factor (labor, capital, and land) specific-factors model. Her model had a single agricultural sector employing labor and land, plus an arbitrary number of manufacturing subsectors employing labor and capital. As discussed further in Deardorff (1984), labor in this model is distributed between agriculture and manufacturing largely based on the stocks of land and capital that are specific, respectively, to agriculture and to manufacturing as a whole. Within manufacturing, however, because both labor and capital are mobile among the multiple subsectors, that part of the model behaves like the HO Model.

Krueger assumed that all goods could be traded on the world market, from which a small developing country would take prices as given. She also assumed that these prices within the manufacturing sector were such as to generate multiple cones of diversification. The latter implies that under free trade, a country will specialize in only a subset of the manufactured goods, those with labor intensities (relative to capital) corresponding to its aggregate employment of labor in the manufacturing sector relative to its capital stock.

A main implication of the Krueger model is the way that patterns of specialization and trade depend on factor endowments. A developing country with a great deal of land relative to both labor and capital will employ so much labor in the agricultural sector that not much labor will be available in manufacturing. As a result, it will actually specialize in the more capital-intensive of the manufacturing subsectors, not because it has so much capital, but because it has so little labor to spare to work with that capital. Thus, within manufacturing, it specializes in less labor-intensive goods. But even there it produces little of them, and may not export them because these sectors are small. The country exports agricultural products, perhaps exclusively.

In contrast, if such a country had a much larger labor endowment, most of that labor would be employed in manufacturing. Its capital-to-labor ratio within manufacturing would then be low, and it would specialize in, and export, labor-intensive goods. Wages, incidentally, would be much lower than in the first case.

The Krueger model provides an appropriate structure for much of Nurkse's analysis, with only minor modifications. We might think of splitting the agricultural sector into two, one producing primary products for export and the other producing food, either for export or for domestic consumption, but that will not much change the behavior of the model. The manufacturing sector can be taken from Krueger's model unchanged for most purposes, including the prediction that labor-abundant developing countries, at least if their agricultural sectors are not large enough to employ too much of their labor, will, under free trade, specialize in and export very labor-intensive goods.

In this form, the Krueger Model does a nice job of explaining the shift that will occur between Nurkse's first two strategies. A natural resource-abundant country with not too large a population will naturally export primary products in exchange for all else. But if the prices of primary products fall, and especially if the countries have much more labor than can be employed in the primary-product sector, the free market will lead to specialization in labor-intensive manufactured goods.

To turn the Krueger Model, thus conceived, into a Nurkse model, then, we need just two more elements. The first is to depart from Heckscher-Ohlin in at least the more capital-intensive manufacturing subsectors to include Krugman-style monopolistic competition. This serves two purposes. First, it adds increasing returns to scale, potentially accommodating Nurkse's concern about domestic market size. And second, by turning these manufactured goods into differentiated products, it allows for the intraindustry trade and the less disruptive exports that Nurkse expected if a developing country were eventually able to export more capital intensive products.

Adding Krugman monopolistic competition into the Krueger model is not as hard as it may sound. That is exactly what Helpman and Krugman (1985) did with the Heckscher-Ohlin model, where they showed that essentially all standard properties of the HO Model survive unchanged when sectors of the HO model are instead made monopolistically competitive under their assumptions. The only exception is that, instead of countries either exporting or importing in these sectors depending on supply relative to demand, they do both. That is, domestic consumers buy products from both domestic and foreign firms, and domestic firms sell to both domestic and foreign consumers, regardless of whether domestic supply exceeds domestic demand or falls short of it. The same will be true if some (or all) of the manufacturing subsectors of the Krueger Model are made monopolistically competitive in the same way.

The other element to be added is political economy. That is, to capture Nurkse's idea that exports of labor-intensive goods will lead to a backlash of protection, we need to endogenize tariffs. Fortunately, we only need to do this for the rest of the world, not for the developing country itself. Although doing the latter might be worthwhile for its own sake, it is not necessary in order to reflect the ideas in Nurkse's Lectures. And since we are not otherwise modelling the rest of world, the addition to the Krueger model will simply be to assume that rest-of-world tariffs on imports of labor-intensive manufactures rise with the level of exports from the developing country. This in turn means that the price the developing country will receive for its exports of these goods must fall as exports rise.

This Nurkse Trade Model, then, generates Nurkse's predictions, as follows. First, following Nurkse's Strategy I, a natural resource- (i.e., land) abundant developing country will naturally export primary products. As long as the prices of these products stay high, and the country's population does not grow unwieldy, it will prosper. But if, as Nurkse expects, the prices of these products decline over time, then the income from these exports will also decline, and the return to any growth that the country manages to achieve will be disappointing.

Strategy II is relevant for a country whose labor force is too large to employ mostly in primary products, either because of population growth or due to decline in the availability of natural resources. And, of course, it may become the strategy of an open economy that was following Strategy I, if the price of primary products falls sufficiently. The Krueger Model, unamended, would have predicted that the country will export the most labor intensive good, importing all other manufactures in exchange. But the Nurkse model goes a step further in predicting an increase in foreign protection and a consequent fall in the price that the developing country can get for its exports. Thus, while the mechanism is somewhat different, the result of a declining terms of trade is the same.

Interpreting Strategy III within this Nurkse Model takes a bit more work. In order to cause all manufactured goods to be produced in the country, tariffs or some other trade barrier will have to be put in place on all such goods that would otherwise be imported. In this model, as noted above, these imported goods may be of various capital intensities depending on the relative abundance in the country of land, labor and capital. A sufficiently land-abundant country, in spite of its scarcity of capital, may import some of the most labor-intensive goods and need to protect them in order to follow Strategy III. Nurkse did not anticipate this, and indeed he would probably say that such a country will escape from the limitation of Strategy II and need not follow Strategy III. Therefore, a developing country that adopts Strategy III is likely to be one whose labor is sufficiently abundant relative to both land and capital that under free trade, it would export only the most labor-intensive manufactured good and import all others.

Strategy III would therefore require tariffs on all but the most labor-intensive manufactures, raising the domestic prices of these goods. That price change will in turn cause the return to capital to rise and the real wage of labor to fall, as explained by the Stolper-Samuelson Theorem. Since the country ceases to import most manufactures, prices will also adjust so that it exports less as well, its remaining exports being either the most labor-intensive manufactured goods in smaller quantity, or perhaps products of the primary-product sector.

What now happens if the country succeeds in growing in spite of the lower income that it now earns producing goods to which it is less well suited? If it grows, its capital stock will rise relative to labor, and gradually, over time, its comparative advantage within manufacturing may move up the ladder of capital intensity. This, it should be said, is not assured, even if it succeeds in increasing its overall capital-labor ratio, since similar growth is probably occurring abroad as well. It must manage to grow faster than the rest of the world in order for its relative factor endowments to favor producing more capital-intensive goods.

If this happens, though, then the developing country will succeed not just in raising its income, but in moving into the monopolistically competitive manufacturing sectors even for export. At first it will not be a net exporter of these goods. But because of product differentiation, it will export at least a small amount of the particular varieties of these goods that it produces, while still importing the more numerous varieties produced abroad. Eventually though, if its growth is successful in this way, it could actually eliminate its tariffs on certain mid-level (in terms of capital intensity) manufactured goods and sustain net export positions in them. This is the outcome that Nurkse described as being less likely to prompt a protectionist backlash in developed countries, since it would not be such a threat to their declining industries.

Nurkse's Track Record

How accurate did Nurkse's model of trade and growth turn out to be, as we look back now with fifty years of hindsight? Some of his predictions have been borne out, but not all.

First, his prediction about a declining terms of trade in primary products has had a mixed record, and at the current moment looks particularly wide of the mark. Prices of primary products have moved both down and up over the last fifty years, in rather large swings. There certainly were times, especially in the first decade or two after he wrote, when primary product prices indeed fell. But in the later period they rose, and today many primary-product exporters are doing quite well, at least with that part of their economies. Not all, however, have so clearly benefited from exports of primary products, even when their prices rose. Many such countries have failed to translate their incomes from exports into savings and investment, suggesting to some that there exists a 'resource curse'. Even some oil exporters have failed to make good use of their oil windfall.

However, as this formalization of Nurkse's model perhaps makes clearer than his own discussion, a country's ability to sustain itself from primary-product exports alone depends not just on their price but on the abundance of the natural resource itself (land, in the model) relative to labor. As populations have grown, the shift to labor-intensive production has become more necessary. Thus, Strategy I has often been inadequate for success.

Nurkse foresaw quite correctly that Strategy II would lead to trade barriers being erected to limit the labor-intensive exports of developing countries. This actually began with restrictions on exports of clothing from Japan, when it was in effect a developing country during its recovery from the devastation of World War II. But these restrictions expanded, both in their coverage of textile and apparel products and in their coverage of developing country exporters, as various countries other than Japan attempted to pursue Strategy II. The barriers ultimately took the form of the Multi-Fibre Arrangement (MFA), which was only terminated in 1995 with the creation of the World Trade Organization, which then phased out the barriers over the subsequent ten years.

What Nurkse did not foresee was that these barriers would not be large enough to prevent quite a number of countries from pursuing the strategy successfully, albeit less successfully than they might have in the absence of the

MFA. One reason for this may have been the fact that the barriers of the MFA took the form of quotas, as well as tariffs, and the rents from the quotas accrued to the exporting countries themselves. Thus, while they could not export as large a quantity as they might have if unrestricted, the price they got for their exports did not suffer. Indeed, because these quotas were allocated country by country, some countries were able to earn more from exports of textiles and clothing than they would have without the MFA.

This advantage should not be overstated. In addition to the MFA, tariffs on textiles and apparel remain some of the highest charged by developed countries. And overall, as noted for example by Schavey (2001) of the US, tariffs on the exports of developing countries are quite a bit higher than the average tariff on all imports into developed countries. The latter was reduced tremendously by the eight successful rounds of multilateral trade liberalization under the General Agreement on Tariffs and Trade, but in part because developing countries were exempted from reducing their own tariffs during these negotiations, they got little in return. And it is no doubt true that resistance to lowering tariffs on their exports was motivated in large part by the disruption to developed country industries that Nurkse predicted.

Nurkse therefore expected Strategy III to be, by default, the one chosen by most developing countries. For several decades after he wrote this was the case, under the label of Import Substitution. As he foresaw, this strategy depended on countries being able to feed themselves, since without exporting they could not count on substantial imports of agricultural goods. Nurkse therefore saw the need for increased productivity in agriculture, although he did not see how this would occur. In fact, agricultural productivity did increase substantially as a result of the Green Revolution, thus forestalling in many (but hardly all) countries the famines that would otherwise have accompanied their rapid population growth.

On the other hand, while many countries pursuing this strategy did manage to grow, they grew only slowly, which would be no surprise to Nurkse. The surprise would have been that countries using Strategy II were able to grow so much more rapidly than the import-substitution countries, in spite of the protection they confronted in the developed world. And it was this example, first by Japan and then by the Asian Tigers (South Korea, Singapore, Hong Kong, and Taiwan), that has gradually led more and more developing countries to shift from Strategy III to Strategy II.

Nurkse might note that the Asian Tigers were small economies, so that their exports never rose to the level that might have prompted a more extreme protectionist response. Indeed, he might also observe that today, as ever more countries pursue Strategy II, including now the very large economies of China and India, the protectionist backlash may be growing. This could account, for example, for the fact that the latest round of multilateral trade liberalization, the Doha Development Agenda, seems headed for failure.

On the other hand, we might also observe that the successful pursuit of Strategy II by an increasing number of countries has led over time to the near disappearance of many of the most labor-intensive industries from the developed world, in spite of efforts to protect them. As a result, the constituent interests for protecting these industries have themselves declined. This is an outcome that Nurkse did not anticipate, but it is one that he would have well understood.

Conclusion

Many things have happened over the last half century, both in the world trading system and in the economies of developing countries. Some of these, Ragnar Nurkse anticipated. Others he did not. But his framework for understanding the interactions between developing countries and world trade was an important tool for interpreting these events, and it continues to be so today.

References

Deardorff, Alan V. 1984. 'An Exposition and Exploration of Krueger's Trade Model.' *Canadian Journal of Economics* 17 (4), 731–746.

Haberler, Gottfried and Robert M. Stern (eds). 1961. *Equilibrium and Growth in the World Economy: Economic Essays by Ragnar Nurkse*. Cambridge, MA: Harvard University Press.

Helpman, Elhanan and Paul R. Krugman. 1985. *Market Structure and Foreign Trade: Increasing Returns, Imperfect Competition, and the International Economy*. Cambridge, MA: MIT Press.

Krueger, Anne O. 1977. *Growth, Distortions, and Patterns of Trade Among Countries*. Princeton Studies in International Finance 40. Princeton, N J: Princeton University Press.

Schavey, Aaron. 2001. 'The Catch–22 of U. S. Trade.' *Knight-Ridder / Tribune News Wire*, 9 March.

Chapter Fourteen:

INDIA AND DEVELOPMENT ECONOMICS: EXTERNAL INFLUENCES AND INTERNAL RESPONSES

J. Krishnamurty and Sumita Kale

An Indian Economics?

Historical Background

When the East India Company, and later the Crown, established peace under a single paramount power, India was confronted, for the first time in its history, with a foreign power that set the economic agenda to suit the long-term interests of the 'home' country. The short-term economic interests of Britain had to be balanced against the need to maintain peace, keep costs down, ensure that British strategic interests were met and, especially after the events of 1857, secure the support of influential groups within the country. As a result, the door was opened to a dialogue with educated Indians on economic and social policies. This was an unequal exercise, as the monopoly of decision- making remained with the colonial power, which could in many cases ignore or override Indian opinion.

Indians nevertheless engaged in this dialogue, partly to try to convince their imperial masters of the need for policy changes and partly to get their compatriots to understand what was holding back Indian development. By the early twentieth century, the debate was best carried out using familiar and generally accepted theory. This made it much more difficult for the government and their sympathizers to refute the arguments of Indian economists who could also draw support from their teachers and counterparts in Britain and elsewhere.

As Indian economists began to pose the Indian development problem, they were naturally most concerned about issues of immediate importance, namely, widespread poverty, the land revenue burden and indebtedness of the peasantry, government monetary and fiscal policies and the decline of traditional industries. Indian economic thinkers kept up to date with the latest theories and works from different parts of the world, and they selectively used modern economic theory that seemed relevant to their cause. As we show later, Indian economists, seeking solutions to the pressing problems of the economy, advocated strategies similar to those of modern development economists.

This is not surprising, since the major issues of development have remained more or less the same across time. Indian economic thinkers in the first half of the twentieth century dealt with problems of balanced growth, surplus labour, human resource development, capital shortage, rigidities in factor markets, promoting activities with increasing returns, the role of values and institutions in the context of economic change, the role of trade and the balance of payments and the critical role of state policy. Much of this took place before such ideas became concretized in what has come to be known as the structuralist approach to economic development.

Early Emphasis on Economic Development

Scholars and leaders, distressed with the regression in the economy under British rule, were quick to recognize the imperative need for economic development. Most of the writers and thinkers of the period before 1900 were not professional economists, but concerned individuals. They understood that development required capital accumulation and the initial focus was on the agricultural sector, the dominant economic activity of the time. For instance, Raja Ram Mohan Roy (1771–1833) stressed that chronic poverty precluded the generation of economic surplus amongst the cultivators, thereby retarding development and modernization. In line with the Benthamite tradition of the greatest good for the greatest number, he advocated radical reforms in land ownership, measurement operations and the revenue regime.

With the spread of English education among the upper classes and increased access to Western economic literature, throughout the nineteenth century there was a shift in the Indian debate towards a clearer articulation of fundamental economic principles. The changed structure of the Indian economy was becoming increasingly apparent; dependence on agriculture was growing and industry was progressively crumbling under foreign competition. The unbalanced pattern of growth and the phenomenon of deepening poverty were challenges that had to be addressed.

As they sought to address these issues, Indian thinkers and writers were well aware of the schools of thought that existed in the Western world. For instance, Bankim Chandra Chatterjee's analysis of the economic situation of the peasant in Bengal used Malthus and Mill's reasoning connecting population growth with the wage-fund theory.[1] G. V. Joshi (1890) used the American economist Carey's concept of a normal ratio between population and production that determines the average standard of living to conclude that the problem in India was one of underproduction and not overpopulation.

When it came to trade, early Indian economic thinkers had advocated free trade, as 'they had been brought up and educated in an academic atmosphere of freedom breathed by Mill, Cobden and Bright and were led to believe in the beneficence of free imports and exports; but they found that the Indian fiscal policy was not genuine free trade' (Kale 1930, 417). The principle of free trade was cited while abolishing import duties on Manchester goods, but excise duty on Indian cotton goods and the import duty on sugar were clear exceptions to the rule. This led economic thinkers to move on towards attempting to formulate economic theory that suited Indian conditions.

Towards an Alternative Methodology – Ranade's Contribution

Justice Mahadev Govind Ranade (1842–1901) was one of the earliest Indians to systematically question the universal applicability of particular economic doctrines and argue against the applicability of standard Western economic theory to the specific Indian institutional and behavioural setting. In his 1892 lecture 'Indian Political Economy', he identified the differences between the Indian context and the Western, and sought to guide thinking in the country on lines similar to the Historical School of Political Economy. Ranade drew upon the traditions in Italy, Germany and the US to advocate that Indian political economy should follow the methodology of these schools of thought, applying not the deductive method but the historical, which accounts for the past while forecasting ahead, and which accepts relativity and not absolutism as the determining characteristic of the economic science.

Ranade's appeal was directed against the prevailing tendency to accept the individualist principle as the foundation for all economic analysis. He cited Cairns, John Stuart Mill, Leslie and Jevons to show that economic thought, even in England, was divided. However, the dogmatic character of economics as practised by the followers of Smith, Ricardo and Malthus was, in his view, the result of basing analyses on assumptions that were not universally applicable. Consequently, solutions to economic problems could not be generalized across all nations. Given the socioeconomic conditions prevailing in India, he said, 'With us an average individual man is, to a large extent, the very antipodes of the economical man' (Ranade 1920, 9). Some of the main differentiating characteristics he cited were the following: In India, the family and caste were more powerful than the individual in determining his position in life; pursuit of wealth was not the dominant motive; custom and state regulation were more powerful than competition; status was more decisive in its influence than contract; neither capital nor labour were mobile or enterprising enough to shift place or vocation; and wages and profit were fixed and not elastic or responsive to changed circumstances.

He also dealt with the question of whether this emphasis on the practical aspects of an economy implied a divorce from theory. 'Theory is only enlarged Practice, Practice is Theory studied in relation to its proximate Causes' (Chandra 1990, 336); and he proceeded to show through various examples how it was important to wed the two. For instance, the law of comparative advantage was being applied to condemn tropical countries like India to serve as sources of raw materials, while the returns from manufacturing and trade were to be enjoyed by European countries, whose resource base was, allegedly, more suited to these activities. Ranade attacked this argument,[2] on the grounds that it pointed to a line of separation in economic activity that was not only unnatural, but also ignored the reality of history. Indian manufactures had enjoyed ready markets in ancient Rome and modern England and the loss of the markets and technology was more an accident of history than a consequence of any pure economic law.

Further, Ranade argued that carrying raw materials across the seas and back to the tropics in the form of finished goods was against the fundamental principle that production should be located where the raw materials and the markets existed. It was therefore important for India to use the natural advantages of a large domestic market and access to resource bases to revive the manufacturing sector that had been destroyed under the British.[3]

Ranade's analysis also incorporated the idea of the impact of different economic activities on growth.[4] Ranade was reacting to a vision of India condemned to a future with economic activity dominated by agriculture. But the use of the word 'industry' in the following sentence is illuminating.

It is further to be noted that such a division of Production, if permanently stereotyped, consigns Asia to an Industry which is under the bane of the Law of Diminishing Returns, while the West of Europe appropriates to itself those forms of Industry which are not subject to any such Law. (Chandra 1990, 339)

This distinction between diminishing and increasing returns was important. Malthus had drawn attention to this and Myrdal and Nurkse had brought it into vogue again as they explored strategies for development. For growth, activities with increasing returns had to be encouraged through protection and other promotional policies, but the application of free trade policies did not allow this to take place.

Ranade set the tone for economic debate in the country for at least a quarter of a century. The emphasis on the Historical Method brought much of Indian work in line with the Realist-Descriptive school of thought, an offshoot of the younger historical school in Germany. The twentieth century saw the emergence of professional economists as important actors in debates on development issues and economic policy. Several prominent economists like Radhakamal Mukherjee and V. G. Kale followed the lead set by Ranade in adopting the methodology propounded in this tradition, i.e., centring economic study on institutions and human behaviour. They and several others undertook detailed studies of the working of Indian institutions that were unique in form or setting, and that often had a productive role.[5]

Mukherjee's Focus on Institutions and Human Behaviour

Radhakamal Mukherjee was struck by the irrelevance of much of accepted theory to India and made valuable contributions to economic theory through his numerous books, particularly *Borderlands of Economics* (1925) and *Institutional Theory of Economics* (1939). In the former he integrated geography, sociology and psychology with economics while putting forth the case for a new economics based on social behaviourism.

> It is true that the economic man is dead, but his funeral rites still remain to be properly celebrated by his legitimate heir, the behaviouristic man, who has emerged from the laboratories of the psychologist but has not yet taken his rightful position in the centre of economics. Behaviourism transforms the psychological notions of economics into objective realities and lays bare the invisible drive that impels economic activities. (Mukherjee 1925, 14)

In his *Institutional Theory of Economics*, where Mukherjee draws on various traditions including Spann and Sombart, he divided the economic environment into three parts: (1) Ecologic – comprising the climate and topography, land resources, mineral and water resources, plants, animals and man's interrelationships with the physical environment as indirectly affecting economic life; (2) Mechanical or technic – tools, weapons, capital and technology, systems of production, mechanisms of exchange, banking, instruments of credit, etc., and (3) Institutional – state, social groups, law, tradition, standards of social values and ideologies, private property, custom or competition, etc.

Mukherjee believed that economics should concern itself with all three and not merely the second, i.e., the price-cost economics. He went on to distinguish between laws, norms and ideals. The ecological environment was governed by laws, which had the same certainty as the laws in physical sciences. Mechanical or price-and-cost economics yielded norms of consistent action, an abstraction that can be justified only on the basis of statistical generalizations of past experiences, or of a necessary law in ecological economics that produces it. The third gives rise to the ideals and policies of what men ought to do in concrete economic situations. He also brought in the aspect of time as being crucial since 'laws', 'norms' and 'ideals' of economic activities are reached by a process extended over time. Without a clear understanding of these three categories, economic analysis and prescription would be confused and divorced from reality.

However, despite his elaborate exposition of theory, Mukherjee's alternative approach to economic growth and development suited for Indian conditions was not widely accepted. He stressed the importance of developing the rural economy, as opposed to the more prevalent notion that growth would occur in the cities,[6] and came up against those who supported a more industrial and urban model. Mukherjee's formulation of the village society, especially in his early work,[7] was often almost idyllic in its description as he contrasted the Indian organization of economic activity and goals of life with the Western way. A strong proponent of Western style industrialism, Brij Narain vehemently criticized Mukherjee's early work in his essay on Indian versus Western industrialism as he wrote, 'One wonders if Professor Mukherjee is talking about this India of ours or some other India, which his own imagination has created' (Narain 1922, 33). Brij Narain did not believe that the average person in India was more spiritual than his Western counterpart.

Despite his conviction that the materialistic Western style of development was not suited to Indian social conditions, Mukherjee did not ignore urban development and modern industry. He advocated town planning, industrial zoning and social welfare measures adapted to the social conditions and needs of workers (See Baljit Singh 1957, 437–438). 'I am convinced,' he said, 'that in sound economic development both large and small industries have their proper scope and importance, and one need not exclude the other' (Mukherjee 1916, xxi).

The Outcome of the Debate on 'Indian Economics'

Unfortunately, despite the work of Mukherjee and some others, very little was achieved in terms of blending different social sciences to develop a more useful discipline. Most economists concentrated on the problems of the day and many contested the need to have an 'Indian economics'. An interesting case is that of the eminent economist D. R. Gadgil,[8] who argued against the idea of a separate Indian economics in 1924, when he had just returned from studying in England. In 1942, however, he endorsed Ranade's views that prevailing doctrines were a product of the socioeconomic conditions in developed countries and were not quite applicable in poor, developing countries like India.

Kale consistently defended Ranade, noting that the latter did not reject all Western thinking:

> It is said that while he rendered valuable services in his time Ranade was 'partly responsible for giving currency to the notion that Western economic theory was utterly useless for interpreting economic phenomenon in India and indicating methods of economic progress,'[9] that he set the fashion in this matter which has continued much beyond its proper time and that what is now needed is comprehension more than dissent. This criticism suffers from a misapprehension as well as from inaccuracy. Ranade set up as a proper guide, one Western school of economist thought against another Western school and never condemned all Western thought, as such, and as pointed out above, we have to do the same thing over again today. He adopted a fashion set by a new school of thought in the West in his time, and it continues in active vogue there at the present moment as a protest against the atomic, mechanical and naturalistic conception of economic activities, which is still favoured by several thinkers. Indian Economics has therefore, its points of agreement as well as differences with the economic thought of the world as a whole, and its aim and instruments are selected to suit the requirements of the people of this country. (Kale 1930, 20)

Kale, like Ranade, had no doubt that the cause of the nation was best served by economists who used a methodology that explored the Indian situation and used Western theory, where applicable, or adapted it appropriately, where necessary. This debate on methodology raged abroad as well, and Indian thinkers were aware of the arguments made in America and Europe, but as was the case everywhere, economic man refused to die.

There was also considerable diversity of opinion on whether Indians responded differently to signals in economic activity. The view that Indians were nonmaterialistic and unworldly was put forth by some, as evidence to support the low level of development in the country.[10] The vision of a rural India, with simple economic activity, as propounded by Mukherjee, Kumarappa and by Mahatma Gandhi was in line with this thinking. However, this contention was also opposed by many, who pointed out institutional reasons rather than cultural as retarding growth. The debate was substantial enough to warrant a whole chapter in a popular textbook of the time that demolished the idea that Hindu spirituality deterred material progress, by pointing out that the 'progress' in England was merely a hundred years old, compared to the centuries of advancement in India before that (see Kale 1918).

The view that the caste system made for labour market rigidities and prevented growth was also denied by many, who blamed British rule for the lack of progress in the nineteenth century. As Brij Narain argued:

> Max Weber judged our caste system from a distance. But he did not know that the influence of the British administration in the past at any rate has been unfavourable to the development of the manufacturing industries in India. It is not the caste system that has hindered the growth of factory industries but Government policy. (Narain 1935, 202)

Indian economics had grown out of a revolt against the prevailing politico-economic situation at the end of the nineteenth century. The majority of the economists from the 1920s implicitly accepted Kale's view that their purpose was not merely to expose weaknesses in Western economic thought, but to collect accurate facts, analyze different social factors and evolve a connected body of thought such that policy in India would relate better to Indian conditions and produce outcomes in line with Indian aspirations. At the same time, Indian economists had to adapt their work to address immediate problems and come up with findings relevant to the policy issues of the day. Ranade's search for a new methodology and an 'Indian economics' was given up by the 1940s.

Economic Development and the Role of the State: Indian Perspectives[11]

An Overview

It should not come as a surprise that Indian economists were concerned with economic development from the start. They realized that their country needed to diversify its production structure so as to reduce the pressure of surplus labour on land and prevent recurrent famines, which were a feature of the period from around 1890 to around 1920. This became what Jehangir Coyajee was to call the diversification argument for protection. Indian economists drew from the experience of Japan and other countries, including Germany, and argued that an interventionist state was needed, which promoted industrial development through all possible means. Following the work of American and European economists, they argued not only for tariff protection based on the infant-industry argument, but also for a whole range of other promotional measures by the state.

While industrialization was seen by most Indian economists as a necessary element of development, there were differences on the policies on which they laid stress, although most favoured a package of policies. Some emphasized lower exchange rates to promote exports; most sought more active state-expenditure policies and involvement in education (especially technical education) and active promotion of new enterprises; and some favoured industrial reform.

A major issue, particularly in the 1920s, was the exchange rate. Many Indian economists argued for a lower rate of 1s 4d to the rupee, while the Hilton Young Commission in 1926 recommended that the rupee should be set at a higher rate of 1s 6d.[12] Those favouring the 1s 4d rupee felt that this was the rate that would have prevailed and that it would stimulate exports. Others, including some Indian economists like Ambedkar, favoured a rate nearer the 1s 6d rupee.[13] The Government obviously preferred the 1s 6d rate as fewer rupees would have to be expended from the budget to make payments in Britain. The Indian cotton textile industry favoured the lower, 1s 4d, rate as it would have improved competitiveness of its exports.[14]

As we attempt to show, the majority of Indian economists in the first half of the twentieth century argued for protective tariffs and subsidies, export promotion through a lower exchange rate, switching public expenditure towards meeting developmental needs and abandoning the policy of balanced budgets in favour of more expansionary monetary and fiscal policies. As with economists everywhere, there were wide differences of opinion among Indian economists of the pre-independence period. At the same time, there was a general consensus in favour of more active state policies for promoting industrialization. However, it was not until after independence in 1947 that a coherent development strategy was developed and policies relating to tariff protection, export promotion, increased public expenditure on education, health, infrastructure, etc., began to be adopted.

While Indian economists before independence devoted considerable attention to the issue of tariff protection, other issues, like the need for public investment in education and infrastructure and more active macroeconomic policies, were not neglected. Several economists held the view that industrialization needed a number of simultaneous measures in different sectors and through different instruments.

Economic Diversification and Balanced Growth

The argument for diversification in the pattern of economic activities was a theme that ran through the work of most Indian economists before independence. Arguments in support of this view were several, including: meeting the needs of defence and the domestic economy during war; averting the risks of monsoon failure; reaping increasing returns through expansion of the scale of production; and ensuring fuller utilization of human resources.

It is interesting that both Mukherjee, in the early twentieth century, and Nurkse, in mid-twentieth century, proposed balanced or multisectoral growth with diversified economic activity for the domestic local market as a solution of breaking the vicious circle of poverty. However, Mukherjee advocated diversified economic activity at the village level, rather than a focus on urban migration as a route for growth. He makes the point that,

> The conditions of our agriculture leave the cultivators out of employment for several months in the year, the vast amount of surplus labour being utilized in favour of home industries. Thus during certain months of the year all the cultivators of the villages are turned into basket-makers, rope-makers, and even weavers of coarse cloths. The industry becomes usually the second string in the bow of the agriculturist. (Mukherjee 1916, 369)

While Nurkse dwelt upon the promotion of complementarity on an economy-wide basis, he did not ignore agriculture. He argued that 'Industrial development for domestic markets requires a complementary advance on the farm front, a rise in agricultural productivity' (Haberler and Stern 1961, 314–315). For Mukherjee, diversification was essential to maintain social stability, while for Nurkse, diversification was part of a strategy of balanced economic expansion for a low income country faced with limited domestic market and low demand for exports of primary products.[15]

Some of these ideas are present in Rosenstein-Rodan's 1943 paper. He viewed complementarity principally in terms of demand for consumer goods as economic expansion took place. He did not place much emphasis, at least for Eastern and Southeastern Europe, on the expansion of basic industries and public utilities in triggering economic growth.[16]

Indian economists of the period appear to have believed that the problem of demand creation could be met by import replacement and export growth, and by more active macroeconomic policies, including greater public expenditure aimed at improving incentives for private investment. Stress was laid on the development of the social and economic infrastructure, education, health, transport, banking and other support services. This is clear from a reading of the work of leading Indian economists like Kale (1918), Jain (1929), Dey (1933) and Thomas (1939). Both P. J. Thomas (1935), in the context of recovery and B. P. Adarkar (1941), in the context of development, stressed the importance of multiplier effects.

Protection to Industry

The long-run objective, for most Indian economists of the first half of the twentieth century, was to have free trade, once protection became unnecessary. The Indian demand, to the extent that one can generalize, was not for across-the-board protection to all industries. This point is worth stressing, for many writers like Lees-Smith (1909) believed that Indian opinion was entirely protectionist and ignored the fact that there were many shades of opinion among Indian economists and leaders. In this section of the paper, we explore the various facets of opinion as the debate over trade and industrial policy evolved over time.

Early Views

During the first four decades of the twentieth century, as the economics profession developed in India, thinking on industrial development policies became increasingly sophisticated. It built upon Ranade's writings at the end of the nineteenth century arguing for greater support for Indian industry. At that time, when tariff autonomy was being denied, he had argued for state involvement in pioneering industry:

> Even if political considerations forbid independent action in the matter of differential duties, the pioneering of new enterprises is a duty which the Government might more systematically undertake with advantage. (Chandra 1990, 344–345)

The great nationalist Gopal Krishna Gokhale, in a speech to the Legislative Assembly in 1915, argued that every country must take care of its economic interests in its own way. The right kind of protection would, in his view, benefit India, but he did not think this could be attempted without representative government (Patwardhan and Ambekar 1962, 331–332).

The view of Indian professional economists, fairly early in the twentieth century, may be taken from an influential and representative Indian textbook by Pramathanath Banerjea, first published in 1911. Countering the view that free trade maximizes the gains from trade and allows every country to develop its natural advantages, he argued that when an industry in one country is threatened with destruction by a similar one in another country, 'it is no solace to the first that the world's wealth is being augmented at the cost of its own' (Banerjea 1911, 209). Far from promoting goodwill (as some free traders might claim), 'Free Trade may produce the result of placing one country in economic subjection to another' (Banerjea 1911, 209).

Banerjea's emphasis on economic subjection accurately reflected the fears and experiences of a country under colonial rule. He noted that it could improve the trade balance, benefit agriculture, raise wages, augment all-round development and industrial independence, counteract unfair competition during the period of growth and prevent extinction. But Banerjea did not completely accept the case for protection. He argued, inter alia, that there was some truth in the view that protection reduced trade and output, destroyed industries it did not protect, diverted capital from its natural channels, benefited the producer at the cost of the consumer, led to state interference and corruption and caused animosity between nations. However, on balance, he felt that free trade should be the general policy; but 'under certain conditions, Protection is not only defensible but is positively beneficial' (Banerjea 1911, 209–210).

Banerjea quoted John Stuart Mill, an ardent supporter of free trade, who admitted that in the infancy stage of an industry, protection is useful. He also quoted List who argued that 'a nation which only carries on agriculture is an individual who in his material production lacks one arm' (Banerjea 1911, 211). From this, Banerjea argued that the development of manufactures was absolutely essential for the well-being of India. A protective tariff, in his view, would not only assist Indian industry but, from a development perspective, would 'also produce the revenue urgently needed for education, sanitation and social reform' (Banerjea 1911, 211–212).

The famous Indian economist, Manohar Lal, had been a student of Alfred Marshall at Cambridge at the turn of the twentieth century. In his correspondence with Marshall in 1909 and 1911 (Whitaker 1966, Letters 935 and 999) Manohar Lal tried hard, but without success, to get from him an unequivocal endorsement of the infant industry argument in relation to India. Also, in his own lectures in Calcutta University, Manohar Lal emphasized the work of the German Historical School, which advocated protection for national development. According to Radhakamal Mukherjee, his student:

> The German Historical School of Economics was given special attention because of the support it gave to the theory of Indian protectionism. List, Knies and Schmoller were given prominence. (Mukherjee 1997, 67)

Debates of the 1920s

When the colonial government finally adopted the principle of tariff autonomy for India, they set up the Fiscal Commission in 1921 to come up with recommendations on how this was to be implemented. John Maynard Keynes was appointed vice-chairman, but finally did not participate. The key economist member was an Indian, Jehangir Coyajee, another illustrious student of Marshall. He played a major role in providing a rationale for the policy of 'discriminating protection' recommended by the Commission. A reading of his private papers and publications on the subject makes it clear that like Banerjea, he had a balanced view on the advantages and disadvantages of protection. He provided the Commission with a summary of the views of major schools of economists and supported a position largely favourable to protection as a means for national development. He also developed these arguments further in his book (Coyajee 1924, Lecture I).

The benefits from protection, in his opinion, were:

(1) Establishment of industries and increased tempo of progress from protection to well-chosen infant industries.
(2) Effective and stimulating effects of diversification of industries and the full utilization of the country's human and other resources due to the same cause.
(3) Increasing potentialities of defence in time of war accruing from help given to key industries.
(4) Advantages and Economies accruing from the increase in the scale of industrial production. (*Coyajee Private Papers*, n.d.)

The losses from protection, in his view were:

(1) Rise of prices …in protected industries.…
(2) Rise of general price level in protectionist countries (both in protected and unprotected articles). The result is that in such countries prices rise faster than incomes.
(3) Protection helps in the formation of trusts and monopolies.
(4) Possibilities of bolstering up of antiquated methods of production.
(5) Possible conflict of interests especially of the manufacturing and agrarian interests.
(6) Growth of selfish political activity. (*Coyajee Private Papers*, n.d.)

Coyajee's background note and balance sheet cite a variety of authorities, including Taussig and Bastable, and also Brown, Grummel, Arnaune, Schmoller, Nicholson and Marshall. In the Report of the Commission, Pigou is cited:

> From these considerations it follows that the case for protection with a view to building up productive power is strong in any agricultural country which seems to possess natural advantages for manufacturing. (Government of India 1922, paragraph 34)

Not all Indian economists were enthusiastic about protection. Thus Professor Gyanchand, in his oral evidence to the Commission, argued:

> Tariff protection can certainly do some good, but in India, under the present circumstances, though I do not want Protection to be banned, I am at the same time not very enthusiastic about tariff protection. I should like the State to give protection to industries in a number of ways, but tariff protection should as far as possible be avoided. (Government of India 1923)

The policies he advocated were: (1) expert advice, (2) state assistance, (3) cheap capital, (4) suitable and cheap communications, (5) subsidies and bounties if necessary, and only then tariff protection. In other words, Gyanchand was advocating a coherent set of development policies that would impact positively on different economic activities, rather than a single-point programme of protection, which had the danger that foreign enterprise could take advantage of high tariff walls. On this last point, Gopal Krishna Gokhale, who was a strong believer in protection, had also opposed the kind of protection 'under which the powerful influences, combinations and interests receive assistance to the prejudice of the general community, the general taxpayer of the country' (Patwardhan and Ambekar 1962, 331–332).

Indian economists generally favoured a conscious and well-developed industrial policy comprising several different elements. But this was not the approach of the government, which dragged its feet on developing an integrated policy to foster industrial development, splitting up contentious industrial policy issues among different committees and commissions so that no integrated policy could emerge. Commenting on this problem, Professor K. T. Shah perceptively noted:

> This is the root vice of the existing system of Government of India. They seem to take an almost impish delight in dismembering a problem of national life, and presenting specific faults for special consideration by commissions of inquiry, whose utility is largely neutralised in advance by such a policy. (Shah 1923, 263n.; see Government of India 1923, 825)

K. T. Shah and C. N. Vakil, both eminent economists writing at the time and arguing strongly for protection, were from Bombay University and were regarded by the British as representing the views of the Bombay textile lobby. Both appeared as expert witnesses before the Commission and argued forcefully that Indian industry needed protection on a sustained basis so that it could compete effectively with British (and other) imports. Shah went so far as to argue that 'As a rule, all industries which are of national importance should be reserved exclusively for Indians' (Government of India 1923, 824). Vakil later argued that the Fiscal Commission's majority had approached protection with 'a free trade bias' (Vakil 1923, 58). Like many others, he did not deny the need for discrimination in granting protection, but felt that that the majorityof the Commission was 'a body of free traders grudgingly yielding the overwhelming pressure of Indian opinion in favour of protection' (Vakil 1923, 128).

Looking back, the difference in positions may not have been that large. Protection was inevitable once tariff autonomy had been conceded and it reflected the acceptance by the colonial rulers, based on the experience of the First World War, that it was in their own interest to develop an industrial base in India. As V. G. Kale noted:

> The difference between the majority and the minority rested on the difference in outlook and on different views regarding the pace with which industrial development should be carried out and the extent of sacrifice that the public should be called on to make for the sake of rapid industrialization of India. (Kale 1929, 90)

More than the principles of protection recommended by the Commission (that were difficult to fulfil in a number of cases), it was their reluctant acceptance by the government that subverted the recommendations. They did not create a standing Tariff Board; they interpreted the rules to Indian disadvantage and, generally, followed a policy of obstruction and delay. Sustained policies and programmes to promote Indian economic development were not on the agenda of the colonial government.

The Debate After 1930

As the work of considering demands for protection were taken up by different Tariff Boards, the problems with the rigid and narrow interpretation of the recommendations of the Fiscal Commission came to the fore. During the 1930s, many Indian economists questioned the success of discriminating protection, while a few argued against protection.

In 1933 H. L. Dey raised the question of whether the cost of protection was justified and equitably distributed and concluded that the burden was inequitably distributed and that it would be better for the government to spend on education, sanitation, agriculture, transport and banking, than on industry itself. This was basically an argument for increasing public expenditure on infrastructure rather than on protection of industries. He also argued in favour of identifying other measures to eliminate what he termed the deficiencies and weaknesses of Indian industry, viz., defective organization, inadequate and unsatisfactory technical equipment and personnel, insufficient supply and extravagant use of capital, lack of adaptation to changing market conditions, labour inefficiency and industrial unrest. He also favoured bounties over tariffs as they were easier to terminate.[17]

In 1941 B. P. Adarkar refuted this position. He argued that not only infant, but even 'embryo' industries needed protection. He questioned the argument that industrialization would not create much employment, arguing that the failure to industrialize was due to the tardy protection policies that had been followed. Perhaps the most important and new argument made by Adarkar, based on the Kahn-Keynes multiplier effects, was that protection created employment both in the industry itself and through its secondary effects on other industries and agriculture. He felt that rationalization of industry or social welfare programmes could not have much impact; industrialization was essential for raising living standards and was not necessarily at the cost of agriculture; and, mining, transport, banking, etc., would not grow unless there was industrialization. Adarkar also produced a number of arguments to doubt the claim that taxes had become more regressive due to protection (Adarkar 1941).

As Bhabatosh Datta notes (Datta 1978, 71), Dey and Adarkar wrote before the papers of Stolper and Samuelson (1941) and Scitovsky (1942) were available. They naturally could not take account of the important contributions made by these papers to the relationship between tariff and social welfare.

Post-Independence Developments

After independence, the Government set up a new Fiscal Commission that reviewed the past experience and concluded that discriminating protection had to be replaced by developmental protection. A standing body, the Tariff Commission, was set up.

However, following a foreign exchange crisis in the latter half of the 1950s, stringent trade restrictions were imposed with a view to reducing imports and promoting exports. These tariffs were often extraordinarily high, far beyond the levels contemplated by Indian economists before independence, leading to serious inefficiencies, and distortions in production and trade patterns in the country. High prohibitive tariff rates of up to 400 per cent were in place. As much as 60 per cent of tariff lines were subject to rates ranging from 110 to 150 per cent. In 1991, following an exchange crisis and initially under an IMF programme, a process of trade liberalization began (Bhagwati and Desai 1970; Panagariya 2002).

We may conclude that the control regime to promote industrial development and conserve scarce foreign exchange, in operation from about 1957 to 1990, had not been contemplated by Indian economists before independence. In their view, protection to a particular industry was a temporary measure, and the cost to the consumer had to be weighed against its advantages.

Macroeconomic Policies

The need for expansionary economic policies in the context of the economic depression in India in the 1930s was highlighted by P. J. Thomas (1935), who argued for a policy to expand public works to create employment and incomes thorough the multiplier process. In the specific context of the depression, he argued that the multiplier effects would be significant and would promote employment and recovery. This was in contrast to the government's policies of 'sound finance' involving curbs of public expenditure and going for balanced budgets. As Keynesian ideas gained ground, many other Indian economists argued along similar lines. From the early 1950s this issue came up repeatedly in many less-developed countries trying to decide on whether shortfalls in resource mobilization should be made up by deficit financing.

Criticism of unproductive expenditure was natural among Indian economists and nationalist politicians going back to the late nineteenth century. These included the nationalists like Dadabhai Naoroji, R. C. Dutt and G. K. Gokhale, but also economists like C. N. Vakil, K. T. Shah and B. R. Ambedkar. The notion became clearer over time that some public spending contributed to development and some did not. By the 1930s development expenditure was defined to include expenditure on education and training, sanitation and health, industry and infrastructure.

Thomas documented the fact that public expenditure for these 'nation-building activities', i.e., development, was minimal in most parts of the country (Thomas 1939). This was because elected Indian provincial governments, even when they were development-oriented, lacked financial resources under the devolution arrangements. This was not an entirely new finding and had been anticipated in 1935 by Adarkar, who predicted that defence expenditure would continue to preempt significant amounts of national budgetary resources. The devolution of functions to elected provincial governments in the late 1930s, without providing adequate resources, made it impossible to promote Indian development in line with her aspirations and needs. Again, as we have noted earlier, there were some economists like H. L. Dey (1933) who argued that rather than spending on industry, government should spend on education, sanitation, agriculture, transport and banking.

Institutions and Paths to Development

Indian economists were aware that the traditional institutions of their economy might be inimical to development. Some argued that India should not follow the Western path of development with all its attendant evils, but develop along a path more suited to it. Some economists, notably J. C. Kumarappa, argued for a return to the village economy based on a large measure of self-sufficiency. This view had some support from economists like Radhakamal Mukherjee, who felt that rapid Western-style industrialization would expose India to all the evils found in the West. However, this view was not accepted by many other economists, like Brij Narain, who felt that only rapid Western-style industrialization could make an impact on Indian poverty.

Criticizing the so-called Western 'model', Radhakamal Mukherjee argued that modern industrialization led to immiserization:

> In the West the problem of distribution is subordinated to the problem of production of wealth. Thus the industrial revolution of the West has set out on a wrong path, and hence it is that the most brilliant achievements in applied science and discoveries in mechanical arts have not increased the general well-being of society. (Mukherjee 1916, 333)

But this was not the dominant view among Indian economists. In his sharp critique, Brij Narain argued for accepting the Western 'model':

> Industrialism alone can save India. And our industrialism will, probably, have to be of the same type as the Western industrialism. We have to fight the West with the same weapons it employs against us. (Narain 1922, 39)

The possible impact of industrial growth on poverty and the quality of life was a cause of concern for some early Indian economists like Radhakamal Mukherjee and J. C. Kumarappa and was also used by some British economists in India like W. Stanley Jevons (1915) to argue against industrialization. A related issue was whether India needed to replace existing traditional economic institutions with modern institutions. As we have attempted to show, Mukherjee and Brij Narain represented two extreme positions on this issue, the former seeking to avoid the Western path to industrialization and development, and the latter advocating its full adoption.

A different approach of thoroughly studying some major Indian institutions not only yielded valuable insights, but also pointed to the possibility of bridging the modern–traditional dichotomy. Two examples, relating to the managing agency system and indigenous banking, may be given.

It was generally agreed that modern rapid industrialization required a class of entrepreneurs, but the question was whether or not Western-type entrepreneurs were required. P. S. Lokanathan in 1935 provided the first thorough understanding of the role of managing agents, a uniquely Indian institution, in industrial development. They were not entrepreneurs of the kind described and idealized by Schumpeter, but products of the unique context in which Indian industry was being developed. He highlighted their pioneering role, their ability to raise funds and provide management to new firms and at the same time pointed out their inhibiting role as the firms grew larger and drew attention to the numerous abuses that occurred (Lokanathan 1935). Significantly, he did not propose their abolition, noting that that they did indeed play a useful role as promoters of nascent enterprises; as controllers, where they had substantial investments in the enterprises; and, as helpful intermediaries between suppliers of capital and demanders of capital. He proposed that they should adapt to circumstances by bringing in fresh talent and by cooperating more with each other.

Again, was the relative absence of modern banking institutions a major constraint on investment and growth? Traditional systems of credit were often blamed for all the ills of Indian agriculture. In 1929 L. C. Jain showed that the indigenous banker, as opposed to the village moneylender, performed a valuable economic function. He proposed a variety of measures to modernize indigenous banking and link it more closely with modern credit institutions. Like Lokanathan, Jain did not reject an existing institution, but suggested ways in which it could adapt to a new context and perform its functions better.

Ecological Aspects of Development

Radhakamal Mukherjee was a pioneer in drawing attention to the impacts of economic change on the environment and natural resources. In this he was well ahead of developments in the West. Ramachandra Guha (1992) has documented French, American and other intellectual influences on Mukherjee and highlights his contributions. According to Mukherjee:

> ...synecology demands that men should work in harmony with balanced relationships in nature, so as to accelerate and not put brakes on nature's continuous operations of recuperation and regeneration. Renewal and enrichment rather than exhaustion and depletion of the region should be man's synecological goal....(Mukherjee 1942, 129)

In his assessment, Mamkoottam sums up his original contributions very well, stating that Mukherjee saw the urgency of using ecological knowledge for better utilization of land, more productive cropping patterns and the preservation of exhaustible resources. He emphasized the need for an appropriate man-land-cattle ratio and for tackling population growth (Mamkoottam 1980). These may seem familiar to us today, but were strikingly original in the early 1930s.

Disguised Unemployment and Surplus Labour

A central idea in the work of both Nurkse and Lewis was the notion that surplus labour existed in agriculture and that it could be tapped to facilitate development. In the case of Nurkse, as is well known, the presence of disguised unemployment represented a potential saving if it could be transferred to the non-agricultural sector, with neither an increase in consumption nor a decline in output by those left behind. Lewis argued that this surplus meant that industrialization could proceed drawing upon the 'unlimited supply of labour' available from the agricultural sector. This section is devoted to disguised unemployment and surplus labour, which were hotly debated issues in India. The origins of the terms can be traced to the late nineteenth century and the debate continued up to the 1970s and even beyond.[18]

Early Origins

The notion of surplus labour is an old one and springs from the common observation that agriculture in many less-developed and overpopulated countries appears to have more persons working than are strictly required. B. R. Ambedkar (1918), in a landmark paper, noted that this was first remarked upon by Sir James Caird, writing in 1884. As Caird puts it:

> A square mile of land in England cultivated highly gives employment to 50 persons, in the proportions 25 men, young and old, and 25 women and boys. If four times that number, or 200, were allowed for each square mile of cultivated land in India, it would take up only one-third of the population. (Caird 1884, 225)

Ambedkar clearly identified the phenomenon of surplus labour in Indian agriculture, when he stated:

> A large agricultural population with the lowest proportion of land in actual cultivation [compared to other countries] means that a large part of the agricultural population is superfluous and idle. (Ambedkar 1918, 473)

Again, Ambedkar realized that there was a need to transfer surplus labour from agriculture to non-agriculture.

> If we succeed in sponging off this labour in non-agricultural channels of production, we will at one stroke lessen the pressure and destroy the premium that at present weighs heavily on land in India. Besides, this labour

when productively employed will cease to live by predation as it does today, and will not only earn its keep but will give us surplus; and more surplus means more capital. In short, strange as it may seem, *industrialization of India is the soundest remedy for the agricultural problems of India.* (Ambedkar 1918, 477, italics added)

This passage reads like many of the arguments made in the 1950s for a balanced pattern of growth involving the transfer of labour from agriculture to non-agriculture.[19] However, perhaps due to the focus of the paper on consolidation of small holdings, there was no discussion of how industrialization would be promoted and financed. While Ambedkar did not outline a development strategy in this paper, he drew sharp attention to the futility of ameliorative measures limited to agriculture and stressed the role of industrialization in not only reducing surplus labour, but also permitting measures to prevent subdivision and fragmentation to be effective.

The concept of underemployment appeared again in a discussion of Indian economic statistics in a paper by the Rajani Kanta Das published in the journal *Welfare*, probably in 1925. This was written in the form of comments on the suggestions of the Indian Economic Enquiry Committee of that year. He defined underemployment thus:

... forced leisure in the case of all persons who employ themselves in industrial enterprises. Among these men might be included cultivators, stock-breeders, artisans, hawkers, peddlers and small shop-keepers. ... Some knowledge on the number of days in which cultivators, artisans and other classes of independent workers remain idle will throw considerable light on the economic condition of the country and help in shaping the policy of the national economy.' (Das 1925, 6)

Not only did Das pinpoint the problem of surplus labour time, but he also made the prophecy that measurement would be 'one of the most difficult tasks to undertake' (Das 1925, 6). He recommended intensive surveys, special investigations and a production census.

The Concept of Disguised Unemployment

There is general agreement that the term 'disguised unemployment' was first used by Joan Robinson in 1936. It is generally believed that Rosenstein-Rodan was the first person to apply it to the problem of development in his landmark paper in the *Economic Journal* in 1943. Among others, Stanislaw Wellisz (1968, 25), R. S. Eckaus (1989), W. C. Robinson (1969) and M. Perala

(2003) credit Rosenstein-Rodan with being the first to adapt Joan Robinson's concept.[20]

Rosenstein-Rodan himself, in a paper dated 30 October 1956, is modest about his contribution:

> The concept of 'agrarian excess' or 'surplus population' or of 'disguised unemployment in agriculture' has, in contrast [to 'optimum population'] a precise meaning, and has only emerged in the late 1920s. Since the 1940s, it has been made one of the cornerstones of the theory of development of under-developed countries. (Rosenstein-Rodan 1956, mimeo, 1)

V. K .R. V. Rao's Contribution

It is not generally known that Professor V. K. R. V. Rao had developed the concept of disguised unemployment in an article published in the *Indian Journal of Economics* in 1938. In this article he acknowledged that Joan Robinson had introduced it in the context of depression in developed countries and proceeded to apply it to India.

Rao defined unemployment thus:

> [The] loss of employment of workers who were previously employed and inability to obtain employment by these and others who might not have been previously employed but who now seek for employment at existing levels of wages or slightly lower levels. (Rao 1938, 628)

In the Indian context, Rao linked disguised unemployment to the decline of Indian handicrafts. He did not estimate the magnitude of disguised unemployment, but asserted that it was large and growing. In this context, he made the statement below, which is remarkable for its anticipation of the 1950s definition of disguised unemployment and surplus labour:

> It is a well known fact that *there are on the land a number of people who do not really contribute to the production of agricultural output and that if they give up agriculture, output would remain much the same.* They are the disguised unemployed of India, and their numbers are large enough to constitute a major problem in India's economy. (Rao 1938, 631, italics added)

Development economists have failed to give Rao due credit for being the first to apply Joan Robinson's concept of disguised unemployment to the context of development. While Rao was not the first economist to identify the existence of excess labour in agriculture, he was the first to argue (1) that the surplus workers were those willing to work elsewhere at more or less the going wage and (2) that their removal would not reduce agricultural output. Given that his paper appeared in 1938, when people in the West did not expect original work to emanate from India, it is not surprising that this major contribution in an Indian journal was missed.[21]

What is, however, much more surprising is that Rao himself had forgotten about it. In a later paper (Rao 1953), he asserted that a UN Committee of Experts was the first to link unemployment with development. This not only ignores his own earlier work in 1938, but that of several others, including Doreen Warriner (1939), Rosenstein-Rodan (1943) and Tarlok Singh (1945).[22]

An Indian Anticipation of Arthur Lewis's Work

Nurkse's 1954 book made a great impact in India. During the late 1950s and the 1960s Indian economists were very familiar with the works of Nurkse and Lewis. During this period, some Indian economists attempted to measure disguised unemployment and surplus labour, but perhaps more important, there was an active debate on the validity of these concepts. Unfortunately, much of this work is unknown to Western audiences today.

Perhaps most extraordinary is the recent realization that A. K. Dasgupta had anticipated Arthur Lewis's 1954 view on development being constrained not by effective demand or labour supply, but by the need for complementary capital. This has been described, by Partha Dasgupta and Amartya Sen, as an example of Merton's 'multiples', i.e., a case where the same idea was developed independently by several persons. (See Partha Dasgupta 2003 and Sen 1994.)

It appears that the ideas presented by A. K. Dasgupta had first been aired in a series of lectures given in Lucknow University, India in 1950.[23]

According to A. K. Dasgupta:

The limiting factor in the growth of employment in an economy such as ours is not so much the shortage of money as a shortage of real capital. With existing capital equipment, even if we have full employment in the Keynesian sense, a large volume of unemployment will still remain in the physical sense. When capital equipment is low and population large, marginal productivity comes down to the level of marginal disutility of labour at a stage where unemployment persists in the physical sense, though not in the 'involuntary' sense. Our economists, misappropriating a term that Mrs. Robinson uses in another context…, often call it 'disguised unemployment.' In fact, however, it is a phenomenon which is not connected in any way with a fall in effective demand, nor does it go along with excess capacity in capital resources. It is there because the maximum capacity of capital equipment is inadequate to fully employ labour. (A. K. Dasgupta reprint 2003, 2921)

We have quoted this passage in full so as to clarify Dasgupta's contribution. It is significant that he did not assume that marginal productivity of labour necessarily dropped to zero. He was also clearly unhappy with the use of the term 'disguised unemployment' when it was related to a fall in effective demand. He was, however, more receptive to another part of the Nurkse doctrine on balanced growth. He believed that in economies like India, capital saturation was far off. In his view:

> For such an economy, an increase in capital resources, if it could be brought about, will make possible a simultaneous development of industries and will have rather the effect of raising the marginal efficiency of capital. (Dasgupta reprint 2003, 2921–2922)

Some Indian Contributions on Disguised Unemployment

There were several important Indian contributions to the debate on disguised unemployment.[24] For the present purpose, we concentrate upon a few representative contributions.

One of the best-known contributions was that of Vakil and Brahmananda (1956), which was reviewed by Nurkse in his paper in the *Quarterly Journal of Economics* (Nurkse 1957). Their major contribution to the debate was the argument that there was a wage-goods gap, which they defined in the following way:

> The surplus of wage-goods available is, therefore, less than the amount necessary to provide employment to all the disguised unemployed at the ruling wage rate. In other words, the unemployment in an underdeveloped economy emerges on account of the disequilibrium between the surplus of employable units measured in terms of wage-goods and the demand for the former measured in terms of the potentially available surplus of work-force. The deficiency between the two is the critical 'wage-goods gap.' (Vakil and Brahmananda 1956, 211)

They also drew attention to the prevalence of 'work spreading' principles and 'make work' schemes in India reflecting, in their view, the presence of disguised unemployment. They argued that unless work opportunities outside agriculture could be found for the disguisedly unemployed, the agricultural reorganization needed for raising productivity could not take place. Nurkse

(1957, 192) agreed with them. It may be added that this was precisely Ambedkar's argument in 1918.

The view that disguised unemployment represented a potential saving, which could be mobilized, was questioned by Chandavarkar among others. He argued that (1) the estimate of potential saving embodied in disguised unemployment was overstated, due to substantial rural indebtedness; (2) the economies of joint consumption would be lost once some workers leave the household, and this would lower potential saving, and (3) the food consumption of unproductive labourers on the farm was an 'unstable quantity' for it depends on marketed surplus and prices. He summed up his position as follows:

Thus the saving potential of disguised unemployment – in itself exaggerated by the economies of joint consumption – is largely a conceptual magnitude which could be said to exist only under the highly restrictive assumptions of constant population, constant marginal propensity to consume of the retained and transferred farm labour, abstraction from the income effects of price changes on food production, and from the implications of large-scale agricultural indebtedness. Furthermore, in practice the costs of mobilising the saving potential of disguised unemployment ... would be greater than the magnitude of such saving. (Chandavarkar 1957, 338)

While Chandavarkar questioned the size of the potential savings and the extent to which it could be mobilized, there were others who questioned Lewis's view that industrialization could proceed using the more or less unlimited supply of labour available to it from the countryside.

K. N. Raj, in his Cairo Lectures (1957), pointed out that part of the time of the so-called surplus workers was spent in the production of nonmarketed goods and services, and if this was taken into account, the number disguisedly unemployed would prove to be less. Allowing for some reorganization of production connected with the transfer would raise the estimate of disguised unemployment. Raj made his most serious attack on Lewis's model by arguing that those who were identified as disguisedly unemployed may not be available for work in the open labour market. Surplus labour was, in his view, context-specific: it depended on the social and economic system prevalent in a country or region and could change over time. Importantly, as traditional social systems weakened, disguised unemployment would increasingly become open.[25]

Amartya Sen (1966 and 1975) questioned Nurkse's view that the marginal productivity of labour would be zero 'over a wide range'. He made the important distinction between 'labourers' and 'labour time' to explain 'work spreading'. Also, he argued that with a positive marginal disutility of work, equilibrium would yield a positive marginal product. Sen emphasized the importance of knowing whether an individual's share in farm income was conditional upon work, and argued that an individual's own perception of his/her employment situation was important in determining availability for work outside the farm.

Concluding Remarks

While Chandavarkar doubted the magnitude of potential saving that could be mobilized, Raj doubted the magnitude of workers under given social and economic conditions that would be available for work at any given time at currently prevalent wage rates. Sen argued that disguised unemployment could be measured under the production approach, but that the magnitudes would change if one adopted the income or recognition approach. This leads us away from the initial position of Nurkse and Lewis, who felt that provided capital could be secured and consumption constrained, nonagricultural production could be expanded more or less indefinitely at the going wage, drawing upon the pool of surplus labour available on the farms. This view was anticipated in some respects, by Ambedkar in 1918 and expressed by A. K. Dasgupta in 1954 or earlier, but it cannot be advanced today without substantial qualification.

The Economics Profession in India

The economics profession in pre-independent India was truly unique: no other country under colonial rule (apart from some countries of recent European settlement) had so many trained economists. While, as we have argued in an earlier section, they did not produce an 'Indian' economics, and while their contribution to economic theory was not large, their understanding of development issues was quite remarkable. This was not surprising, for they lived in a country that they believed had had a glorious past and they could see that the current economic situation and prospects under British rule were not favourable.

It is almost a truism to say that they understood the Indian economy better than their rulers. They felt that the problems of caste, religion and attitudes to economic activity were serious barriers. They were also aware that some of the prerequisites for development were missing: literacy was extremely low, modern technical education almost nonexistent; production infrastructure, credit and marketing arrangements were weak; and government economic policies were not directed towards promoting industrialization.

Most viewed this state of affairs as unsatisfactory; while some felt that it could be changed even without the achievement of independence, others felt that political independence was a prerequisite for development. Again, the vision of development varied from one of rapid modern industrialization to one based on reviving traditional and village industries.

Students of Indian economics of the period were exposed to a wide range of intellectual influences as their teachers were exposed to Western ideas, but were prepared to reject or modify them as they felt fit. Some of the teachers of economics at the major centres were trained abroad, but many famous Indian economists were entirely indigenous products. However, even those who had not left the Indian shores were exposed to the ideas of a wide variety of European and American economists, past and present. This was reflected in the training provided, not only to the next generation of economists, but also to civil servants and other influential groups.

A number of Indian economists, notably Brij Narain, V. G. Kale and Benoy Sarkar, could read books in several European languages and maintained contacts with centres of learning around Europe and the US. Again, as we have stressed earlier, even when writers like Ranade pointed to the unique features of the Indian economy and society and contrasted them with those of the West, the intention was not to turn away from Western economics, but to draw upon other (not necessarily non-Western) traditions. This was stressed by V. G. Kale (1930) and was implicit in the work of many Indian economists, including Kale, Radhakamal Mukherjee, Benoy Kumar Sarkar, Jehangir Coyajee and Brij Narain, who were influenced by economic and sociological thinking from many different parts of the Western world.

As we have noted earlier, the examples of two influential teachers, Manohar Lal and Coyajee, indicate that training in economics at Cambridge did not mean that they were unaware or unsympathetic to ideas emanating from continental Europe and the US. There was also an active discussion in the early volumes of the Indian *Journal of Economics* on the content and relevance of syllabi in relation to the needs of Indian students.

Among British professors appointed to Indian universities, many like W. Stanley Jevons and A. R. Burnett-Hurst in Allahabad, W. H. Myles in Punjab and Gilbert Slater in Madras, came from an empirical tradition and actively promoted applied work on the local economy. An important exception among expatriates teaching in India was C. D. Thompson, an American-trained theoretical economist and an influential teacher in Allahabad.

Again, many Indians who had studied abroad, often in Britain, specialized on empirical subjects. They and their students appear to have been quite willing to take on board ideas from different places if they felt these were valid and useful. There were also some Indian economists who concentrated on economic theory, including J. K. Mehta and A. K. Dasgupta.

One view on the issue of teaching material was that of Radhakamal Mukherjee. Looking back on his career as a teacher at Lucknow University, he claimed:

> Throughout the past few decades the study and teaching of economics at the Indian Universities were shaped by textbooks in economics obtained from Cambridge and Oxford. In the early years of my own teaching, I deeply felt the necessity of relating economic theories and doctrines not only to economic history but also to the crying issues of economic disintegration and economic recovery. (Mukherjee 1997, 119)

This heavy reliance on textbooks from Cambridge and Oxford appears to be overstated. Mukherjee's own experience in Calcutta University, quoted earlier, belies this claim. Anecdotal evidence suggests that good teachers at major centres like Calcutta, Bombay, Allahabad, Lucknow, Madras, Poona and Mysore did not depend so much on such textbooks.

As economic literature developed in India and elsewhere, the content of economics courses, especially by the late 1950s, became heavier and more specialized. The practice of reading a wide range of books on a subject was gradually replaced by dependence on textbooks, even at the more reputed centres of learning. The evolution of economic ideas, as a subject, began to be put in a straitjacket by the textbooks. Certainly by the early 1960s, the use of new textbooks replaced the practice of reading the original writers. Economic theory texts tended to focus on specific techniques and results, without much discussion of how they came about or what kinds of thinking lay behind these developments. This process of change was gradual, the pace of change varying by university and teacher.

Concluding Remarks

Since the nineteenth century, Indian economists applied their minds to the problems of growth and development, as they saw while there was rapid economic development occurring in many countries, their own country did not progress under British rule. In the process they pioneered thinking on a wide range of development issues that they found relevant to the Indian situation. Among the topics on which they contributed to the literature were surplus labour, trade and industrial policy, social and ecological impacts of industrialization, alternative paths to development, the role of traditional institutions working in new contexts, and problems of shortage of capital and land.

A remarkable aspect of the work of these early economists was that they lived and worked in a country under imperial rule, where it was not easy to secure the attention and respect of the alien government. In order to do this, they had to keep abreast of the latest theories and events in the other countries, and select and apply those parts of Western theory that best reflected Indian conditions and addressed Indian concerns. This practice of reading original work from different parts of the world, often in languages other than English, and adapting the findings to India, was a hallmark of Indian economists before independence.

Drawing strength from empirical approaches prevalent in Europe and the US, Indian economists worked hard to develop a better understanding their own economy and society. The results enabled them to refute arguments used by their rulers, reflecting their own interests, to suggest that India could not develop or should remain agricultural.

Indian economists in the first half of the twentieth century generally argued for protective tariffs and subsidies, export promotion through a lower exchange rate, shifting public expenditure towards meeting developmental needs and abandoning the policy of balanced budgets in favour of more expansionary monetary and fiscal policies. As with economists everywhere, there were wide differences of opinion among Indian economists of the pre-independence period. At the same time, there was a general consensus in favour of more active State policies for promoting industrialization.

Indian economics had grown out of a revolt against the prevailing politico-economic situation at the end of the nineteenth century. By the 1930s, most Indian economists agreed that their purpose was not merely to expose weaknesses in Western economic thought, but to collect accurate facts, analyze different social factors and evolve a connected body of thought such that policy in India would relate better to Indian conditions and produce outcomes in line with Indian aspirations. By the 1940s Ranade's search for a new methodology and an 'Indian' economics was given up. The approach was adopted of using received theory, adapting it, and applying it to Indian contexts.

We may conclude that Indian economists did not create a new school of thought.; They produced some theory and introduced some new concepts; their view of economics was essentially a practical one. In Ragnar Nurkse's words,[26] 'An economics unaffected with real world problems would court the danger of sterility;' Indian economists did not fail this test.

References

Adarkar, B. P. 1941. *The Indian Fiscal Policy.* Allahabad: Kitabmahal.
———. 1935. 'The Economic Aspects of the Indian Constitution.' *The Economic Journal* 45 (177), 177–183.
Ambedkar, B. R. 1925. 'Statement of Evidence to the Royal Commission on Indian Currency.' At http://www.ambedkar.org/ambcd/30.%20Statement%20of%20Evidence%20to%20the%20Royal%20Commission.htm Accessed November 2008.

————. 1918. 'Small Holdings in India and their Remedies.' *Journal of the Indian Economic Society* 1. Reproduced in V. W. Moon (ed.). 1979. *Babasaheb Ambedkar: Writings and Speeches*, Vol. 6. Bombay: Government of Maharashtra.

Ambirajan, S. 1991. 'Ambedkar's Contributions to Economics.' *Economic and Political Weekly* 34, 46–470, 3280–3287.

Arndt, H. W. 1972. 'Development Economics before 1945.' In Jagdish N. Bhagwati and Richard S. Eckaus (eds). *Development and Planning: Essays in Honour of Paul Rosenstein-Rodan*. London: Allen and Unwin.

Balachandran, G. 2003. *India and the World Economy, 1850–1950*. Delhi: Oxford University Press.

Banerjea, Pramathanath. 1911. *A Study of Indian Economics*. Calcutta: Calcutta University.

Bhagwati, J. N. and S. Chakravarty. 1969. 'Indian Economic Analysis: A Survey.' *American Economic Review* 59 (4), Part 2: Supplement, 1–73.

Bhagwati, J. N. and Padma Desai. 1970. *India, Planning for Industrialization*. London: Oxford University Press.

Caird, James. 1884. *India, the Land and the People*. London: Cassel and Company.

Chandavarkar, A. G. 1957. 'The Savings Potential of Disguised Unemployment.' *Economic Journal* 67 (266), 335–338.

Chandra, Bipan (ed.). 1990. *Ranade's Economic Writings*. New Delhi: Gian Publishing House.

Coyajee Private Papers, n.d., National Archives of India, New Delhi.

Coyajee, J. C. 1924. *The Indian Fiscal Problem*. Patna: Patna University.

Das, Rajani Kanta. c. 1925, 'An Opinion on the Suggestions of the Indian Economic Enquiry Committee.' *Welfare*. Calcutta.

Dasgupta, A. K. 2003 [1954]. 'Keynesian Economics and Underdeveloped Countries.' *Economic and Political Weekly* 38 (28), 2919–2922.

Dasgupta, Partha. 2003. 'The Social Analyst: A. K. Dasgupta (16 July 1903–14 January 1992).' *Economic and Political Weekly* 38 (28), 2916–2918.

Datta, Bhabatosh. 1978. *Indian Economic Thought: Twentieth Century Perspectives, 1900–1950*. New Delhi: Tata McGraw Hill.

Dey, Hirendra Lal. 1933. *The Indian Tariff Problem in Relation to Industry and Taxation*. London: George Allen and Unwin.

————. 1950. *Policy of Protection in India: A Retrospect*. Pune: Gokhale Institute of Politics and Economics.

Eckaus, Richard S. 1989. 'Rosenstein-Rodan, Paul Narziss (1902–1985).' In John Eatwell, Murray Milgate and Peter Newman (eds). *The New Palgrave: Economic Development*. London: W. W. Norton and Company, Ltd, 296–297.

Ganguli, B. N. 1977. *Indian Economic Thought: Nineteenth Century Perspectives*. New Delhi: Tata McGraw Hill.

Goheen, J. 1958. 'A Comment on Professor Singer's 'Cultural Values in India's Economic Development', *Economic Development and Cultural Change* VII (1), 1–3.

Government of India. 1923. *Indian Fiscal Commission: Minutes of Evidence Recorded by the Indian Fiscal Commission*, Volume I. Calcutta: Government of India.

————. 1922. *Report of the Indian Fiscal Commission, 1921–22*. Calcutta: Government of India.

Govindu, V. G. and D. Malghan. 2005. 'Building a Creative Freedom: J. C. Kumarappa and his Economic Philosophy.' *Economic and Political Weekly* 40 (52), 5477–5488.

Guha, Ramachandra. 1992. 'Prehistory of Indian Environmentalism: Intellectual Traditions.' *Economic and Political Weekly* 27 (1), 57–64.

Haberler, G. and R. M. Stern. 1961. *Equilibrium and Growth in the World Economy: Economic Essays by Ragnar Nurkse*. Cambridge: Harvard University Press.

Hamilton, C. J. 1916. 'Economic Development of Japan.' *Bengal Economic Journal* 1, 26–43.

Jain, Laxmi Chandra. 1929. *Indigenous Banking in India*. London: Macmillan and Co.

Jevons, H. Stanley. 1916. 'The Teaching of Economics.' *Indian Journal of Economics* 1 (1), 95ff.

Jevons, W. Stanley. 1915. 'Capitalist Development of Agriculture.' Paper read at the Indian Industrial Conference, December 1915. [cited in Ambedkar 1918]

Joshi, G. V. 1890. 'Economic Situation in India.' *Sarvajanik Sabha Journal* (January).

——. 1930. *An Introduction to the Study of Indian Economics*, 7th edn, Vol. I. Poona: Aryabhushan Press.

——. 1929. *Economics of Protection in India*. Poona: Aryabhushan Press.

——. 1918. *Introduction to the Study of Indian Economics*, 2nd edn. Poona: Aryabhushan Press.

Karve, D. G. 1958. 'Comments.' *Economic Development and Cultural Change* 7 (1), 7–9.

Krishnamurty, J. 2009. *Towards Development Economics: Selected Indian Contributions, c 1900–1945*, New Delhi: Oxford University Press (forthcoming).

——. 2008. 'The Indian Antecedents of Disguised Unemployment and Surplus Labour.' *Indian Journal of Labour Economics* 51 (1), 53–62.

——. 'Labour Force Concepts and Employment: Some Impacts of the Cairo Lectures.' 'In A. Vaidyanathan and K. L. Krishna (eds). *Institutions and Markets in India's Development*. Delhi: Oxford University Press, 265–285.

Kumarappa, J. C. 1935. 'Philosophy of Village Movement.' Rajahmundry: Razan Electric Press.

Lees-Smith, H. B. 1909. *Studies in Indian Economics*. London: Constable.

Lindley, Mark. 2007. *J. C. Kumarappa: Mahatma Gandhi's Economist*. Mumbai: Popular Prakashan.

Lokanathan, P. S. 1935. *Industrial Organization in India*. London: George Allen and Unwin.

Mamkootatam, Kuriakose. 1980. 'Radhakamal Mukherjee's Contributions to "Man and his Biosphere." New Delhi: Indian Council of Social Science Research (mimeo).

Mukherjee, Radhakamal. 1997. *India: The Dawn of a New Era (An Autobiography)*. New Delhi: Radha Publications.

——. 1950. *Planning the Countryside: First Report*. Bombay: Hind Kitabs.

——. 1942. *Social Ecology*. London: Longmans, Green and Co.

——. 1939. *Institutional Theory of Economics*. London: Macmillan and Co.

——. 1925. *Borderlands of Economics*. London: George Allen and Unwin.

——. 1916. *Foundations of Indian Economics*. London: Longmans Green and Co.

Narain, Brij. 1935. *Tendencies in Recent Indian Economic Thought*. Delhi: University of Delhi.

——. 1922. *Indian Economic Problems*. Lahore: Punjab Printing Works.

——. 1920. *Essays on Indian Economic Problems*. Lahore: The Punjabee Electric Press.

Nurkse, Ragnar. 1962. *Patterns of Trade and Development*. Oxford: Basil Blackwell.

——. 1957. 'Reflections on India's Development Plan.' *The Quarterly Journal of Economics* 71 (2), 188–204.

Panagariya, Arvind. 2002. *Indian Economic Reforms: What Has Been Accomplished? What Remains to Be Done?* Asian Development Bank Research Department Policy Brief.

Patwardhan, R. P. and D. V. Ambekar (eds). 1962. *Speeches and Writings of Gopal Krishna Gokhale, Volume I, Economic*. Poona and Bombay: Deccan Sabha and Asia Publishing House.

Perala, Maiju. 2003. 'Allyn Young and Early Development Theory.' At http://www.arts.cornell.edu/econ/75devconf/papers/Perala%202003.pdf

Price, Ralph. 1966. 'M. G. Ranade's Theory of Development and Growth.' *Explorations in Entrepreneurial History / Second Series* 4 (1), 40–51.

Raj, K. N. 1957. *Employment Aspects of Planning in Under-Developed Countries*. Cairo: National Bank of Egypt.

Ranade, M. G. 1920. *Essays in Indian Economics*. Bombay: Thaker and Co.

Rao, V. K. R. V. 1953. 'Full Employment and Economic Development.' *Indian Economic Review* I (2), 43–57.

———. 1938. 'The Problem of Unemployment in India.' *Indian Journal of Economics* 18 (4), 627–634.

Robinson, W. C. 1969. 'Types of Rural Unemployment and Some Policy Implications.' *Oxford Economic Papers* 21 (3), 373–386.

Rosenstein-Rodan, Paul. 1956. 'Disguised Unemployment and Under-Employment in Agriculture.' Cambridge: Center for International Studies, Massachusetts Institute of Technology (mimeo).

———. 1943. 'Problems of Industrialisation of Eastern and South-Eastern Europe.' *Economic Journal* 53 (210/211), 202–211.

Scitovsky, T. 1942. 'A Reconsideration of the Theory of Tariffs.' *Review of Economic Studies* 9 (2), 89–110.

Sen, Amartya. 1994. 'Amiya Kumar Dasgupta (1903–1992).' *Economic Journal* 104 (426), 1147–1155.

———. 1975. *Employment, Technology and Development*. Oxford: Clarendon Press.

———. 1966. 'Peasants and Dualism with or without Surplus Labour.' *Journal of Political Economy* 74 (5), 425–450.

Shah, K. T. 1923. *Trade, Tariffs and Transport in India*. Bombay/London: National Book Depot/P.S. King and Co.

Singer, M. 1956, 'Cultural Values in India's Economic Development.' *The Annals of the American Academy of Political and Social Science* 305 (1), 81–91.

Singh, Baljit. 1957. *The Frontiers of Social Science: In Honour of Radhakamal Mukherjee*. London: Macmillan.

Singh, Tarlok. 1945. *Poverty and Social Change*. 1st edn. Toronto: Longmans Green and Co.

Slater, Gilbert. 1918 'Higher Economics Courses I.' *Indian Journal of Economics* 2 (1), 92–95.

Sovani, N. V. 1991. *Indian Economics: Some Theory, Some Practice*, Gokhale Institute Studies No. 72. Pune : Gokhale Institute of Politics and Economics.

Stolper, W. F. and P. A. Samuelson. 1941. 'Protection and Real Wages.' *Review of Economic Studies* 9 (1), 58–73.

Thomas, P. J. 1939. *The Growth of Federal Finance in India, Being a Survey of India's Public Finance from 1833 to 1939*. London: Oxford University Press.

———. 1935. 'A Plan for Economic Recovery.' *Indian Journal of Economics* 15 (4), 447–457.

Vakil, C. N. 1923. *Our Fiscal Policy*. Bombay: D.B. Taraporevala Sons and Co.

Vakil, C. N. and P. R. Brahmananda. 1956. *Planning for an Expanding Economy: Accumulation, Employment and Technical Progress in Underdeveloped Countries*. Bombay: Vora and Co.

Warriner, Doreen. 1939. *Economics of Peasant Farming*. Oxford: Oxford University Press.

Wellisz, Stanislaw. 1968. 'Dual Economies, Disguised Unemployment and the Unlimited Supply of Labour.' *Economica* 35 (137), 22–51.

Whitaker, John (ed.). 1966. *The Correspondence of Alfred Marshall, Economist, Vol. 3, Towards the Close, 1903–1924*. Cambridge: Cambridge University Press.

NOTES

1. The Relevance of Ragnar Nurkse and Classical Development Economics

1 We would like to thank Yves Ekoué Amaïzo for his help with the data used in Figures 1.2 and 1.3.

2 To be precise, Rodrik and Skidelsky, similarly to many others, mean mostly poverty reduction in this context.

3 The following paragraphs draw on Reinert (2007).

4 There are a number of other thinkers that played key roles in early development theory who could be mentioned here as well; for instance Raul Prebish, W. W. Rostow. A good collection of recollections by the key figures in this tradition is gathered in Meier and Seers (1984) (although this does not include Nurkse, as he had passed away by the time of this publication).

5 We are necessarily generalizing; for more detailed accounts we refer the reader to subsequent contributors in this volume.

6 While Nurkse (1961) is a collection of his various works, we refer to this publication as a whole.

7 For Nurkse, key passages are Nurkse (1953, 19–25).

8 Krugman (1994), for instances, discusses only the aspect of increasing returns and fails to note how this is related to financial issues.

9 Hirschman discusses his relationship to Nurkse and Rosenstein-Rodan most explicitly in Hirschman 1984, see especially 96–97.

10 Shleifer 2008; see Galbraith 2008 from the opposite perspective.

11 Classic reference is Williamson 2002 summarizing "what Washington means by policy reform', originally published in 1990; see also Williamson 2008.

12 For accounts from rather different perspectives, see Toye 1987 and Klein 2007.

13 Wade 2004 is an excellent overview.

14 Blecker 2000 provides an overview of export-led growth strategies.

15 A useful discussion of international agreements and industrial policy space is Rodrik 2007, 129–148. For Augmented Washington Consensus, see Rodrik 2006.

16 It is interesting that China's development strategies over the last few decades exhibit the results of this skewed learning process in international development mainstream: while in the 1980s, China seemed to be on the path towards the East Asian type of capitalism where a mix of competitive markets and technology targeting is a key element, then, reflecting the rise of the Washington Consensus in the 1990s, China switched to an export-led growth strategy that, however, also exhibits certain elements from the Latin American type of development: nepotism and static rent-seeking in the policy environment and uneven income distribution. For an intriguing study of Chinese capitalism, see Huang 2008.

17 Excellent and authoritative summary is Cimoli et al 2006.
18 Somewhat ironically, it was Viner who called Nurkse to Princeton faculty just before the latter's death (Nurkse accepted the call, but never started to work in Princeton, however; this is the reason his archive is in Princeton). See Viner's letter to Nurkse from December 22, 1958, in Viner's archive in Princeton, II Correspondence, 1. General correspondence, NI-NY.
19 An excellent summary on the rise and fall of New Public Management is Drechsler (2005); see also Pollitt and Bouckaert (2004).
20 See in particular Evans and Rauch 1999, also Wade 2004.
21 On the role of the state and institutions in economic growth, see, e.g., Evans and Rauch 1999, Wade 2004 and Amsden 1989.
22 The most recent summary of such arguments is Rodrik 2007. For public choice, see most recently Buchanan and Yoon 2008

2. Life and Time of Ragnar Nurkse

1 In *Internationale Kapitalbewegungen* Nurkse (1935) rather opposes himself to Keynes: 'Für die Epoche des internationalen Kapitalismus kann man die zwischenstaatliche Unbeweglichkeit des Kapitals nicht mehr mit gutem Recht annehmen. Im Gegenteil: hohe Autoritäten (wie z. B. *Keynes*) haben in unseren Zeitalter wiederholt Anlaß gefunden, sich über die *übermäßige* Wanderlust des Kapitals zu beschweren.' (7); 'Überhaupt bedeutet die Keynessche Lehre in dieser Hinsicht eine bedenkliche Annäherung ...' (79); '*Keynes* scheint an dieser Stelle außer acht zu lassen, daß in die Indexziffern nicht nur die Preise, sondern auch die Mengen der Güter – als Gewichte – eingehen. Seine Feststellung würde nur für Durchschnitte, die die Rundprobe (circular test) bestehen, insonderheit also für ungewogene oder völlig gleichartig gewogene Preisdurchschnitte Geltung haben.' (151–152)
2 Reprinted from: Haberler, Gottfried and Robert M. Stern (eds). 1961. *Equilibrium and Growth in the World Economy: Economic Essays by Ragnar Nurkse*. Cambridge, MA: Harvard University Press, 365–69. Complemented by Kalev Kukk and Kalle Kukk.

3. Nurkse and the Role of Finance in Development Economics

1 Compare Hollis Chenery (1955) writing in 1955, 'Industrialisation is the main hope of most poor countries trying to increase their levels of income. It is also the most controversial aspect of the problem of economic development.'
2 They were countered by, e.g., Streeten (1959) and Hirschman (1958). Hirschman shared Nurkse's view that developing economies were not capital supply constrained, but expressed doubt that they had the entrepreneurial capabilities to generate balanced growth. A balanced, but negative, assessment is given in Singer (1960), who considers the approach 'premature rather than wrong'.
3 The term was coined by Albert Hirschman (1981) in his *Essays in Trespassing* for those who believe a single economic approach – the neoclassical – applies to all economic problems. This has a very different meaning depending on whether 'mono' is interpreted as Greek or Spanish.
4 See the comments by Alan Winters, Anne Krueger and others to the 21 July 2007 review of Reinert's book by Martin Wolfe in the *Financial Times*.

5 Nurkse himself speaks of the difference between 'allocation' and 'mobilization' reflecting the confrontation between comparative advantage and growth. In Nurkse (1961) the entire discussion is on the demand or mobilization aspect, and he takes supply not representing a constraint on the development problem. See his reply to his discussants (272).

6 Following Rosenstein-Rodan, he classified this as an 'academic' solution, but today it does not, in fact, appear so academic.

7 However, it is interesting to note that he proposed industrialization simply as a means to improve capital accumulation, and although he makes reference on occasion to the possibility of intensive (as well as extensive) capital accumulation, he does not appear to make use of the microeconomic supply-side explanation of increasing returns, but rather emphasizes the macrodemand side – just as disguised unemployment represented potential savings, investments in industry represented potential gains in productivity that could only be realized in a balanced expansion—that is, a higher level of overall activity, rather than economies of scale (see the discussion of the origin of these in the works of Allyn Young).

8 Nurkse (1953, 37). Keith Griffin (1969) questions the assumption that peasants cannot save because they are too poor. However, Nurkse's argument is not that peasants cannot save, for implicitly they do when they support unproductive labour, it is that their savings cannot be directed to development.

9 The question of whether labour could be removed from agriculture without decreasing output has been the subject of much subsequent debate. In 'Reflections on India's Development Plan', Nurkse (1957, 190) notes that the Indian Second Five-Year Plan estimates that 'one-fourth to one-third of the existing labour force in agriculture may be surplus to requirements'.

10 Joan Robinson (1936, 226) assumes that a 'decline in demand for the product of the general run of industries leads to a diversion of labour from occupations in which productivity is higher to others where it is lower. The cause of this diversion, a decline in effective demand, is exactly the same as the cause of unemployment in the ordinary sense, and it is natural to describe the adoption of inferior occupations by dismissed workers as disguised unemployment.' Although never given as reference, Robinson's analysis of the concept appears to be the source of the term that seems to have been first introduced into the development literature by V. K. R. V. Rao in 1938 and popularized by Rosenstein-Rodan in his classic 1943 paper 'Problems of Industrialisation of Eastern and South-Eastern Europe'.

11 Note the similarity with the classical savings assumptions that would quickly appear in the work of the post-Keynesian growth and distribution theory. In Nurkse's analysis, the workers in the agricultural (consumption) and capital goods sections have a unitary propensity to consume while the rest of the population has a propensity to save that is positive. Also note that one could interpret this analysis as similar to Lewis's assumption concerning differing marginal productivity in agriculture and industry. This would not be correct, for in Nurkse's analysis there need be no difference in the marginal product of labour in agriculture and capital goods production. It is sufficient that the disguised unemployed have a marginal product that is equal to zero, and although he refers to the possibility of both extensive and intensive capital accumulation, differences in productivity between agriculture and industry do not appear to have played a significant role in his argument. Sir Arthur Lewis (1964) informs us that he came upon the idea of unlimited supplies of labour and increasing productivity in the industrial sector in August 1954 in Bangkok, while Nurkse's ideas were set out in 1951 in lectures in Rio and Cairo,

but published in summary in the *American Economic Review* 'Papers and Proceedings of 1952'. It is interesting that in his recollections, Lewis discusses Nurkse's ideas as a means to avoid the inflationary consequences of expanding production, but he seems not to have understood the proposal, presenting it as one in which the disguised unemployed labour works for no remuneration.

12 This article also had a profound impact on the ideas about cumulative causation found in the work of Nicholas Kaldor.

13 Rosenstein-Rodan (1943) advocates a policy of treating the economy as if it were engaged in the planning of production within a single large firm.

14 Note that this is not the same as the increasing returns that result from the scale economies of physical consumption (e.g., the relation between volume and surface) since it requires both interdependence across industries and demand.

15 A position that is echoed in both Hirschman's defense of unbalanced growth and Alice Amsden's (1989) description of the role of the state managers in Korean economic development in *Asia's Next Giant: South Korea and Late Industrialization*.

16 Keith Griffin (1969, 37) has criticized this approach as presuming that developing countries are poor because they have always been poor, when, in fact, most developing countries had a developed past that was disrupted by conquest and colonization. Thus, the external factors that cause 'undevelopment' are ignored in addressing the strategies to promote development. While this is undoubtedly correct, it seems that Nurkse and others who referred to the vicious circle of poverty were more interested in the idea of cumulative causation than to argue that the major problem facing developing countries was their history of poverty. Myrdal (1956) notes the increasing divergence between the implications of trade theory and the actual increase in income disparities across countries as being associated with the term 'vicious circle.' Myrdal cites Nurkse's use of the term in his 1952 Cairo lectures as the stimulus for his own attempt at a virtuous 'cumulative causation' theory.

17 Nurkse (1961, 250). In Nurkse 1954 he makes a strong case for foreign investment in providing such infrastructure investments, as he considered to have been the case in the nineteenth century. 'There is no question that ample scope exists for international financing of public improvements in the poor countries today' (755).

18 Nurkse (1953, 1954). Indeed, in the latter he calls for a revival of 'public-utility type of international investment' (754).

19 An early proponent was J. M. Keynes (1946): 'It is obvious that no country can go on forever covering by new lending a chronic surplus on current account without eventually forcing a default from the other parties.' This reflects what was a dominant view in the period, even in official circles such as the IBRD. See Alter (1961). Alter was on the economic staff of the bank and appears to have started analysis of the problem. See also the analysis of Dragoslav Avramovic (1958).

20 See http://www.othercanon.org for background references.

21 See http://www.cfeps.org and http://www.levy.org/forums for references to the relevant literature.

4. Early Development Theory from Sun Yat-sen to Ragnar Nurkse

1 The *San Min* Principles were actually written in 1897 during Sun Yat-sen's exile in Europe, where he studied the social, economic and political systems of the European countries.

The published lectures Sun Yat-sen gave in 1924 are said to be incomplete, as he died in the beginning of year 1925. (For a biography on Sun Yat-sen, see Perälä *A Development Pioneer Unappreciated* (2007a.) The earliest English language publication of *San Min Chu I* was released in 1927 (Dr. Sun Yat-sen Memorial Hall). The 1953 version of *The Principles* was used in writing this paper, but given that the time period of the original publication is important, 1927 is referred to in the text in addition to 1953 to remind the reader of the relevance of chronology in the appearance of economic ideas. Furthermore, the central ideas of *The Principles* were formed earlier and published in 1923 in the Kuomintang Declaration. Last, but by no means least, *The International Development of China* was published in 1922, though the author of this paper only had access to the second edition published in 1929, after Sun Yat-sen's death. The text cites 1922 again to emphasize the chronological order of the texts discussed and gives the exact citations for the second edition in brackets when necessary. The publication dates of the articles complied in the *Fundamentals of National Reconstruction* vary between 1905 and 1924.

2   Sun Yat-sen's views on land policy (Lin 1974, Schiffrin 1957) and Chinese socialism (Lai and Trescott 2005, Gregor and Chang 1982) as well as various historical contributions focusing on Sun Yat-sen and the early Chinese political developments have been published. Yet the recognition of his economic development vision is lacking in the literature with the exception of a brief article by Weaver (1939) in the *Historian*.

3   See Perälä (2002, 2006) for a thorough discussion on the classical endogenous growth process.

4   The choice of emphasis in this section is based on the idea that despite the fact that Rosenstein-Rodan has been attributed as having given the impetus for the development economics to form as a sub-field of economics, his collection of ideas that consist of the theory of the big push are fragmented and do not comprise a comprehensive vision of development and growth process. In fact, they are difficult to understand without the knowledge and understanding of the classical endogenous growth theory and Ragnar Nurkse's theories of the vicious circle and balanced growth. See Perälä (2002, 2006) for a discussion of these theories with a comparative view of the classical endogenous growth and the early development theories.

5   That is, some economic perspectives are clearly underlying his vision. Though not cited according to modern academic standards due to stylistic differences in writing, as some of his contributions were not intended as academic publications and the academic citation standards were distinct at the time from that of the contemporary ones, Sun Yat-sen's perspective confirms to the classical endogenous growth vision, a growth perspective that began forming with the publication of Adam Smith's (1776) *The Wealth of Nations*. This brief discussion on the biographical aspects that have influenced Sun Yat-sen's development thought is based on chapters two and three of Perälä's *A Development Pioneer Unappreciated* (2007a).

6   More appropriately, Perälä (2007a), in *A Development Pioneer Unappreciated: Sun Yat-sen's Thought on Economic Development* establishes Sun Yat-sen among the prominent twentieth century pioneers of development.

7   For an in depth discussion on this 'dynamic mirror effect' of Say's law, see *A Development Pioneer* (Perälä 2007a).

8   An example of behavioural externality is a case in which a poor household, previously without electricity, is brought under its municipal provision. The availability of electricity then changes the behavioural patterns of the household, as cooking and other household chores can now be conducted with the help of the electrical appliances. Furthermore, in the case of a rural farm household, electricity enables the use of a water pump instead

of having to carry water for irrigation and for farm animals and so forth. Before the availability of electricity, these needs were fulfilled by labour, and hence, their contribution to the actual consumption and capital goods market demand was nonexistent. For an in-depth discussion on this and the operation of Say's law in the process of economic development, see *A Development Pioneer* (Perälä (2007a).

9 This is due to the fact that simultaneous market expansion caused by supply increase is needed for the law to hold. As argued by Rosenstein-Rodan in his shoe factory example, the 'diversity of human wants' creates complementarities, prevalent pecuniary externalities, between wage good industries and hence complementary, coordinated expansion is needed for the supply to create its demand. Though one must note that the market expansion as represented by the wages of the labourers in these industries is smaller than the actual value of the supply increase and hence, an external market is needed to avoid the excess supply of goods. From this perspective, Rosenstein-Rodan also focused on the problem of economic development as one of generating a sustained market expansion at the subsistence level.

10 Similar to the social and economic policies of most European countries in the beginning of the twentieth century, after which Sun Yat-sen formulated his development perspective and goals and the policies needed to achieve them.

11 It originally was his Presidential Address, which he used to contribute to a prevailing discussion on increasing returns to scale, defending a neglected perspective of their relevance to economic growth.

12 See his discussion in 'Big Business: How Economic System Grows and Evolves Like a Living Organism' (Young 1999, 412–413).

13 An extension of the market as understood by Allyn Young entails externalities that lead not only to internal returns captured by an individual firm, but also to external ones, external benefits to firms operating on the market. In reality, any expansion of the market leads to external economies, pecuniary and technological (nonpecuniary), as well as demand-side behavioural changes and associated externalities.

14 Competition creates limits to internal returns, spreads pecuniary and technological (nonpecuniary) externalities and maximizes market expansion through competitive price-setting that increases purchasing power on the market.

15 Young discusses the notion in such broad terms that it entails both horizontal and vertical pecuniary external economies. Basically, horizontal pecuniary external economies occur between wage-goods producing firms, while vertical pecuniary external economies occur between suppliers and final goods producers. These terms were introduced to economic development by Rosenstein-Rodan (1961, 1984).

16 It is worth remembering that Young was writing on the eve of the Great Depression and hence his vision was formed based on the growth and development experience of the advanced economies during the past century; a case of generalized or even partial market failure was not considered by him.

17 Though Young (1999, 416) refrains from analyzing a case of market failure, in a different contribution when discussing the growth of the economic system with reference to business enterprises, he makes explicit reference that this growth, which is like an evolution of a living organism, cannot by itself, if left to the competitive forces alone, assure that balance is achieved on the market. This point is further discussed when comparing Young's and early development theorists' views with respect to policy.

18 Pecuniary externalities are market-price-mechanism-transmitted inter-firm or inter-industry interdependencies, while technological (nonpecuniary) externalities are interdependencies between the production functions of firms or the sectors of economy,

e.g., industrial training in labour. The discussion and terminology was first formalized within the literature by Tibor Scitovsky (1954).

19 This capital investment-reducing dynamic in underdeveloped economies reverses its nature in economies at more advanced stages of development, where the dynamic fuels endogenous growth.

20 In classical economics, the separation between supply and demand sides in economic analysis is not as explicit as in neoclassical economics. Evidence of this is that the economic phenomenon is analyzed through concepts, such as Say's law, that address explicitly the relation and interrelatedness between supply and demand. For a more in-depth discussion on classical economics and its relevance, see Perälä (2007b).

21 In the historical context of Young's contributions, this is a direct criticism of the Soviet development model, as it violated the inherent characteristics of classical growth process that relies on market transactions and dynamics as a source of growth.

22 Though from the perspective of Sir Arthur Lewis (1988), 'much of emergence of economics is that of development economics', hence the classical contributions are more characteristic of the continuum of development from low-income economies to advanced industrialized ones. It can be argued that given that the economics profession emergence and its knowledge creation was (and has been) concentrated in Western academia, at the time of writing Smith's (1776) *The Wealth of Nations*, these countries were affected by vibrant economic changes, namely the industrial revolution, and were developing rapidly. Hence, the focus of economics throughout much its emergence was rapidly developing economies, going through the process of structural transformation from agrarian economies to industrialized ones. With this transformation of economies and their long-term sustained improvements in the standards of living, the focus of economics increasingly became the economic problems, challenges and dynamics of high-income nations and hence, the persistence of underdevelopment and the dynamics promoting it in low-income nations were abstracted away from by the profession due to its geographical location and research emphasis as well as other historical occurrences in political and economic history such as the presence of colonialism, which created a bias against the regions subjected to foreign rule in terms of economic and political analysis.

23 As an exception within the field is reference to Sun Yat-sen by H. W. Arndt (1987).

24 For a further discussion on this see *A Development Pioneer Unappreciated* (Perälä 2007a).

5. The Roots of Unequal Exchange: Mihail Manoilescu and the Debate of the 1930s

1 To cite only the best-known names.

2 He is not mentioned, for instance, in the 4,800-word Wikipedia entry, 'Unequal Exchange'.

3 Sir R[eginald] Hoare to Foreign Office, 21 June 1940, FO 371.24992, Public Record Office, London.

4 Later renamed the Polytechnic.

5 Whether Manoilescu was motivated by antisemitism or sound financial judgment in letting the Banca Marmorosch-Blank fail is debatable, but a recent study has supported the latter view. See Popisteanu, Preda and Retegan (1982, 38–44).

6 Manoilescu. 'Memorii.' Manoilescu had a private audience with Salazar. 'Memorii,' 614.

7 Diamandi ([1936?], 268). Similar opinions were held by French and British observers. The French Minister in Bucharest reported a rumor that Manoilescu had secretly sent

government funds to Switzerland while he was minister of commerce. French Minister in Bucharest [G. Puaux] to Foreign Minister, 29 June 1931, Quai d'Orsay Archives, vol. 170, 28. The British Embassy reported in 1939, 'He [Manoilescu] is said to be venal.' 'Records of Leading Personalities in Roumania.' Bucharest, 31 July 1939, FO 371.23855, 17.

8 In the 1920s, at least, Manoilescu had had no objections to working with Jewish partners in a Transylvanian mining venture in which he had invested his wife's fortune (Manoilescu, 'Memorii,' 41, 499, 576).

9 For details, see Vasile (1979, 368–91). Romania's export prices to Germany rose 123 per cent from 1939 to 1944, while import prices from Germany rose 614 per cent, giving the lie to Manoilescu's vision of how the 'Großraumwirtschaft' would work. See Lampe and Jackson (1982, 532).

10 E.g., see Condliffe (1933, 358). Condliffe opined that it was the industrialized countries that had the most to lose by pursuing autarkic policies, a view M. Manoilescu had also expressed

11 Cassel (1927, 43–44) put the larger share of blame on trade union monopolies rather than on 'monopolistic combines of enterprises', but argued that the two were mutually reinforcing.

12 There was also the cost of increased unemployment in the West, in Cassel's view, partly owing to labour unions' insistence on the introduction of the eight-hour day Cassel (1927, 28, 29 (quotation), 32).

13 Manoilescu (1933a, 121). In the same passage Manoilescu added that Cassel had 'absurdly' proposed free trade as a solution, but the Romanian ignored Cassel's principal recommendations for the West to provide expanded credit and capital investment for agricultural and colonial countries.

14 He defined productivity as value added per worker in terms of international prices.

15 Manoilescu 1986, 125; see the same point in Manoilescu 1929, 177. I will refer hereafter primarily to Manoilescu 1986, the expanded Romanian edition of Manoilescu 1929. The work was revised in 1946–48, but only published in 1986, thirty-six years after the author's death. The Romanian edition is a reworked version of the 1937 German edition. Though the 1986 edition is the definitive one, it is necessary to refer to others, especially the original French one, because of its reception by critics and Manoilescu's attempts to answer them in later editions. Note that the first words of the title of the revised work (national forces of production) emphasize the productivity issue, as did the title of the 1937 German version. 'The productivity of labor is the fundamental ['capitala'] notion in our work,' he wrote in Manoilescu 1986, 97. In a given economic activity or branch of industry, if C = fixed capital invested, and K = liquid capital, and T = total number of workers, then 'specific capital' (or q) = $(C + K)/T$, or capital per worker. Further, if P = value of production, and S = total wages, then p = value of output per worker, or P/T, and s = average wages, or S/T. Output per worker, or 'productivity', equals average wages plus specific capital multiplied by i, the average rate of profit in that industry, or $p = s + q(X)i$. This formula was not included in the French and French-derived editions in English, Italian and Portuguese. Manoilescu 1986, 124.

16 Manoilescu 1986, 131–32. These calculations were based on the assumption that only male adults worked in agriculture. If, said Manoilescu, one more realistically added the additional labour inputs in agriculture by women and children, the ratio of productivities would reach 9 to 1 See Manoilescu (1986, 130). Generalizing for 'backward agricultural countries' in the latter work, Manoilescu believed labour productivity in industry was, on average, four times greater than in agriculture (127).

17 Rosenstein-Rodan noted that the private investors would maximize the private, not the social, marginal net product. See Rosenstein-Rodan (1984, 215).

18 The coefficient of quality was equal to average net production of an industry (roughly, value added) divided by the square root of the product of the number of workers times the amount of fixed capital, or $Q = P/\sqrt{A \times C}$. Manoilescu (1986, 147).

19 Manoilescu 1986, 160. Agricultural and industrial countries were so distinguished by their exports. Manoilescu (1934a, 28, note 2).

20 Manoilescu (1986, 160–61). Manoilescu thought that the price scissors of the Great Depression was a 'passing' phenomenon (353). On this important matter, his analysis differed sharply from that of Raul Prebisch and the UN Economic Commission for Latin America (ECLA).

21 In 1954 Lewis '… independently advance[d] the argument first made by the Roumanian writer Manoilescu … that protection is justified in [lesser developed countries] on the ground that wages in industry are excessive in relation to agriculture' (Findlay 1980, 70). See Lewis (1954).

22 The formula in note 26 could be modified to include land, by replacing the square root of AxC by the cube root of AxCxO, where the last term represents the amount of land cultivated in a given branch of agriculture. Manoilescu (1986, 149).

23 Manoilescu (1986, 330) ('relative utility'). He had nothing to say about other components of the service sector, such as government or professional salaries and fees.

24 Manoilescu (1986, 304; 1929, 342). He added that there was no sacrifice by society under a protectionist regime, as List's theory had indicated; on the contrary, the whole nation benefited, because of the higher productivity gained. 'In that regard, the bourgeoisie, following its own interests, has helped the whole people …' Manoilescu (1986, 304).

25 Manoilescu (1986, 302). They might persist, one assumes, because of greater technological change in industry over the middle term.

26 Manoilescu (1986, 365). In fact, however, Manoilescu did momentarily defend autarky after the London economic conference of the League ended in failure in 1933. See Manoilescu (1934b, especially 15–19).

27 Manoilescu (1986, 44). A division of the world into plutocratic and proletarian nations had already been identified by the Italian proto-Fascist Enrico Corradini (1910) and the Chinese theorist who introduced Mao Tse-tung to Marxism, Li Ta-Chao (1920). See Corradini (1973, 146; Meisner 1967, 144). Modesty aside, Manoilescu believed that just as Marx had explained the exploitation of social classes, he had explained the exploitation of peoples. Manoilescu (1934a, 29).

28 As late as the 1940s, Manoilescu still had not abandoned the idea of 'raising the purchasing power of agricultural countries', at least as a rhetorical device. Manoilescu (1986, 375). This goal would be successively taken up by ECLA and UNCTAD later.

29 In Manoilescu (1934a, 368), Manoilescu recommends a policy of exporting manufactures, but it is not clear that he is directing his advice only to agrarian countries trying to industrialize; see p. 20.

30 In an implicit contradiction; see p. 20.

31 For example, in *Revue Economique Internationale* (by Leon Hennebicq), *American Economic Review* (by Leo Pasvolsky), and in a medium of *haute vulgarisation*, the *Times Literary Supplement* (anon.).

32 It may have been Manoilescu whom Oskar Morgenstern (1937, 122), later known as the father of game theory, had in mind when he wrote, 'In the esoteric circles of "pure theory" the division between real science and amateur economics is quite clear: The

occasional outbursts from outsiders, especially people trained in mathematics and engineering, who advance monstrous ideas, does not alter this to any great extent ....'

33 With Eli Hecksher, Ohlin demonstrated how comparative advantage is derived from differences in factor endowments among countries and how a country could profit by exporting goods whose production made the most intensive use of its most abundant factor.

34 Ohlin 1931, 36. In the subsequent Romanian edition, Manoilescu (1986, 287) answered Ohlin by saying that certain industries would never be created in agrarian countries without artificial price incentives; however, this defense only amounts to List's infant-industry argument, though elsewhere, Manoilescu defends new high-productivity industries from their first day of operation. Furthermore, Manoilescu misread Ohlin in saying that the latter approved of tariffs to the extent that they maintain high salaries, obtained through the activities of trade unions as non-competing groups (293).

35 Viner (1932, 121–25 (quotation on 125)). Manoilescu responded to Viner in the posthumus Romanian edition of his work (1986, 252–54), but did not address the issue of trade union monopoly as the reason why wages, prices and productivity (by Manoilescu's definition) might be higher in those industries for which Manoilescu found empirically higher cross-national data to support his case.

36 Viner (1937, 498, note 12). Nicholas Georgescu-Roegen, the most important Romanian economist after 1945 and a major figure in the American profession, wrote: 'Viner kept decrying Manoilescu's thesis ... Yet even Viner ... finally weakened, as he sought to justify the classical doctrine by the difference in occupational disutilities.' Georgescu-Roegen (1987, 300).

37 On the Tasca-Manoilescu debates, see Paiusan and Busa 1990, 291–320.

38 Tasca 1937, 40–41. The exploitation of Romanian peasants by urban ethnic minorities was a process Manoilescu had condemned. In a reply to Tasca, Manoilescu stated that his programme would benefit Romanian agriculture – an allegation that was correct in the long run, if wages in agriculture eventually rose as workers sought jobs in industry, and relative prices and wages in agriculture rose (Manoilescu 1937, 56). However, long-run terms of trade data available at the international level down to 2000 seemed to indicate the predicted process was not occurring (See Ocampo and Parra 2003).

39 See the reference to Sombart implying his approval of Manoilescu's doctrine in Manoilescu (1986, 44).

40 Brinkmann (1938, especially 276–79). Viner had made similar criticisms. In fact, Manoilescu inconsistently employed both the (classical) labour theory of value and the (neoclassical) marginalist price theory, based on the utility and availability of goods (and inversely on their scarcity). He accepted the neoclassical concept of economic equilibrium based on a marginalist explanation of prices. Manoilescu distinguished between 'internal' and 'external' values: The former were derived from the creation of goods, accounted for costs of production and were explained by the labour theory of value, as modified by his 'qualitative' stratification of labour inputs, based on capital per worker. 'External value' was derived from utility and expressed a quantitative relation between the utilities of two goods; it was therefore explained by marginalist considerations. Manoilescu (1986, 73; 1940b, 22–25).

41 Manoilescu referred to members of the liberal professions and civil servants as a 'pseudo-bourgeoisie' in Manoilescu (1942b, 110).

42 Hagen (1958, 498–503, 511 (quotation), 513). Hagen also shows that a policy of subsidies will, in theory, raise real income higher than protection will, and the *optimum optimorum* is a combination of free trade and subsidies (498).

43 Based on his analysis of international trade. See Manoilescu (1940a, 16–26).
44 Romer 1990, 71–102. Also Murphy, Shleifer and Vishny 1989, 1003–1026. For a discussion of the significance of Romer's article, see Warsh 2006.

6. Nurkse and the Early Latin American Structuralists: A Reflection on Development Theory, Industrialization and their Relevance Today

1 See Dahlman (2007) for a synthesis of the current global scenario.
2 See, among others, Pisano (2006).
3 On the reshaping of global IP regimes and on the emergence of new markets for knowledge see Cimoli and Primi (2008).
4 See Rodríguez (2001) and Bielschowsky (2006) for a review on the validity of the contributions of Prebisch and Furtado to the contemporary development debate.
5 See Pérez and Soete (1988).
6 See Williamson (1990) for the Washington Consensus and World Bank (1991) for the concept of market friendly policies. For an analysis of the structural reforms and Their impact in Latin America, see Stallings and Péres (2000).
7 In this respect, see Bhagwati (1988) and Krueger (1990). In Latin America, for example, several facts contributed to the delegitimization of development policies: (1) the public enterprises that had traditionally invested directly in new sectors were either privatized or closed, reflecting the new view that the state should only play a subsidiary role in economic growth; (2) the need to balance public finances meant eliminating subsidies, particularly fiscal ones, and the subsidy components of credit operations; and (3) there was a (sometimes controversial) perception that many investments suffered from bad planning, poor project management and corruption, and in some cases were considered responsible for high inefficiencies – the so-called 'white elephants'. This loss of legitimacy of policy, however, did not occur homogeneously in all the regions of the world. It has been much pronounced in Latin America. For example, in several countries of East and Southeast Asia, active sectoral policies, sometimes even with targeting at the firm level, remained in force until the mid 1990s, fading gradually, and at different rates, as domestic production and technological capabilities were gaining competitiveness, engendering a gradual joining of those countries to the free-market game and to the international trade regime. See Peres and Primi (2008).
8 See Cimoli, Dosi, Nelson and Stiglitz (2006) for an interesting and provocative assessment on how institutions and policies shaped industrial development.
9 The Production Development Policy launched in May 2008 in Brazil, the Industrial Policy of South Africa of 2007, the Indian strategic management of intellectual property rights for favouring accumulation of technological capabilities and domestic industries are only some examples of this tendency. See Peres (2006) and Peres and Primi (2008) for an analysis of the Latin American experience.
10 See Furtado (1985) for an almost 'personal tale' on the creation of the Economic Commission for Latin America. For an overview of the evolution of ECLAC ideas see Bielschowsky (1998, 13, table 1). The history of the economic ideas inspiring the activity of the ECLAC and the evolution of the Latin American development tradition are interlinked. The boundaries between the '*pensamiento cepalino*' and the Latin American development tradition blur; however, it is possible to trace the evolution of Latin American structuralism in a quite precise way. The Latin American development

tradition includes different contributions, from those belonging to the dependency theory, to the structuralism and the body of literature produced by ECLAC. For an extensive review of the evolution of the Latin American structuralism see Rodríguez (2006). The volume CEPAL (1998) collects a series of selected contributions of main ECLAC works since its foundation.

11 Basically, it was recognized that investments impacted the economy though two complementary channels. Investments produced, on the one hand, a supply effect through the creation of production capacities (capital accumulation); on the other hand, they engendered a demand for capital goods. Given the almost nonexistent domestic supply of capital goods, the demand effect was completely transferred abroad through increasing imports, leading to frequent stop and go cycles derived from recurring trade imbalances. This process and the recognition of the potential spillover effects derived from technical progress embedded in capital goods production, were the rationale behind the policies in support of domestic production of capital goods in various countries of the region (Fajnzylber 1983).

12 The term 'monoeconomics' was coined by Hirschman to refer to the neoclassical attitude of considering that a unique theoretical approach would apply to all circumstances (Hirschman 1981).

13 Even though the historical approach is common to all structuralists, it is Furtado (1956b and 1961) who dedicated most of his efforts to link economic development with historical trajectories.

14 This issue is extensively treated in Nurkse (1957 and 1959b).

15 Here there is a reference to the Marshall external economies, even though in a different meaning. In Nurkse's interpretation the external economies inducing increasing returns represent the increase in market size derived from the interrelation between different production activities, not the kind of external economies like communication, transports or average techniques of production. (Marshall 1890)

16 In making reference to the Japanese experience, Nurkse quotes Tsuru (1941), a Shumpeter student at Harvard. Tsuru, S., Economic fluctuations in Japan 1868–93, Review of Economic Statistics.

17 The third conference makes reference to the concept of disguised unemployment and the relative issue of disguised savings that could be mobilized if labor could be transferred to more productive activities. In this respect, even though the discussion between Furtado and Nurske do not focus on this point, it is interesting to note an implicit similarity. This point of Nurkse's analysis finds many similarities with the ECLAC analysis of structural heterogeneity (Pinto 1970, 1971 and 1976). The concentration of labor in low-productivity activities (mainly agricultural and natural resource-based activities) was seen as a major determinant of low aggregate productivity. Structural heterogeneity was identified as one of the major barriers to sustained growth in Latin America. A transformation of production structure aiming to reduce heterogeneity would have induced increases in productivity, and consequently in output.

18 See Prebisch (1981) for an excellently worded imaginary dialogue between the structuralists and Friedman and Hayek, where, in what constitutes one of the most 'didactic' articles in heterodox economics, Prebisch shows why neoclassical theory is not apt to explain capitalistic development in peripheral countries.

19 See Arthur (1989), David (1985) and Pérez and Soete (1988).

20 In this process, both Prebisch and Nurkse identify 'à la Lewis' models, stressing the role of disguised unemployment (as in Nurkse) or the ill- or unemployed (as in Prebisch and Furtado) as source of productivity increase in the new industrial sector.

21 For a critical review regarding different stances towards industrial policy, see Chang (1994) and Péres and Primi (2008).

22 For an interesting review, see Adelman (1999).

23 See Prebisch (1950), Furtado (1956a) and (Fajnzylber 1983) among the structuralists. See, among others, Nelson (1959), Atkinson and Stiglitz (1969), Dosi (1988), Bell and Pavitt (1993), Cohen and Levinthal (1990), Cimoli and Dosi (1995) for evolutionary analysis on patterns of learning and technical change.

8. Ragnar Nurkse and the Law & Economics of Development

1 Nurkse (1958, 73) was quite clear in stating that he was the one who applied Duesenberry – 'as Duesenberry formulated and I applied it.'

2 By and large, the term 'Governance' has become a more or less neutral concept that focuses on steering mechanisms in a certain political unit, emphasizing the interaction of State (First), Business (Second) and Society (Third Sector) players. 'Good Governance', on the other hand, is not at all neutral; rather, it is a normative concept that embodies a strong value judgment in favor of the retrenchment of the State, which is supposed to yield to Business standards, principles and – not least – interests. In that sense, 'Good Governance' privileges the Second over the First Sector, even in First Sector areas.

The concept of 'Good Governance' arose in the 1980s in the International Finance Institutions (IFIs) such as the World Bank, the IMF, UNDP and OECD, as a positive extrapolation from the negative experiences that these organizations had had in the developing countries by observing that their financial aid seemed to have had no effects. From this, they deduced an absence of institutions, principles and structures, the entirety of which was called 'Governance' – and 'Good Governance' when they worked well. This means, however, that the 'Good' in 'Good Governance' is not good in any general or generalizable sense, but as pertains to what most of the IFIs in the 1980s thought was good – a perspective that these days is not shared by many experts anymore, including those within the IFI's themselves. But while a unitary definition of the concept 'Good Governance' never existed, not even within the respective individual IFIs, 'good' principles usually encompassed such concepts as transparency, efficiency, participation, responsibility and market economy, state of law, democracy and justice. Many of them are indubitably 'good' as such, but all of them – except the last one – are heavily context dependent, dependent not only on definition and interpretation, but also on time and place. (This note after Drechsler 2004, 388–389, with references.) Nurkse's focus on domestic capacity is the opposite of paternalism; in his hard-nosed economic approach, he takes the developing countries, including the least developed ones, seriously and at eye level.

3 The following segment is an only slightly revised version of Drechsler (2000a, 237–238), as this covers precisely the same matter.

4 Basu (1987, 687 claims that the 'lack of formalization in Nurkse's work led to much misunderstanding – handsomely contributed to by Nurkse himself – about the policy implications of the poverty-trap doctrine.') But the lack of formalization arises from Nurkse's realism, and the policy implications are clear *because* of it.

5 But it does not even end here. In turn, such restrictions make domestic supply come under pressure to produce and thus lead to inflation (Nurkse 1964 [1953], 112–113). Yet again, as inflation creates forced saving, that might – depending how far it goes – also be good for capital formation. Politically, it is a very dangerous road to take, however, for well-known reasons (1953, 116).

6 Although Nurkse (1953) does not make this connection here, he would have certainly been supportive of it, for the same reason he was for tax on consumption, rather than earning (146–148), which makes sense anyway, from an aggregate perspective. Naturally, this would preclude social engineering to some extent, but never mind that: 'Not a change in the interpersonal income distribution but an increase in the proportion of national income devoted to capital formation is the primary aim of public finance in the context of economic development' (147). If we want to develop, we must live with some people to be rich, and because these fortunes are gained via investment, these are, after all, the 'good guys' and not the inheritors. That entrepreneurs in the classical sense should actually be rewarded for the sake of all, is one of Schumpeter's main lessons for social democracy and (in the American sense) liberal thought that Nurkse strongly agreed with.

7 Nurkse is no legal thinker at all; legal institutions do not seem to interest him. To call him a Law & Economics thinker, therefore, must refer to the wider concept of 'law' within this context.

8 This is the saying attributed to Campbell-Bannerman, as any quick Google search will tell, but his actual expression was, 'Good government could never be a substitute for government by the people themselves' (speech at Stirling, 23 November 1905, in the *Daily News*, 24 November 1905, according to *Oxford*, 1993, 3.13). This is quite a different phrase, but the more popular, abbreviated one serves our purpose better to focus on the economic prerogative in development economics.

9 Not necessarily, though; one can also easily envision an economics that is beneficial to the 'deserving' countries or people as well (either a priori or because they are economically successful) – something that on a higher level could be called Nietzschean economics (but see Backhaus and Drechsler 2006).

10 For the context of the discourse of British colonialism, see Webster 2006. As quite frequently, some of Nurkse's arguments that appear on first sight to be a bit 'reactionary' turn out, after careful investigation of discourse, arguments and tropes, to be, if anything, rather 'ahead'.

9. Ragnar Nurkse's Development Theory: Influences and Perceptions

1 In fact, Nurkse himself was understandably not happy with this term (Nurkse 1953, 1).

2 For details regarding his studies at Edinburgh see University of Edinburgh (2007) as well as the correspondence between Nurkse and Dr Rankin, such as Nurkse (unpublished 1941) and Nurkse (unpublished 1945).

3 Formalist economics argues that economics is the study of utility maximization under conditions of scarcity and therefore it is about making choices – be it Robinson on his island or the globalized world of the twenty-first century. Substantivists argue that economics is about societies organizing their production, distribution and consumption. A society's strategy as an adaptation to its environment and its resources may or may not involve utility maximization (Polanyi 1944). Probably Nurkse and Polanyi knew each other: Karl Polanyi was at Columbia University in New York from 1947 to 1953 (teaching general economic history) – while Nurkse worked at Columbia from 1945 to 1958.

4 The term in its narrower sense was originally coined by Duesenberry, but later, with respect to the international dimension, often ascribed to Nurkse.

5 The idea of 'disguised' unemployment can be traced at least to Keynes' disciple Joan Robinson (1936).

6 It is interesting to note the qualification of this argument in a letter by Nurkse to Jacob Viner: 'I wonder who has maintained that disguised unemployment is prevalent in Brazil. For my own part, of course, I excluded Latin America. ... The fragmentation of peasant holdings typical, for instance, of Indian farming may be viewed as being, to some extent, a reflection of surplus farm labor' (Nurkse unpublished 1956).

10. Nurkse Meets Schumpeter: Is Microfinance a 'Silver Bullet' to Economic Development?

1 In this context, Schumpeter refers to the historical soundness of his financing thesis, especially by the example of the brothers Pereire (founders of the Crédit Mobilier in the nineteenth century), which is seen as the starting point of the modern banking system.

2 The neoclassical growth paradigm includes the idea of money neutrality, meaning that financial capital does not affect the process of economic growth. This opinion is supported by monetarism (Friedman) and by several theorems of neoclassical capital market theory (e.g., irrelevance theorem, separation theorem). According to the well-known theorems of Modigliani and Miller, Tobin and Fama, modern capital markets theories ('Capital Asset Pricing Model'; 'Option Price Model') refer strongly to assumptions of a perfect capital market and its information efficiency to analyze risk-adequate prices under uncertainty.

3 See, e.g., King and Levine (1993). With regard to our evolutionary perspective, based on Schumpeter's framework, the title of King and Levine's work is noteworthy: 'Growth and Finance: Schumpeter might be right.'

4 According to these problems, the use of external financing resources is always connected with 'hidden costs of other people's money.' (Bhidé 1992)

5 The categorization in resource- and relationship-oriented bootstrapping refers to Winborg and Landström (2001).

6 For empirical evidence, see Harrison and Mason (1992), Freear, Sohl and Wetzel (1995), Coveny and Moore (1998).

7 For a characterization of these different phases, see, e.g., Benjamin and Margulis (2000, 96).

8 Whether the origin of the bank-operational credit system can be determined is a disputed question. At least the step from the clearing bank to the deposit and credit bank can be clearly observed. Banks spread like wildfire across industrialized nations.

9 'Involution' means a loss of entrepreneurial capabilities (see next chapter). The main goal of American Research and Development Corporation (founded in 1946) – the first venture capital intermediary – was 'to marry some small part of our enormous fiduciary resources to the new ideas which are seeking support'. (R. Flanders, quoted in Bygrave and Timmons 1992, 17) Thus, Schumpeter's image of a risk-transforming intermediary became a new character, since venture capital funds were opened to receive money ('input') from different kinds of depositors (insurance companies, pension funds, private investors, etc.).

10 See Bygrave and Timmons (1992), Murray (1999), Gompers (1998), van Osnabrugge and Robinson (2000).

11 For a deeper understanding of the difference between 'input logic' and 'development/ evolutionary logic' see Röpke (2002, 2005) and Siemon (2006a), (2006b).

12 According to Kirzner(1992, 1997), innovation is just another form of temporal arbitrage.

13 An example for interfunctional evolution is a routine entrepreneur who evolves to an arbitrage entrepreneur (or innovative entrepreneur). An example for intrafunctional evolution is an arbitrage entrepreneur who learns within his arbitrage function to innovate to keep his arbitrage function.

14 This line of economic thought can be interpreted by theoretical insights of Ashby, Varela and Maturuana. They refer to system theory as a basis to explain the process of evolution of biological systems. Ashby considers the need of subsystems' variety in order to dominate environmental variety ('Ashby's Law'). Of course, much work has been done by economists previously (like Adam Smith and Friedrich August von Hayek) to explain social phenomena explicitly and implicitly by system theory (Röpke 1977), but without referring to the aspect of autopoietic reproduction of systems. Maturana and Varela created the theoretical idea of closed, inputless ('autopoietic') self-reproduction of systems. Thus, this line of thought refers to the epistemology of 'constructivism' (Röpke 2002; Siemon 2006b): For the paradigm of constructivism, reality is not 'out there'; it has no ontological quality independent of human experience. Knowledge is not objective and constructed by each individual. In a further sociological approach, this can be connected to the work of Luhmann (1999), who – in contrast to most godfathers of modern system theory – demands an interpretation of social systems (i.e., economy, politics etc.) as autopoietic, 'structurally linked' systems that reproduce by communication. But Luhmann never brought up a differentiation of functions within the system 'economy'; thus, the explanation of evolution and development seems empty without a deeper entrepreneurial analysis.

15 Concerning the 'task difficulty' in the McClelland model, the optimal degree of challenge is a 'modest' one, not too difficult and not too easy to master.

16 See Siemon (2006b). Regarding a 'Theory of Financial Intermediation' see the contributions of Diamond (1984), Scholtens and van Wensveen (2000), Allen and Santomero (2001). For a neoclassical approach see Fama 1980. An important critique of the theory of financial intermediation based on traditional (neoclassical and/or institutional) theories has been brought up for discussion, e.g., by Scholtens and van Wensveen: 'the financial intermediary provides consumer and business households with a variety of services that fulfil their different needs, the financial intermediary is involved in a complex process of financial transformation. In the course of qualitative asset transformation – with respect to maturity, liquidity, risk, scale and location – it adds value for ultimate savers and investors. *This active role contrasts sharply with the passive intermediating of savings to investments within the economy, a thought that prevails in the traditional theory of financial intermediation*' (Scholtens and van Wensveen 2000, 1250; emphasis added). Despite their demand for a dynamic perspective on financial intermediation, these authors clearly admit that they 'cannot present here a complete modern theory of financial intermediation yet' (Scholtens and van Wensveen 2000, 1251).

17 This has to be mentioned for understanding Allen and Santomero's approach from an evolutionary logic standpoint. They refer to the intrafunctional evolution of banks, i.e., being innovative within their arbitrage function (Siemon 2006b).

18 The property rights of a bank embody a series of protection rules and other constraints, thereby causing them to lose their financing ability. Because of this historical institutional path, financial intermediaries have to refer to the vitality of informal financial networks in order to reconnect to the entrepreneurial ability they once enjoyed. They lose their innovation abilities for typical Schumpeter financings, particularly if they evolve from closed informal business angel syndicates to an open formal fund that is receiving money from different kinds of monetary sources. If these

sources represent entrepreneurial routine and arbitrage, the business charta of the syndicate/fund loses its innovative identity. This is also the evolutionary interpretation of formal venture capital market's inclination to remove innovation, because their problem of involution can be attributed to this input-logic problem ('flow of routine and arbitrage money into an intermediary's funds') as well. I regard this effect as a 'Dutch Disease of Financial Intermediation', relying on a term that is used in the theory of international trade. I see some entrepreneurial parallels, but of course other terms referring to 'Crowding out' or 'Gresham's law' might suit as well.

19 According to Granovetter's term of 'social embeddedness', bootstrappers can additionally rely on 'strong ties' by receiving help and resources from their social networks (family, friends). Business angels usually rely on these 'positive signals' before they undertake their investments.

20 Most of this work – see, e.g., Fiet 1995, van Osnabrugge 2000 – has been influenced by mainstream economic thought (neoclassical capital theory, institutional economics) comparing advantages of Business Angels with regard to venture capital firms, but these attempts to explain business angels' role in economic development do not suffice

21 This can be illustrated by statements of venture capitalists: 'Venture Capitalists invest someone else's money, so they have to work to criteria they've promised their subscribers they're going to work to.' 'Venture capitalists are investing money on behalf of pension funds; we get our money of raising funds. They don't want us goofing off and having fun. We're not here to enjoy ourselves or satisfy our egos; we're here to make capital gains to benefit pension funds. That sort of constraints what we do' (all quotations in van Osnabrugge and Robinson, 2000, 102).

22 According to the theoretical framework of Deci and Ryan, a crowding out of intrinsic motivation occurs additionally as a result of strict regulations and incentive structures.

23 In the same sense, this has been elaborated by Sohl (1999, 109): 'There are indications that this complementary relationship also extends to a two-way flow of investment opportunities. In this context, venture capital funds will refer investment opportunities to angels with which they maintain a professional relationship. These deals, deemed to be early-stage for the venture capitalist, would meet the stage requirements of the private investor. The reverse flow of information follows the complimentary relationship and occurs when angel-financed firms mature to the stage-appropriate venture-capital level and are referred by the business angels to the venture capital firms with which they have an established relationship'[23].

24 This illustrates the ability to explain, or at least to understand, innovation financing with reference to aspects of the neoclassical as well as the institutional economic theory. However, such an explanation is only effective with reference to socio-technological aspects. It already contains elements of 'entrepreneurship' that can be seen as the line of connection between these two branches of theory. Evolutionary Economics thereby represents a progressive shift of the scientific problem in in the sense of Imre Lakatos.

25 This has been stated by Hirschman as well: 'Nevertheless, our diagnosis has one special characteristic: it is not concerned with the lack of one or even of several factors or elements (capital, education, etc.) that must be combined with other elements to produce economic development, but with the deficiency in the combining process itself' (Hirschman 1958, 25).

26 Dutch Disease is representing the potential loss of entrepreneurial skills by focusing on industries after gaining/detecting *and* making use of low-energy inputs. Dutch disease is an economic phenomenon in which the discovery, exploitation and export of natural resources ('nature capital') de-industrializes a nation's economy. In countries that are rich

in resources like Iran or Middle Eastern or African countries, Dutch Disease prevents the emergence of a substantial industrial sector and the wide range of learning processes that are connected with industrialization and the export of manufactured goods. These phenomenona were also observed in the Netherlands in the 1950sand 1960s, when large reserves of natural gas were first exploited. Therefore, the term 'Dutch Disease' emerged. The phenomenon of Dutch Disease is – like our problem of losing entrepreneurial skill in the realm of financial intermediation – strongly connected with Ricardo's theorem of 'comparative advantage' as described by Caves and Jones (1981, 111): 'The role of the doctrine of *comparative* advantage is crucial in understanding the phenomenon of the Dutch Disease. A country exports those commodities in which it possesses a *comparative* advantage, and it may lose such an advantage in some commodities even if its technology is unchanged if, in other sectors, its technology (or price) improves' (original emphasis). Countries infected with Dutch Disease are mostly too weak to climb up the ladder of industrialization. Under free trade, resource-rich countries are crowded out by market mechanism from the production of low-technology and increasingly medium-technology products. There is thus a mismatch between the entrepreneurial competencies available and products that are mostly sufficient to produce and primarily export-oriented products on the one hand and technologically simply processed resource-based manufactures and the competencies needed for higher value-added resource-based manufactures on the other hand. Many countries endowed with natural capital are locked into a development trap. They have difficulties in transforming their static into a dynamic comparative advantage. This requires the infusion of entrepreneurial energy, which creates new knowledge and competence (see Röpke 2005, 28–37).

27 Abramowitz extends the simple catch-up hypothesis to analyze the fluctuating strength of the process and explores the connections between convergence itself and the relative success of early forerunners and latecomers.

28 By referring to J. M. Clark, Nurkse has already stressed the role of innovations and innovative capabilities in order to convince consumers from new products: 'A true pioneering investment is made not to meet an existing need but to create one' (Nurkse 1962, 265). Nowadays, modern system theory allows interpreting Schumpeter's 'innovation' aspect as an 'entrepreneurial function' (see chapter 2). Thus, the latter aspect has to be amended: Schumpeter stressed that the innovative function has not to be embodied by people in private markets.

29 Nurkse states that a very 'important determinant of the volume of international trade in the long run is the 'of the market' and the level of productivity. Balanced growth, as a means of enlarging the market and stimulating the incentives for higher productivity through capital investment, is an essential basis for expanding trade' (Nurkse 1960, 21).

30 Elsewhere, he states, 'The theory of international specialization as such is a static analysis. It assumes a given pattern of comparative advantage, given levels of domestic productivity and given amounts of productive resources. The theory can be and has been supplemented by considering the way in which factor supplies may react to the opening up of trade, but even in this form it remains an exercise in comparative statics' (Nurkse 1962, 254). Furthermore, 'This type of trade theory is absolutely basic; it can be extremely useful. It is, however, limited in scope; and the more clearly we recognize its limitations the better for the realism and relevance of international economics. Dynamics, by contrast is concerned with effects of continuing changes with rates of change' (ibid., 326).

31 'We therefore envisage industrial activities, whether for export or for home use, as being set up on top of the existing export sectors, so long as in these sectors a country still enjoys a high, 'established' comparative advantage even though, as a consequence

of sluggish expansion of external demand, its 'incremental' comparative advantage in these lines may be low' (Nurkse 1961, 36).

32 Thus, we have stongly to distinguish Ricardo's two strands of arguements regarding a theory of international trade: (1) His theorem *of* comparative advantages and (2) his theorem of causes *for* comparative advantages (natural goods). From an evolutionary perspective the first aspect is still persuasive, but the second point has to be revised by combining and integrating Schumpeter's aspect of innovativeness and existing theories of international trade (Heckscher-Ohlin, Stolper-Samuelson, Product Life Cycle, etc.).

33 Nurkse stresses in this context the role of the concept of income elasticity of consumer demand – a concept that is implicitly referring to Engel's law (Nurkse 1961, 42). Nowadays, the role of high income elasticity and a low price elasticity of demand is often stated as important tools to ayalyze and characterize the meaning of innovations within the process of economic development and growth.

34 Haberler states that 'Nurkse does not draw the conclusion that the poorer countries should cross bridges before they are reached; he does not recommend that they should restrict trade artificially on the ground that at some (uncertain) future date their export market will decline and their terms of trade deteriorate' (Haberler 1962, xii).

35 To break out of the forces of allocative X-Efficiency doctrine, the free trade doctrine has to be left in case of a strong gap of competencies between countries, which is followed by excessive demand due to perceived strong task difficulties.

36 Thus, we use the term 'poorest' or 'very poor' to refer to people living on less than $1 per day or in the bottom half of those living below their nation's poverty line. We will use the term 'poor' to mean those living in poverty above $1 per day or in the upper half of those living below their nation's poverty line.

37 The interest covers the high cost of making very small loans and personally servicing each client every week. It also covers the cost of managing the 'centre meetings'; the peer support group process; and providing information on social services, personal development, health and other critical information that helps clients improve their lives and the future of their families. Their rates are also affected by the rates microfinance institutions themselves pay for borrowing the funds that they in turn lend to their clients.

38 Although many types of price regulation might be wellmeaning, in reality they can cause a fatal blow to the microfinance institutions that they affect. When microfinance institutions are required to charge a predetermined interest rate, which is usually much below the costs, the microfinance institutions are often forced to go out of business.

39 Savings and credit groups that have operated for centuries include the *susus* of Ghana, 'chit funds' in India, *tandas* in Mexico, *arisan* in Indonesia, *cheetu* in Sri Lanka, 'tontines' in West Africa and *pasanaku* in Bolivia, as well as numerous savings clubs and burial societies found all over the world. Formal credit and savings institutions for the poor have also been around for decades, providing customers who were traditionally neglected by commercial banks a way to obtain financial services through cooperatives and development-finance institutions. One of the earlier and longer-lived microcredit organizations providing small loans to rural poor with no collateral was the Irish Loan Fund system, initiated in the early 1700s by the author and nationalist Jonathan Swift. In Indonesia, the Indonesian People's Credit Banks or 'The Bank Perkreditan Rakyat' (BPR) opened in 1895. The BPR became the largest microfinance system in Indonesia with close to 9,000 units. Another early pioneer, ACCION International, was founded by a law student, Joseph Blatchford, to address poverty in Latin America's cities. Begun as a student-run volunteer effort in the shantytowns of Caracas with $90,000 raised from private companies, ACCION today is one of the premier microfinance organizations in

the world, with a network of lending partners that spans Latin America, the United States and Africa. ACCION helped found BancoSol in 1992, the first commercial bank in the world dedicated solely to microfinance. Today, BancoSol offers its more than 70,000 clients an impressive range of financial services including savings accounts, credit cards and housing loans – products that just five years ago were only accessible to Bolivia's upper classes. BancoSol is no longer unique, since more than 15 ACCION-affiliated organizations are now regulated financial institutions.

40 Recent evidence gathered by Timothy Guinnane, an economic historian at Yale demonstrates that the success of Friedrich Wilhelm Raiffeisen's village bank movement in Germany, which began in 1864 and reached 2 million rural farmers by 1901, resulted in large part from its ability to confirm the hypothesis that people can be relied on to repay their loans, and that it is possible to provide financial services to poor people through market-based enterprises without subsidy. Raiffeisen's and his supporters' altruistic action was motivated by concern to assist the rural population to break out of their dependence on moneylenders and to improve their welfare. From 1870, the unions expanded rapidly over a large sector of the Rhine Province and other regions of the German states. The cooperative movement quickly spread to other countries in Europe and North America and, eventually, supported by the cooperative movement in developed countries and donors, also to developing countries.

41 While the aim of such rural finance interventions was usually defined in terms of modernizing the agricultural sector, they usually had two specific objectives: increased commercialization of the rural sector by mobilizing idle savings and increasing investment through credit, and reducing oppressive feudal relations that were enforced through indebtedness. In most cases, these new banks for the poor were not owned by the poor themselves, as they had been in Europe, but by government agencies or private banks.

42 There are many reasons why women have become the primary target of microfinance services. According, to the World Bank World Development Report 2000/2001 ('Attacking Poverty.' New York: Oxford University Press, 2001), at a macro level, 70 up to 75 per cent of the world's poor are women. Women have a higher unemployment rate than men in virtually every country and make up the majority of the informal sector of most economies. They constitute the bulk of those who need microfinance services. Targeting women has also proved to be a successful, efficient economic development tool. Research performed by the United Nations Development Programme (UNDP) and the World Bank, among others, indicates that gender inequalities inhibit overall economic growth and development. A recent World Bank report confirms that societies that discriminate on the basis of gender pay the cost of greater poverty, slower economic growth, weaker governance and a lower living standard for all people.

43 Meanwhile different forms of fund raising via electronic ways have been established. The electronic forum 'Kiva', e.g., democratizes the microfinance concept. If you have a PayPal account, you can extend credit to borrowers in developing nations. Your money goes straight to them, and they pay you back.

44 As Stiglitz (1990, 361) suggests: 'with a large group there is a free-rider problem – each would prefer that others expend the energy required to monitor and incur the ill will that would result from reporting offenders who have misused the funds lent to them.'

45 In the following, I refer to an internal working paper of Prof. Dr Jochen Röpke (University of Marburg). I am very grateful to able to make use of some of his hints regarding Grameen Bank's entrepreneurial efforts to play a vital role in order to overcome the problem of poverty by financial intermediation.

46 'During our fieldwork,' Hulme and Mosley (1996, 125) report, 'it was common to find BRAC, TRDEP and Grameen Bank offices and branches in close proximity.' More than 200 credit programmes have been identified, by far the largest being the Grameen Bank (ibid., 99).

47 In addition, we have to ask: How much of the wealth created, if any, during this period can really be attributed to lending from Grameen, given other factors that impact on poverty? During ten years, a country as Indonesia has been able – without anything resembling financial institutions of the Grameen type – to reduce the number of people living below the poverty line by 30 million between 1970 and 1980 and by a further 15 million between 1980 and 1990, 90 times the number of people Yunus claims have moved above the poverty line due to Grameen's efforts.

48 A second feature of Grameen's credit mechanism is the open conducting of all transactions. This again will dampen the enthusiasm of any innovator: to qualify for a credit, he would have to give away crucial knowledge on which the success of his innovation depends – or cheat the members by hidden action (doing something else with the money than previously said). But given the tight social control and high information transparency, hiding innovative ambitions is difficult. Innovators introduce a wedge between members in terms of income and wealth. Inquality between members increases, destroying the bond of solidarity and enfusing envy in the nonanonymity of small group interaction.

49 In a similar vein, the Bank states in one of 'The Sixteen Decisions' members need to enculturate in their daily behaviour, 'We shall collectively undertake bigger investments for higher incomes.' Whether collective investment plays any role among members, we do not know. If innovative projects become included, the outcome is likely failure. It is not this practice, per se, that is debatable. But Grameen's vision of eradication of poverty among its members does not harmonize with the credit delivery scheme as practiced so far. Loans are short term, requiring weekly repayments and stable cash flow. Default is severely punished by the bank and peers. Such procedures rule out any waiting for future income increases, longer-term and innovative investment. A relatively low impact on income and employment generation is the price paid by a low default rate.

50 While women have taken a high percentage of the loans and invested in their households, improving the health and education of their children, this has had a cost. Running a business has added to their workload and changed their role in the family, sometimes putting a strain on their marriage. Moreover, in some cases, husbands have used the loans, but expected the women to repay it. Yunus states, that in a heavily Muslim society this triggered opposition. The first opposition came from the husbands, who thought Grammen was insulting them. Second were the mullahs, who started preaching that taking money from Grameen Bank was against the religion.

51 It is not a matter that innovation would be absent in the villages where Grameen operates; far from it. The Green Revolution has taken a deep hold in Bangladesh, creating a vast field of opportunities for creative entrepreneurship (Hossain and Sen 1992; Lewis 1996).

52 Thomas Dichter is the author of *Despite Good Intentions: Why Development Assistance to the Third World Has Failed* (Amherst: University of Massachusetts Press, 2003). He has worked in international development since 1964 in a variety of institutions including the World Bank, the United Nations Development Programme, the Peace Corps and numerous nongovernmental organizations.

11. Stockpiling of International Reserves and Development: A Misguided Link

1 In an earlier period, during the 60s, as a consequence of the plans to provide the international financial system with greater liquidity, the debate focused on defining the optimal level of international reserves necessary to maintain the value of a currency within the fixed exchange rate system. A decade latter, during the 70s, when most countries adopted freely floating foreign exchange rate regimes, international reserves were seen as buffer to absorb a transitory current account shock (see Edwards, 1983 and García and Soto, 2004).

2 Reducing the likelihood of suffering a speculative attack implies an increased *policy credibility* of the government, which in turn, might attract capital inflows both portfolio and direct, which might be expected to generate growth.

3 Proposed initially by Pablo Guidotti (then deputy finance minister of Argentina) and then refined by former US Federal Reserve Chairman Alan Greenspan in 1999.

4 The same can be said about the ratio of international reserves to imports (R/M), which suggests that an adequate level of reserves can be established as that level of reserves which are able to cover at least three or four months of imports. More importantly, however, the criterion suggested by the ratio R/M became inappropriate when most economies moved to a freely floating exchange rate regime and/or when they could borrow foreign currency in the international markets. In a freely floating system, the need to keep reserves is reduced considerably (even for fully open economies) because, in theory at least, the external imbalances can be corrected through adjustments of the exchange rate or, in the last resort, through the ability to borrow from the international markets.

5 Despite the lack of a theory for reserve adequacy, there are studies that have applied econometric techniques to try to determine it. These include, among others, Ben-Bassat and Gottlieb (1992) for a selected group of 13 economies, Ramachandran (2004) for the case of India and García and Soto (2004) for Chile and other Asian economies.

6 A cost that, as Mendoza (2004, 73) himself stresses, needs to be taken in the proper context. For example, for a large country like Brazil or Malaysia it may be infinitesimal, but large for a small country like Uganda.

7 There are also some studies that have considered the *total* vulnerability of the balance of payments, but have only focused on estimating reserve adequacy, neglecting the cost of excess reserve accumulation. For example, the study of Wijnholds and Kapteyn (2001) estimates optimal reserve adequacy for a group of emerging economies, including in its estimates the vulnerability emanating from the capital account, taking account of potential capital outflows by domestic and external residents, but without stressing the cost of reserve accumulation. Their conclusion in this respect is '… that it is not accurate to generalize, as some authors do, that borrowing to strengthen reserves is quite costly for emerging market countries, assuming that such borrowing is all done in long-term bond markets' (25).

8 The central idea of this threshold comes from the fact that during the boom of crises of the 90s, both the current-account deficit and the short-term external debt, both expressed as a fraction of GDP, reached levels beyond which the historical record indicates financial markets start to get nervous and, on that basis, decide to withdraw their capital out of the country. In this sense, the authors suggest that a level of reserves that could maintain financial investors in calm could be of an order of around 5–6 per cent of GDP. Any level of international reserves in terms of GDP above that threshold can be considered an excess, and this in turn allows an estimate of its cost.

9 In this respect, for example, the Bank of England highlights (10) that 'even a positive return may not be optimal; the key question is whether higher returns, after allowance for risk, could be made elsewhere (e.g., through investment in the country's domestic infrastructure).' See *Handbooks in Central Banking* No. 19 of the Bank of England. Available at: http://www.bankofengland.co.uk/education/ccbs/handbooks/ccbshb 19.htm#top (accessed: 28 September, 2006).

10 It might be the case that the country might not need to use their excess of international reserves to accelerate growth (outstanding examples of this among developing countries are Singapore, China and Korea). This does not imply that the resources are left unproductively. These economies, for example, are maximizing returns through investing the resources in investment funds (see Singh, 2006).

11 But not only costs in terms of forgone developmental projects. These resources can also alleviate the constraint of domestic supply finance that most developing countries face (see Nurkse, 1962), so when the excess of reserves is sitting unproductively, the country has to look for sources of finance, which usually are external and which usually come with high costs.

12 According to Rodrik (2006, 8), 'the process of accumulating international reserves… makes clear that the relevant counterfactual in most instances is not one dollar of additional public investment, but one less dollar of short-term foreign debt.' Also, so far, there is no evidence that international reserves have been used to finance infrastructure projects, especially when the aims of reserves accumulation are liquidity and protection (see Singh, 2006).

13 Brazil, for example, has started to show some negative signs, identified as the 'Brazilian disease'. The domestic currency (the Real), as a result of the high accumulation of international reserves, has risen steadily from R$1.84 to the US dollar in 2002 to a recent R$1.95. This has made Brazilian goods less competitive, particularly manufactured ones (Wheatley, 2007).

14 Mexico, for example, has increased reserves by around 300 per cent since the 1994–95 peso crisis. However, manufactured exports have risen, on average, at a 12 per cent rate during 1996–2005, which is much lower than the 20 per cent rate achieved during the 1981–1994 period.

15 Recall that the danger of the contagion risk, defined as 'the threat that a country will fall victim to financial and macroeconomic instability originat[ing] elsewhere' (Grabel, 2003, 320), will depend upon the vulnerability of the recipient emerging economy (i.e., its current levels of flight, currency and fragility risk) relative to the specific form and size of the shock (trade, foreign income or financial, i.e., cost of finance, investor herd behaviour) as well as any responses by policymakers and investors (see Chui et al, 2004 and ECLAC, 1998). Additionally, the effect of the contagion risk will vary in duration and intensity according to the linkages that the country under consideration maintains with the country (or region) where the crisis originates.

16 Recall, however, that the neo-iberal strategy of financial liberalization is growth-distorting, because it promotes the creation of new opportunities for risky investment practices and a corresponding misallocation of credit toward speculative activities, with destabilizing macroeconomic effects (Grabel, 1995, 129). Furthermore, 'abandoning financial repression may lead to an explosion of government debt, economic instability and lower economic growth' (Fry, 1997, 768).

17 Only the most optimistic studies emphasize the fact that despite currency crises, financial liberalization can be linked to boom-bust cycles (see Tornell, Westermann

and Martinez, 2004) or argue that developing countries can benefit from financial liberalization, but with many nuances (see Kose et al, 2006).

18 According to Thirlwall (2003, 79), the historical experience of the last 30 years or so points to an important exchange-rate regime policy conclusion: 'intermediate positions between rigidly fixed rates (or hard pegs) and floating (what might be called 'soft' pegs) are not sustainable without capital controls.'

19 See Singh (2003) for a comprehensive exposition of the disadvantages of foreign direct investment and why it should be regulated.

20 Alternatively, charging a higher domestic price for foreign currencies than the official rate for investing abroad in capital assets such as shares and properties might inhibit flight risk (see Thirlwall, 2003).

21 For a more complete discussion concerning the benefits of the dual exchange rate system, see Mikesell (2001).

22 However, these studies do not show causality.

23 According to Grabel (2004), the precedent for the tripwires-speed bumps approach is in US stock markets and futures exchanges.

24 In addition to monitoring the evolution of the ratio, an attempt should be made to monitor the level of the variables under concern as well as their rate of change. This may allow having more accurate indicative signals.

25 See Cruz, Amann and Walters (2006), where some trip wires are proposed and analysed for the Mexican economy for the period 1988–1994.

12. International Currency Experience and the Bretton Woods System: Ragnar Nurkse as Architect

1 'Different than anything the capitalist world had seen before' (Ikenberry 1992, 289).

2 Nurkse 1944. Chapter 6, on exchange stabilization funds, was written by William Adams Brown, Jr.

3 Early dissenters included James Meade and Milton Friedman. It is not quite right to set Haberler against Nurkse as making the cases for and against, respectively, flexible currencies. Haberler at this stage merely noted the theoretical merits of a flexible currency, as did Nurkse himself. See Haberler (1964, 441) and Nurkse (1944, 14).

4 According to Haberler, 'The most coherent theory of the depression along these lines' belongs to Richard Von Strigl (see Strigl 2000).

5 For a paean to the sterling bloc, one could do worse than Nurkse (1944, 47–65).

6 Nurkse (1944, 99) cites White's 'well known' thesis on French international accounts.

7 This is when both sides began exchanging plans. The British team first transmitted their plan to the US team in mid-July 1942 (see Dormael 1978, 57).

8 Nurkse (1944, 218, 224) explicitly cites the 1943 British and US plans for a postwar monetary system, the Canadian plan to reconcile the two and the Joint Statement.

9 Nurkse (1944, 117) cites in particular the French floating episode after WWI.

10 On capital controls: 'What used to be a heresy is now endorsed as orthodox' (Dormael 1978, 148).

11 Lord Beaverbrook in a memorandum to Cabinet, 9 February 1944. Dormael 1978, 131.

12 To be precise, these are reserve requirements of the central bank vis-à-vis the currency, which is distinct from the banking system's reserve requirements vis-à-vis its depositors.

13 German-born American jurist Arthur Nussbaum (1950, 118) refers to a 'calamitous intrusion of early paper money' in medieval times.

14 Nurkse (1944, 11).
15 Nurkse (1944, 97).
16 Nurkse (1944, 12).
17 Nurkse (1944, 12).
18 A chronology of the repeal of cover statutes is sought by the author. Any help would be appreciated.

14. India and Development Economics: External Influences and Internal Responses

1 Bankim Chandra Chatterjee's 1879 Bengali essay 'Equality', quoted in Ganguli (1977).
2 Here he applied the methodology propounded by the Historical School but used the arguments carefully to reach his conclusions.
3 This has similarities with the argument presented by Nurkse in his industrialization for domestic markets strategy of growth.
4 Diversification of economic activity was a policy recommendation repeated many times, as outlined later in this paper, from the Famine Commission in 1880, which recommended diversification as a risk reduction strategy, to Mukherjee (1939) who saw this as necessary for the revival of the village economy. Ambedkar highlighted both surplus labour and capital shortage and argued for rapid industrialization to reduce pressure on land. This was also the basis for Nurkse's balanced growth strategy in the early 1950s.
5 To name a few examples: village studies in Madras, Hyderabad and Mysore (Gilbert Slater and his students, and Kesava Iyengar), indigenous banking (L. C. Jain), village government (John Matthai), managing agencies/industrial organization (P. S. Lokanathan).
6 The debate continued with the Gandhian model being contrasted with the 'modern industry' path of development, which India eventually did take up after independence. J. C. Kumarappa was a leading proponent of Gandhian economics (Kumarappa 1935).
7 For an example, see Mukherjee (1916) and for a later view, Mukherjee (1950).
8 Gadgil's articles written in the local language Marathi have been summarized in Sovani (1991).
9 Jathar and Beri, Indian Economics cited in Kale (1930, 20).
10 See Singer (1956), Goheen (1958) and Price (1966) for more modern presentations of this position, and Karve (1958) for a refutation.
11 These issues are discussed at length in Krishnamurty (2009).
12 The 'lower' and 'higher' exchange rates of 1s 4d and 1s 6d respectively are the sterling to rupee ratio.
13 See http://www.ambedkar.org, 'Statement of Evidence to the Royal Commission on Indian Currency.'
14 For a full discussion of this issue, see Balachandran (2003).
15 'The solution seems to be a balanced pattern of investment in a number of different industries, so that people working more productively with more capital and improved techniques become each others customers. … a low income country through a process of diversified growth can seek to bring about upward shifts in domestic demand schedules by means of increased productivity and therefore by increased real purchasing power. In this way a pattern of mutually supporting investments in different lines of production can enlarge the size of the market and help to fill the vacuum in the domestic economy of low income areas. This in brief is the notion of balanced growth' (Nurkse 1957, 247).

16 Rosenstein-Rodan mentions both approaches, but favours wage good expansion to public investment in basic industries and utilities for East and Southeast Europe. (See Rosenstein-Rodan 1943, 205–208)

17 Dey (1933, 38–41). It may be added that Dey changed his position on the utility of protection after independence (Dey 1950).

18 In this section, some post-1950 Indian writing on the subject is discussed as it reflects important responses to the Nurkse-Lewis contribution.

19 Ambirajan (1991) also regards this as an anticipation of later work by other economists on surplus labour.

20 See Krishnamurty (2008) for a more detailed discussion of the Indian antecedents of the concepts of disguised unemployment and surplus labour.

21 See, for example, H. W. Arndt (1972, 21–22) who, on very little evidence, dismissed the contribution of Indian economists before 1945.

22 He was referring to the UN Report, *National and International Measures for Full Employment*, published in 1949.

23 See A. K. Dasgupta (2003). This is a reprint of his paper 'Keynesian Economics and Underdeveloped Countries', which appeared in the *Economic Weekly* in 1954.

24 A good bibliography and discussion of the concept of disguised unemployment is available in Robinson (1969). The contributions of non-Indian economists are critically discussed here. Also see Bhagwati and Chakravarty (1969) for an extended discussion of the Indian literature on surplus labour.

25 For an extended discussion of K. N. Raj's contribution to employment issues, see Krishnamurty (2007).

26 Nurkse, Seminar in Stockholm School of Economics, 13 April 1959, reproduced in Nurkse (1962, 62).

www.ingramcontent.com/pod-product-compliance
Lightning Source LLC
Chambersburg PA
CBHW022347280326
41935CB00007B/103